abbreviation
and contraction of my
are right ; but let me
general rule or
and occasions, he
should look at
(Penguin edition),
such serpentine

1985

The Old Rectory
Didcot
Oxon

14 Aug. 1988

you are married
happy. Marriage,

3

CHIEFSWOOD,
MELROSE, SCOTLAND.
MELROSE 72.

lifting and cutting trees ( I love trees)
though I have to travel great distances to
nte but protracted marriage of minds with
anting of creatures, the Asiatic water-
nst / omit those other indolent delights
dlice , or organising snail-races, or
y, engaging badger into dialogue ; or
convivial
slow,
and
atively —
es, where
asure, to
duchesses
mai
by m
to
p
!
ent!
the
; at
mist,
etrine
s and
by
J
Perhaps

ONE HUNDRED LETTERS
FROM HUGH TREVOR-ROPER

One
Hundred
Letters
*from*

# HUGH TREVOR-ROPER

*edited by*
Richard Davenport-Hines
*and* Adam Sisman

OXFORD
UNIVERSITY PRESS

# OXFORD
## UNIVERSITY PRESS

Great Clarendon Street, Oxford, OX2 6DP,
United Kingdom

Oxford University Press is a department of the University of Oxford.
It furthers the University's objective of excellence in research, scholarship,
and education by publishing worldwide. Oxford is a registered trade mark of
Oxford University Press in the UK and in certain other countries

Published in the United States of America by Oxford University Press
198 Madison Avenue, New York, NY 10016, United States of America

British Library Cataloguing in Publication Data
Data available

Library of Congress Control Number: 2013947868

ISBN 978–0–19–870311–2

Printed in Italy by
L.E.G.O. S.p.A.–Lavis TN

# ACKNOWLEDGEMENTS

Our paramount debt, one beyond measure, is to Blair Worden, Hugh Trevor-Roper's literary executor, who encouraged us to undertake this book, and who has given us far more help in the preparation and revision of it than the editors could expect or adequately thank.

Judith Curthoys, the Christ Church archivist, who has charge of the Dacre papers, has been a wonder of patience and efficiency throughout our work. Rodney Allan has translated, identified, and glossed passages from Greek and Latin, and has done sterling work in correcting the transcription of documents. We are profoundly grateful to both of them.

We are also grateful to Jeremy Cater, Jeremy Catto, Edward Chaney, Frank Giles, the late Earl Haig, Sir Michael Howard, James Howard-Johnston, Alan Macfarlane, Peter Miller, Alasdair Palmer, Richard Rhodes, Zeev Sternhell, the Hon. James Stourton, Geoffrey Wheatcroft, and Blair Worden, who supplied us with letters and consented to their publication.

We thank those who have given permission to reproduce letters to their relations: the Hon. Deborah Blake (to her father Lord Blake); Susan Chater and William Stuart (their father Charles Stuart); Jane Clark (her husband Alan Clark); Alastair Hamilton (his father Hamish Hamilton); Alexandra Henderson (her father Sir Nicholas Henderson); Sarah Holdsworth (her mother Valerie Pearl); Mary Lefkowitz (her husband Hugh Lloyd-Jones); Robin and Vivien Perutz (their father Max Perutz); and Helen Szamuely (her father Tibor Szamuely). Oliver Ramsbotham has kindly allowed us to quote correspondence between his father, Sir Peter Ramsbotham, and Trevor-Roper.

Other debts of gratitude are to the Beinecke Library at Yale, for the letters to Wallace Notestein; the Library of King's College, Cambridge, for the letters to Noël Annan; the Harry Ransom Center at the University of Texas at Austin, for the letters to Gerald Brenan; Claudia Wedepohl, archivist of the Warburg Institute, for consent to reproduce letters to Frances Yates; Henry Hardy and the Isaiah Berlin Trust; the Brotherton Library, Leeds (Special Collections), for the letter to Lord Boyle of Handsworth; the Wellcome Library, for the letter dated 24 February 1973 to Sir Peter Medawar (PP/PBM/D/12); Gertrude Himmelfarb for permission to quote a letter by her of 25 August 1965; Anthony Thwaite for supplying and allowing us to quote a letter to him of 3 September 1976; and the Syndics of Cambridge University Library, for permission to publish an extract from a letter to J. H. Plumb. The quotation from Sir Isaiah Berlin on p. xii is from Henry Hardy and Mark Pottle (eds.), *Isaiah Berlin, Building: Letters 1960–1975* (Chatto & Windus 2013), pp. 84–5 © Isaiah Berlin Literary Trust.

Many amendments were made after Henry Woudhuysen's invaluable scrutiny of the typescript. Numerous other individuals have helpfully answered queries or volunteered information, among them John Adamson, Jeremy Cater, Jeremy Catto, Edward Chaney, Xenia Dennen, Gavin Fuller, Timothy Garton Ash, Mark Greengrass, Miriam Gross, Henry Hardy, Edward Harrison, James Howard-Johnston, Lord Kennet, Paulina Kewes, Mary Lefkowitz, John Maddicott, Peter Miller, John Morgan, Jan Morris, Alasdair Palmer, Philip Pattenden (who has taken particular trouble in answering questions about Cambridge), Christopher Phipps, Richard Rhodes, Norman Stone, James Stourton, Gina Thomas, William Thomas, Geoffrey Wheatcroft, David Wootton, and Brian Young. We are grateful to them all.

# CONTENTS

# LIST OF ILLUSTRATIONS

## Plates

'You understand the nature of history better than any of your contemporaries in England, and I dare say in Europe, and there is no reason for concealing this fact.'

Sir Isaiah Berlin to Hugh Trevor-Roper, 6 March 1962

# INTRODUCTION

These hundred letters, a selection from the many thousands that Hugh Trevor-Roper composed, were written over fifty-eight years, from September 1943, when he was 29 years old, to December 2001, when he was 87 and had thirteen months to live.[1] The first letter was written in his period as an intelligence officer, who found in correspondence, and in the solitary meditations that were published in 2011 as *The Wartime Journals*, forms of self-expression that were excluded by the secrecy and mechanical preoccupations of his work. When he wrote the last of his letters he was living alone, widowed, almost blind, and mortally ill, in a Victorian rectory in the town of Didcot in south Oxfordshire. This volume traverses a career in academic life which roamed far beyond it. A Tutor in History at Oxford from 1946, he became Regius Professor of Modern History in 1957; was ennobled in 1979 as Lord Dacre of Glanton; and moved to Cambridge in 1980 as Master of Peterhouse, an office he held for seven years until his retirement. Seventeen of the letters are written from his Oxford college, home, or office; eleven from the Master's Lodge at Peterhouse; seventeen others during his many travels. The letters describe visits to Greece, to Spain, to Portugal, to Iceland, to Israel, to the United States, to the West Indies, to Australia, to Pakistan, to Soviet Russia, to Czechoslovakia.

---

[1] The most substantial biographical source is Adam Sisman, *Hugh Trevor-Roper* (2010). Shorter accounts are Blair Worden, 'Hugh Redwald Trevor-Roper', *Proceedings of the British Academy*, 150 (2007), and James Howard-Johnston, 'Lord Dacre of Glanton', in Angela Huth (ed.), *Well Remembered Friends* (2004). The advice of Blair Worden has been indispensable in the writing of this introduction.

Trevor-Roper wrote to enliven. As he declared in a BBC radio programme (described in his letter to Noël Annan of 20 October 1988), he believed that history should be not 'a boring private subject for the specialists' but a vital force that animated general readers: 'I would like people to feel that they're part of history…to feel…the movement of it and themselves in it, and not to see the past as a dead deposit but as a living continuity.'[1] His vitality, which was indomitable in both his historical work and his extra-curricular diversions, is evident throughout these hundred letters selected for publication at the time of the centenary of his birth. Our selection illustrates the range of his life and preoccupations: as a historian, a controversialist, a public intellectual, a legislator, a lover of literature, a traveller, a countryman. It depicts a life of rich diversity in public activities and private avocations; a mind of intellectual sparkle and eager curiosity; a character that relished the comedies of his time, and revelled in the absurdities, crotchets, and vanities of his contemporaries. It reveals the complexities of an exceptional personality. And it will gladden readers who value wit, erudition, and intellectual vigour. The playful irony of his correspondence places him in a literary tradition which stretches back to the correspondence of Madame de Sévigné in the seventeenth century and Horace Walpole in the eighteenth. Like them he takes pleasure in enlightening and amusing his correspondents. Like them he has a vivid power of pictorial imagery. Yet in a letter of 7 March 1959 we find Trevor-Roper wearying of the superficiality of de Sévigné's correspondence. His power of analysis brings something more searching. He, no less than they, is an aesthete, but his aestheticism is combined with fierceness of intellect, with an inexhaustible curiosity of enquiry, and with a passion for lucid analysis.

Trevor-Roper's correspondence amounted to millions of words. A book needs reasonable bounds, but a volume containing many hundred more letters could easily have been compiled without a diminution of

---

[1]  *Desert Island Discs*, BBC Radio 4, 21 August 1988. We owe this quotation to Rory Allan, of Christ Church, Oxford.

quality. Had the editors had an eye to the stature or fame of the recipients rather than to the intrinsic interest of the letters, we might have included letters to such men as George Orwell, Anthony Powell, Cyril Connolly, Malcolm Muggeridge, Lord Cherwell, Solly Zuckerman, and Harold Macmillan. Yet Trevor-Roper, who was no respecter of celebrity, wrote the great majority of his most memorable letters to less prominent people.

Hugh Trevor-Roper was born in January 1914 in the small village of Glanton in the Cheviot Hills, close to Northumberland's border with Scotland. As he recounted to his future wife in his letters of August 1953, a chill loneliness numbed his childhood. His visual alertness and pictorial imagination, which through his life would feed his unquenchable appetite for metaphor, were present in his boyhood, as was the myopia which perhaps intensified those qualities. 'I can't understand anything', he explained in 1942, 'that I can't present to my imagination in a pictorial form; and when I comprehend anything vividly, it is always in the terms of some visual image.'

A physically strenuous child, he had little physical contact with his parents, and his adult relationships would sometimes be hampered by bodily tension or awkwardness. He discovered for himself during his solitary childhood those consolatory resources that would also sustain him in adulthood: reading, and observation of the natural world. The first letter in this collection, to Logan Pearsall Smith in 1943, is written from his parents' house in Alnwick, the Northumberland town to which his parents moved when he was a small boy. It mentions, *inter alia*, the trout-streams, woodlands, stubble-fields, and partridges of the neighbouring landscape. In another letter, written to his future wife on 8 August 1953, he recalls his boyhood love of the wild flowers, crustaceans, tadpoles, caterpillars and butterflies that he found on forays in Northumberland or near his boarding-schools. Nearly four decades later, in a letter written on 14 July 1991, he describes his struggle to save the lives of an array of orphaned hedgehogs. The emotional isolation of his childhood leaves its mark on his letters. They are a reaching out for contact. The craving is so strong in the sequence of letters to James Howard-Johnston, his stepson, that the recipient often felt unequal to replying. It is more discreetly present in letters to Peter Ramsbotham (19 March 1947), Dawyck Haig (28 January 1951), and others. It is implicit, too, even if less transparently so, in his exchanges with Valerie Pearl, Felix Raab, Blair Worden, Alasdair Palmer, and Edward Chaney. He longed for his correspondents to reply. 'Do write again: I love your letters, and I long to hear of you, and from you,' he urged Gerald Brenan, on 11 March 1968. Many of the letters published here are expressions of tenderness or affection from an inhibited man who—even by the standards of his emotionally well-drilled generation— had difficulty in expressing his feelings. The high spirits of the letters can have a serious purpose, which has care and thought behind it. We see it in the humour of his letter to Alan Yorke-Long (21 September 1952), which was written to amuse a dying friend, or in his letter to James Howard-Johnston (21 May 1960), which was intended to revive the spirits of a depressed teenager.

'The satirist may laugh, the philosopher may preach,' wrote Trevor-Roper's preceptor Edward Gibbon in his autobiography, 'but...knowledge of our own family from a remote period, will be always esteemed.' Where our ancestors are concerned, Gibbon continued, 'we wish to discover them possessed of ample fortunes, adorned with honourable titles, and holding an eminent rank in the class of hereditary nobles.' Trevor-Roper enjoyed (but not too seriously) the facts that he was a collateral descendant of William Roper, the son-in-law and biographer of Sir Thomas More, and a direct descendant of a younger brother of the tenth Baron Teynham. As a boy he was aware that only a dozen lives (several of them those of elderly bachelors) separated him from inheriting the Teynham peerage, which had been created in the reign of King James I. His ironical pleasure in imagining his remote relations bedecked in their coronets is detectable in the references in his letters to Lady Dacre, Lord Carlisle, Lord Hampden, Lord St Oswald, and others, and in his hopes of buying family portraits from his distant connection Lady Ford. He had early acquaintance with an aristocratic society, for soon after his birth his father, a country doctor at Glanton, bought an additional practice at nearby Alnwick, a town dominated by the Duke of Northumberland and his towering castle. The Trevor-Ropers' house in a picturesquely named street, Bondgate Without, was a short walk from the ducal ramparts. The social position of medical families in King George V's England was precarious: the status of physicians depended on that of their patients; doctors' wives were notorious for their anxiety to exact due respect in their communities; the class-consciousness in a little ducal town was intense; and Kathleen Trevor-Roper surpassed most of her kind in fretful snobbery.

Trevor-Roper was sent at the age of 9 to a barbarous preparatory school in Derbyshire, and a year later to a more tolerable but still Spartan establishment, Belhaven Hill near Dunbar. As a boy from Northumberland, imbued with romantic visions of Borders history, in which the English were valiant patriots repulsing the raids of barbarous Scottish marauders, he was captivated by Walter Scott's *Tales of a Grandfather*, with its account of Jacobite rebels and such Reiver families as the 'Dacres of the North', who from their garrisons contended against the lawlessness of the Borders. At Belhaven Hill the minority of English children were subjected to xenophobic Scottish bullying by their fellow pupils. Trevor-Roper's hostility to Scottish nationalism, manifest in his letters to Nan Dunbar (17 April 1980), James Stourton (5 October 1986), and others, may owe something to rebuffs of his early years.[1]

Trevor-Roper thrived in examinations. At the age of 13 he won a scholarship to Charterhouse, a major public school on the outskirts of Godalming in Surrey, where he excelled as a classicist. He made the first of his appearances as a contributor to weekly magazines while a schoolboy. On 27 May 1931 'H. R. Trevor-Roper (Charterhouse)', aged 17, featured in *The*

---

[1]    Colin Kidd, 'Lord Dacre and the Politics of the Scottish Enlightenment', *Scottish Historical Review*, 84 (2005); William Ferguson, 'A Reply to Professor Colin Kidd on Lord Dacre's Contribution to the Study of Scottish History and the Scottish Enlightenment', and Colin Kidd, 'On Heroes, Hero-Worship and Demonology in Scottish Historiography', *Scottish Historical Review*, 86 (2007); Jeremy Cater, 'Editor's Foreword', in Hugh Trevor-Roper, *The Invention of Scotland* (2008).

*Listener* as co-winner of its Greek crossword (in which all the answers were from the *Iliad* or *Odyssey*). A month later, on 24 June, he was one of the prizewinners for the Horace crossword. These modest triumphs testify to the exacting and unashamed standards of culture that still prevailed in the 1930s, and to the spirit of playfulness that accompanied Trevor-Roper's academic training. Classical literature was always his first love, even after he had changed, as an undergraduate at Christ Church where he was a classical scholar, from a degree in that subject to one in history. He had great tracts of Greek and Latin poetry—and of English and European poetry too—by heart. His adult correspondence is suffused with classical quotations and allusions, which came so readily to him, which indeed he could scarcely keep out of his head. The beauty and purity that language can achieve, its power of allusiveness, the limitless range of its resources—those were his constant sustenance. He cared for language for another reason too, as an instrument of lucidity and mental discipline. He felt 'moral hatred', he told his former pupil Blair Worden in April 1977, 'for rhetoric, slovenly language, ambiguity, emotive obscurity'. Once, he added, he had supposed that his obsession with clarity of prose had originated in his reading A. J. Ayer's *Language, Truth and Logic* after its publication in 1936; but four decades later, 'when I look back I think perhaps my classical education was the original cause of this attitude. At the back of my mind, I still see every sentence as demanding to be put into Latin. If it cannot be put into Latin, I know that it is, at best, obscure, at worst nonsense.'

Probably as compensation for being bookish in habits and appearance, Trevor-Roper was a rowdy, hard-drinking undergraduate and graduate student, who ran with the beagles and hunted with the hounds. Exultant with drink one night, he hurled an empty champagne bottle from a first-floor window of the Gridiron club which narrowly missed his fellow pupil and future ally Robert Blake, who was walking on the pavement below. Always he guarded against solemnity, which he never confused with seriousness. In his wartime journals he wrote, in a characteristic strain of self-mockery: 'In moments of silent meditation, sitting in the

sun on hay-stacks or by river-banks, or roistering over pots of ale, or waiting by covert-sides, I am often astonished by the depth and extent of my
learning. "Hugh Trevor-Roper", I say to myself, when this bewildering
revelation breaks upon me, "you must be careful or you will be buried,
obliterated, beneath the burden of this stupendous erudition. Go slow!
Be canny! In the interests of learning, you should devote more time to
beagling, foxhunting, drinking, fishing, shooting, talking; or, if you must
read, read Homer, Milton, Gibbon, who cannot harm the brain.'" Even in
his thirties he had dissolute bouts. After George VI and Queen Elizabeth
visited Christ Church for its 400th anniversary celebrations in 1946, he
told his wartime colleague Solly Zuckerman: 'I signalised Their Majesties'
visit by extreme intoxication. My hand still trembles, my mind is cloudy,
and I am crippled by mysterious bruises.' Trevor-Roper's pleasure in bois-
terous nights underlies several letters before his marriage in 1954. His
pleasure in physical exertion and rough journeys is voiced in his letters to
Nim Church (28 August 1946), Dawyck Haig (2 April 1951), and his wife
Xandra (21 September 1960).

The letters in this volume show Trevor-Roper as a writer first, a historian second. Yet they have much to tell us about his historical work and
outlook. They illuminate lines of historical investigation, developments in
his interests, and the premises of his historical philosophy. They are witnesses, too, to the unassailable independence of his historical judgement.
That characteristic marked his work from the start. Having secured a first
in history in 1936, he began work as a graduate student on Charles I's Archbishop of Canterbury William Laud. Under the nominal supervision of
the Regius Professor of Ecclesiastical History, Claude Jenkins, he was left
to go his own way. He never saw himself as a member of a historical school
or tried to create one. His historical thinking was formed largely in reaction against prevailing orthodoxies. Though in his earlier career—'my
marxisant phase' as he would later call it—he accepted the premise of
R. H. Tawney that the political changes of the sixteenth and seventeenth
centuries originated in economic and social conflicts, he would become repelled by the determinist spirit of Marxist and other progressive historical

thinking, which denied or belittled both the freedom of the human will and the role of contingency in history. Economic history in any case lost its appeal to him, and gave way to his studies in the history of ideas. 'I used to think', he admitted in 1951, 'that historical events always had deep economic causes: I now believe that pure farce covers a far greater field of history, and that Gibbon is a more reliable guide to that subject than Marx.'

Of all the things for which he revered Gibbon, none influenced him more than the eighteenth-century historian's gift for historical comparison. His mind, like Gibbon's, searched restlessly for analogies and contrasts that would illuminate one age by the light of another. With Gibbon he saw the past in the present and the present in the past. It was partly for the same capacity that he admired Gerald Brenan (with whom he maintained a correspondence throughout the 1950s and 1960s). Brenan's *The Spanish Labyrinth* was a study of the Spanish civil war; and yet, as Trevor-Roper told Bernard Berenson in February 1954, 'I make my best pupils studying 16th and 17th century Spain read it, for I think there is more profound analysis of 16th and 17th century Spain between the lines of Brenan's book than in the explicit statements of any work written directly on the subject.' 'The richness of the historical knowledge, the heroic intellectual integrity, the rejection of all ready-made formulae, the monumental learning behind it, the burning lucidity of the style—it made everything else written on Spain seem pitifully shoddy.' To Trevor-Roper's mind the breadth of Brenan's perspective achieved what specialization, which has nothing to compare its findings with, cannot. The present book includes a letter of 13 December 1956 to J. C. Masterman, the Provost of Worcester College, Oxford, which decries narrow and unadventurous specialization in terms that anticipate Trevor-Roper's inaugural lecture as Regius Professor of Modern History at Oxford the following year. He was dismayed by the introversion of the proliferating sub-disciplines of historical study, as he was by the decline in the knowledge of foreign or classical languages among historians.

Trevor-Roper's interest in international politics is a recurrent presence in the volume. A letter of 8 November 1956 to his former pupil Edward

Boyle, who had just resigned as a minister in protest at the mishandling of the Suez crisis, voices Trevor-Roper's dismay at the ineptitude of the Eden government. By now Trevor-Roper had excoriating language both for Marx—'historically, he remains a huge fossil lodged in a living stream, discolouring indeed a thin trickle of it, but without influence upon its future course'—and for his adherents: 'Modern Marxists, with a million mass-produced needles, busily stitch and mend the system, which perpetually splits and shrivels at the touch of events.'[1] His statements provoked responses from Communist Party members including Eric Hobsbawm, Christopher Hill, and Andrew Rothstein (the last a figure of contempt to Trevor-Roper, as shown in a letter of 6 August 1986). The ensuing controversy ran in the correspondence columns of the *New Statesman* for nine issues, from 20 August to 29 October 1955, with Isaiah Berlin joining Trevor-Roper against Hobsbawm. Trevor-Roper's combative letters to the press over the decades include tussles with Evelyn Waugh in the correspondence columns of the *New Statesman* in the winter of 1953–4 over the character and history of English Catholic recusancy, and a protest in *The Spectator* in 1955 against newspaper distortions in the coverage of the Burgess–Maclean spy story.[2] The present volume confines itself to private letters, but his public ones are not a negligible part of his output. Among them are those penned under the name Mercurius Oxoniensis and published first in *The Spectator* and then, in 1970, as *The Letters of Mercurius*. In this book letters to Wallace Notestein and James Howard-Johnston in the summer of 1968 supply privately circulated *addenda* to that collection. Trevor-Roper wrote spoof letters, private and public, under other names, though those documents too, again having separate qualities, are not represented here.

Trevor-Roper relished controversy and was a master of controlled invective. He felt vivified when waging war on Lawrence Stone, Tawney, Arnold Toynbee, and other scholars whose use of evidence, or whose

---

[1]  H. R. Trevor-Roper, 'Marx as a Historian', *New Statesman*, 27 August and 22 October 1955.
[2]  See appendix in Mark Amory (ed.), *The Letters of Evelyn Waugh* (1980); H. R. Trevor-Roper, 'The Establishment', *Spectator*, 21 October 1955.

premises or interpretations or priorities, he found defective. Yet although he and A. J. P. Taylor battled in print and on television over the latter's *The Origins of the Second World War*, the two men remained on reasonably cordial terms. After his opponent's death Trevor-Roper retained an interest in the personality and conduct of his erstwhile foe, as is attested by letters to Adam Sisman of 21 June 1991 and Geoffrey Wheatcroft of 12 January 1994.

Other controversies arose from Trevor-Roper's interest in wartime intelligence. In the first months of the Second World War he was recruited to a newly formed section of the War Office's communications department called the Radio Security Service. There he became expert in interpreting the decrypted radio transmissions of the German secret service, the Abwehr. When peace returned he retained his intelligence contacts, and in the 1950s he answered their enquiries about younger Oxford men who were considered suspect—the future cabinet minister Edmund Dell among them. From the 1960s he published reviews and essays about intelligence matters in terms that vexed some officials of MI5 and MI6 by their criticisms, mockery, and indiscretions. This aspect of his life is covered in letters to Kim Philby of 21 September 1968, to Michael Howard of 5 November 1981, and to Noël Annan of 17 November 1981 and 28 September 1994. Although he resisted the more implacable postures of the Cold War, as is indicated by his letter to Isaiah Berlin of 18 February 1955, he loathed the brutal stupidity of Communist regimes, and was shocked by their incarceration or mental subjugation of scholars (see his mention of Mikhail Bakhtin in his letter to Frances Yates, 28 December 1969). In the post-war era he saw both Communism and the Roman Catholic Church, which he likewise assailed in print, as enemies to the freedoms of thought and action which they denied to their members. His excitement at the collapse of Soviet domination of Russia and central Europe in 1989–90 is evident in his letters of the period.

Dick White, who was head of MI5 in 1953–6 and of MI6 in 1956–68, was Trevor-Roper's lifelong friend. It was while the two men were downing bottles of hock with H. L. A. Hart in occupied Germany during the summer of 1945 that White decided that Trevor-Roper should deploy his formidable powers as an assembler and analyst of evidence to prove beyond doubt that Hitler had died in the Berlin bunker in April 1945 rather than (as rumour-mongers insinuated) being spirited away by submarine to South America, secreted on a Baltic island, or kept as Stalin's captive in an oubliette. This was an ideal task for a young man who had already proved his investigative and analytical skills. He drew on his findings to write *The Last Days of Hitler*, which became an instant bestseller after its publication in 1947. It secured his reputation among commissioning editors in the 1950s as England's pre-eminent expert on Nazi documents. He provided a long essay, 'The Mind of Hitler', to introduce a volume of Hitler's table-talk which George Weidenfeld published in London in 1953; he wrote an introduction to the letters of Martin Bormann; and enjoyed meetings with François Genoud, who controlled the literary estates of Bormann and Joseph Goebbels, and with Himmler's Estonian masseur Felix Kersten. His interest in the complex psychology of such rogues as Genoud was comparable to his attraction to those malicious old men Logan Pearsall Smith and Bernard Berenson, and to his curiosity about the mainsprings of character of such confidence tricksters as Kenneth de Courcy, Robert Peters, and Edmund Backhouse—all of whom are mentioned in these letters.

Trevor-Roper's refusal to be confined to a single historical period or to monolingual sources, still less to any specialist topic, set him apart from those of his contemporaries who wrote big books on the subjects on which they had concentrated at length. Bernard Berenson, Wallace Notestein, and other friends urged him to write a long masterpiece on the period of the English Civil Wars. They complained of his readiness to be diverted by intrigues within his college or faculty, or on behalf of candidates for academic posts, or against the rival machinations of his antagonists. They noted that his former Christ Church ally Robert Blake, although no less busy in academic politics, had managed to write two big biographies of Conservative prime ministers as well as heading an Oxford college and completing other important books.

When Trevor-Roper was elected as Master of Peterhouse, a journalist (prompted by informants who had spoken non-attributably) wondered if he 'may now find the time to write the magnum opus on the English Civil War which has been promised for many a year. Even his greatest admirers would agree that his published output in his own specialist academic field of the seventeenth century has been disappointingly slight after the considerable promise of his first book on Archbishop Laud.'[1] That was a partial view, not merely in the light of Trevor-Roper's revulsion against the idea of having 'his own specialist academic field', but because there was nothing 'slight' about his output. The bulk of his publications is formidable. There are, it is true, far more essays than books, a pattern for which he would not have apologized. Historians, he maintained, should write essays on subjects on which they are not qualified to write books, and so bring a comparative perspective to them. Some of his essays are of Victorian length. All of them reduce large subjects to their essence. Many of them, such as his 'Religion, Reformation and Social Change', 'The Religious Origins of the Enlightenment', and 'The Scottish Enlightenment', have lastingly transformed their fields.[2]

Trevor-Roper was a great figure of twentieth-century Oxford, and a luminary in the generation of public intellectuals that also included Isaiah Berlin, Stuart Hampshire, H. L. A. Hart, and A. J. P. Taylor. Only a small selection of his letters about the affairs of the university where he spent most of his working life is included here, for inevitably they have their parochial aspects; but there is more than ephemeral interest in the three letters on academic matters to J. C. Masterman (13 December 1956), Valerie Pearl (4 April 1969), and Robert Blake (17 August 1970). Another of Trevor-Roper's academic correspondents, with whom he exchanged letters over several decades, was Hugh Lloyd-Jones, who had been elected Regius

---

[1] Ian Bradley, 'Oxford Loss, Cambridge Gain', *The Times*, 20 December 1979.
[2] John Robertson, 'Hugh Trevor-Roper, Intellectual History and the "Religious Origins of the Enlightenment"', *English Historical Review*, 124 (2009); Trevor-Roper, 'The Scottish Enlightenment', reprinted in the posthumous volume *History and the Enlightenment*, ed. John Robertson (2010).

Professor of Greek in the university and a Student (Fellow) of Christ
Church in 1960, but who moved to the United States after his retirement
in 1989. Lloyd-Jones was 'a striking example of the kind of brilliant, vivid
and anarchic figure whom it is hard to imagine holding a major chair in
the modern, managed and managerial university', wrote Robert Parker,
Wykeham Professor of Ancient History at Oxford, of Lloyd-Jones after
his death in 2009. Readers of *One Hundred Letters*, which contains three
letters to Lloyd-Jones written during a sequence of exchanges that followed Trevor-Roper's move to Peterhouse in 1980, will feel Parker's words
are applicable to him too. Likewise Parker's picture of Lloyd-Jones in reluctant attendance at committees—'it was always a pleasure at sub-
faculty meetings to watch him ostentatiously working his way through
the week's crop of off-prints while the routine business droned on'—
recalls other observers' memories of Trevor-Roper writing letters in his
immaculate handwriting (or producing deft drawings of animals or car-
toons of his colleagues) during the drudgery of board meetings of the
Oxford History Faculty. Like Trevor-Roper, Lloyd-Jones was a formidable
polemicist who strove to enlist his extensive foreign contacts (in Parker's
words) 'to combat the provincialism of Oxford'.[1] The two men resembled
each other in their scholarly zeal, in their thirst for intellectual enquiry,
and in the intensity of their diction and gaze. Both men brought colour to
an increasingly monochrome academic environment.

Trevor-Roper's activities were never restricted to the university. He lectured abroad, reviewed in the weekly magazines and Sunday newspapers,
plunged deep into public debates, inspirited an easily demoralized wife,
went abroad for weeks at a time as a special correspondent, travelled back
and forth between Oxford and his Scottish home (a journey made more
arduous by the Beeching cuts, which closed the Carlisle to Edinburgh
railway, and with it Melrose station, in 1969). After 1979 some of his letters
describe his attendance, as Lord Dacre of Glanton, in the House of Lords.
He took the Conservative whip but was not inhibited by it. He seldom

---

[1] Robert Parker, 'Sir Hugh Lloyd-Jones', *Guardian*, 9 December 2009.

spoke in the chamber, where he may not have felt at ease as a performer. His rare interventions—as in the debate on oversight of the Security Services held in December 1986—are striking for their concision, elegance, and authority. It is, however, his relish for the individual tempers, the quiddities, and group loyalties of his fellow peers that he savours in his letters to Edward Chaney of May 1988, to Noël Annan of 20 October 1988 and 28 September 1994, to Alasdair Palmer of 24 December 1989, and in others. Three letters in this volume were written in the Lords.

It was a few months after his elevation to the peerage as Lord Dacre of Glanton in 1979 that he was elected Master of Peterhouse. Some fellows of the college, content to regard him as a Tory, hoped for a reign of peaceable immobility. Instead, he did battle against what seemed to him to be reactionary, obscurantist, and introverted tendencies within the fellowship. He had admirers and allies among the fellows, but others were dismayed by his implacable insistence on his interpretations of the college's rules, as well as by the freedom with which he regaled the high tables of other colleges with his colourful accounts of life in Peterhouse. Even among detached onlookers, some questioned his characterizations of his adversaries and his interpretations of their beliefs, and felt that the stormy disputes in the governing body, which were broadcast in the press, had become too dominant an obsession with him. His use of the word 'mafia' to describe some of the fellows not only indulged his satirical instincts. It exaggerated the cohesion—intellectual and political—of the figures concerned.

Yet his battles at Peterhouse were not mere personal fixations. In his mind fundamental issues of intellectual and educational principle were at stake. His commitment to liberal values and secular premises was incompatible with 'the Peterhouse school of history', and especially inimical to the outlook of Maurice Cowling, the historian who had been his kingmaker at Peterhouse but became his chief opponent. His historical credo, as he stated years after his retirement from the mastership of Peterhouse in 1987, was: 'stand firm on our own Western Tradition—the tradition of the Enlightenment, the open society, pluralism'. He strove to expose the college to outside influences, and supported rationally argued reforms. He particularly confounded expectation first by accepting the arguments for the admission of women to the college, and later by proposing the successful motion in governing body which achieved that result. His mind, although ineradicably the product of a male intellectual world, was not confined by it: he enjoyed communicating with intelligent, strong-minded female colleagues, as his letters to Valerie Pearl, Nan Dunbar, and Frances Yates attest.

There was another convulsion in Trevor-Roper's sixties. Much of his public impact had been achieved by his exposure of the errors, elisions, misquotations, slipshod deductions, or outright frauds of other scholars. Yet at the age of 69 he made an egregious mistake which humiliated him across the educated world. The fiasco of his authentication of the forged Hitler diaries is recounted in his letter to Frank Giles dated 10 July 1983, and in later comments to Edward Chaney of 20 April 1991. Here it is enough to note that his failure was caused less by arrogance than by his remoteness, heightened by the encroachments of age, from the world of journalism with which he was contending. In the estimate of Neal Ascherson, who was a journalist on *The Observer* from 1960 until 1990, the danger for Dacre in 1983 was that 'he had no idea of the frantic haste, secrecy, and pressure of a big exclusive, in which there is no room for second thoughts. His first glance at the diaries suggested to him that they could be real, but a first glance was all he got. His instinct was not to authenticate them until he had taken more time to reflect, to examine, to wait for the ink and paper tests to be confirmed. But that was not on offer. His mistake was to allow himself to be hurried into stating that the diaries were genuine…A sort of innocence, rather than the famous arrogance, brought the catastrophe about.'[1]

Trevor-Roper's letters, written between 1947 and 1959, to Bernard Berenson, who was his mentor in the history of art and an early guide in

---

[1] Neal Ascherson, 'Liquidator: Hugh Trevor-Roper', *London Review of Books*, 19 August 2010; Ascherson, 'Hugh Trevor-Roper', in W. Roger Louis (ed.), *Resurgent Adventures with Britannia* (2011), 178.

his reading about the history of ideas, were published as *Letters from Oxford* in 2006. That was a substantial book, but there were others to whom he wrote a still greater number of words. There were also innumerable brief exchanges of letters with other correspondents, usually prompted by particular events or publications: the letters in this volume to Peter Medawar, Tibor Szamuely, and Zeev Sternhell are examples. It might be supposed that a man who wrote so much must have written hurriedly. The supposition is confounded, even in letters written when the pressures of his work were strongest. Writing letters was an essential pleasure of his life, and in them, no less than in his other writings, his careful ordering of his ideas, his marshalling of his vocabulary, and his precision and concision of expression brought satisfaction even when time was short—and even as he protested his ineptitude at setting a calm pace for his paper-work. 'I am congenitally incapable of preparing lectures, articles, anything, ahead of time,' he told Robert Blake in 1977. 'I always work best under the lash; and so I leave everything until it simply *has* to be done. Then my scholarly perfectionism comes into play: I hate doing anything badly; so I go through agonies of tumultuous industry at the last minute.'[1]

Some correspondents told him that they were keeping his letters for posterity (though not all of them did); but while his correspondence is part of his literary legacy, he might not have savoured its publication. He was always more interested in writing than in publishing. The letters were private documents, in which he trusted to their privacy. He was aghast when he heard that an irreverent letter he had sent Berenson in 1952 about the death of King George VI had been handed around among visitors to Berenson's Italian villa, I Tatti—one of whom was a journalist. He was irritated when told that a private letter of 1963 about the candidates for the Regius Chair of Modern History at Cambridge had been copied by its recipient to the incumbent Regius Professor, Herbert Butterfield, in whose papers in Cambridge University Library it could be read by

---

[1]   Trevor-Roper to Robert Blake, 1 August 1977, Dacre papers; Richard Shannon, 'Robert Norman William Blake', *Proceedings of the British Academy*, 153 (2008) is a fund of information on Trevor-Roper.

anyone with a reader's ticket; indignant when warned that private letters which he had written from Peterhouse in the 1980s were being circulated; shaken, too, to learn that his correspondence with Wallace Notestein was available in Princeton, and being photocopied. One of the editors of this volume can recall Trevor-Roper letters being read aloud, with hilarity, to him by one of the recipients in the 1970s. Tibor Szamuely's children remember their father reading aloud newly received letters from Trevor-Roper at the breakfast table. Indeed, a *samizdat* of the letters developed. Trevor-Roper's wartime subordinate and Christ Church colleague Charles Stuart loaned to Robert Blake a twelve-page letter, which has since gone missing.

Why, in so crowded a life, in which he had to fight for time for his historical writing, did Trevor-Roper write so very many letters? The tempting answer is that this was easier than writing works of sustained historical scholarship. Yet his problem was not to write books. It was to persuade himself to publish them. He drafted much which was never published, including the huge book on the Civil Wars. It was dissatisfaction with the outcomes, not laziness or indifference, that kept so many of his writings from print. Truancy for Trevor-Roper was not an evasion of labour, but a principle of conduct, essential to mental equilibrium and to adventure of thought. To allow the mind to run idle was to escape from the pressures of conformity, social and professional, which his whole cast of mind resisted. In a letter to Wallace Notestein on 21 July 1968 he rejoices in the 'pleasure of total vacancy'. Nine years earlier, at the close of his inaugural lecture as Regius Professor in 1957, he praised one of his predecessors in the chair, Frederick York Powell, 'the friend of Mallarmé and Rodin and J. B. Yeats and Verlaine', whose life had likewise escaped the confines of academic employment: Powell 'contributed impartially to the *Encyclopaedia Britannica* and the *Sporting Times*', and conned the boxing reports in the *Licensed Victuallers' Gazette* as conscientiously as he did *Beowulf*.

If letter-writing was a form of truancy, it also gave scope for another necessary antidote to the earnest daily round: frivolity, an indulgence which ran deep in his nature. 'Who of us', he asks in a letter of 21 June 1991 to his future biographer, 'would wish to be judged by our private letters, in which one is licensed to be frivolous and irresponsible?' Frivolity is not a uniform feature in these letters: there are passions and earnest convictions; but the tone of mischievous comedy is seldom absent for more than a few pages. He wrote his letters off duty. They did not demand the research or the dogged accuracy necessary to his historical writing. The more exuberant of them allowed unfettered scope to caricature, distortion, even fantasy. Yet if there are those essential differences from his professional work, there are no less essential similarities. Behind the two forms of writing there lie the same powers of mind and observation; the same range and exactitude of learning; the same impulse for historical comparison; the same assured movement of thought between the concerns of the past and those of the present. The letters are distillations of a historian's wisdom.

Readers of the letters assembled in this book, where they are arrayed with elucidatory footnotes, will experience them differently from their recipients. Many of his correspondents might have spurned our provision of translations and glosses as fussy or condescending. Hugh Lloyd-Jones, Trevor-Roper's fellow classicist, annotated a draft of *Letters from Oxford* with pungent marginalia expressing his distaste for explications which, he felt, should be unnecessary to anyone of culture. But for other recipients, particularly younger ones who had been educated amid the decline of classical studies, Trevor-Roper's allusions and quotations must have been a test, as they might be to unaided readers now. He liked to stretch the minds of his younger correspondents. There are deliberate challenges as well as beguiling tutelage and confiding scholarship in his affectionate, generous letters to them. As he told his future wife in August 1953, he admired youthful spontaneity, curiosity, receptivity, flexibility, and unspoilt imagination. It was to these qualities that he appealed in letters written to guide and widen and brighten their recipients' minds, to steer his young friends towards fresh intellectual pursuits or literary pleasures. A letter from him also posed the challenge of reply, itself an instructive exercise. He once urged his young friend the historian Jeremy Catto, an eager recipient of his letters, to reply more often, not merely to give Trevor-Roper himself pleasure but because of the benefit one can derive from the necessary trouble. It is a measure of his yearning for contact that he so much relished letters from people who could not begin to match his epistolary gifts.

He strove to instil a concern for freshness and exactness and clarity of language into the young, and to deter them from the slipshod conformism of cliché and jargon. Those purposes are clear in letters to James Howard-Johnston during his education at Eton and Oxford and his later training at the Dumbarton Oaks Centre for Byzantine studies; to the graduate students Felix Raab in September 1962 and Alan Macfarlane on 22 January 1967; and in the literary precepts entitled 'The Ten Commandments' which he sent to Edward Chaney on 11 May 1988. For Trevor-Roper, as for Gibbon, style was the image of character. It could not be attained without discipline. In a letter of 1 May 1993 to his former pupil Richard Rhodes, he drew a parallel between the anarchic tendencies of modern English usage and the practices of the 'anti-monastery' of Rabelais's *Gargantua and Pantagruel*, whose votaries lived as they wished and as their instincts demanded, free of laws and regulations: 'I think it began in the '60s, with the general doctrine of permissiveness, as at the Abbey of Thelema: *Fais ce que voudras*: it doesn't matter about rules, technique, clarity, meaning, so long as you express yourself; as also in the other arts: splosh the paint about and the result is art because it is *you*. Horrible egotism!'

Most of these hundred letters exude a sense of self-possession. Cool, clear thoughts have been ordered and polished. Possible lines of resistance to Trevor-Roper's arguments have been anticipated, and potential obstacles demolished by uncompromising, sometimes merciless logic. Yet rationality was only one dimension of his mind. There is an intense literary sensibility at work in these letters, which is caught in evocations of poetry and landscape and the natural world. And while the rationality proclaims confidence, there are inner uncertainties. Occasionally in these letters the reader can divine, behind the habitual élan, the shyness that could inhibit him in conversation. In familiar company, it is true, he could be a brilliant talker, but his exuberance had a way of turning conversation into monologue. Letters, being written monologues, permitted the shaping of thoughts and words which impromptu discussion forestalls. Moreover, though he generally shunned emotional self-exposure in letters as in company, his correspondence does not always mask the loneliness, the self-doubt, and the depression that often accompany the comic temperament. In two letters of 1953 taken from his huge correspondence with his future wife Xandra, an exchange whose emotional intensity surprised all who had known him on its discovery after his death, he exposes raw feeling.

The letters reveal another feature of his temperament that the world did not often see: the tug of self-reproach. Despite his many worldly successes there is in some of the letters an undertone of inner censure. He blames himself for frittering time, for misdirecting effort, for a failure to bring his life under organizational control. When he was in Oxford, in his college rooms or his office in the History Faculty Building, even in his house in St Aldates, he felt bombarded by the administrative documents which demanded his attention, and mislaid or forgot the personal correspondence that he cherished. As he put it to J. H. Plumb in 1970, 'I am a hopeless writer of letters—or at least, a hopeless organiser of the paper which falls like a gentle but continuous blizzard of snow on my various desks. Some of them congeal into solid, lasting ice; others somehow get pushed off into great drifts at the table-side; others simply melt away and no trace is left of them. Yours has suddenly emerged from beneath a drift, and fills me with shame for my long silence.'[1]

Twenty-nine of the letters in this volume, including some of the gladdest ones, were written at Chiefswood, the house in the Scottish border country which the Trevor-Ropers owned from 1959 until 1987. On solitary visits to the house, or on days alone there while his wife visited her

---

[1] Trevor-Roper to J. H. Plumb, 7 March 1970, Plumb papers, Cambridge University Library.

titled friends in Scottish country houses where he might be bored or (in the case of Catholic families) ill at ease or unwelcome, he studied and thought and wrote in assuaging peace. He read big or difficult books that required intensity of attention: 'seven stout quarto volumes' of the correspondence of Hugo Grotius in July 1968, for example, or the works of Ssu-ma Ch'ien in April 1979. In his quiet interludes at Chiefswood he would sit in his study and write long, conversational letters which ranged over university business, personal news, intellectual preoccupations, world affairs, travel plans, and gossip. Andrew Marvell's poem 'The Garden', where 'Society is all but rude | To this delicious solitude', would come into his mind. The letters to friends and younger scholars from Chiefswood savour solitude—and are simultaneously retreats from its burdens. On 16 July 1966 he wrote to the graduate student Alan Macfarlane, with whom he shared an interest in seventeenth-century witch-hunts: 'I am enjoying being alone, with no more exacting conversation than that of the gardener: and do not understand why Xandra makes such a fuss about cooking (to the extent, now, of fetching a Chinese cook from Hong Kong): I live on ham, tongue, pork pie, spring onions and strawberries & cream, & cheese, white wine and brandy, and I find that the preparation of meals takes no time or trouble at all, & I am working like mad on witches. If you feel in need of a change & can live on such fare, come & visit me. I should not entertain you: you would work on *your* witches next door.' The invitation, at once to company and to separation, signals the ambivalence towards solitude of a man in whom it could be so creative but also so despondent a condition.

In these letters, readers can visit Trevor-Roper in his study at Chiefswood, hear his monologues, savour his ideas, weigh his judgements. If the wit sometimes has the sharpness of spring onions, at other moments—with its irony, its inventive and elaborate metaphors, and its unquenchable delight in human absurdity—it is pure strawberries and cream.

# PREFATORY NOTE

With a mind to continuing sensitivities we have omitted some phrases or paragraphs from a small minority of the letters that were written during the last quarter-century of Trevor-Roper's life. The deletions have been made silently, for the indication of omissions might carry its own unkind imputations, and would anyway be a distraction to readers. Occasionally other passages have been omitted from the volume because they deal only with humdrum or practical matters which even the most artistic letter-writers have sometimes to address.

We have preserved the variety of his spellings, uses of capital letters, and so on. Normally we have corrected his rare slips of the pen, though not the slight errors in his quotations, from memory, of Greek texts. We have not reproduced the full addresses of letters, or postcodes.

# THE LETTERS

*In 1940 Trevor-Roper, then aged 26, made the acquaintance of the writer Logan Pearsall Smith (1865–1946), with whom he formed an immediate rapport, despite the difference in their ages. In the summer months, when on leave from his war work with the Radio Intelligence Service, Trevor-Roper would often visit Smith at his house in Chelsea. Smith liked to tease Trevor-Roper and to be teased by him. In the summer of 1941 Smith wrote to him, 'I will allow myself to say that I find your company the most delightful in the world', but added, 'I am not entirely sure that you are altogether a nice person.' Smith found (or affected to find) the younger man's enthusiasm for country pursuits absurd. A bond between the two men was their passion for literary style and their interest in the properties and resources of language. 'Words and phrases are the only things that matter,' he told Trevor-Roper early in their friendship. The following letter was written while Trevor-Roper was staying with his parents in Northumberland.*

## To Logan Pearsall Smith, 18 September 1943

20 Bondgate Without, Alnwick

My dear Logan

There'll be no trout for anyone this time, I'm afraid, unless I can get enough with a minnow tomorrow. The wind and the rain have driven them all down to the river-bed, and no flies hatch; or if they do, at once, like the infant of Saguntum,[1] they huddle their broken shells about them & scurry off to warm bolt-holes in the banks. So instead of breaking my heart by those unavailing, immitigable streams, here I am sitting in the warm & the dry, reading St Simon,[2] and playing with those will-o'-the-wisps that dance and beckon so temptingly before me,—I mean *Things to Write About*, ghostly forms which beguile and mock me, as you, I believe, are mocked, by *Wicked Things to Say*, clamouring behind the barrier of your teeth. (But I'm a bit sceptical about your version, for I notice that they don't need to clamour long for release in my presence, protest I never so much).

---

[1] Pliny, *Natural History* 7.3, describes how 'an infant at Saguntum…at once went back into the womb in the year in which that city was destroyed by Hannibal'.

[2] The *Mémoires* of Louis de Rouvroy, Duc de Saint Simon (1675–1755).

Well, you have added more to the number of these inviting Will-o'-the-Wisps, with your *Famous Sins*, and *Portraits of the Deans of Christ Church*; but I'm not heeding yours, for another has already captivated me: having discovered in myself a flair for characterisation, I'm contemplating a short sketch of the *Sage of Chelsea*.[1] And so I will fill my time till this month ends, and then, behold, I shall be hunting again, getting up early in the morning & riding to the great russet woods, & feeding my horse on windfall crab-apples, while I read my Horace at the covert-side, until I hear the cry of hounds rising & falling in the wood, like the cry of sea-gulls around a ship. O ravishing music! and of course I shall get slightly drunk afterwards, & come & see you, & talk inconsequently about it all; but you won't listen, for you'll be polishing, polishing away till there is nothing left of your portrait of Sir Hubert Parry—which why haven't you published?[2] This urgent query flashed suddenly across my mind as I listened to Handel's Water Music in my bath this evening, and wished I had been George I, to glide down old Thames in a procession of barges, with Nymphs & Porpoises frisking alongside, & Handel & his players playing the Water Music in another barge; but I'm afraid old George I was paying little or no attention, but sitting, bored & boring, eating black-puddings & spinach all the time...and at this point in my meditations, the bathwater having become cold, I thought of your character of Sir Hubert Parry. Why haven't you finished & published it? What's the good of my floating you as a Chelsea Sage if you won't play your part? And anyway, what right have you to pose as a retired, retiring Sage at your age? Why, you're not even 80 yet; your active years are still to come; all the governors of Europe are now between 80 and 90. Perhaps I'd better come back a day early & prod you into a sense of your duty.—But no,—I had forgot—that word, I now remember, has long since dropped

---

[1]   T-R wrote a pen-portrait, 'Logan Pearsall Smith in Old Age', which he sent to his subject for approval. T-R adopts for Pearsall Smith a phrase coined for Thomas Carlyle.
[2]   Pearsall Smith endlessly revised waspish character sketches of his contemporaries. Sir Hubert Parry (1848–1918), composer and Director of the Royal College of Music, was among them.

from your selective vocabulary; though even Basic English, with its 850 words, probably contains it.[1]

You see I'm in a holiday mood. I have leisure for all things. Why, I even turned up one of my early publications the other day (they are few, but they bear infinite re-reading; do you find the same quality in yours?). It was an article on William Somervile, the poet, published in *Country Life*,[2] that excellent paper; and from it I learned that, on his death, Somervile was described by Shenstone as 'conscious (at least in one production) of having pleased the world'.[3] Will this do for your epitaph—even though, in your Chelsea philistinism, you haven't read that one work which so pleased the mid-18th century world?

Well, I'm falling asleep. I've trailed through the turnips & stubble-fields of Chillingham all day after partridges, & am weary. If you see Marjorie Madan,[4] give her my love, & over her troutless breakfasts let her remember the River Till, that enchanted, but temporarily fishless, river. But to the American sergeant, a coldish shoulder is all that I can offer.[5]

yours ever

Hugh Trevor-Roper

---

[1]   The linguist and bibliophile Charles Kay Ogden (1889–1957), co-founder and editor of the international journal of psychology *Psyche*, devised a simplified language, 'Basic English', with 850 words, as a standardized means of international communication. He published *Basic English* (1930), *Debabelization* (1931), and other works known to Pearsall Smith's Chelsea set.

[2]   'William Somervile, the Poet of the Chase' (10 June 1939).

[3]   William Shenstone (1714–63), essayist, poet, and landscape gardener, helped Somerville revise his poem 'The Chase'. The passage of his to which T-R refers reads as follows: 'Our old friend Somervile is dead! I did not imagine I could have been so sorry...I can now excuse all his foibles; impute them to age, and to distress of circumstances...For a man of high spirit, conscious of having (at least in one production) generally pleased the world, to be plagued and threatened by wretches that are low in every sense; to be forced to drink himself into pains of the body in order to get rid of the pains of the mind, is a misery...I loved him for nothing so much as his flocci-nauci-nihili-pili-fication of money.'

[4]   Marjorie Madan (1896–1987), wife of the literary dilettante Geoffrey Madan, had spent Edwardian holidays at Chillingham, the Northumberland castle which her grandfather Sir Andrew Noble, the Newcastle armaments manufacturer, leased from Lord Tankerville.

[5]   T-R portrayed Pearsall Smith's protégé Stuart Preston (1915–2005), a sergeant in the US Army, as snobbish and pretentious in a character sketch in his *Wartime Journals*.

*In the summer of 1946, after finishing his book* The Last Days of Hitler, *Trevor-Roper left for a holiday in Iceland. He spent three weeks there, mostly alone, strolling along the seashore, walking in the mountains, watching birds, fishing for trout and char, and camping in the wilderness. Naomi Church (b. 1913) was the daughter of Canon Roland Allgood, rector of Ingram, a village in the Cheviots a few miles from Trevor-Roper's birthplace and on the higher reaches of the river Breamish, where he fished as a young man. She married on 15 September 1939 John Cunningham Church (1914–71). The Churches shared Trevor-Roper's zest for country sports.*

## To Naomi 'Nim' Church, 28 August 1946

[Iceland]

My dear Nim,

You see I have got to Iceland. It took a good deal of organisation, but *everything is possible*.[1] I hope it will even be possible to get back when I want to; I haven't considered that yet. The fishing situation is very different now from what it was. After a few hundred years of passively watching eccentric Englishmen tossing flies & minnows into their rivers, the Icelanders have taken to it themselves, with great zeal; the farmers have sold their rights to corporations, joint-stock-companies, catchment boards, & preservation-trusts; and there is no casual fishing to be had anywhere. As I had set out from Alnwick with an assortment of casts like hawsers, flies the size of sparrow hawks on hooks like meat-hangers, and a net big enough to land a porpoise, you may think I have been had. Not at all. Suppress the welling tear. Providence never lets down her pet lambs. While I was waiting for the boat at Fleetwood, Lancs., there was delivered to me a letter from a complete stranger in Devonshire, pressing me to the use of his two rivers in northern Iceland, and enclosing letters to his sub-lessees.[2] So now I am living in a farm in the valley of the river Fujoska. There are no fish in this part of the river (at least none that I can find),—it is the unvalued part

---

[1]  Nim Church would have recognized this as a favourite phrase of T-R's.

[2]  Lionel Fortescue (1892–1981), an Eton master who had retired to a village on the edge of Dartmoor.

which hasn't found a sub-lessee,—but it is very beautiful, & I am having next weekend on the best part. At present I find fishing rather exhausting. The rivers are very fast and clear, and the pools, if any, are separated by miles of volcanic rubble and overgrown lava-humps. The other day I had to walk eight miles over such country, in waders, with tackle, & carrying a 4 lb bull-trout. After a mile, I sat down on a lava-hump and cleaned the creature with a pair of nail-scissors to reduce its weight; I thus reduced it to about 3 lb 15¼ oz. I was thoroughly bored with the animal by the time I got back. Next day I decided it would be better to take a pony. The pony was infinitely slow. My own elegant racehorse would have got there in a twentieth of the time (admittedly at the cost of seven or eight catastrophic falls and the drowning of both of us in one of the swirling torrents we had to ford). It was pouring with rain and bitterly cold—the sort of day which possibly dawns on the Cheviots sometime towards the end of November, at which you give one shuddering glance through the Rectory window, and at once bury your nose for the rest of the day in *Archbishop Laud*.[1] (At least I hope this is what you do. Perhaps you really embroider nappies). When I found some likely water, I would hobble the pony and start struggling, in a high wind, with casts & flies. Just when I had reached that familiar stage when the cast was entangled into a quite inextricable cocoon, and the flies had hooked themselves in a quite inaccessible part of my mackintosh, I would hear a dull thud to the rear, & looking round, would see that the pony, attempting surreptitiously to unhobble itself, had looped the loop, and was lying on its back among the lava-humps, with its feet in the air, and a dissatisfied expression on its face. After this had happened twice, I tried leaving the pony unhobbled and trusting to its good sense. A fatal confidence! It would wait till my back was turned, and then wander away at a speed which it had never shown on any other occasion. Altogether, I think it is easier to fish without a pony.

After describing these humiliations, perhaps you will indulge me in a Boast. The whole of Iceland has been swept up in a cyclone of inflation,

---

[1]    T-R's first book; it was published in 1940.

and everything costs the moon (consider that I am forgoing a meal to pay the postage on this letter, and then ask yourself if christian charity could go further; your father might preach a sermon on this text to the critical worshippers of Ingram). Thus I found that my whole allowance of money had gone in two days. What does the enterprising man do on such an occasion? Well, I investigated the nature of the financial situation in Iceland, & found that wages were on the same scale as prices, so I decided to make some money instead of buying it, & losing it all in the exchange. First I made stucco (very good stucco too) for two hours in the Arctic port of Akureyri. This got me 15 kronur & a meal. (15 kronur will buy two working-class meals, or one bourgeois meal; it costs 15/- to buy). Inspired by this scoop, I went to consult the chairman of the local fishing-board about the fishing. When I introduced myself he said, 'Are you related to the great Trevor-Roper whose literary works are read so enthusiastically on this forlorn polar sea-shore?' or words to that effect; and at once he produced a copy of the *New York Times* and pointed to an article that seemed to be by me, although at first I failed to recognise it under its title of '*New Light on a Bloodstained Mystic*'.[1] He then explained that he was editor of the local weekly, and asked if I would write a special article for it, for which he paid me 200 kronur. Since then I have made no more stucco, & can boast that my works have been translated even into Icelandic.

I believe I said above that everything is possible. There is one matter to which I think this otherwise universal rule may not apply: the Icelandic language. I intended to get on without it, but as no one on this farm speaks a syllable of any other language, there is no help for it, I must scratch my way along in it. It is a very eccentric tongue, and seems to bear no relation to any known system of speech. The books say that is similar to Old Norse, but I don't believe it. My old norse[2] was a Scots body from Brechin, and was perfectly intelligible, especially when she forbade us to put both butter and jam on our bread.

---

[1]  An article about Himmler, published on 21 July 1946.
[2]  T-R plays on an archaic alternative to the word nurse, 'norsh'.

This is the end of this letter. It's a great mistake to write more than two pages. Who knows but you may have stopped in the middle through sheer physical exhaustion, as people do in *Gone With the Wind* & Tolstoy's *War & Peace*; & then what a waste to have written so much.

Love to Phyllida, John & Nigel.[1]

yours ever

Hugh

—∞∞∞—

On 18 March 1947, near the end of an exceptionally harsh winter, Trevor-Roper celebrated the publication of The Last Days of Hitler with a dinner in Oxford, to which he invited several of those who had helped him to investigate his subject or write the book. His friend Peter Ramsbotham (1919–2010) was unable to attend as he was serving in Hamburg with the Control Commission. Ramsbotham, who would be British Ambassador to Iran and the United States during the 1970s, was a graduate of Magdalen College, Oxford, who had served in the wartime Intelligence Corps. He had coordinated the search for witnesses from the bunker during Trevor-Roper's investigation into Hitler's last days, had assisted him in the quest for Hitler's will, and was now providing material for a book that Trevor-Roper was thinking of writing about the July plot of 1944 to assassinate Hitler. In the previous month, Ramsbotham had arranged for the Intelligence Department to loan Trevor-Roper, via MI5's Guy Liddell, their files on the July plot. Trevor-Roper was, however, about to abandon this book, as he did so many others.

Ramsbotham had written to Trevor-Roper from Hamburg on 8 February 1947: 'my pedestrian wit can never do justice to the sparkle and gaiety of your epistolatory favours. The recipient of the Song of Solomon must have felt as I do—embarrassed by being the occasion for such a wealth of words, but determined that others shall also enjoy the riches offered. Your letters are a source of very real pleasure; they regale me in moments of deep depression in this city of misery, self-pity and frustration. If you have written many such letters to other friends, I look forward to the time when we can each assemble our possessions and publish a collection of "belles lettres" to codify your wit and embalm the fragrance and charm of your literary style between slim (and expensive) covers!' Unfortunately Trevor-Roper's other letters to Ramsbotham were lost.

---

[1]    Nim Church's husband and children (Phyllida was T-R's god-daughter).

## To Peter Ramsbotham, 19 March 1947

Christ Church, Oxford

My dear Peter,

How are you? What has it been like in Germany? Have you too been buried in snowdrifts, congealed like a prawn in aspic, in mountain-walls of solid ice, overwhelmed in blizzards? and are you now swimming aimlessly, hither and thither, in infinite oceanic floods? Conceive, if you can, my term,—eight weeks of it—not only pupils (that bane of a university) but these unabated climatic horrors. Have I done so much as one short day's foxhunting? Not one. I have moped in my room while my unhappy horse, like some disconsolate reindeer in the Lapland solitudes, standing knee-deep in the snow, and pointing its nose fondly out of its igloo in the direction of Bicester,[1] has almost forgotten the sound of the hunting horn. Sadly, I sometimes blow my own in my rooms, at 2.0 a.m., after a light snack with my friends in the hope that the noise, having deafened a brace of canons in Tom Quad in their stertorous slumbers, will drift ethereally over the intervening woods & pasture into Buckinghamshire, and cheer that poor forlorn quadruped. Now, at last, the snow is past: what is the result? Eton College, your old *alma mater*, has been evacuated by boat from upper windows; the young of our ancient aristocracy, top-hatted and coronetted, have been rescued from quattrocento pinnacles and Palladian clock-towers & have gone home. Here, in Magdalen College, your other *alma mater*, the tower indeed, like some disdainful lighthouse in Sestos or Abydos,[2] still stands serenely overlooking the floods; but elsewhere what an infinite watery waste greets the eye! The elms are all down. A great gale swept over the world the other night, and almost every elm in Oxford is flat. Their age, poor things, was some 250 years, & their roots being in the water, what could they do? They sighed a seventeenth-century metaphysical sigh and collapsed, one after the other; and now their

---

[1]  T-R rode to hounds with the Bicester hunt. His horse Rubberneck was stabled at Quainton in Buckinghamshire.

[2]  Towns on opposite shores of the Hellespont. In 1810 Byron swam from Sestos to Abydos in four hours, as Leander was said to have done in his pursuit of Hero.

shattered hulks, like drowned giants, lie this way & that in the floods; & the Magdalen deer, like dappled dolphins, swim timidly to & fro in their changed, watery world. But why do I dwell thus maliciously on your college? Mine is in no better plight. There are 20 elms down in that part of the Ch Ch Meadow alone which is still visitable without stilts, waders, or native canoes. Indeed all Oxford is under water. Swans swim in the streets. There is no life save in upper storeys. Cattle are herded on the Magdalen Tower, and racehorses neigh incongruously in the Christ Church belfry, and college messengers ply from tower to tower in graceful gondolas, singing improbable *amoretti* as they glide over the submerged colleges of the Turl. But here I am beginning to exaggerate slightly, I will desist, & turn to the next item, only observing that there is one man in Oxford at least who is quite untouched by the calamity—your former colleague Robert Blake.[1] He, like Nero, is an aesthetic soul, indifferent to the price at which artistic sensations are bought. The gurgles of the drowning, the total submersion of whole colleges, is immaterial to him, so long as his East Anglian aestheticism can be satisfied by the spectacle of infinite endless floods; & he spends whole afternoons surveying the deluge with serene complacency.

But now I turn to my book. It is out. Why were you not here for my party on the (theoretical) day of its publication? It was a splendid party. From the ends of the earth they came, Solly Zuckerman from the remote septentrional north of Birmingham;[2] Dick White from the Mahomeddan East of London;[3] & Herbert was there,[4] & Denys Page,[5] & Charles

[1] Robert Blake (1916–2003), later Lord Blake, Student—Christ Church's equivalent of Fellow—and Tutor in Politics at Christ Church 1947–68 and Provost of the Queen's College 1968–87; a close ally of T-R's in college and university intrigues.

[2] (Sir) Solly Zuckerman (1904–93), later Lord Zuckerman, Professor of Anatomy at Birmingham University 1943–68, wartime Scientific Adviser to Combined Operations HQ.

[3] (Sir) Dick White (1906–93) had prompted T-R to write *The Last Days of Hitler*. Like T-R, he had been a pupil of J. C. Masterman at Christ Church. White joined the Security Service in 1936 at Masterman's instigation, and became a lifelong friend of T-R when they worked as wartime colleagues. He headed MI5 1953–6 and MI6 1956–68.

[4] Herbert [H. L. A.] Hart (1907–92) was a wartime intelligence associate of T-R who had been present when White proposed that T-R write *The Last Days*. He was a Fellow of New College, Oxford, Professor of Jurisprudence 1952–68, and Principal of Brasenose 1973–8.

[5] (Sir) Denys Page (1908–78), Classics Tutor at Christ Church 1932–50, had been involved in deciphering wartime enemy signals at Bletchley. He was elected Regius Professor of Greek at Cambridge in 1950, and Master of Jesus College, Cambridge, in 1959.

Stuart;[1] & the oysters that were eaten, & the infinite succession of wines that were drunk, went on till 2 a.m.,—a Sardanapalian beano;[2] I wish you had been there; but alas, you were in Germany, flighting the wild duck on those great lakes among those haunted woods of Schleswig Holstein,[3] which to me are more beautiful than all the dreary vineyards and ridiculous gothic follies of the Rhineland, and all the suburban scenery of the Black Forest. And now the position is reversed; for I (I think) am going to Germany on 27 March, armed with a transatlantic abundance of dollars, while you, whom I would rather see than all Germany, are coming home for precisely the duration of my stay. Klop[4] has given me a letter to Prince Bismarck, at Friedrichsruh, near Hamburg,[5] and an introduction to Stauffenberg's cousin Count Albedyll,[6] who lives (I understand) in an enchanted castle on a mist-enshrouded island in the forgotten Baltic Sea; but what is the use, if you aren't there to meet me, to look after me, to listen to my boasts, to walk with me among those ancient lakes, & divert any access of Nordic melancholy by your conversation? I shall have to turn aside and go to the wretched old Rhineland with its vulgar bric-à-brac castles faked for the coal-&-chemical kings who have ruined Germany & Europe. Shall I find the friendly face of Leo Long in one of them?[7] Do you think he would receive me as a casual visitor? I should like to visit him and pick his brains.

[1]  See p. 14.

[2]  The legendary Assyrian king Sardanapalus was renowned for luxurious excess.

[3]  T-R's journeys there, while conducting his investigation into the death of Hitler in 1945, are described in his *Wartime Journals*.

[4]  Jonah Freiherr von Ustinov (1892–1962), known as 'Klop' (the Russian for bedbug), was press officer in the German embassy in London until 1935, when he was recruited by MI5. His son was the multi-talented Peter Ustinov.

[5]  Count Gottfried von Bismarck-Schönhausen (1901–49) had known in advance of the July plot to kill Hitler, although he had not participated. His manor house of Friedrichsruh was destroyed by RAF bombing in 1945.

[6]  Graf Claus von Stauffenberg (1907–44), German war hero and instigator of the July 1944 plot to kill Hitler, was related to the ancient Estonian noble family of Albedyll, who had become leading Prussian military junkers in the 19th century and several of whom held influential military posts during the Second World War.

[7]  Leonard ('Leo') Long (1916–2002) was a Holloway carpenter's son who won a scholarship to Trinity College, Cambridge. He was taught by Anthony Blunt, elected to the Apostles in 1937, and recruited by the NKVD (the precursor of the KGB) around the same time. After the outbreak of war he joined the War Office's military intelligence department. There he became

By the way, have you received your copy of my book? I think I told my publishers to send it straight to Hamburg; I hope they have. As for my next, I don't think it will be on the Plot after all; and that although[1] you have so kindly sent (I learn from Dick White) a great haystack of papers to S.J.[2] for me. But an American has got in ahead of me,—Allen W. Dulles, who was head of OSS in Switzerland during the war.[3] He has published the book in America, & my publisher here asked me to read it for him. It is a good book, & I have advised Macmillan to publish an English edition. This makes me doubtful about the need for another. But there are still problems connected with the Plot which seem to me of great interest, & which he has left unanswered; so my researches will continue, & your devotion in sending those huge files of documents will not, I hope, have been in vain. I have in fact written a turn on the Plot in *Polemic*, which isn't out yet; so you will see (if you want) what stage my views on that subject have reached.[4] Incidentally, if you are in England on 4 April, & happen to turn on the wireless, you may hear me dogmatising on the subject of Disraeli; but don't be deceived.[5] Of course I know nothing about Disraeli. All I have done is to tell my two faithful friends Robert Blake & Charles Stuart about my predicament, and they retired to their several hermitages, & in a few days, behold! they returned, bringing in their hands, one the six volumes of Monypenny & Buckle,[6] the other all the other relevant works, all neatly flagged and indexed; & now, by this cooperative effort, the truth has been obtained. I think I shall adopt this system for everything in

---

the source of Ultra and other military secrets supplied to the Russians. Appointed deputy head of intelligence at the British Control Commission in Germany in 1945 (therefore a colleague of Ramsbotham's), he remained active as a Soviet agent until 1952.

[1]   i.e. even though.

[2]   Not identified.

[3]   Allen Dulles (1863–1969) was Director of the Central Intelligence Agency 1953–61. T-R called on him at Claridge's Hotel in May 1947.

[4]   T-R, 'The German Opposition, 1937–1944', published in the shortlived journal *Polemic*.

[5]   'Disraeli—the Political Virtuoso', *Listener*, 17 April 1947.

[6]   William Flavelle Monypenny and George Earle Buckle, *The Life of Benjamin Disraeli, Earl of Beaconsfield* (1910–20).

future; I believe it is called 'the organisation of study'. Of course it depends entirely on having good organisers; fortunately I have.

Now my dear Peter I am going to end this tedious letter; I expect that you have long ago ceased to read it, and already sleep is descending upon my eyes. Only let me know what your movements really are, and remember that if you are in England and I am not in Germany, there is no one I would rather see than yourself. The fatted oyster will be opened; the cherished bottle will be uncorked; & for as long as you will visit me I will even (if your credulity can be stretched to entertain this absurd proposition) not talk but listen.

yours ever

Hugh

---

*The following two letters, to his fellow historian and Christ Church colleague Charles Stuart (1920–91), were written during Trevor-Roper's foreign travels. On Boxing Day of 1947 he left for Prague with his pupil Alan Clark (1928–99), later a historian, politician, and diarist, in an open-top Lagonda belonging to Clark's father, the art historian Kenneth Clark. In the spring of 1949 he would spend some weeks travelling in the United States with another pupil, Francis Dashwood.*

*Stuart, who had worked alongside Trevor-Roper analysing radio intercepts and other intelligence during the war, was an ally of his in post-war Christ Church. Together with the young politics don Robert Blake, they saw themselves as Cavaliers fighting Oxford's pleasure-loathing Puritans, and as a Party of Gaiety to relieve the life-diminishing austerities adopted during the war.*

## To Charles Stuart, 31 December 1947

Prague

My dear Charles

I hope you are having domestic high-jinks for the New Year at Ashtead[1] while I make do on the slender fare of Czechoslovakia; and that if (as

---

[1]  T-R liked to tease Charles Stuart about the dull respectability of Ashtead, the quiet, moneyed town in the Surrey stockbroker belt where Stuart's family had a comfortable villa.

seems possible) I fail to return to Oxford in time, you will somehow find, in the unsorted jumble of the Junior Censor's[1] rooms, the documents necessary to the launching of the year's historical studies at the House.[2] You will find the tutor's book in my Tallboy, and other relevant files in one of my big files labelled *Ch Ch & University*. But don't be alarmed. In view of the impossibilities which have been surmounted to get here, I believe that I shall solve the minor problem of return.

The problems began with the incompetence of the RAC, who lost those essential documents, the *triptych* & *carnet*, without which it is quite impossible (they said) to move a car across any frontier anywhere, & then closed down for Xmas, merely sending us a wire that they would send them direct to Harwich for us to pick up on our way abroad. In fact they never arrived, & the only advice we could get was to wait five days for the next boat, when a new set would be prepared.

This of course we rejected out of hand, & in spite of the protests of the Port Officer, I ultimately prevailed (by a feat of diplomacy which I cannot now understand) on the Landing Officer at Harwich to write out an authorisation for 'temporary export', on the basis of which we were ultimately able to get the car on to the ship. Unfortunately the customs officials at Antwerp, being Flemish, were less easy to talk to, and were quite inexorable. No sooner had we got the vehicle ashore, than they firmly padlocked it into a necessarily capacious iron cage; and after a whole morning's argument they only yielded so far as to agree to release it provided that the sum of £600 was deposited, in Belgian currency, as a pledge of its return. Fortunately we found a rich shipping magnate who, by touting round his business friends on Saturday afternoon, raised and deposited this sum for us. Thereupon the iron bars creaked open & we were able to drive on to the German frontier.

This of course presented a special problem, which was solved by a careful plan elaborated over a dozen oysters in the Century Bar, Antwerp. Rightly

---

[1]    Christ Church Censors are the college officers responsible for the supervision of studies and for the discipline of undergraduates.

[2]    Members of Christ Church often call their college 'the House', after its Latin name *Aedes Christi* (the House of Christ).

deducing that no British official would yet be on duty at such an hour, we craftily drove up to the frontier at 7 o'clock on Sunday morning, having previously taken the precaution of flying a union jack from the bonnet, thus suggesting the presence of a British general within. In these circumstances, a few sharp words in German to the German on duty had an electrical effect on his conditioned reflexes, and we floated effortlessly into Germany. There I contrived to get American military orders for the car, which got us as far as the Bohemian frontier; and there, thanks to the complete ignorance of the English tongue which disabled the Czech customs officials from detecting that the details which I gave them rested on no authority whatever, we slid through the iron curtain,—much I hope to the chagrin of the RAC, who still protest that we must necessarily be waiting at Harwich. You will realise from this that I am fairly confident of getting the relics of the car back in due course.

I am sorry that I should have to say *relics*; but veracity compels me to admit that after a head-on collision with the chauffeur-driven limousine of the Minister of Labour for Land Gross-Hessen on top of the snow-bound Spessart, no other word is strictly applicable. Fortunately, at the time of this misencounter, we had slowed down slightly from the optimum cruising-speed recommended by the makers of the car (104 m.p.h.) so that the impact was less disastrous than it might have been, & we inflicted rather more damage than we suffered.

If you see Menna,[1] tell her that Prague is delightful, & the absence of other travellers makes it particularly attractive. I paid a visit to the Wallenstein Palace this afternoon,—a fascinating place—I will send her a picture-postcard of it if I can find one—& intend to go on pilgrimage to Jičin if the roads are free. Indeed everything here is most attractive; it is also excessively cheap, since although the bank-rate for the dollar is 48 crowns, I find that I can always get 270 crowns for it on the black market; which makes a considerable difference.

---

[1] Menna Prestwich, née Roberts (1917–90), Tutor in Modern History at St Hilda's College, Oxford, 1946–83, Fellow 1947–83, and University Lecturer 1962–83, married another historian, John Prestwich (1914–2003), Fellow of Queen's 1937–81. She was both an ally and occasional bane of T-R.

I have a few more boasts, but perhaps I had better keep them in reserve till I see you on 15 Jan.

yours ever

Hugh

P.S. You should not deduce from the above narrative any reflections on my chauffeur. He is above praise.

⌾

## To Charles Stuart, 24 March 1949

The Preacher's Room, Lowell House, Harvard University

My dear Charles,

You will assume from the letterhead that my devotional tendencies have at last got the better of me; but perhaps I had better explain that accident rather than complete conviction has brought me to this address. I was in fact staying in comfort with a hospitable Bostonian family until the maid's boy-friend, smoking when tight in the maid's bed, set the entire house ablaze and himself escaped from the debris in my clothes; so Isaiah Berlin, by a quick appropriate gesture, lodged me here. *Five Kings of the American Pulpit* is my bedside book,[1] and when I saunter out of this spacious suite, expletives wither on the lips of suddenly reverent undergraduates. Otherwise it doesn't matter much where I stay, as my life is spent in a succession of cocktail parties organised by Francis Dashwood.[2] I can scarcely open my mouth to speak without a Bronx or Manhattan being shot into it. In New York I went to dinner with

---

[1]   Clarence Macartney (1879–1957), pastor of the First Presbyterian Church of Pittsburgh, published *Six Kings of the American Pulpit* in 1942. Perhaps T-R was remembering the five kings of the Amorites in the book of Joshua.

[2]   Francis Dashwood (1925–2000), who had been educated at Eton and Christ Church, was studying at Harvard Business School. He inherited the West Wycombe estate in Buckinghamshire and the premier baronetcy of Great Britain in 1966.

Mrs Cornelius Vanderbilt—see Gustavus Meyers *ad loc*—where 26 bores sat down to dine off gold plate and 26 Irish footmen stood behind their chairs.[1] Most of the guests were people who also tried to give grand parties and were therefore invited not out of love but in order to humiliate them by the show of superior magnificence. After dinner, in order to escape the tedium of talking or listening to each other, we were all shepherded into a state-room, & made to look at an indescribably dull colour travel film taken in Europe by Cornelius Vanderbilt jr. This I find is a regular feature of American dinner parties—one better, because less effort, than bridge.

Isaiah is a great success here, but the Warden of Wadham, you will no doubt be sorry to hear, less so: in fact his lectures, crowded at the beginning, have attracted a steadily dwindling audience, as a sad reminder that so little intellectual capital, unrefreshed by continual speculation, can't really be made to go very far, even in America.[2] He returns to Oxford next week, to watch the Dean of Ch Ch (whom he never names without undertones of hostility) operating as V.C.[3] I don't feel that he relishes the presence here either of Isaiah or of myself; but I can't think why, since we are both so discreet.

The day before I left England I sold my last horse.[4] From now on I shall devote myself to pure (or almost pure) scholarship, compared with which I find the cocktails of Boston & the high-life of New York as dust and ashes and dead-sea-apples in my unresponsive mouth. Still, as even

---

[1]   The journalist Gustavus Meyers (1872–1942) wrote *History of the Great American Fortunes* (1909), *History of American Idealism* (1925), *The Ending of Hereditary American Fortunes* (1939), and *History of Bigotry in the United States* (1943). Grace Vanderbilt (1870–1953) lived at 1048 Fifth Avenue. Her son Cornelius Vanderbilt IV (1898–1974) had seven wives and was a tabloid journalist.

[2]   In the autumn of 1948 and spring of 1949 (Sir) Maurice Bowra (1898–1971), Warden of Wadham 1938–70 and Professor of Poetry 1946–51, gave a series of lectures which became his book *The Romantic Imagination*. He complained at the time: 'My lectures are attended by large crowds, who have a reverential look, as if they were in church. The girls knit, the boys look at the girls. At intervals, elderly ladies come in, stay for ten minutes, and then go out. Small boys come from the street, playing hide-and-seek.'

[3]   John Lowe (1899–1960), Dean of Christ Church 1939–59 and Vice-Chancellor 1948–51.

[4]   To one of his pupils, Tommy Baring (1927–2009). T-R liked to recall that the transaction was settled during a tutorial.

dead-sea-apples are quite enjoyable while they last, I go back to New York next week before penetrating the south.

I had quite a good journey here except that we ran into snowstorms which made landing in Gander impossible & we had to go hundreds of miles out of the way and land on our last drop of petrol in a desolate snowbound waste called Goose Bay, Labrador. I intend to begin a common-room gambit with the words 'When I was in Labrador...'

How is scholarship in Ashtead?

yours ever,

Hugh

---

*In the spring vacation of 1951 Trevor-Roper set out on a walking holiday in Greece. The country was recovering from the bitter civil war which had ended in October 1949; few tourists yet visited it, or at least dared to stir outside Athens. The result was that he never met another foreigner. 'It was heaven,' he wrote. In one three-day trek he covered eighty miles: 'the most terrible, but also the most wonderful walk,' as he described it. 'I rather like discomfort, and sleeping out-of-doors, or in peasants' huts.' He had an alarming experience in the Peloponnese town of Megalópoli, when his hotel bedroom was invaded at 3.00 a.m. by enraged soldiers who stabbed his mattress with their bayonets. They accused him of being a Communist spy—'not for the first or the last time', he reflected wryly, years later.*

*Trevor-Roper tried to persuade his friend Dawyck Haig[1] to accompany him on this and other trips abroad. They had come to know each other in the late 1930s, when Haig had been an undergraduate at Christ Church, and Trevor-Roper a young don. Haig was always known as Dawyck (pronounced Doyick), after the courtesy title which he bore until, as the only son of the Field Marshal, he inherited his father's earldom at the age of 9. After his capture by the Italians in the Western Desert in 1942, he was consigned to Colditz, where he was among the prominente, those well-connected prisoners whom the Germans had selected as potential hostages. After the war, he studied at Camberwell School of Art, where he was a pupil of Victor Pasmore, Lawrence Gowing, and William Coldstream. In the years after the war Trevor-Roper was a welcome guest at Bemersyde, Haig's estate in the Scottish Borders, which had been presented to his father by a grateful nation in 1921. When Haig asked him to undertake the thorny task of editing the Field Marshal's diaries, Trevor-Roper instead proposed Robert*

[1]   George Alexander Eugene Douglas Haig, 2nd Earl Haig (1918–2009).

*Blake, who thus became another regular visitor. For Trevor-Roper, Bemersyde was a haven,
and Haig an ideal host. 'There is no place that I visit with such pleasure, or leave with such
regret,' he wrote after a visit in the spring of 1950: 'My dear Dawyck, infinite thanks: your
house is the humanest place I know,—you make it so.' In 1954, Trevor-Roper would marry
Haig's eldest sister, Lady Alexandra Howard-Johnston (1907–97), known as Xandra.*

## To Dawyck Haig, 28 January 1951

Christ Church, Oxford

My dear Dawyck,

I am of course disappointed that you can't accompany me, if I can go, to
Greece. It will be my loss. But after all (I say to myself, when I seek to ra-
tionalise these profound matters) why should you? You were never, I
think, a classical scholar: you have never read Homer, that unforgettable
poet (and a man who has never read Homer, according to Bagehot,[1] 'is like
a man who has never seen the sea: there is a great object of which he is unaware'); so how can I expect you to sympathise with the desire I have to
visit, before it is too late, those romantic templed shores, the shame I feel
at never yet having visited them or proceeded from the intoxicating fore-
taste in Italy to the authentic feast beyond the Adriatic? Even so, do you
feel no temptation? Do not even the broken rocks of Crete, which thrust
themselves up in the background of El Greco's early pictures—and sometimes, disguised as Spanish rocks, in his later pictures too—do not even
these draw you thither? Evidently not. You prefer riding in point-to-
points. Well, I must not demur:

> To turn and wind a fiery Pegasus
> And witch the world with noble horsemanship[2]

is a respectable and traditional ambition, especially in the peerage;
and therefore, although I now regard horses in general as superficially

---

[1]   In his essay on the poet William Cowper.
[2]   Shakespeare, *1 Henry IV*, IV.i.114–15.

attractive but fundamentally dangerous creatures (and so am apprehensive of my most valued friends having much to do with them),[1] I hope that you will nevertheless enjoy your springtime snorting headlong across the unperceived flowering countryside, and will be (since you avow this ambition) universally admired—always allowing me privately to admire you for other reasons—by the tweed-clad matrons, goggle-eyed maids, immobile massive farmers and sonorous bookmakers of three counties; and if—as cannot always be avoided—some unfortunate mishap should occur: if you should be impaled, like a shrike's larder, on a blackthorn hedge, or plunged, like a dipped sheep, in a water-logged ditch, or deposited suddenly on the flat in a ludicrous and humiliating posture,—then I would console you in advance by reminding you of the profound observation of R. S. Surtees, when the Earl of Scamperdale lamented inconsolably the death, in a steeplechase, of his favourite and parasite: 'When an Earl is in distress, comforters are seldom far to seek...'[2] I, of course, undeterred by your choice, am still hoping to go—if necessary alone, if necessary for years—to Greece; so I, though willing enough, can hardly be among such possible comforters (of which anyway I hope you will have no need); but I will send you, from Sunium or Mycenae, a postcard of some romantic ruin crumbling desolately upon those ancient cliffs or among those pastoral solitudes, as a reminder of the injudiciousness of your choice.

You see, already after a fortnight of term, I am suffering from fugitive moods, from nostalgia for remote rivers and silent rural scenes—that disastrous emotion which has twice taken me to Iceland, but which cannot be exorcised. But all is well: you need have no alarm nor fear for my health or reason. These gentle emotions are, I must sadly admit, only half of my nature. Meanwhile the physical circulation of the blood is kept going by furious battles on every front,—war against the clergy at home, war against impertinent adversaries abroad, controversies in the learned journals, battles in the university, and of course deep and regular potations of

[1]   T-R had broken his back in a hunting accident in 1948.
[2]   From Surtees's *Mr Sponge's Sporting Tour* (1853): 'When a lord is in distress, consolation is never long in coming.'

exhilarating champagne and stupefying port. A few days ago I had just, by a dexterous manoeuvre, contrived to eject from this college an interfering popish monsignor, and had sealed his exclusion by legislative action, and so, as you can imagine, I was beginning sadly to apprehend that flatness in life which always follows total victory, when behold! the dull calm was happily broken by a foolish American judge publishing, in England, statements about me which my legal advisers (Mr Justice Blake and others) have assured me are libellous, damaging and actionable.[1] What luck! at once an exhilarating whiff of life has ruffled again the rapidly stagnating pool: the quiet well-feathered nests of lawyers in the discreet legal lanes of WC1 and EC2 are all astir; sharply-worded ultimata are flying hither and thither through those cosy boskages; and the air above Chancery Lane is already thick with the musty odour of horsehair wigs wagged this way and that in learned, sententious altercation. The judge is in full retreat and I am obliging his publishers to recall all copies of the book from the book-sellers, to delay publication, and to make costly changes,—all of which will not of course save the residue of the book from being reviewed by me when it does come out. Naturally this is all very wearing to the health, but it is absolutely necessary to the morale. On my visits to Scotland I have learnt one phrase which I am prepared to teach to others: *Nemo me impune lacessit.*[2]

I have just re-read my last paragraph. How frightful you must think I am,—how frightful perhaps I really am! I am ashamed (momentarily, & in your presence) of these sudden deviations into aggression and bellicosity, these unseemly interruptions of a demure & scholarly life, which no doubt (if analysed by a highly-paid psychologist) would be shown to have a sinister and unfavourable significance. One day I must seek, by introspection (that delicious but dangerous adventure) to solve this problem, to exorcise this demon, of which you, I am sure, must gently disapprove. But alas, though I always intend to improve my character, I never do; & now it is indubitably

[1]  Michael Musmanno (1897–1968), Judge of the Supreme Court of Pennsylvania 1952–68. His account of Hitler's end, *Ten Days to Die* (1950), attacked T-R and was scathingly reviewed by him in *The Spectator*, 16 March 1951.

[2]  This is the motto of Scotland's highest rank of chivalry, the Knights of the Thistle, meaning 'No-one attacks me with impunity'. Dawyck Haig's father had been invested as a KT in 1917.

too late. You must take me as I am—I am grateful to be taken at all—and if you, being unable, for good reasons, to leave—indeed why should you leave—your paradisiacal hermitage by the Tweed, will nevertheless still allow me sometimes to visit you there, then perhaps (apart from the perfect pleasure that I derive from it) your influence will correct or reduce these outrageous elements in my behaviour. Meanwhile I am reminded of you by a visit from Denys Dawnay[1] who is staying with Roy Harrod.[2] I missed him at Bemersyde when he was with you last summer and have greatly enjoyed meeting him here, though the spectacle of such physical frailty is almost terrifying to me and I cannot look upon it without apprehension. I suppose it is a sign of cowardice that I like people to look well and not to remind me quite so obviously of the precariousness of life & health!

I hope you are looking after yourself, and painting—which is a far safer & more suitable activity than horsemanship, about which— as you see—I have a slight *phobia* since my own accident. It is only a slight one, but I cannot altogether charm it away!

yours ever<br>Hugh

—∞—

## To Dawyck Haig, 2 April 1951

Olympia, Greece

My dear Dawyck,

Exhausted, my feet blistered and torn by the rocky ground of the Peloponnese, my face burnt and blackened by its sun, having walked eighty

---

[1] Denys Dawnay (1921–83) painted several prominent Oxonians: his oil portrait of A. L. Rowse is now in the National Portrait Gallery. David Hockney wrote the foreword to Dawnay's collection of pastiche portraits of dachshunds dressed as German nobles, *The House of Tekelden* (2005).

[2] (Sir) Roy Harrod (1900–78), Student in Modern History and Economics at Christ Church 1924–57.

miles in three days, starting every morning at dawn, and having—to me the most painful experience of all—today waded through the waist-high and infinitely wide river Alpheus, dragged by my relentless guide over a series of razor-like stones—I have arrived in Olympia; which being the Newmarket or Epsom of the ancient world naturally reminds me that you might possibly have been with me here, are perhaps at this very minute madly engaging in those equestrian competitions whose dangers were so often and so eloquently celebrated by the Greek writers,—without however thereby dissuading their aristocratic friends from continuing to take part in them. And would you, I ask, by a natural sequence of thought, have enjoyed the expedition into which I sought to lure you? Frankly, I think, No. I would like, of course, to say Yes, and to repeat yes until I had made you regret your refusal; but in fact my respect for the truth obliges me to say that though there have been momentary illuminations which, among my friends, only you would have fully appreciated, nevertheless the cost of experiencing those illuminations—the dust and heat, the squalid inns, the physical exhaustion of travel on foot (it is often the only way) is one which none of my friends (who after all are mostly luxury-loving intellectuals) would have paid. There have been times (and especially today, half-way across that terrible river which the ancient Greeks rightly credited with a divine capacity for resentment) when I have almost forsworn myself & wished myself back in England. But now that I have reached the known world again, & can travel easily to Athens in a train, and have no need of discomfort thereafter, but will either fly to Crete to salute those pictorial pre-historic water-closets which were so ingeniously designed by the late Sir Arthur Evans[1] to forget his social predicament (he was discovered, in a compromising position, on a park-bench with a boy, and fled to Crete where he discovered—or invented—a whole civilisation), or will retire for a comfortable week-end to the house of rich friends in unintellectual Boeotia on the

---

[1]   Sir Arthur Evans (1851–1941), Keeper of Ashmolean Museum 1884–1908 and patron of Oxford Boy Scouts, undertook the archaeological excavation of the Cretan city of Knossos, and pioneered the study of Minoan civilization.

edge of that (now drained) Lake Copais—the embargo on whose eels caused all the Athenian epicures to weep,—now that I have only these sybaritic experiences to look forward to, and can look back on the hardships and horrors of the last week,—how delightful it has all been! Where shall I begin, where end? The Temple of Bassae, still almost perfect, eight miles from the nearest road, hidden high up in the romantic Arcadian mountains? The brutal Frankish fortresses poised on great teeth of rock dominating the beautiful valleys of the Alpheus and the Eurotas? The hospitable crag-bound nuns of byzantine Mistra who, when I panted up to their precipitous empinnacled nunnery, pressed upon me water of delicious freshness, exquisite liqueurs of Kalamata, and crystallised grapes, their own confection, of unparalleled sweetness? Or should I mention those places of overwhelming emotional significance—Agamemnon's castle at Mycenae, the scene of those enormous tragedies, or the romantic cross-roads at the foot of Parnassus where Oedipus murdered his father and thereby supplied such unlimited material to Sophocles and Freud? All these I think you would have liked, & I should like to have shared the experience of seeing them with someone who would also have appreciated them. But I don't think you would have enjoyed getting there: it would have reminded you, at times, too much of your forced marches from prison-camp to prison-camp in Germany. And yet one painter visited & painted these & far more inaccessible places in Greece, in days of far greater discomfort: Edward Lear, in whose paintings of Greece & Calabria, I hear, there is now a boom in England. Are you an admirer of his work? Some of his paintings are here, but alas, unpurchasable, being immobilised in a library—the whole set of about thirty having been bought in London for £25 by an enlightened Greek ambassador: but that, of course, was before the boom.

But meanwhile what of you? Have you won any races? Have the tweed-clad matrons of the north applauded your horses and horsemanship and so slaked your thirst for admiration? The last item of news that I read before leaving England was of Johnnie Dalkeith's accident: I was sorry to hear of it and hope he is better; but it confirms me in my hardening conviction that horses are dangerous creatures.[1] And yet so, I suppose, are cars; so I will allow the conviction to soften again into a mere pose which, no doubt, under your influence, I shall ultimately abandon.

When shall I see you? When the point-to-point season is over, I suppose. Will you be in the south after I am back in England (I spend a week at I Tatti[2] & return on 17th April)? If not, the Bentley[3] will be polished as for a state visit, & I shall come & ask to spend one with you, at mid-term, outraging those censorious ex-censors of Ch Ch who hold it as a doctrine which whosoever keepeth not pure & undefiled shall without doubt perish everlastingly, that censors of Ch Ch must always be in Oxford. I rather enjoy outraging them in general, & in this particular should taste a doubled (or rather squared) enjoyment.

yours ever

Hugh

———∞———

## To Dawyck Haig, 20 October 1951

Christ Church, Oxford

My dear Dawyck,

Lest you should say of me, as of Robert, in some moment of *ennui* or petulance engendered by my silence, that I have 'gone out of your life', I sit down, on sudden impulses, though perhaps at long intervals, to write you

---

[1] John Montagu-Douglas-Scott (1923–2007), known by the courtesy title of Earl of Dalkeith, studied at Christ Church in the late 1940s after wartime service as an ordinary seaman in Royal Navy destroyers. He became the largest private landowner in Europe after succeeding his father as 9th Duke of Buccleuch in 1973. He recovered from his hunting mishap in 1951, but after a worse accident in 1971 was left paralysed from the chest down and confined to a wheelchair.

[2] Bernard Berenson's villa near Florence, where T-R was a welcome visitor.

[3] T-R had bought himself a grey Bentley from the proceeds of *The Last Days of Hitler*.

a letter; hoping thereby to elicit from your remote, silent, meditative hermitage on the Tweed that even rarer phenomenon: an answer. Further I hope that you will, to the particular question which I now put to you, answer Yes. Will you come to the Censors' Dinner?[1] It will be held on Christ Church on Monday 10ᵗʰ December; and I hope I need not say that Robert and I, as hosts on that occasion, would be delighted if we thought you could come. I hope to fetch Parson Lloyd from Alnwick;[2] can I fetch you from Bemersyde? So we hope, but alas, I apprehend that you, looking across the Tweed at that infinite distance, that vast intervening winter wilderness of hills and floods and cities and moors and mists and, in one word, *England*, will retreat again to your studio and never be seen at these remote southern occasions. But do say yes if you can. Possibly you will find some other occasion which can be combined with this. Possibly other hosts will press you southwards at the same time (though none can be more eager to receive you). If you think it possible I shall send you a formal card, pompously inscribed with florid lettering and armigerous emblems—I would send it now if it were yet printed—and we will both rejoice in anticipation of that rare visit, as ornithologists (I understand) rejoice when the Arctic tern descends similarly from the icy north to spend its winter in these milder latitudes.

I wanted to ask Johnnie Dalkeith too; but he, of course, with ill-timed perversity, will be hunting foxes at your gates.

I sent you a brief message from Spain, as one that drops a pebble into a bottomless well and listens automatically but without serious hope for evidence of its arrival. I greatly enjoyed my unexpectedly rearranged visit to that strange peninsula for which I have now conceived, perhaps

---

[1]  T-R had been appointed Junior Censor of Christ Church in 1948, and Senior Censor in 1950—both busy administrative posts in the life of the college. There was an annual dinner at which the Senior Censor and Junior Censor reported on college business during their terms of office. The dinner was exclusively for Students, with neither the Dean nor any of the cathedral chapter present. When a Senior Censor demitted from office after two years, he was 'buried' at the dinner while the Junior Censor was installed as his successor. This custom dated from the time of John Locke, who was 'buried' at the end of his censorship.

[2]  William Lloyd (1899–1986), vicar of Alnwick and domestic chaplain to the Duke of Northumberland 1944–65.

because of its novelty (for I had never before been there), a romantic passion. You, I think, having declined to visit it with me, flew secretly and alone to Madrid, visited the Prado, and flew immediately home again, averting your eyes from the rest of the country. O inconceivable aversion! I was delighted with the place,—with those infinite golden uplands: everything was golden,—stubble-fields, golden hillocks of grain being winnowed on every village floor, golden corn-dust suspended in the air of those hard, cold, impersonal sierras; with those vast churches echoing night and day (as it seemed to me), like some Tibetan lamasery, with the interminable, hieratic, nasal mumble of bald-headed priests immobile in their huge carven stalls; and above all, with the antique grave dignity of even the poorest peasants when one spoke to them among those vast empty fields. Italy now seems, through familiarity, almost vulgar to me—and Portugal is disgustingly vulgar—after that experience of Oriental strangeness and Homeric simplicity. And to think that you flew over it, with sealed eyes, undeviating between Madrid and Melrose...But then even Greece, even the mysterious beauty of Delphi, failed to lure you out of your hermitage. How then (I sadly ask) can I possibly lure you to the familiar quadrangles of Christ Church? Nevertheless, I hope you will come.

Send me anyway a brief note. Tell me how you are, and whether you are hunting or painting. I hope you are painting. All Earls hunt; it is far more distinguished to paint!

yours ever
Hugh

———ᗗᗗᗕ———

In the 1950s Trevor-Roper was courted by the publisher Hamish ('Jamie') Hamilton who, after the success of The Last Days of Hitler, was keen to recruit him to the Hamish Hamilton list. The letter that follows was written in response to Hamilton's suggestion that someone should write a life of Trevor-Roper's Christ Church colleague Frederick Lindemann (1886–1957), Lord Cherwell. 'The Prof', as Cherwell was widely known, had been Professor *of Experimental Philosophy—that is, physics—at Oxford since 1919. He was elected as a Fellow of the Royal Society at the age of 34. He had learnt to fly in 1916 so that as an experimental pilot he could confirm, by his own valiant empirical tests, his theoretical calculations as to how aviators could get their aeroplanes out of deadly spins. The Prof had the unusual, and possibly unique, distinction of competing in the Wimbledon tennis tournament when holding an Oxford chair. He was also a fine pianist. He had a reverence for historic families, and was proud when the Duke of Westminster introduced him in 1921 to Winston Churchill, whose intimate confidant he became (despite being a rigid teetotaller and vegetarian). He reached the highest influence as the Prime Minister's wartime scientific adviser. He was also principal Opposition spokesman on financial affairs in the Lords during the Attlee years, and sat in Churchill's peacetime Cabinet in 1951–3. Cherwell expressed himself forcefully, believing himself to be a realist surrounded by fools. After they had spent an evening together in 1937 Trevor-Roper realized that his host believed him to be more conservative in his opinions than he really was, 'and so is welcoming me with open arms, as an offset to all these young socialist dons!'*

## To Hamish Hamilton, 19 February 1952

Christ Church, Oxford

My dear Jamie,

A biography or an autobiography of the Prof is equally out of the question.[1] An autobiography he would never write,—official secrecy and personal secretiveness would alike prevent it; while for a biography the material would be hard to find, and, if found, would ultimately, I think, prove to be dull. For the Prof, though an amusing companion, has not a rich personality: he has made himself appear interesting by elaborate concealment of his real character, and revelation would only reveal its ultimate jejunity. By this I mean that he lacks all those human interests and weaknesses which make people interesting to other people: he is a machine which has adjusted every part of itself to ensure mechanical efficiency (a dull enough attribute) and has eliminated every interesting

---

[1]  Roy Harrod's memoir, *The Prof*, was published by Macmillan in 1959. Lord Birkenhead's official biography followed in 1961. A further biography by Adrian Fort appeared in 2003.

quality which might interfere with that result. Drink,—he scientifically rejects it; family ties,—he has none; human relationships,—he has few, if any, whose bases (as distinct from their superficial form) are really human. There is nobody, I think, to whom he ordinarily speaks unguard-edly. All energies have been canalised for the pursuit of power and respect (perhaps to compensate for lack of affection), and such friendships as he recognises have been acquired in the course of that pursuit, or mark stages in it: none precede it or are quite irrelevant of it. An indirect conse-quence of this is that whereas he will speak of such parts of his life as are incidents in the successful advance towards power, or illustrations of it, he never speaks of any other parts of it,—early life, the days (which must have occurred) of social pushing and political intrigue, failure, etc. He never mentions his parents or his home; conceals his age (see *Who's Who*); acknowledges only one brother (the successful one; there is a black-sheep brother whose existence was accidentally discovered by me during the war, but whom I dare not even mention to the Prof); conceals the source of his wealth (I have evidence that his father owned the Dresden water-works, but again would never dare to question the Prof on this); and, in general, as he is utterly incommunicative on these and such subjects, so he is a master of skilful evasion if anyone should be so hardy as to show interest in such forbidden subjects. Further, being a defensive and se-cretive character, he is utterly unintrospective, never detaches himself from himself, never criticises himself, never laughs at himself (and there-fore never reveals, as entertaining, his own failures or misfortunes), and has no sense of historical accuracy or impartiality whatever. He is a par-tisan whose partisanship transforms every incident which he may nar-rate. He does not know what objectivity is. For instance, he has protested to me because I brought Frank Pakenham[1] back here to teach when he ceased to be a Socialist Minister, insisting that Christ Church ought to be

---

[1] Francis ('Frank') Pakenham (1905–2001) was a politics don at Christ Church 1934–46. As a newly created peer, he served in the Labour government of 1945–51 (latterly as First Lord of the Admiralty). He returned to teaching in Christ Church 1951–5, and succeeded as 7th Earl of Longford in 1961. T-R customarily referred to him with affectionate contempt.

politically impartial,—i.e. only containing, among its teachers, uncompromising conservative ministers like himself! It is a tragedy, in my opinion, that this secretive partisan should be the executor who will control the papers of Winston Churchill after his death.[1] Such, in my opinion, is the real character which is studiously protected by impenetrable reserve, hieratic, unapproachable mystery as to all interesting subjects, carefully smooth social manners, and a notorious capacity for barbed repartee. So you will see that he would never divulge the material for an official biography, and has so carefully covered his tracks that an unofficial biographer would have to do a great deal of research to uncover them again. What, for instance, are his origins? He is so violently anti-Semitic and anti-German that I suspect them to be German-Jewish,—it would fit with his general concealment and repudiation of his unsuccessful past; but he always insists that they are Alsatian, and quickly discourages any attempt to penetrate behind that generalisation. I probably know him as well as anyone (except Winston, his most intimate friend); but the result is to convince me that nobody really knows him. He is impersonal, inured against the revelation of weakness by a systematic asceticism, an undeviating pursuit of power, a carefully fabricated aura of mystery.

I like the old wretch myself, because I like wicked men (others pretend to like him because they like to know powerful men), but I can see why those who don't share my perhaps curious taste regard him as a real menace, especially if they dislike his politics—which indeed are the blackest reaction. Fundamentally the Prof believes in an absolutely mechanical society, managed with scientific efficiency, and therefore without any concessions to liberalism, in the interest of the old ruling classes: a sort of 1984 run by the House of Lords. For the Prof, as a rootless immigrant, has a secret hankering for the deep-rooted ancient security and long-established respect of the British Peerage, in whose complex, variable constellation (or nebula) he now himself—to the astonishment of astronomers—coldly shines, a new, incongruous star. He likes being a

---

[1]   In the event Cherwell predeceased Churchill by over seven years.

Peer, and likes casually and perfunctorily to tinkle coronets in his conversation; but of course it is the olympian security rather than the ancient tradition or whig history of the British aristocracy which appeals to him. He has no interest in tradition, and no liberal ideas,—none whatever. He does not even allow that liberalism is a cheaper and more efficient system of government than despotism, as some illiberal political thinkers would nevertheless reluctantly concede; for as a trained scientist and bureaucrat he believes that really scientific despotism could be made cheaper and more efficient still, without any of that waste of energy which toleration, liberalism, and such untidy systems necessarily entail and which exact scientists always deplore. But it is fundamental to the Prof's political views that this ruthless mechanical bureaucracy must be run in the interest, and by the agents, of the classes, not the masses. The Prof's attitude towards the masses is quite clear: he hates, despises, and—above all—fears them. His insulation from their world is complete. The Churchillian idea of 'tory democracy', of sharing any of their emotions (he has no emotions) or enthusiasms (he hates enthusiasms) or pleasures (he despises their pleasures) is incomprehensible to him. His only contact with the lower classes is with butlers. He only moves in limousines. He has never been seen walking in a street. His life is spent, carefully secluded from the tiresome evidence that humanity exists, in luxury-hotels, great houses, carefully-run laboratories, and in his own inaccessible rooms in college. These rooms are of an indescribable hideousness (for the Prof is an utter philistine), furnished like a first-class steamship saloon, hung with endless photographs of views available to rich tourists travelling by that line.

As for his laboratories (and indeed, I understand, his London offices), these are run on the principle of a sixteenth-century Turkish galley. Hundreds of slaves, mostly foreign,—prisoners of war or fugitives from justice—are battened below the hatches and there labour night and day at the oar: colourless creatures (for they never see the light) whose passions have long been atrophied by disuse and whose rowing efficiency, by unremitting practice, has become phenomenal; while the Prof, like a nautical pasha, telescope under arm, saunters on the bridge, confident of success in any encounter. Incidentally, to return to his politics,—he is quite the worst politician I have ever known. He has no idea whatever of winning over the floating vote (which is, after all, the essence of politics). His scientific impatience of amateurs and individualism makes him a hopeless diplomatist. He has only to open his lips for opposition at once to harden and all the floating voters to paddle unanimously away to the other side. Fortunately, as a peer, he does not need to woo the public vote; and when he speaks in the House of Lords, he is speaking to the converted. He is also generally inaudible, and this is a great advantage to his cause.

My colleague Robert Blake, who has just come in, and who is also a great friend of the Prof (for he also appreciates wicked men), has patiently allowed me to read this letter to him. He confirms its general tenor, but thinks that I have not done sufficient justice to the old boy's urbanity. The Prof is a genial conversationalist, an attentive listener, and creates a most favourable impression, especially on the young when they are first introduced to this legendary figure from whom they have generally apprehended a very different reception. He likes the young, provided they show no leaning to dangerously liberal views,—likes them much better than the old who, although generally conservative, tend to include in their conservatism an element of sentiment and tradition hateful to the icy realism of the Prof, and who may even, before 1939, have been odious Chamberlainite heretics, unforgivable by God or man. This urbanity is a comparatively recent development in the Prof,—since 1939 in fact, when he first became sated with power and fame and could first afford to be indulgent to the less successful. But it is now an obvious and genuine quality. I like introducing my guests to him, and they seldom fail to be charmed by him.

I mentioned the Prof's hatred of Germans. During the war he was the strongest advocate of two clearly defined policies in respect of Germany. One was the policy outlined in the 'Cherwell Minute' of 1942, which meant bombing all German cities to rubble regardless of military objectives; the other was the Morgenthau Plan of 1944, which meant turning the remains of Germany into a sheep-walk and reducing the surviving population by 75%.[1] He does not much like being reminded of these plans now, and indeed will not forgive Henry Morgenthau for having had a secret recording made of their private discussion of the Morgenthau Plan. This is not of course because the Prof repents of the inhumanity of these plans (he does not know what words like 'repentance' or 'inhumanity' mean), but because they proved unsuccessful and impracticable. He only likes to remember the (admittedly numerous) occasions when he has been proved right. He once challenged a colleague to a bet, which is recorded in the college betting-book. He lost the bet (he bet that colour-films would have replaced other films in England by 1940), but has always refused to pay up, for that would be an admission that he had been wrong. Instead he maintains that he was really right in some highly metaphysical sense, although certain limitations of his colleagues' understanding may have prevented them from realising the fact.

I hope I have convinced you that the Prof has fundamentally a dull mind and that no biography of him could be interesting. Certainly none would be possible. I only know two sources for his early life. One is an elderly London stockbroker, who told me about the Dresden waterworks, but who (since he is now aged 96) may not be indefinitely available. The other is Freddie Birkenhead,[2] who, though only 44, may well (to judge from his state when we last met) find, like his distinguished father (and from the same cause), an untimely end. Of course, though dull, the Prof is also outrageous; but that is another matter. I like him for being outrageous. I also like him because he has been a friend and ally: his block of voters on the Christ Church Governing Body have always had clear and authoritative orders to vote with the Party of Light (i.e., with Us). He has been a loyal

[1]  The Morgenthau Plan, named after the US Secretary of the Treasury Henry Morgenthau, was accepted by the Western Allies at the Quebec Conference in 1944, although never fully enforced. It proposed a punitive policy towards post-war Germany, including the loss of territory, partition of the remnant into two autonomous states, demilitarization, the dismantling of heavy industry, and reparations.
[2]  Frederick Smith, 2nd Earl of Birkenhead (1907–75), biographer, eventually mastered his dependence on alcohol (unlike his father, the formidable barrister-politician F. E. Smith, whose death in 1930 was hastened by drink). Freddie Birkenhead, who had been educated at Christ Church, was a lifelong friend of T-R's.

enemy of my enemies,—and what more can be demanded of any man? If one asks the ultimate question, is it better that such a man should be/not be? I answer uncompromisingly, Yes,—provided, of course, that he has no direct control in politics. This, in spite of his enormous personal influence with Winston, the Prof (in my opinion) has not, and never will have. His political incapacity—which is heroic—cancels itself out. The plain fact is that he is not English and has not even the remotest understanding of English political life, and though *in* British politics is no more *of* them than was (for instance) Baron Stockmar in the time of the Prince Consort.[1] Winston uses him simply as a technical adviser. For political views and tactics Winston does not need advice,—or at least (as some of his subordinates have sometimes sadly complained) will never take it. But even they are no doubt glad that he doesn't take it from the Prof.

yours ever

Hugh

P.S. *On no account leave this letter lying about,* or I shall be in the law courts, and the Prof (who denounced a colleague to M.I.5 for uttering dispirited observations on the progress of the war, over the port, in 1940) would have, I fear, little mercy. Our friendship is a longstanding alliance of interest rather than an emotional relationship capable of surviving any such strain!

P.P.S. 'The less appetising liqueurs' are Van Der Hum. I daren't say so in print lest the distinguished (and presumably rich) Dutchmen who distil the nauseous brew from who knows what pestiferous mundungus[2] should have me in the law courts too!

P.P.P.S. I am in bed; hence the inordinate length of this letter.

---

[1]  Christian Friedrich Freiherr von Stockmar (1787–1863), physician to King Leopold of the Belgians and his confidential agent, mentor to Leopold's nephew Prince Albert of Saxe-Coburg-Gotha before and after his marriage to Queen Victoria, and resented for his unofficial influence at the British court.
[2]  Stinking tobacco; more generally, spoiled merchandise. A word often used by T-R to mean something distasteful or repulsive.

*Alan Yorke-Long (1924–52) died of cancer about a fortnight after this letter was written. The child of Plymouth Brethren parents, Yorke-Long was an ebullient, joyful character, who planned to produce a comprehensive history of eighteenth-century court music, and seemed inexhaustible as he studied and wrote during long days at the British Museum. He renovated a mews house in Park Crescent Mews West, near the Regent's Park and Broadcasting House, where he held evening concerts: he was a striking host, standing well over six feet tall, and proportionately broad, with an unruly shock of very fair hair. He also delivered BBC commentaries, and befriended music-lovers including Trevor-Roper's brother Patrick (known as Pat), Edward Sackville-West, and Desmond Shawe-Taylor. His health failed before he could finish his book, fragments of which were published posthumously, with a preface by Pat Trevor-Roper, by Weidenfeld as* Music at Court: Four Eighteenth-Century Studies *in 1954. Hugh Trevor-Roper, who helped to prepare the book for publication, wrote the following letter to amuse a dying man.*

## To Alan Yorke-Long, 21 September 1952

Christ Church, Oxford

My dear Alan

I was very sorry not to see you the other day when I was in London,—especially as I afterwards heard that you didn't have your treatment that afternoon after all; so I must write to you instead, being at the moment in Lincolnshire, where the churches (I find) all smell rather high: doubtless a residuary whiff of our old friend the Clerical Student of Ch. Ch.,[1] who first preached the Word (incrusted indeed with a good deal of superstitious rubbish) to the web-toed inhabitants of these dismal marshes. How different, I am sure, was good old great-aunt Adelaide who, in her quiet distaff way, was no doubt a sound two-bottle-orthodox evangelical church-woman (the two bottles being of home-brewed parsnip wine!).

Meanwhile, what gossip can I tell you from Oxford? Has Pat told you of the great Lewis Carroll *trouvaille*? If so, skip the next few paragraphs; if not, attend and I will expound.

[1] Eric Mascall (1905–93), a mathematical wrangler at Cambridge who became an Anglo-Catholic priest, was sub-warden of Lincoln Theological College 1937–45; then a Student of Christ Church 1945–62, and University Lecturer in the Philosophy of Religion, before becoming Professor of Historical Theology at King's College London. Among his profuse writings was a volume of verses, *Pi in the High* (1959).

The day I left Oxford for Constantinople there appeared in Ch. Ch. a drab-looking figure whose accent, accoutrements and nose all betrayed a Glaswegian origin: and indeed a little research soon revealed that he was in fact Prof. Norman Black, of that great university on the Clyde, the Athens—or should I say rather the Thebes—of the North.[1] He was, he said, engaged on academic research; and when he elaborated further, it did indeed seem to me very academic indeed; for not only was he preparing a thesis on the subject (which in itself I regard as pitifully unpractical) of Proportional Representation, so dear to the hearts of Liberals, Commonwealthsmen,[2] Plymouth Brethren, & other minorities; but he was particularly seeking to rediscover for posterity a particularly abstruse form of Proportional Representation mathematically devised, *anno* 1870 or thereabouts, by Lewis Carroll, as a suggested method of electing Students of Ch. Ch. However, even the Students of Ch. Ch. thought it too academic for actual use, and it was rejected by a few unanimous canonical snorts, and the precious secret was, as it seemed, lost in everlasting oblivion...

But no, for we have forgotten Prof. Black. This tiresome scholar (not to put too fine a point on the matter) nagged away like a gadfly, if I may mix a metaphor or two, until the Clerk of the Ch. Ch. Treasury, exasperated by his importunity, ultimately agreed rather testily to open a dusty old crate on which tenant-farmers had been accustomed, on visits to their landlord, to deposit their sheepdogs, saddles, wives, vegetable-marrows and the other usual impedimenta of bucolic life. And what was discovered therein? What indeed but a couple of thousand or so MSS in the holograph of Lewis Carroll, the value of which, in America, has now been estimated at some £30,000.

But who, you naturally ask, is the owner of this rich *cache*? The answer is simple. Lewis Carroll deposited these documents in his

---

[1]  Actually Duncan Black (1908–91), Lecturer at Glasgow University 1946–53 and Professor of Economics at the University of Wales, Bangor, 1953–68. He was author of *The Incidence of Income Taxes* (1939) and *The Theory of Committees of Elections* (1958), but numerous articles and treatises that he wrote in the intervening period were rejected by refereed journals or academic publishers. *A Mathematical Approach to Proportional Representation: Duncan Black on Lewis Carroll* appeared posthumously.

[2]  17th-century republicans.

capacity *not* of Student of Ch. Ch., or of C. L. Dodgson *tout court*, but of Curator of the Senior Common Room. *Ergo*, the documents belong exclusively to the S.C.R. Therefore the proceeds cannot constitutionally be used for any such improper purpose as, for instance, educating the proletariat, or buying incense for cathedral, but *must* be invested in *port*! Think of the debates about to break out now at the crowded SCR meeting specially summoned to discuss this important topic on the very first day of term! I particularly look forward to the painful dilemma of Mich. Foster.[1] What course will he advocate? Keep the papers as treasured exhibits? But how often has he inveighed against any suggestion that Ch. Ch. should add to its store of books, pictures, MSS, furniture, or any other dangerous reminders of those insidious and pernicious pursuits, so rightly condemned by St Gregory and other Fathers of the Church, *Culture* and *Learning*! Sell them at market rates? But might we not then be in danger of elevating our standard of living on the proceeds, and thus causing grievous offence to Almighty God? It is a sad quandary for the old bird. I expect he will advocate burning the lot, as useless vanities, in a great bonfire in Tom Quad, like Savonarola,[2]—and yet might there not then, as in the case of that tiresome Florentine killjoy, be, in the same place, a little later, another bonfire...? But I think Michael Foster would *like* to be burnt—he would enjoy both the pain and the opportunities of forgiving them as knowing not what they do....

I hear that you, with exquisite 18th century elegance, are choosing your own epitaph. May I take part in this competition and offer this lapidary but, I hope, premature inscription:

---

[1]   Michael Foster (1903–59) was Student in Philosophy at Christ Church from 1930 until he gassed himself in his college rooms. His stinting of pleasures and austere, self-mortifying Christianity were often derided by T-R.

[2]   Girolamo Savonarola (1452–98), Dominican friar and zealous Florentine preacher against luxury, whom T-R likened in *Renaissance Essays* to a grim ayatollah. In 1497 he organized the public incineration of books, art works, and ornaments in the most famous of the bonfires of the vanities; but a year later his body was burned after a public hanging, and his ashes cast into the river Arno.

Here lies
Alan Yorke-Long
a Scholar
Whose intimate knowledge of Operatic Music
at the Courts of Europe
was, alas!
unseasonably required
at the Court of Heaven

or do you prefer Latin, marble's language as the poet affectedly expresses it?[1]

Sub hoc Tumulo
Alanum Yorke-Long
in sectam Fratrum Plymouthianorum natum
post vitam epicuream
et mortem scepticam
Anglicanissime sepelierunt
Amici insolabiles.[2]

I am getting pretty facile at this branch of art, for although I began this letter in the flats of Lincolnshire, I am now finishing it among the disconsolate ruins of Jedburgh Abbey; although the inscription on the tombs of Cheviot shepherds are, I pique myself, less exquisitely turned than those compositions of mine.

I hope you are comfortable. Get better; and I shall visit you, if you will see me, on my return to the South.

yours ever
Hugh

---

[1] Robert Browning, 'The Bishop Orders His Tomb at St Praxed's Church': 'And marble's language, Latin pure, discreet'.
[2] 'Under this mound | Alan Yorke-Long | born in the sect of Plymouth Brethren | after an epicurean life | and a sceptic death | was buried in the proper Anglican manner | by his inconsolable friends.'

*Trevor-Roper revered Gerald Brenan (1894–1987), whom he described to Bernard Berenson as 'a hero of mine'. Brenan was an autodidact, without university education. He had a tempestuous affair with Dora Carrington, figured on the fringes of the Bloomsbury set, but lived in Spain until the civil war forced his return to England. Brenan's account of this period,* The Spanish Labyrinth: An Account of the Social and Political Background of the Civil War *(1943), became one of Trevor-Roper's favourite books. In 1952, soon after sending this letter, Trevor-Roper visited Brenan and his wife in Wiltshire, and liked them both 'enormously'. He extolled Brenan for 'an almost heroic integrity, a hatred and impatience of humbug which reminds me of George Orwell; than whom however he is much more genial and sociable'. In 1953 the Brenans returned to Spain and settled in Andalusia, where he would remain, almost continuously, until his death at the age of 93. Trevor-Roper paid several visits to the Brenans' simple Andalusian home, where he found the talk more uninhibited and intelligent than anywhere he knew.*

*In this letter Trevor-Roper adumbrates the thesis of a conflict, in the sixteenth and seventeenth centuries, between 'Court' and 'Country'. The argument was expounded in his essay 'The Gentry', which he was then just completing: an attack on the neo-Marxist interpretation advanced by R. H. Tawney and his followers of the class struggle between the gentry and aristocracy that led to the English Civil Wars. T-R's 'Court and Country' thesis would inform his influential essay 'The General Crisis of the Seventeenth Century' (1959; reproduced in his book* Religion, the Reformation and Social Change, *1967).*

## To Gerald Brenan, 23 November 1952

Christ Church, Oxford

Dear Mr Brenan

Are you still where you were? Since I have been unable to persuade you to visit Oxford, and since my admiration for your works grows rather than diminishes with time (as does my curiosity about certain problems of Spanish history which, I become more & more convinced, only you can relieve), may I consult you, either in writing, or, if that is not even more inconvenient to you, by personally calling on you if you should be at leisure? (I must go to Marlborough School some day soon, & anyway the distance is not so very great). But perhaps I should outline to you the subject in which I am at present interested.

It seems to me that in the 16th & 17th centuries there is, in Western Europe, on the one hand, a general cult of 'the court', represented socially by the great scramble for offices, the competition for titles, the character of education, the waste and display of official life (as opposed to the economical conventions of the 19th century), the tone set by such writers as Castiglione, Gracián, etc. etc., and, on the other hand, an opposite cult which can conveniently be called of 'the country': a cult (often also nurtured among failed courtiers or officials) of self-respecting parsimony and idealisation of an aristocratic attitude.[1] The more I study the social background in England before the Great Rebellion, the more I become aware of this as the fundamental antithesis of society—far more fundamental than religious opposition. For instance, it seems to me that so far from recusancy & puritanism being opposite to each other, both are rival formulations of the anti-court attitude. This, I think, can be shown in detail if one studies the actual families concerned. Now it seems to me that in contemporary Spain, where the extravagance of Court life was far greater—e.g. under Philip III—than in England even under James I, there must have been some comparable attitude among the *hidalgo* class[2]—unless they were all effortlessly drained off by immigration or sank into quietism. Was there? Is there any work in which one can study the attitude of the Spanish *hidalgos* of 1600–1650 as one can study, in so many memoirs & family histories, the attitude of the English gentry? It is a world that seems to escape the books—or at least the books known to me. I can find no Spanish *social* historians; and yet just as English history would be to me unintelligible without some understanding of the Puritan squires, so I suspect that the Castilian *hidalgos* must have had some greater significance in Spanish social history than merely as soldiers & colonists abroad—questions of local office, agriculture, church-tithes, etc.

---

[1]   T-R explored this theme in his essay 'Country House Radicals 1590–1640', published in *History Today* in July 1953.
[2]   Spanish lesser nobility.

Do you know any works in Spanish on this topic (if it is a real topic)? I regard you & Braudel[1] as the only Hispanists (or Hispanologues) who seem to think of these & such matters; and Braudel is even more inaccessible than you! So I hope you will not mind my sudden random intrusions into your peace.

yours sincerely<br>Hugh Trevor-Roper

P.S. I hope to go back to Spain in the spring & make some studies there—but time is so short that it is a great help to know in advance where to look & what to look for!

———

*While staying at Bemersyde in April 1953, Trevor-Roper met Haig's eldest sister Xandra, who lived nearby in the Borders. She was unhappily married to a naval officer, by whom she had three young children. After Trevor-Roper's return to Oxford she visited him in Oxford, and within a couple of months of meeting they were lovers. Because they lived so far apart they were able to meet only rarely, and communicated most often by correspondence, sometimes writing each other as many as three letters in a single day. Their sixteen-month affair, originally clandestine, would culminate in marriage, but it was marked by frequent trials and misunderstandings. The following two letters were written during a crisis in their relations, after Xandra had taken her brother into her confidence, who had advised her to continue with her husband if possible.*

## To Xandra Howard-Johnston, 8 August 1953

8 August 1953                                         Christ Church, Oxford

My dearest Xandra

You think I am ironical when I am serious and serious when I am ironical—or at least you pretend to do so; is it just calculated feminine

---

[1]   Fernand Braudel (1902–85), leader of the *Annales* School of historians, whose book *La Méditerranée et le monde méditerranéen à l'époque de Philippe II* (1949) was admired by T-R.

perversity, or is my language really so 'ambiguous'? Of course I was perfectly serious when I said James should read natural history books and become observant. You say that those are two things that I have *not* done. But (if you are right in saying so) may I not even so suggest that a boy avoid the omissions that I perhaps regret having made in my early studies? In fact I don't think you are right. When I was a small boy I was an enthusiastic naturalist: I read numbers of books on natural history (some of which I will now give to James if you think he will like them); knew all the wild flowers that grew in Northumberland, all the kinds of crustaceans, molluscs, sea-mice, marine-spiders, etc., that crept and clung upon its coast; collected butterflies and moths (I even once caught a White Admiral after days of stalking in Gatwick wood, Surrey); kept hedgehogs, tadpoles, caterpillars and mice; and (unlike Billa)[1] *can* tell the difference between a weasel and a stoat! If you were ever to come on a country walk with me, I believe I could add *considerably* to your knowledge of the details of animal and vegetable life! Of course I have forgotten a good deal—especially about birds at which I was never so good, as they are less easy for a short-sighted boy to see; and then I think I interested myself in such things the more because I was a solitary child (neither my brother nor my sister had, or has, the slightest interest in nature; and I was very ungregarious!), and took less interest in them later when I found other subjects to concern myself with; but even so I think it is a good thing for a boy to study, and I was not being ironical at all!

Now you ask what I think of your letters: are they ungrammatical, ill-expressed, naïve, platitudinous? I am, you say, 'a famous writer', and you expect a judgment. Dearest Xandra, I *hate*, I really, genuinely hate, being treated as 'a famous writer', and I can assure you that there is no more certain way of driving me back into an opaque, impenetrable reserve than by treating me as such.[2] It maddens me when people introduce me in such terms: I'm afraid I always retreat into a sulky silence and create a very bad

[1]  Wilhelmine ('Billa') Harrod (1911–2005), wife of T-R's Christ Church colleague Roy Harrod.
[2]  In earlier letters Xandra had complained of his reserve.

43

impression if they do! I feel it is false in itself, a misuse of language, and also it makes people treat one in a different way, a kind of inhuman, deferential way; and whereas I know you will say I don't respond much at any time, nevertheless I do think that I can respond just a little in society if treated as human, not as a kind of exhibit or slot-machine! That is one reason why I like undergraduates, at least some of them. It is not for the reason that you supposed,[1] but because they haven't yet acquired that deferential attitude which people so soon acquire when they think in terms of public dignity. Of course there are other reasons too—they are energetic, willing to rough it and do chores, and interested in experiences: they like seeing and learning and discovering new things and don't look on everything with that *blasé* affectation of boredom which older people so often do. All this makes them good travelling companions; I think you are a good travelling companion too; because you are still capable of being delighted and surprised and instructed by new worlds; but you must have noticed how most people, once grown up, lose that freshness of approach, and when they travel are more apt to complain at the interruption of customary routine than to be exhilarated by experiencing something new.

Now, your letters: need I really say it? I *love* receiving them; they make it perfectly possible for me to live alone here, in this sullen climate, surrounded by deserted rooms and halls, and quadrangles full of apparently inhuman tourists, taking my identical cold meals in solitude and silence while the echoes of their brazen, inappropriate, transatlantic misobservations drift in through my open window. I have tried to work here alone in August before; and always before I have had to give up through utter dispiritedness; but this time I feel I can go happily on and only wish it could go on longer; and this difference is entirely due to the sustaining hope and confidence that next day, at breakfast, I shall find a flat blue envelope with a Melrose postmark and a spidery inscription! I can assure you that my sensitive skin has not yet shivered at an infelicitous adjective, that I never notice your punctuation (which is surely a sign that it is

---

[1]  Xandra had thought that T-R might be physically attracted to young men.

correct), and that I would rather have a mixed metaphor (as in your last letter) than no metaphor at all! If there are any platitudes, I will shudder and tell you; but so far—in some 769 pages—there have been none! So please don't write to me as if submitting exercises to a critical pedagogue; write as you do, and as fully, and as often, and I am delighted!

And now comes the question what I shall say to Dawyck. I keep putting off my reply to him, because it is so difficult; and perhaps in the end I shall not reply, it being too difficult. How can I explain the position? The fact is that I feel a kind of complex where Dawyck is concerned. He has been a very good friend to me for a long time, and I owe him a great deal and have a genuine respect and deep personal affection for him, and yet I now feel that perhaps we have been on false terms, and that I, insensitively, have been unaware of it.[1] You know, he is very uncommunicative (in some ways less communicative than I am), and when he writes letters they are so brief and bald that they suggest a positive physical difficulty in writing, as if he were writing with treacle or tar instead of ink. Nevertheless he always behaves with such kindness that one tends to deduce his sentiments from that, and in fact, deducing from his behaviour, I have allowed myself to suppose that he both understood me & liked my company more than I now feel that he does. I now feel that he has in his mind a picture of me which, in some respects, I believe to be wrong (for although I am always chary of supposing that I am right about myself, I do feel that there are some points on which one can be a judge), and, further, that he finds me a more difficult companion than he had allowed me to suppose; and therefore I feel that I have exploited his kindness too much in the past; and when he writes suggesting that I write fully and openly to him, I feel that whereas I could have done so before, when I believed there was a greater basis of understanding between us, it is much more difficult now, across the great cloud of incomprehension which seems to me suddenly to have revealed itself between our minds. This is the basis of my difficulty. One can unbare one's soul (though at the best of times it is a painful

---

[1]   Xandra had informed him that Haig thought him 'quite neuter'; and had suggested, *inter alia*, that Haig found his company boring.

enough operation) to someone with whom one feels complete sympathy of understanding; but without that sympathy it is, I think, impossible. Please don't tell this to Dawyck—that would only add a social misunderstanding to a private difficulty; but if he complains that I have not answered, I hope you will see my difficulty and contrive that he does not blame me for my omission!

Dearest Xandra, these are some of the difficulties that inhibit my expression; and when I try not to thrust before you such a dreary tangle of insoluble emotional and intellectual problems, but to extract with such precision as I can the essential, practical conclusions, then you find these conclusions clear perhaps, but cold. No doubt you are right; but I think that I am also right in supposing that clarity—at least if it is about a complicated and tangled matter—must be rather cold and surgical. However, if you don't mind the tangle, I can assure you of the warmth. I do indeed love you deeply, more deeply (I am sure) than anyone before, and I now feel that I should be unhappy without you and without your letters in a sense in which I have not been unhappy before. I have often enough wanted to express this, but always I have been inhibited by the great practical difficulties of doing anything about it—so many grim, invincible, irremovable figures project their prohibitive shadows relentlessly across what might otherwise be a simple relationship giving happiness to both of us; or else (I must admit) you have pressed me for short, simple answers and then, perversely, feeling that complex situations don't provide such simple answers, I have dodged the pressure and slid maliciously away; but at least I have tried to show by other means than words how much your love means to me. I couldn't have enjoyed our holiday more, and I am ashamed to think that perhaps I have not properly thanked you for it, and for coming with me to visit my friends, and sharing also with me the discomforts which I sometimes so arbitrarily imposed.[1] May I do so now, and ask to be forgiven for my reticence hitherto?

---

[1]    They had met in Paris in mid-July, and had fled to Florence when warned that Xandra's husband was looking for her. They stayed three nights with Berenson at I Tatti, and two more nights in Siena and Urbino. Afterwards Xandra complained that T-R had been 'cold and distant' at I Tatti.

I am beginning to be ashamed of this letter, it is so confused and com-plicated and egotistical. I will end it. I'm afraid also it is the last I will write for a few days, so for that reason too I wish it were better; but as it will catch the late post tonight, Saturday, I don't suppose you will get it before Monday afternoon, and since you go to Wales on Tuesday, I daren't write a letter that may miss you. But I will write again on 13th, to reach you in Wales on 14th; and I shall hope that you will be able, even in these inter-vening days, to find some opportunity to send me some note, however brief, to tell me that you have had a good journey and are well and some-times thinking of me, as I shall be of you.

All my love

Hugh

P.S. I return Mr Boyce's sensible letter.[1]

⸺∞⸺

## To Xandra Howard-Johnston, 11 August 1953

2.30 a.m.                                                    Christ Church, Oxford

My dearest Xandra

I have been quite unable to sleep thinking of your monstrous letter—my reason, my general philosophy make me think that I must have deserved it, but my wounded prejudices still insist that it was monstrous—so I am now going to give up the effort and write to you fully about it. I shall not argue any points with you—I did that in my letter which I sent express to you during the day—but I shall try to explain. You know, I hate exhib-itionism, the egotistical display of mental nakedness; I feel that it is em-barrassing also to the witnesses, as in the case of the Princess de Noailles'

---

[1]  A letter from her solicitor.

lover at that famous Paris ball.[1] But you have forced me to do it, and I think I must.

I must admit that I have terrible, almost physical difficulty in expressing emotion. I wish this were not so, but it just is. When I was a child, I never saw, in my own home, any evidence of any emotion whatever; and it was somehow conveyed to me that any show of it was not only improper but ridiculous. I felt that if I ever showed any, I would be publicly mocked; and mockery made me very miserable. I am not actuated by any unkind feelings in saying this: it is simply true. I can simply say that I never heard a word of affection pass between my parents, or from either of them to any of their children. This fact has often astonished me in retrospect; but it had at the time an effect which it is very difficult to overcome. I have always been extremely defensive about showing emotion (I also hate having to explain this, because I feel that it obliges me to say things about my own parents which I do not want to say). This has been a great personal difficulty for me and has interfered with every emotional affair I have had. When I was genuinely in love with the girl whom you, perhaps prudently, declined to meet, I felt terribly inhibited by this difficulty, and the facts that I was still involved in another affair at that time, and that her parents eyed me with chilling disapproval, of course made it even more difficult. I have always regretted this, and so, I think (but perhaps I am vain in so thinking) does she. Every tentative beginning of an affair tends to founder on this difficulty; although in fact I am so fastidious (or should I say complacent?) that no serious problem has occurred since then.

Then you come along. We find common interests; I find I am delighted with your conversation and company and gaiety; I also find that you are terribly unhappy and have long concealed that unhappiness under that gaiety, and I am terribly sorry for you; I find that you are in love with me; I am delighted to have such affection; and insensibly (this is the order of events: I have no secrets from you and pretend nothing to you) I find that

---

[1]    Marie-Laure Bischoffsheim, Vicomtesse de Noailles (1902–70), banking heiress and patron of the *avant garde* in literature, art, and music, gave many balls and collected histrionic admirers. At her famous *fête costumée* of 1951 the guests were dressed in the style of 1900.

I am in love with you. What then do I do? When one is in love, one wishes to give everything one has and more than one can; but in this case fearful limitations surround us—the brick-wall of your marriage, the oppressive cactus-thicket of past liabilities and omissions, the maddening necessity of secrecy. Shut in and pressed down by these external limitations, internally inhibited by a physical or psychological difficulty which I have admitted, what do I do? In language, I find the easy solution which, I'm afraid, has become second nature to me, my automatic reaction to an insoluble problem: I use a private language, patter away upon the twigs of things, and leave the root to be deduced from my actions. For if my language has been ambiguous, have my actions not been clear?

But you will not have this, and here is my grievance which I must express. I give my heart to you—rather a complicated object, you may say, like a sea-urchin, prickly outside and untempting within; but you asked for it and must connive at some of its limitations. If you would take it without too many questions (since you agree that the questions are unanswerable) then, by not raising too many difficulties, or knocking our heads against the brick walls, or rushing against the thorns, and by not insisting on detailed declarations which you must see that I have difficulty in expressing, we might have some happiness together without fruitlessly and endlessly discussing the terms of it; and gradually, by use and practice, some of the problems might even become less insoluble. But no; you insist on prodding the sensitive angularities of my heart; you try to tear off the skin to see what is underneath; you report on it to Dawyck and compare notes; you invite me to exhibit it to Dawyck so that he can make further observations—and you invite me to do so just at a time when the bridge upon which I have so often and so pleasantly met Dawyck—a delightful, half-serious, sham-gothic, rural estate-bridge—seems, by the internal gnawing of invisible death-watch-beetles, to have dissolved; so that if I go to meet Dawyck I now feel that I shall find only an unbridged gulf between us, and then (since I suffer from social vertigo) I shall draw back from the edge and be able to say nothing. And then, when I, being in pain from this pressure, utter what is perhaps an undignified squeak (I do not defend that

49

letter that so enraged you; I don't remember its contents; I just remember, at the end of the day, sending you a brief note which was not meant to be cold at all, but just something so that you should not say that I had not written, something to explain away the coldness that I felt you were imputing to me), then you direct against me that terrible document. And yet, even if I didn't and couldn't love you (which is not the case), even if I had merely out of friendship tried to alleviate your difficulties and give you some comfort in them, would this even then have been a fair reply?

When I received your letter I thought, when I was capable of thinking, that I had been wrong to turn the other cheek six weeks ago, when you sent me that formidable postscript. Such indeed is the advice of Our Saviour; but it must be admitted that in practical matters he is a very bad adviser. After all, he regulated his own affairs very badly and came to a most unfortunate and premature end in consequence. I felt that I should have resisted then, and that perhaps I should resist now. Well, before I take to the *maquis* here is my manifesto. It is not very defiant because, as I have said, I always have a secret rational conviction that, whatever my spirit protests, in fact I must be to blame for anything that is said about me. If it had not been for this secret rationality, I would just have slammed the gates, drawn up the drawbridge, issued boiling oil to the battlements, and launched a *défi*. But since I do feel that I must have been partly—and in that part seriously—to blame, I have put out instead this expostulation. You cannot believe what it costs me to utter this egotistical autobiography. I *hate* it. I have never said so much to anyone before. I have never mentioned my previous affairs—either the AFFAIR or the *crise de coeur*—to anyone; but you have forced this out of me, and as the mandrake is said to scream when dragged up by the roots, so you must not complain if the noise of this uprooting is also unmusical.

Dearest Xandra, *je suis navré*,[1] but you have still

All my love

Hugh

---

[1] 'I am so sorry.'

At the Congress for Cultural Freedom held in Berlin in 1950 Trevor-Roper had joined with the philosopher A. J. Ayer in resisting the prevailing spirit of anti-Communist hysteria. He disliked all forms of witch-hunt. He nonetheless objected to the subservience of members of the Communist Party, who, he felt, sacrificed their intellectual independence to party discipline. He recognized that some Marxist historians (such as his Oxford colleague Christopher Hill)[1] had made contributions to historical understanding, but felt they had never done so as Marxists.

His position was tested by the case of Moses Finley (1912–86). Finley had been dismissed in December 1952 as an assistant professor at Rutgers University in New Jersey after pleading the fifth amendment against self-incrimination when interrogated by the House Un-American Activities Committee. He again invoked the fifth amendment when summoned before the Senate Subcommittee on Internal Security in 1954. Shortly after this experience, he left for England, where he was considered for a studentship (fellowship) in classical studies at Christ Church. When this letter was written he was staying in Oxford.

## To Isaiah Berlin, 18 February 1955

Savile Club, 69 Brook Street, London

My dear Isaiah,

I meant to ask you this morning, and forgot, whether you either know or can find out reliable information about *Moses I. Finley*, a Greek historian, Jewish by origin, American by nationality, and now resident at New College, whom we are seriously considering to succeed Dundas.[2] Evidently he has fled from America, where he was until recently employed at *Rutgers University*, having pleaded the fifth amendment. He says that he was not a communist but kept open house and was not prepared to deny on oath that he had entertained communists, lest he run into a charge of perjury. I presume he is a fellow-traveller. He says that Rutgers University supported him in the affair and will tell us the facts.

---

[1]   Christopher Hill (1912–2003), a Communist Party member 1934–57, historian of early modern England, Fellow and Tutor of Balliol from 1938; Master, 1965–78.

[2]   Robin Dundas (1884–1960), who had taught Greek history as a Student of Christ Church for 46 years, reached retirement age in 1955. He was notorious for his fretful interrogations of undergraduates about their sexual habits.

My personal impression of Finley is favourable; his reputation as an intellectual is good; he seems to be a man who extends the frontiers of his subject, rather than sitting (like so many of our colleagues) in the well-cleared middle of it; and his book *The World of Odysseus*, which I am reading, seems to me lively and good.[1] If we elect him there is a good chance that an apoplectic stroke will carry off McCord Wright, which will be excellent,[2] and perhaps Lord Cherwell will be usefully mortified. For all these reasons I am in favour of Finley.

On the other hand I do think that the question of his politics is important. On this subject, my view is fixed: fellow-travellers, apolitical sillies,—yes, if they are good enough; party members,—no, however good. This is a view I am prepared to defend, and which I am not prepared to change.

So, for the making up of my own mind, the essential question is *what exactly happened at Rutgers?* Since Finley himself says that Rutgers will support his version, I have no great urge to write to that (to me) unknown university. I would like clear evidence from some source which *cannot* have fixed it with him. Have you any means of discovering the true facts? If you have, please do.[3]

yours ever,

Hugh

—∞—

*Trevor-Roper was dismayed by the British invasion of the Suez canal zone in November 1956, following its nationalization by the Egyptian President, Gamal Abdel Nasser. He was*

[1] T-R was reviewing the book for the *New Statesman*, where he would describe it as 'most exciting, most readable'.

[2] David McCord Wright (1909–68), Professor of Economics at the University of Virginia, who during the mid-1950s also held a post at Christ Church.

[3] Once he had satisfied himself that Finley was not a Party member, T-R determined to bring him to Christ Church: after a hard struggle, and despite Robert Blake's opposition, he succeeded in persuading the Governing Body to offer Finley a post. But by then Denys Page had recruited Finley to Cambridge, where he eventually became Professor of Ancient History, Master of Darwin College, and (as a naturalized British subject) ended his days as Sir Moses Finley.

*especially critical of the Prime Minister, Sir Anthony Eden. The next letter was written to congratulate his former pupil Sir Edward Boyle (1923–81), who had resigned from his post as Economic Secretary to the Treasury in protest against government policy In a subsequent letter Trevor-Roper would urge Boyle: 'Do get rid of Eden. It seems to me our only hope of ever being considered honest again lies in repudiating that disastrous liability!' He told Berenson that 'all my worst suspicions of Eden are confirmed'. This 'vain, ineffectual Man of Blood' had thrown his weight about 'with the uncontrolled, panic-stricken, bewildered irresponsibility of a last-minute convert' to the anti-Arab cause. 'So we are condemned by all, haven't secured the canal, have put it out of action, haven't got rid of Nasser, and look like making a present of the Middle East to Russia. Was ever a good case so wantonly bungled?'*

*The letter below was written from a house belonging to Christ Church, 8 St Aldates, into which the Trevor-Ropers moved early in 1956. Though Trevor-Roper would cease to be a Student of Christ Church when he became Regius Professor the following year, they would continue to occupy the house for the next quarter of a century.*

## To Sir Edward Boyle, 8 November 1956

8 St Aldates, Oxford

My dear Edward

Two days ago I decided to write to you, and then I thought, No, you are too busy to be troubled with the reading of letters; so I didn't. Now I hear on the wireless of your resignation, on which I congratulate you, and feel less inhibited.

I was in Dublin when the attack on Egypt took place. I was at a dinner-party for 12 people and the 9 o'clock news was turned on, describing that attack. I have seldom felt so embarrassed. I said to myself: but the whole cabinet has approved, no spectacular resignation is announced, therefore there *must* be a good reason. Where the govt. is at fault is in its handling of information & its preparation of opinion. The evidence, about immediately impending Arab attacks on Israel, will be produced in a day or two: it ought to have been produced now. So I reserved judgment until I got back to England. But such evidence has never been produced and I am now forced to conclude that it is not available.

My own view is perfectly clear. This situation—I mean, an Israeli preventive war—was predictable a year ago. The evidence that it must happen at any time from May 1956 onwards, and probably before January 1957, was overwhelming. I cannot understand why the govt. did not educate opinion to think in those terms. I quite agree that the overthrow of Nasser was desirable and that force might have to be used. But it seems to me inconceivable that the govt. should not have so managed opinion at home and abroad that such intervention should be interpreted as legal and legitimate, not unprovoked, illegal and outrageous. And, above all, it had to be effective. I fear that as things have gone it will not be effective. In fact, I foresee very black possibilities. I am forced to conclude that Eden, led by the nose by the Arab-appeasers, including America, only jumped on to the anti-Arab 'bus when the extent of his failure became clear; and jumping, could not control the 'bus. He was in the position of Chamberlain in 1939, converted to an opposite policy by facts, not of Churchill in 1939, systematic & consistent in that policy. I do not know if this is a correct interpretation, but it seems—on such evidence as I have—the obvious one.

Now what will follow? At worst, Russian domination; if not that, probably the loss of all British influence in the Middle East; and as for internal politics, a gift of Britain to the Socialists with their unreal, disastrous economic policy. It is a very gloomy prospect.

In these circumstances, I have taken no part in any petitions, manifestos, demonstrations. I feel that I cannot join the Socialist & Liberal hue-&-cry which is based on lack of realism about the Middle East. Nothing—not even idiocy by Eden—can alter the fact that Nasser is a menace and the rotten Arab states are a standing invitation to Russian control. On the other hand I cannot join the die-hards who insist that this move was in some way 'statesmanlike'. I should like to think that some kind of rational tory policy could be saved from the wreck and could prevail without waiting—as happened when Disraeli wrecked the tory party— for a generation. We simply haven't a generation to wait now. For this reason I was dispirited to find that no one resigned from office over this issue (I hardly count Nutting,[1] I'm afraid): for it seems to me that only those who disassociate themselves can hope to provide an alternative nucleus. For the same reason I was glad to hear of your resignation.

I would very much like to see you if you are in these parts or free in London; and if I can be of any help to you I should be glad to do anything I can. I hope your constituents will support you; if they do, it will be a mark to both them and you; if they don't, it will be one to you only.

yours ever

Hugh Trevor-Roper

~~~

*The medievalist Vivian Galbraith (1889–1976) was due to retire as Oxford's Regius Professor of Modern History in 1957. A former Fellow of Balliol, Galbraith had held the post—the most senior post in the History Faculty—for ten years. He had opposed Trevor-Roper's candidacy for the vacant chair in modern history in 1951. In July 1956, Trevor-Roper opened his campaign to succeed Galbraith. He conferred with Blake and sounded possible rivals, including Steven Runciman and Professor C. R. Boxer of King's College London. The latter disclaimed any interest. 'You are the obvious choice for the Chair,' he replied. Runciman, on the other hand, responded that he would not refuse the Regius Chair if it were offered. Trevor-Roper did not confer with his most obvious rival, A. J. P. Taylor.[2] He called on his former tutor J. C. Masterman, now Provost of Worcester, who greeted him with the words 'I'm not such an old fool as you think', pointing to a file marked 'Regius Chair of History' which he had ready. In discussion Masterman and*

---

[1]   (Sir) Anthony Nutting (1920–99) resigned as Minister of State for Foreign Affairs on 31 October 1956 and as MP for Melton on 16 November (a week after this letter was written). Nutting, whose two elder brothers had been killed in the Second World War, was an advocate of United Nations peace-keeping both in the canal zone and internationally.

[2]   Alan John Percival [A. J. P.] Taylor (1906–90), History Tutor at Magdalen 1938–63 and Fellow of Magdalen 1938–76; University Lecturer in Modern History 1946–54 and in International History 1953–63. A fluent and powerful writer, he was the author of more than thirty books, including *The Struggle for Mastery in Europe, 1848–1918* (1954) and *English History, 1914–1945* (1965). His revisionist *The Origins of the Second World War* (1961) provoked outrage, especially from those who had misread its arguments, and brought him into conflict with T-R on television and in print. The success of Taylor's frequent broadcasts and newspaper columns, which was resented by many of his colleagues, made him the best-known historian of his time. Sir Lewis Namier, who had been his friend and mentor in pre-war Manchester, told

*Trevor-Roper dismissed the claims of Richard Southern,*[1] *whom Galbraith regarded as his proper and natural successor. Trevor-Roper mentioned Runciman's name; Masterman, who stroked his nose sagely at this suggestion, declared that he would write to his former pupil, David Stephens, now the patronage secretary responsible for advising the Prime Minister on such appointments. 'My suspicion is that J.C. may want to run me,' Trevor-Roper confided to his wife Xandra. 'I am making a tremendous effort to be discreet,' he told one of his pupils.*

*In mid-December Masterman summoned Trevor-Roper for another talk. He was due to go to London to see 'them' on the subject of the Regius Chair, and asked Trevor-Roper for a letter giving his views on the subject. He then made one of his 'carefully calculated indiscretions' and produced a letter from his former Worcester colleague, Asa Briggs, whom he had consulted on the matter. Briggs, who had recently taken a Chair of History at Leeds, wrote that there was only one obvious name: Trevor-Roper. Both Southern and K. B. McFarlane of Magdalen were too narrow, and Taylor too irresponsible. Briggs's support was especially encouraging, because he was neither a personal friend nor a natural ally. This interview convinced Trevor-Roper that Masterman planned to put his name forward.*

*Perhaps the letter Trevor-Roper wrote at Masterman's request can be interpreted as a disguised manifesto.*

## To Sir John Masterman, 13 December 1956

[marked] Not sent. Replaced by (discreeter) typed letter

8 St Aldates, Oxford

My dear J.C.

Of course I will gladly give you my views about the Regius Chair, though you may find that, by opening this little vent, you have liberated a larger blast of warmer air than you had expected.

---

Taylor, whose gifts were so extraordinary, had disappointed him by...his addiction to popular journalism'. Taylor was bitterly disappointed that Namier did not back him robustly for the Regius Chair.

[1]   (Sir) Richard Southern (1912–2001) had served in the Political Intelligence Department of the War Office before returning to his fellowship at Balliol in 1946. He had established his high reputation as a medievalist with *The Making of the Middle Ages* (1953). His inaugural lecture as Chichele Professor of Modern History at Oxford in 1961 called for change in the Oxford history school. As Peter Brown recalled, Southern noted that '"a school founded on the model of classical studies, based upon literary texts, had been taken over by German methods of archive-based scholarship". He said little more; but...we knew that he had sounded the death-knell of the Pipe Roll.' Southern was President of St John's College, Oxford, 1969–81.

I believe that we need a summary break with the present Oxford tradition, a tradition which has now continued itself, *vi inertiae*,[1] for thirty years. During those thirty years, in which the aims and methods of historical study have been profitably re-examined abroad, and important works published and new horizons envisaged, Oxford (as it seems to me) has become a backwater left ever further behind by the intellectual tide. Can anyone point to any serious historical book, or school of thought, or set of ideas, as being typical or worthy of Oxford in those years? Our professors who, on the whole (except in this case of the Regius Chair), tend to elect each other, seem to think it positively indecent to risk error by writing anything: for may not some plodding pedant one day discover some new document which will overturn their rash conclusions? How much safer to edit, with factual and bibliographical footnotes, some hitherto deservedly unnoticed monastic laundry-book! Given this philosophy in the Chairs of the Elect, it is hardly surprising if historical writing, historical thought, has dwindled to a standstill in Oxford just when it has been rising, and raising most interest, in the rest of the world.

Does this seem too radical a statement? Consider the facts. Of our seven historical professors today, only one (the Chichele Professor) has written so much as one original book on a historical subject.[2] His books are not very galvanising, and they are of course in the tradition of the period: but at least (like those of Powicke[3]) they represent that tradition when it was alive. They exist. Of the other six professors, two (the

---

[1]   'By the force of inertia'.

[2]   The medievalist Ernest [E. F.] Jacob (1894–1971), a former Student of Christ Church, was Professor of Modern History at Manchester 1929–44 and Chichele Professor of Modern History in Oxford 1950–61. He had published *Studies in the Period of Baronial Reform and Rebellion* (1925), *Henry IV and the Invasion of France* (1947), and essay collections. In the late 1950s he was working on a volume in the Oxford History of England, *England in the Fifteenth Century* (1961).

[3]   (Sir) Maurice [F. M.] Powicke (1879–1963), who was born and (like T-R) reared in Alnwick, was Professor of Medieval History at Manchester 1919–28, and Galbraith's predecessor as Oxford's Regius Professor of Modern History 1929–47. Although he tried to rescue medieval history from insularity, and encouraged his pupils to take account of European scholarship, his own work was stolidly grounded in English constitutional and institutional history. He too wrote a volume in the Oxford History of England series.

Professors of Military History[1] and International Relations[2]) have not, so far as I can discover, written so much as one article between them. The Professor of Modern History has usefully edited some documents but never ventured an opinion.[3] The retiring Regius Professor, in his full career, has edited a text and published two short treatises on the prohibitive danger of seeking to interpret any such text. The Professor of Economic History has written three articles, all more or less on the same subject of aristocratic marriage settlements in the time of Queen Anne;[4] and I believe that, had we but world enough and time, we could find, in obscure parish journals, one or two learned *trivia* by the Professor of Ecclesiastical History.[5] Of course I know that there are articles which, though short, can be of disproportionate significance and can by themselves justify a career, like Notestein's Raleigh Lecture[6] or Maitland's Rede Lecture;[7] but I do not think that anyone would put the few articles of our Professors in that class. It mortifies me to think that this is Oxford's contribution to historical study today, and that Namier—who on any account

[1] (Sir) Norman Gibbs (1910–90), Chichele Professor of the History of War 1953–77, had been appointed as one of the Cabinet Office's war historians in 1943, although his unwieldy volume in the Grand Strategy series of the official history of the Second World War was not published until 1976. He had published little by 1956.

[2] Agnes Headlam-Morley (1902–86), Montague Burton Professor of International Relations 1948–71, had published *The New Democratic Constitutions of Europe* (1929) and edited her father's literary remains.

[3] Bruce [R. B.] Wernham (1906–99), who had served in the RAF Photographic Interpretation Unit 1941–3, had written an official history of RAF Bomber Command to 1938, which was never published. He had edited two calendars of state papers, and co-edited a volume of documents, at the time of his election to the chair in modern history in 1951.

[4] (Sir) John Habakkuk (1915–2002) had published three articles at the time of his election as Chichele Professor of Economic History in 1950. During his 17 years in the Chichele Chair he produced an article every year. His first book, *American and British Technologies in the Nineteenth Century*, appeared in 1962.

[5] Claude Jenkins (1877–1959), librarian of Lambeth Palace 1910–34, Regius Professor of Ecclesiastical History and Canon of Christ Church 1934–59, had supervised T-R's doctoral researches on Laud, but neglected his pupil. T-R disliked his fusty obscurantism, frugality, scavenging of food, and grubbiness. In J. I. M. Stewart's novels, Dr Stringfellow is modelled on Jenkins, whose eccentricities are also recounted in the memoirs of E. L. Mascall (see p. 36).

[6] Notestein's 'The Winning of the Initiative by the House of Commons' was the Raleigh Lecture of 1924, and published in *Proceedings of the British Academy*.

[7] Maitland's 'English Law and the Renaissance' was the Rede Lecture at Cambridge in 1901, and was published with copious notes later in the year.

must surely be admitted to be England's greatest living historian—has been kept out of every Oxford chair in turn, in order not to upset these quiet lives.[1]

It can be argued that a Professor reveals his quality not merely in his own writing but in the work of his pupils, in the 'school' he creates, so that a Professor who writes nothing at all may nevertheless be important by his influence. I agree. But where is the 'school' of any present Oxford professor? There is no such thing. Historical research here is not really organised at all. No Professor has a research seminar. Students wishing to do historical research are not directed to problems: they are told to find some neglected pool and paddle in it. They are farmed out to supervisors on the principles of Buggins' turn. So real problems are left untouched and human labour and intelligence are wasted on that miscellany of trivial theses which makes the Report of the Committee for Advanced Studies such a shameful document.

Now I know that unambitious archivists are very useful creatures, and what would we do without them in their proper place? But I suggest that their proper place is a Record Office, not a University. In a university I feel that we ought to have professors who aim a little higher and are not afraid to interpret evidence and even, by publishing their interpretations, to run the gauntlet of public criticism and risk being proved wrong. After all, history is a science, and the sciences advance by hypothesis and criticism, not by accumulation and piety; through the

[1]    Sir Lewis [L. B.] Namier (1888–1960) had been Lecturer in Modern History at Balliol in 1920–1 and Professor of Modern History at Manchester University 1931–53. He wrote penetrating essays on 19th- and 20th-century European diplomatic history, was a doughty propagandist for Zionism, but was supremely a historian of Hanoverian England. He advocated painstaking archival research to provide close structural analysis of political alliances and voting patterns ('Namierization') and denied the significance of political ideas. He hated abstract schemes, philosophical historians, and 'fine writing' (though his own prose was distinctive and powerful). *Ideengeschichte*, the history of ideas, was (he once told Isaiah Berlin) 'what one Jew cribs from another'. According to Plumb, Trevelyan muttered of him, 'Great research worker, no historian'. Despite his pre-eminence Namier had been excluded from positions at Oxford or Cambridge: initially, because of anti-Semitic prejudice; later, because his domineering monologues drove colleagues out of common-rooms. His tendency, in the Oxford historian John Cooper's words, to 'rather adolescent obscenity in exclusively male company' was also disliked.

laboratory, not the museum; by public controversy, not secret relic-worship. And I should also like to see someone in a position to influence study in Oxford who is aware of the important historical work being done abroad, and who is capable of inspiring some purposive research, such as Namier inspired at Manchester and Neale and Tawney[1] in London, such as Hamilton does at Chicago[2] and Braudel in Paris. Stockholm and Florence, thanks to Heckscher and Sapori,[3] have thriving historical schools: why not Oxford? This is admittedly aiming high,—higher than can be achieved by merely one appointment,—but it would be something to make a start. I would like to see a start made by the introduction, at the top, of someone who is right outside the dismal Oxford tradition of the last thirty years. Why should we not import someone from outside, from Cambridge, London, Aberystwyth, anywhere, to re-fertilise this sterile school?

Naturally I have thought a good deal about names, and have thought of some names which, by causing an epidemic of apoplexy in several comfortable chairs, would precipitate several other useful vacancies. But I will not bother you with doubtful candidates. My considered nominee is a Cambridge man: Steven Runciman.[4] I do not suppose that he could do all that I have required of the ideal Professor: that would be to expect too much of him or of any man; but at least the process of reform could begin with him. He would be a Professor of the right kind: a distinguished

---

[1]  (Sir) John [J. E.] Neale (1890–1975), Astor Professor of English History at University College London, 1927–56, who specialized in Elizabethan England. R. H. Tawney (1880–1962), economic historian, social critic, and Christian socialist, whose interpretation of the social changes leading to the Puritan revolution established itself as orthodoxy for a generation of historians. According to A. L. Rowse, 'Tawney exercised the widest influence of any historian of his time.'

[2]  Earl Hamilton (1899–1989), who held a chair at Chicago 1947–67, was an economic historian of colonial Spain and pioneer of quantitative economic history.

[3]  Eli Heckscher (1879–1952) and Armando Sapori (1892–1976) were both economic historians.

[4]  (Sir) James Cochran Stevenson Runciman (1903–2000), who wrote as Steven Runciman, revivified the study of Byzantium. He believed that it was the task of historians to make history readable, and deprecated academics who wrote only to impress their contemporaries. Having inherited money from his shipping magnate grandfather, he had no need of university posts.

historian who has written original, scholarly and highly readable books, and who would lend distinction to the chair instead of merely owing any distinction he had to it.

I know there is one objection that will be made to Runciman and which therefore I hasten to forestall. He is a medievalist. Our last three Regius Professors, covering the last thirty years, have all been medievalists, and all of the same school; and Aristotle, Ibn Khaldoun[1] and other such political philosophers seem agreed that three of a dynasty is always enough and generally too much. However, there is such a difference between Runciman and our home-bred parochial medievalists that I have no hesitation in pronouncing them to be of an entirely different species. Look at Runciman's books—*The First Bulgarian Empire, The Medieval Manichee, The History of the Crusades* (3 volumes), *The Eastern Schism*. These are large subjects, largely treated: how can one put such works in the same category as an edition of the Anonimalle Chronicle[2] or an Unpublished Act Book of an Archdeacon of Taunton?[3] Runciman is a real scholar, but also a cosmopolitan scholar, whose studies range in space from France to Persia, in time from the Fall of Rome to the fall of Byzantium. And he can write. There is a liberalism, an elevation, a vitality about his work which makes that of our local antiquaries, nibbling away in their narrow sectors, look mean and stale. For mere interest, give me an obscure Bogomil heretic enlivened by the wit and scholarship of Runciman rather than the most outrageous Angevin adventurer reduced, even by Jacob, even by Powicke, to prim and spinsterish conformity. Of course I know that history doesn't consist of style only, and our present Regius Professor would say that any historian who writes well *must* be a bad historian; but in fact, if one looks at the admittedly great historians, one finds that they all had style as well. It goes with the character, as the bouquet goes with the wine, inseparable

[1]   Ibn Khaldūn (1332–1406), courtier and historian of the Berbers, to whom T-R devoted a chapter of his *Historical Essays*.

[2]   V. H. Galbraith's edition of this anonymous account of English history 1333–81 had been published by Manchester University Press in 1927.

[3]   *Act Book of the Archdeacon of Taunton*, ed. T. Atkinson Jenkins (1868–1935), in *Collectanea*, vol. ii, ed. Thomas F. Palmer, Somerset Record Society (1924).

if the substance be good. It would be refreshing to have a Regius Professor in that good old tradition; and therefore, on all points, without much more ado (for I have already covered too much paper), Runciman is my man. I hope I can persuade you to make him yours?

yours ever,

Hugh Trevor-Roper

⸺◦⸺

On 6 June 1957 it was announced that Trevor-Roper had been appointed Regius Professor in succession to Galbraith. The competition for the post attracted exceptional interest, as several prominent candidates, including Taylor and Trevor-Roper, were well known to the general public. The view that Taylor was the best qualified was expressed by many, including Taylor himself.

Soon after the announcement the Trevor-Ropers travelled to Russia, at the invitation of the recently installed British Ambassador, Patrick Reilly. While staying at the British Embassy the Trevor-Ropers were warned that they would be followed on every expedition, and that all conversations would be bugged. Although they were comfortable at the Embassy, conditions elsewhere were bleak. At a new 'Intourist' hotel they were devoured by bedbugs. None of the hotels provided soap or lavatory paper. There was no plug for the bath or handbasin. Servants were happy to accept Trevor-Roper's nylon socks instead of tips. Restaurant food was unpalatable and took up to ninety minutes to arrive: the Trevor-Ropers were told that the delay was caused by bureaucratic procedures devised to prevent pilferage. Xandra, who wore haute couture garments at home, had been advised by Lady Reilly to bring only old, plain clothes to Russia, but women stared at her as if she were a creature from another galaxy and sometimes fingered her clothes as they passed. After returning to England, Trevor-Roper wrote to his brother describing that 'grim, prison-like country which I find it so interesting to have seen, and from which I am so glad to have escaped'.

From Russia Trevor-Roper wrote to Wallace Notestein (1878–1969), a specialist on seventeenth-century English history and for many years Professor of English History at Yale, who had spent the academic year 1949–50 in Oxford as a visiting professor. The two men were linked by their acquaintance with Berenson: Notestein's wife Ada Comstock (the first full-time President of Radcliffe College) was a close friend of Berenson's sister, and the couple had made the first of several visits to I Tatti in 1950. Notestein admired Trevor-Roper's prose. 'There is a new star in the historical world,' he had written to him during the previous year: 'No-one, not even Namier, can write like you.'

## To Wallace Notestein, 25 July 1957

British Embassy, Moscow

My dear Notestein

I have long owed you a letter of thanks; but I have delayed writing it until I had despatched some 280 other letters of thanks: for I wanted to keep to the last, for a period of relative ease and freedom, the pleasant task of writing, at greater length, to those particular friends whose letters gave me the greatest pleasure. I was altogether delighted by yours. Thank you very much indeed for it. There is no support, in these matters, that gives me greater pleasure than yours.

I must admit that I really think A. J. P. Taylor's qualifications were the highest, and I would have been glad if he had been nominated (Rowse, of course, would have been a humiliating disaster); but I suppose it was impossible, especially as the P.M.'s *eminence grise* in such matters, Namier, seems to have turned against him. The circumstances are, in my opinion, entirely creditable to Taylor. He dared to criticise, in a review in the *Manchester Guardian*,[1] the ridiculous lengths to which Namier's army of industrious hacks are now carrying his methods, 'namierising', at tedious length, the insignificant members of obscure assemblies and their trivial tactics. After that, it seems, all past links were broken: of no avail was Taylor's devoted energy in preparing and writing for that *Festschrift*:[2] the Master requires absolute obedience; and this gesture of independence was fatal. The sad fact is that Taylor is really too independent to have *any* support from *any* Establishment. The Labour Establishment is even more hostile than the Tory: when there was a Labour Government, Herbert Morrison prevailed on the BBC to cut Taylor off the air, and now Lord Attlee has written a mean and factually incorrect review

---

[1] 'The School of Namier', a review of John Brooke's *The Chatham Administration 1766–1768*, appeared in the *Manchester Guardian*, 16 November 1956.

[2] Richard Pares and A. J. P. Taylor (eds.), *Essays Presented to Sir Lewis Namier* (London, 1956). Both Taylor and Trevor-Roper contributed essays to this volume.

of Taylor's last work (his Ford lectures) dismissing him as 'a well-known television star'.

However, if Taylor is, as it seems, simply not *papabile*,[1] and if my other candidate, Steven Runciman, is disqualified as a Cambridge man and a medievalist (but how different from our Oxford medievalists!), then who am I to spurn this unexpected crown? I see an immense amount of work to do, of which the prospect appals me. One of my first acts, after the announcement of the nomination, was to call on Galbraith. It was the first time that he has ever spoken to me since he came to Oxford as professor, and he had offered to give me advice on my new position. The experience was rather pitiful. He told me what Latin formula I should use on being admitted as a fellow of Oriel; he told me that I would find myself *ipso facto* a trustee of certain insignificant trusts; he bewailed the inadequacy of his predecessor and of the Provost & Fellows of Oriel; but of the rights and duties, the difficulties or opportunities of a Regius Professor of Modern History in Oxford he said nothing, nothing at all. I got the impression that he has never attempted to do anything in that chair, which he accepted, he said, as 'an old man's retiring job'. The consequences can be imagined: there is no faculty centre, no direction of research, no publication of theses, no rational control or direction of any kind. The Professor hasn't even a secretary... However, as I can't use the excuse of 'an old man's retiring job', I suppose I shall have to find an answer to these problems.

We are greatly enjoying our visit to Russia, though glad to be staying in the comfort of the Embassy after a few experiences of Russian hotels. In spite of all that one reads about the vast economic growth and new efficiency of Russia, the overwhelming impression is of ancient squalor only temporarily beaten back by spasmodic pretentious construction. Of course there is undoubted efficiency in certain directions: but it is in directions generally hidden from the public, being the directions leading to state power only. As far as the ordinary daily life of the citizen is

---

[1] 'Eligible to be elected Pope', usually said of a cardinal.

concerned, this is still the seedy, oriental country of Gogol or Turgeniev—
without any of that *douceur de vivre* which depends on an aristocratic
society.

One respect in which efficiency is shown, and shown to the public, is
the field of 'culture'. 'Culture' is an absolute fetish here, and the sums of
money which are released for 'cultural' purposes are inconceivable to us.
Is an 18th century palace tumbling down? It is restored, if necessary, from
the ground upwards. Is an old church or monastery in ruins? It is rebuilt
according to the original plans, the mosaics re-copied, the dome regilded.
The fact that there are no Tsars, no princes, to live in the palaces, no
priests, no monks to occupy the churches or monasteries, is quite irrelevant. The Tsar's palace at Peterhof, near Petersburg, was shelled to pieces
by the Germans, who carried off the works of art and melted down the
dozens of 18th century statues, all of gilded bronze, in the formal gardens.
Today all has been rebuilt, replaced, regilded: marble pillars, crystal and
gold chandeliers, fountains and effigies and colonnades are once again
*herrlich wie am ersten tag.*[1]

On the other hand, once one has admired, or, more properly, been stu-
pefied by these experiences, one soon realises that this 'culture' is entirely
dead. I mean, it is totally divorced from ideas. The aesthetic deposit of the
past, once it has been warranted 'correct' by experts, is carefully preserved and publicly venerated and deliberately imitated: railway-stations,
tube-stations and public buildings are now built in stereotyped classical
form; but the ideas behind these forms, or indeed any ideas at all, are still
totally banned. The repression of ideas, even in the comparatively liberal
atmosphere which has developed in the last few years, is still extraordinary. In consequence there is absolutely no intellectual or aesthetic life,
no modern art, no modern architecture that is not either dreary and
mechanical or mere imitation of the past; and the armies of 'culture'-
seeking Russians who fill the museums, guided in parties by 'experts'

[1] 'As glorious as it was on the first day' (from the prologue, set in heaven, to Goethe's
*Faust*).

who know what is 'correct', gape with an exactly identical *rictus* at 13<sup>th</sup>-century Russian ikons, Italian Renaissance paintings, 18<sup>th</sup>-century portraits, and the ghastly petty-bourgeois chocolate-box representations of forward-looking workers and peasants which fill entire galleries under the name of 'socialist realism'.

But if I try to tell you about Russia, I shall never stop; so let me reserve the remainder of my impressions till we meet, when my grave comments on industrial production etc., will be punctuated and perhaps enlivened by Xandra's graphic account of the army of bed-bugs which inflicted on her not very extensive surface, in the most pretentious *Intourist* hotel in Vladimir, the 403 bites which still, every day, I have to re-count and re-anoint. I hope also there will be plenty of other topics of conversation. So do please let us know when we can see you, remembering that by the time you receive this letter we shall already, if all goes well, be back in Oxford.

yours ever

Hugh Trevor-Roper

———⟨⟩———

*'In order to disperse my critics, I am now writing a huge book, in three volumes,' Trevor-Roper told Berenson in December 1957. He had been contemplating a history of England during the English Civil Wars and interregnum since 1949. He had promised Berenson in 1955 that he would start a big book on the seventeenth century 'as soon as we have a house'. The 'huge book' had been deferred twice, in favour of other works, which he then abandoned. Now he planned a major work on the Puritan revolution of the seventeenth century, which he expected to be his magnum opus.*

*Several of Trevor-Roper's letters of 1959 declare that he is 'furiously writing' and 'writing, writing, writing—or rather, re-writing, re-writing, re-writing'. He once told a graduate student that he wrote everything four or five times over before he would let it go to print. Many of his letters mentioned the difficulties he was encountering with the form of his book. The challenge of interweaving an analysis of the social structure with a narrative of especially complex events would eventually defeat him.*

*Trevor-Roper often complained about the distractions of family life. The house in St Aldates was not big enough for him to elude his three stepchildren in the school holidays.*

*Xandra considered southern England 'suburban', and preferred the Borders, where she was keen to find a replacement for Birchfield, the cramped house near Melrose, which was too small to provide Trevor-Roper with a study and which was partly owned by her first husband. At first Trevor-Roper resisted and remonstrated: 'You often seem to forget that I have my work to do, that all my books are at Oxford, that to earn money I have to keep in touch with London, even in vacation, and that all this makes me want to live, for preference, reasonably near London.'*

*But Xandra would prevail. A few months after this letter was written they bought a gabled villa outside Melrose, only a few miles from Bemersyde. Named Chiefswood, it had been built by Sir Walter Scott for his daughter Sophia after her marriage to his biographer John Lockhart. Though the Trevor-Ropers were delighted by their acquisition, it was recalled by Xandra's elder son James Howard-Johnston as 'a gloomy house, with small windows, in a hollow where damp and cold gathered, without much joie de vivre inside'. Trevor-Roper equipped himself with a study there, with Aubusson carpet on the floor and upright Aubusson chairs by the fireplace.*

*Xandra devised an elaborate decorative scheme, and converted the kitchen into a striking dining-room, with red and white striped awning slung under the ceiling and crimson parachute silk on the walls giving the illusion of being inside a tent. She furnished the house with fine English and French pieces from the late eighteenth and early nineteenth centuries. It would be Christmas before the house was ready for their occupation.*

## To Wallace Notestein, 7 March 1959

Hotel Métropole, Beaulieu-sur-Mer

My dear Notestein

You sent such a kind message in your Christmas card that I am ashamed of not having written earlier to thank you: but we have had a pretty difficult time ever since mid-December and everything is behindhand. It began at the end of the Michaelmas term, when we prepared to move to Scotland: a seasonal migration which, for organisation, number of wagons, beasts of burden, persons, bales of luggage, fodder for the journey, presents to bestow on the chiefs of hospitable tribes *en route*, compares with any of the nomadic journeys of Abraham, setting out from the rich, sophisticated cities of Chaldaea to the bare and stony solitudes of rural Palestine. On this occasion the tribe duly set out, but when it reassembled at Melrose to the noise of tribal gongs, ram's-horn trumpets, and the nasal call to prayer of the local minister of the kirk, the children and the parcels were there, the camels and the concubines, but one person was missing. Xandra had been taken ill at Oxford just before her turn came to leave. So I had to go back; and on arrival found she had been removed to hospital with virus-pneumonia. Nor was that all. After a fortnight, when she seemed on the way to recovery, the doctor, by an excess of zeal, nearly killed her with penicillin. It would, he said, save her from hypothetical complications: in fact, it caused a real illness far worse than the pneumonia had been and kept her another three weeks in hospital. Meanwhile I was living alone in our house in Oxford, without food or servants, surrounded by obstinately closed colleges until the term and the horrors thereof, and of a particularly nasty winter, returned: so by the time Xandra was out of hospital and fit to be taken for a recuperative holiday, I felt almost as much in need of one myself.

However, all that is now past. Ten days ago Xandra's health and the University statutes both allowed us to go, and here we sit, our drooped spirits reviving in the Mediterranean sun, our purses leaking rapidly through invisible seams, but health and peace of mind as silently returning. Xandra is already infinitely better, and although I complain of being like a battery-hen in this place, stuck on a narrow perch between the mountains and the sea, deprived of any hen-run in which to exercise myself, and gorged with huge and regular meals of rich and fattening food, nevertheless, when the sun is out my temper becomes benign again and I read not-too-serious books and write not-too-serious letters. Of the books, I began with Madame de Sévigné's letters; but after the first 900 pages I began to find her rather an old bore: I grew tired of the recurrent pregnancies of French countesses and the second-hand compliments of gouty French dukes, and *ma bonne* and *ma mie* and the dear tame *abbé* at Livry and Les Rochers; and so I have turned to Bertie Russell's *History of Western Philosophy*. What a splendid old thing he is! My veneration for him grows and grows: for the vast range of that unageing intellect, and the sovereignty of reason over that range, and that marvellous style with its economy and clarity and good temper and wit. I have had to stop reading him in bed because Xandra says I wake up our neighbours when I laugh, as I did, rather loudly, over Empedocles.[1] As for my not-too-serious letter-writing, well, you see here an instance of it.

Of course serious writing has been almost completely suspended amid these misfortunes; which is tiresome, for I was getting on with my book and was pleased with it. I had written some 500 pages, and found it was getting too long and too formless, so had begun again: now I am pleased with it and see it falling into shape. But it is no good trying to write here: I can only write in a large room, full of my own books, and with space to walk up and down while I meditate the *clausulae*[2] of my sentences. Xandra says this is very inconvenient to her: she would like me to be able to write unobtrusively in an attic bedroom, leaving the rest of the house free for the uninhibited self-expression of three children furiously competing on their discordant musical instruments.

Meanwhile how are you both, what are you doing, what hearing in that universal intelligence-exchange in Edwards Street? Write to me some time, to Oxford, and tell me all. How fared Galbraith in your great country (I am sure you will report only good things of a fellow-Scot), how Rowse (about whom you can feel no such inhibitions)? I have seen neither of them in the last year: Galbraith, I suppose, because I so seldom go to Oriel College—it is incredibly dull, friendly but dull, like a country club in Carlisle; Rowse because, for some reason, I have been struck out of his Book of Life forever. However, no doubt I shall feature—no doubt we shall all feature—in his Book of Death. For you know that Rowse, for

---

[1]  Russell described Empedocles (*c.*490–430 BC) as a 'mixture of philosopher, prophet, man of science and charlatan...a democratic politician, who at the same time claimed to be a god'. His summary of Empedocles' proto-theory of evolution pictured a world of wondrous creatures: 'heads without necks, arms without shoulders, eyes without foreheads, solitary limbs seeking for union. These things joined together as each might chance; there were shambling creatures with countless hands, creatures with faces and breasts looking in different directions, creatures with the bodies of oxen and the faces of men...only certain forms survived.'

[2]  The shaping of perfect cadences or endings.

years, has been keeping a huge diary—a diary, we are led to understand, which, in bulk and all other qualities, will leave the Goncourt Diaries nowhere.[1] In this diary all his enemies are to be portrayed, and to receive their final portraits, for the gallery of history. Whatever we may be like in real life, history is to know us, if it knows us at all, only as we are definitively etched in the classic pages of Rowse's Journal—just as 17th and 18th century Oxford and its characters are now immutably, even if inaccurately, portrayed in the pages of Wood and Hearne.[2] But who knows? Perhaps someone will go and spoil it all by writing an even more preservative portrait of Rowse,—who, after all, is a character, though an odious character, and deserves, as Wood and Hearne deserve, a brief portrait. I like to think of him, that once radical peasant, the would-be Lenin of England, the preacher of proletarian revolution among the Methodist miners of Cornwall, now sitting in isolated splendour, surrounded by *objets d'art* and aristocratic pictures, in Castle Grind-the-Faces-of-the-Poor, his pen hurrying, hurrying over the endless pages, creating, for the future, an imaginary present, to solace his frustrated soul. For long periods the pen glides smoothly, as if the inkwell contained only balm and oil, for it is describing the virtues of duchesses, and the sound of their coronets is tinkling musically in his ears; but now and then the nib is suddenly crossed, the purple ink splutters, the crested writing-paper is torn: for his olympian thoughts have been disturbed by some disgusting intrusion: he has seen, through the iridescent aureole of his heaven—like some Father of the Church who looks down through the parting clouds of the Empyrean[3] and sees the faces of heretics growling from the Pit— the faces of his enemies: of you or me or those more generalised enemies 'carping intellectuals' and 'the idiot people'. I suppose all the great prolix

---

[1]  The journals of Edmond Goncourt (1822–96) and his brother Jules (1830–70) provide a frank, often biased portrait of the Parisian literary intelligentsia.

[2]  Anthony Wood (1632–95) and Thomas Hearne (1678–1735) were both Oxonian antiquaries who kept diaries. Wood, who was as ill-tempered as Rowse, compiled a series of Oxonian biographical sketches, *Athenae Oxonienses*. In his inaugural lecture as Regius Professor T-R referred to the 'snarling old antiquaries...Antony Wood and Thomas Hearne, the hermit-crabs of Merton College and St Edmund Hall'.

[3]  i.e. from heaven.

diarists—those who wrote diaries for posterity—the Goncourts, Greville[1] as well as Wood and Hearne—were really like this: embittered, frustrated men seeking a posthumous revenge on the society which disdained them. But in your great country I believe he is not disdained—at least not West of the Alleghenies. There, there, he now says, in Madison (or is it Denver, or Kansas City?), is his spiritual (and financial) home, among the admiring, enlightened, embattled women of the Lecture Clubs, the true *Kulturträger*[2] of the 20th century. 'If the Socialists win the next General Election', says this former socialist candidate for a Cornish constituency, 'I shall become an American citizen.' So you may yet have him, and for keeps.

We are going to stay here for a few more days—making a fortnight in all—and then will probably move to Aix-en-Provence, a charming town, for a few more days, before going back, via Paris, to England. We had meant to pay a short visit to B.B.[3] in Florence, but I now fear, from Nicky's last letter, that he is past seeing people, or at least having guests, so we must preserve him in our memories as we last knew him, which is perhaps best. It is very sad to think of the dissolution of I Tatti: it had become so much part of our lives; and of course I regard its impending institutionalisation as little better than dissolution: at least it is a metamorphosis so complete that all continuity will be broken. How BB himself would hate the sight of all those calf-eyed specialists in *Kunstgeschichte*[4] niggling away in the corners of his house! How he can create such a coffin for himself bewilders me: but I suppose it is mere piety: Harvard made him: Harvard gave and now Harvard shall take away…I feel I can safely say this to a Yale man: you can say what you like to me of the folly of old Willy Stone, the millionaire owner of the Albany, leaving everything to Peterhouse, to

[1] The meticulous diaries of Charles Greville (1794–1865), Clerk of the Privy Council 1821–59, are an important source for British political history from the Regency to the Crimean War and are spiced with sharp social observations.

[2] Someone or something that transmits cultural ideals, especially from one generation to the next.

[3] Bernard Berenson, who, as his health failed, was more than ever dependent on his companion Nicky Mariano.

[4] 'Art history'.

raise the standard of living of Postan, Butterfield, Wormald, Brogan *et hoc genus omne.*[1]

I must stop now. Even in this Phaeacian spot[2] one sometimes becomes conscious of the passage of time—even if only through the sudden tinkle of glasses or cutlery, reminding the serried battery-hens on their maritime perch that new mounds of meal and maize are about to be thrust before their crammed and twitching gullets. But I hope that by this exercise—the only exercise I can take—I will at least provoke you to write to us and tell us all about yourselves, with a peripheral frill of gossip, and give us news also that you will be coming over to Europe in general, and Oxford in particular, this summer, where we long to see you both again. Xandra repeats these sentiments, like Echo in my ear, and adds her love to mine, for you both.

yours ever,

Hugh Trevor-Roper

───⟨∞⟩───

*Trevor-Roper was a remote figure to his three stepchildren during the early years of his marriage. However, he developed an increasing intimacy with the two eldest, James (b. 1942) and Xenia (b. 1944), as they became bright, intense teenagers whose intellects he could stimulate, enrich, and guide. The following two letters were written when James was a 17-year-old pupil in his final term at Eton, estranged from his father and in low spirits. Encouraged by his stepfather, Howard-Johnston would study classics at Christ Church,*

---

[1] 'And everyone of that kind'. William Stone (1857–1958) had been the first scholar in natural sciences at Peterhouse, but declined a fellowship. During the 1940s he bought many sets of chambers in Albany, Piccadilly. He bequeathed the freeholds together with £100,000 to Peterhouse, which erected an eight-storey brick tower to house fellows and undergraduates and funded studentships and a research fellowship—all named after him. The historians Michael Postan, Herbert Butterfield, Brian Wormald, and Denis Brogan were fellows of Peterhouse.

[2] It was on the land of the Phaeacians that the storm-tossed Ulysses, or Odysseus, found refuge in the *Odyssey*. For T-R, a Phaeacian landscape was one whose enchantment suggested the presence of mythological figures. If the Greeks had had such a river as the Thames, he reflected when wandering by it during the war, they 'would have peopled it with nymphs, and invested it with divinity and divine associations…and I thought of Odysseus' address to the river of the Phaeacians at whose mouth he landed'. T-R also used the adjective to denote the delights of epicurean living.

*beginning in the Michaelmas term 1960. Howard-Johnston would go on to become a Fellow of Corpus Christi College, Oxford, and University Lecturer in Byzantine studies 1971–2009. Trevor-Roper's correspondence with him draws on their shared knowledge of Greek literature.*

## To James Howard-Johnston, 21 May 1960

Boughton House, Kettering[1]

My dear James,

Your letter arrived this morning just before we set off for a week-end at Boughton. I am so sorry you are ill, and I do hope you will be better quickly. Meanwhile here is a brief booklet (please don't lose it) on an 18th century Bluestocking for your list of those tiresome creatures. They began, I'm afraid, long before Molière. There were some famous Renaissance Bluestockings. At the Reformation there was another crop of them. The Duchess of Suffolk, the Queen of Navarre, etc. In England the most bluestocking generation, I think, was that of queen Elizabeth. Her contemporary, Lady Jane Grey, for instance, when they came to offer her the crown instead of Bloody Mary, was reading the *Phaedo* in Greek.[2] Queen Elizabeth herself of course was tremendously learned, and on one famous occasion reduced a Polish Ambassador to speechlessness by a brilliant extempore tirade in Latin.[3] And then, in the 17th century, there is Lady Conway,[4] who knew everyone who was anyone in the intellectual world, and had famous incurable headaches, and ended a Quaker. But as a general rule I think that Bluestockings flourish in ages of Reform. They

[1]   Where the T-Rs were staying as guests of the Duchess of Buccleuch.
[2]   Plato's *Phaedo* is the dialogue in which Socrates contemplates the immortality of the soul before being forced to drink hemlock.
[3]   At Greenwich, in 1597, Elizabeth delivered impromptu in Latin a famous denunciation of Spanish trading practices coupled with a fierce rebuke to Paweł Działyński, the uncouth and blustering ambassador of Sigismund III Vasa, King of Poland.
[4]   Anne Conway (1630?–1679), Viscountess Conway. During the war T-R had read, at Pearsall Smith's recommendation, Marjorie Hope Nicolson's edition of *The Conway Letters* (1930). The book inspired him with the wish to write a history of the English ruling classes; see *Wartime Journals*, 150–3.

take to Reform in a big way, and then, being feminine and conscious of not having the rest of their sex with them, and of seeming eccentric, they overdo it. Look up Harriet Martineau in the *Dictionary of National Biography*.[1] She was a particularly tiresome Unitarian Bluestocking, a little later than Mrs Macaulay.[2] You might do a turn on her: I expect she was related to your classics tutor.[3] And finally, of course, there are the Suffragettes.

You asked for Lucian. I haven't sent him for I only have him in four volumes. If you think he might interest you, why not get Fowler's translation—or the Loeb edition—out of the Library (it must be there) & see whether you like him first? I nearly sent you a book, Dill's *Roman Society at the End of the Roman Empire*,[4] but I didn't feel sure that you would be interested in it. I thought of this because you suggested looking at some period of antiquity outside the famous centuries. If you are, I really will.

In fact I wrote you a long letter about a week ago, but Mummy came & read it and then made a fuss and said it would upset you and I mustn't send it—although in fact I can't think it could have had any such effect since it only concerned books and such things! But she evidently thinks I upset you, and she wouldn't let me come and see you, which I wanted to do. I am terribly sorry if I do upset you. I hope I don't. I only want you to find your own feet and gain confidence in yourself, as I am sure you will do if only you don't bother about yourself too much and will learn to speculate a bit and take risks.

I didn't want you to see the psychiatrist, but perhaps I am prejudiced. During the war, I was ill & was sent to a military hospital. They couldn't discover what was wrong with me—it was something internal—so, as

---

[1]  Harriet Martineau (1802–76), author of *Illustrations of Political Economy* (1832–34), *Society in America* (1837), and *Laws of Man's Social Nature* (1851).
[2]  Catharine Macaulay (1731–91), who wrote a Whig narrative history of 17th-century England.
[3]  Richard Martineau (1906–84), classics master at Eton, was appointed in 1967 as College Lecturer in Classics at Magdalene College, Cambridge, where he was a Fellow and Director of Studies in Classics 1969–74.
[4]  Sir Samuel Dill (1844–1924), Professor of Greek at Queen's College, Belfast, 1890–1924, published his great work on *Roman Society* in 1898.

institutions always do, they passed me on to someone else. They said it must be imagination & therefore I was a psychiatrist's case. I saw the psychiatrist, who pomped and pumped away and doubtless made some grave report about my *ego* or *id*. Then I got out of the hospital and went to a proper doctor who at once said that I had got appendicitis. So my appendix was cut out, and I lived happily ever after, with a very low view of psychiatrists. But I mustn't prejudice you against them.

Do get better quickly and write again. I do really like hearing from you and am sorry I don't hear very much.

Don't take *any* views from Juvenal! I really think he was an odious man. All that flogging of dead horses... And as for the satire on women—No 6, I believe—I thought it was always expurgated from school texts!

All love from
Hugh

---

## To James Howard-Johnston, 19 June 1960

8 St Aldates Oxford

My dear James

I was delighted to hear from you. Never apologise for long letters: I love them, especially from you. It is very sad that so few people write long letters now: the telephone and the motor-car have killed them by removing half the need for them: one sees one another, or talks to one another, so much more. And yet it is such a pleasure to receive genuine letters. I even like writing them, though of course one is always so short of time. I think it is a good thing to write them. If one never writes real letters one can never acquire the art of expressing one's self; and at times it is such a relief to do so.

I am sorry you feel so inhibited with some people (especially since I am evidently one of them!). But don't worry. Probably half the time when you feel you can't make contact with the people you would like to know, they are doing exactly the same in respect of you. I remember when I was your age I felt exactly the same. I admired people (generally for wrong reasons) and felt that they despised me. How could they fail to do so when they were so successful, so good at games, so popular, or whatever it might be, while I was so unsuccessful, so unathletic, so awkward? It is true I was quite clever at books, but I only felt that people despised me the more for that, and I tried to conceal it and show that I, too, however unskilfully, did unintellectual things. But then I discovered that my whole view of the world was wrong, and really people don't go round looking for the same qualities which they have themselves and despising other people. More often they despise themselves. What everyone in the world really wants, whether they are fully aware of it or not, is to be loved, and a character capable of inspiring or giving affection is *never* despised. This is one of the (many) reasons why I am very fond of you: I think you have a genuinely affectionate nature. Don't you notice how people like you? It is quite obvious, for instance, that Mr Taylor is very fond of you. So, I am sure, are half the people of whom you are afraid and who you think despise you. So cheer up!

So you see what a shock it was to me when I was told that you were frightened of me, that I upset you, was the cause of your depression etc. I have felt unhappy about it ever since. But I hope you will not feel that in future. I am determined, within my limited means, to do everything I can for you. Of course I shall continue sometimes to show impatience, to be short-tempered etc., but you will understand, I hope, that this is merely my mood, and be tolerant of me.

I don't really think you will retreat into a hole at Oxford. I think you will find it a new world, liberating rather than restricting. I hope so anyway. Most people do. But don't bother yourself about it: at least not yet.

I look forward to going abroad with you. I hope our tastes will not be *too* different. We can talk about it at long leave. Will you renew your own passport? Please do: I have so much to do at present! It is quite simple. But please let me know when you do it and through what agency. This is important because, as you know, there have been difficulties about your passport in the past. All will be well because I have now got a legal certificate to protect it, but I must know when and where to use it.[1]

I expect your essay was excellent really. Don't always assume you do things badly: you don't. As for Shakespeare, don't read too many commentaries. In reading any great work one must read as much as is necessary to appreciate it: one must know the language, understand the allusions, or at least the important allusions, appreciate the *nuances*. But once one can do that, it is the great work, not the commentary that matters. I think Logan Pearsall Smith's *On Reading Shakespeare* is a wonderful book in that way: it carries one along, makes one look at Shakespeare from different angles, appreciate *both* the language *and* the dramatic quality, and see new aspects of both, and see them freshly, not overlaid with too much learning.[2]

I knew Logan Pearsall Smith very well. In fact he was the man who had more personal influence on me than anyone else. He even left me all his money—but then, at the last minute, there came a ghastly young man,[3] *much* less worthy than I, and flattered him and pretended to be interested in literature, and Logan, with a stroke of his pen, lying on his death-bed, half-mad (he suffered from a kind of mild temporary insanity which comes and goes, bringing alternation of exhilaration and depression, called 'manic depression'—he wrote his books, as one can sometimes see, when exhilarated), struck me out and left everything to the ghastly young man. Then he died. Of course it didn't end there. There were

---

[1]  Following his divorce in 1954, Rear Admiral Clarence ('Johnnie') Howard-Johnston (1903–96), James's father, had raised legal objections to James's possession of a passport, in an attempt to prevent him from travelling abroad with his stepfather.

[2]  Published in 1933. The first chapter poses a provocative question: 'This barbaric medley of bombast and ribaldry, of blood and melodrama—is this really the top of human achievement, the noblest memorial, as we are told, that our race can leave behind it of our existence on this planet?'

[3]  John Russell (1919–2008), then a *Sunday Times* book reviewer; later art critic for the *New York Times*.

terrible scenes. Someone else, who *thought* that if the last will could be declared invalid, he would scoop the inheritance, tried to get Logan certified insane. Logan's sister, Alys Russell (Bertrand Russell's wife), joined in. There was drama upon drama. I kept right out of it because I thought it was all so sordid. Finally there was an agreement between the ghastly young man and the 'someone else', and they split the swag. Neither of them realised that really the money hadn't been left to the 'someone else' before the ghastly young man turned up, but to me. Then the 'someone else' wrote a book about Logan saying what a monster he was![1] I reviewed the book on the wireless and said he wasn't a monster at all, and was furiously attacked! The whole episode was a horrible illustration of human behaviour and has made me feel very strongly about wills and will-shakers (Logan's word): I often think of it when it is a question of humouring grand-mère[2] or when I see anyone sacrificing their lives, or part of them, to the illusory hopes of legacies!

What a marvellous play *Antony and Cleopatra* is! Shakespeare's poetry, as it got less pure and limpid (in the early poems it is so unbelievably pure and limpid), seems to me to get deeper and deeper: depth opens below depth: it is like Aeschylus, multi-dimensional; and in *Antony and Cleopatra* I feel that there is an altogether new dimension

> Let Rome in Tiber melt, and the wide arch
> Of the rang'd empire fall…
>
> Eternity was in our lips and eyes,
> Bliss in our brows' bent…
>
> Oh, my oblivion is a very Antony…
>
> Give me to drink Mandragora
> That I might sleep out this great gap of time…

---

[1] Robert Gathorne-Hardy (1902–73), bibliographer, botanist, and Smith's former secretary-companion, wrote *Recollections of Logan Pearsall Smith* (1949).
[2] Dorothy du Breuil de St Germain (née Baird; 1882–1971) was Admiral Howard-Johnston's rich mother, a clever but uneducated woman, who lived most of her life in France.

> But let determin'd things to destiny
> Hold unbewail'd their way...
>
> darkling stand
> The varying shore of the world...

Don't you feel this new dimension, this sense, suddenly evoked, of a vaster, wider, deeper, not more complicated but more unfathomable, more mysterious world than hitherto one had assumed?

What a mystery Shakespeare is! I often wish I could penetrate it. But always I remember Logan's warning, which you have read, about the lunacy in which all such fond ambitions end.

Now I must stop. Let my last words (for the time being) be these: don't be frightened. If in doubt, if in depression, if in anxiety, say so without fear. We have invented language, refined it so that it can express even the subtlest thought, even the obscurest sensations; why then should we not use it, and dissolve difficulties by articulating them? I have the greatest confidence in you; there is nothing I would not say to you with trust, or hear from you with sympathy.

> All my love from
> Hugh

---

*Trevor-Roper's wife Xandra, the eldest daughter of Field Marshal Haig, was sensitive about her father's reputation, as was her brother. Trevor-Roper was nervous of her reaction when he learned that Alan Clark, who had been his pupil in the late 1940s, and with whom he had been friendly ever since, had written a book about the British Expeditionary Force in the First World War. This proved to be an indictment of British military leadership. Its title, The Donkeys, alluded to the saying that the British troops on the Western Front had been 'lions led by donkeys', though it seems that Clark, who attributed the remark to a member of the German general staff, may have coined it himself. The Donkeys would prove to be an influential work, which reinforced the negative stereotype of Haig as a callous incompetent. Before the book had appeared, Clark sent Trevor-Roper a copy of the September 1959 issue of the magazine History Today, which contained an article extracted from the book describing*

*Sir John French's dismissal in 1915. The magazine exacerbated the offence by mistakenly giving the book's title as* The Donkey.

## To Alan Clark, 31 August 1960

Chiefswood, Melrose

My dear Alan,

Thank you so much for your letter and for sending me your article. How well you write! I read it with real pleasure.

Of course, largely, I agree with you. If I used the phrase 'the great man'[1] on the telephone, that was not indeed ironically, but certainly not seriously; it was a convenient neutral, anonymous formula, in invisible inverted commas, inspired by the fact that the study door was open and Xandra in the next room, and proper names are always overheard! I am regarded as 'anti-Haig' by the family, although I only consider myself to be objective; and so, for the sake of peace, I keep very quiet on the subject. That is why I am so craven about being too openly brought in on it!

I believe a great work could be written on the politico-military drama of the first war, on both sides, by someone who could get out of the futile spiral of personalities. Lloyd George behaved abominably to Haig, going behind his back, etc. etc. Agreed. Lloyd George conspired against his political, Haig against his military colleagues. Agreed. But do not these facts simply illustrate a larger problem? Winston Churchill told Bob Boothby that he was determined, in the second world war, not to be put in the position of Lloyd George in the first, afraid to sack his generals. But what was this larger problem, and why was Lloyd George afraid? The answer seems to me to be that in the period 1870–1914 the British generals had got inflated reputations cheaply. They had mopped up colonies, defeated Afghans and Chinese, Egyptians and negroes and even, in the end, Boers, and governments at home had allowed them to be built up as national heroes just because the distant theatres and foreign troops which they had dominated made it

---

[1]   i.e. Haig.

impossible for them to be politically dangerous at home. (Halévy[1] makes a similar point about the popularity of the British Navy in the 18th century.) And this popular build-up of the colonial generals worked. Think of the scenes when Gordon was killed, and the British public and Queen Victoria (that faithful mirror of its most vulgar prejudices) howled for Gladstone's blood! In 1914, it seems to me, the myth came home to roost. Generals with inflated colonial reputations and immense power through popular support, suddenly found themselves fighting a war which they were incompetent to win, being no longer against fuzzy-wuzzies but against the greatest military and industrial power in Europe, but over whose conduct they had a monopoly which the politicians could not openly break. Hence an insoluble dilemma leading to morally tortuous behaviour. The generals, convinced by the myth of which they were the beneficiaries, genuinely believed that they and they alone could win the war. Within their caste-bound limits they were honourable men. But when they found that the war did not respond to their treatment, they had to grope and plunge outside those narrow limits. Hence the unedifying excursions into politics. Similarly the politicians found themselves faced by a political problem (the independence of the Army) which they could not control. So they too groped and plunged, in an unfamiliar world, and resorted to tactics which, when afterwards exposed to the light of day, looked pretty bad. Of course by the 1920s, when the problem no longer existed, politicians and generals had retreated in good order back again into their conventional worlds, and each could express horror at the shocking behaviour (in the past) of the other, suppressing or explaining away their own...

The same point can be made (*mutatis mutandis*) about the other side. The German generals were also confident. Had they not, by *Blitzkriege* in 1864, 1866, 1870, made the empire? They too had great prestige and believed themselves indispensable; but the difference was that since their wars had been in Europe they could be a much more real threat to the civilian

---

[1]   The French historian Élie Halévy (1870–1937) wrote a multi-volume *History of the English People in the Nineteenth Century*, published from 1913 onwards.

government. And they too, when they proved incapable of a *Blitzkrieg* in 1914, entered into politics and floundered and intrigued in that strange world. In the end, since there was no Lloyd George, they triumphed in politics though they failed in war. See Wheeler-Bennett,[1] *passim*.

Altogether, I see the first world war as a tremendous drama in which human beings, faced with problems beyond the range of their capacity or conventional ideas, were driven into desperate expedients quite outside their conventional patterns of behaviour; and I feel that if this formidable background, which dominated the merely human foreground, is recognised, it should be possible to treat the whole subject in a way in which the personal controversies, which can be tiresome, find their place.

Perhaps this is what you are doing. I hope so. Anyway I greatly look forward to seeing the book, though I shall have to be very careful with 'the great man's' family—except my stepson, with whom I can discuss these matters and who has also read and enjoyed your article. As I say, I think you write excellently and I long to see more of your writing. What is the real title of the book? And I was delighted to hear from you, and would be delighted to see you again. Are you ever in Oxford in term-time? Do you live in Devonshire, and on a farm, and do you actually farm—Jersey cows and all that? I am taking my stepson James to Greece on 15 Sept, but will be back in Oxford on 10 Oct: he is then coming up to Christ Church. So do let me know when I can see you. Perhaps you are sometimes in London? Anyway, I should *love* to see you again.

yours ever
Hugh

---

[1]   Sir John Wheeler-Bennett (1902–75), author of *The Nemesis Of Power: The German Army in Politics, 1918–1945* (1953).

*After James Howard-Johnston had been accepted to read classics at Christ Church, Trevor-Roper surmounted opposition from the boy's father and took his stepson to Greece. James enjoyed the visit, and appreciated his stepfather's kindness in taking him, though in retrospect he judged it thoughtless of him not to return until the last possible moment, so that he reached Oxford later than the other new undergraduates.*

## To Xandra Trevor-Roper, 21 September 1960

Poros, Greece

My darling,

I am beginning this letter in the island of Poros, though it would be folly to post it anywhere but in the centre of Athens. We sent you postcards from Venice and one from Athens on arrival yesterday. The Greek steamer was, like most Greek organisations, thoroughly inefficient. We wasted almost a whole morning struggling for attention in the Venetian office of the company, only to be told that the ship on which we were booked was not sailing and we were being put in another, which started later and proved both smaller and slower. However we reached Piraeus yesterday morning & spent the morning in Athens. As I said in our postcard, Freya[1] is here (rather piqued that she has to stay at a hotel, as we are in the Pawsons'[2] only spare room) and she was badgering Mrs Pawson to go with her to Poros today and Troezen tomorrow. Mrs Pawson can't come till tomorrow and James prefers to stay somnolently in the suburbs of Athens eating English food, at least for today; so in the end we agreed that I should go with Freya to Poros today and James will be brought by Mrs Pawson to join us tomorrow, if necessary to rescue me from so formidable a companion. So far I have kept on my own. On the boat, Freya told me with

---

[1]  (Dame) Freya Stark (1893–1993), explorer and travel writer, author of more than two dozen books on her travels in the Middle East and Afghanistan, as well as several autobiographical works and essays.

[2]  The Pawson family had lived at Shawdon, a tower house between Alnwick and Glanton, during T-R's boyhood, and were related to his sporting acquaintances, the Milvains of Eglingham. David Pawson ran the Athens bus company, and had married Pamela Lovibond (1907–81), a friend and travelling companion of Freya Stark.

relish that Derek's trip to Persia had been 'even more disastrous' than Derek's famous trip to Turkey,[1] and that Derek's companion, Furse,[2] had found him so impossible that they had quickly parted: 'really, he is the most unsuitable person in the world to be a traveller. Why he hadn't learnt a word of Turkish!' whereupon she settled down to study an English–Turkish dictionary and I followed suit and studied my Modern Greek grammar...

What a beautiful place Greece is! I had thought that in the autumn, it would be disappointing, all burnt up. But today, after arriving in Poros and having lunch and a siesta, Freya and I walked over the hills to see the remains of the old temple of Poseidon in which Demosthenes, after the fall of Athens, took poison. Everywhere the air was astringent, almost disinfectant, with the smell of thyme, sage, rosemary; the autumn cyclamens were in flower; there were flowering squills and scented lemon-groves and pine-woods (but Greek pine-woods, like larch woods) from which resin was being tapped for that delicious resinous *vin ordinaire* on which I rely for the smooth working of my digestive system here; and except for a circular stone threshing-floor, there was no sign of human life. It was enchanting. And then there is that air, that sky, which makes Greece, to me, so infinitely more beautiful than Italy: those subtle colours, that touch of cloud and mist that carries the outlines of mountains and seas out of clarity into mystery, a kind of divine mystery! I was altogether carried away by it. John Sparrow,[3] when we last saw him, said, 'I shall be in Bergamo, eating pasta, and you will be in that strange, difficult, uncomfortable land'; but how much rather would I be here than in Bergamo or even Vicenza or Florence or anywhere else in Italy! I wish I felt that James would enjoy it as much as I do, but I cannot help feeling that he

---

[1]  Derek Hill (1916–2000), landscape and portrait painter, and an inveterate gossip, who lived in the early 1950s in the *villino* in the grounds of I Tatti. T-R's comments about him invariably carry a satirical edge. 'The thought of his trivial *couturier*'s mind makes me shiver,' he confessed to Xandra during their courtship.

[2]  Roger Furse (1903–72), painter and costume designer for stage and film, including Olivier's *Hamlet* and *Henry V*.

[3]  John Sparrow (1906–92), Warden of All Souls 1952–77.

is really an American tourist who will condescend to accept beauty only if it is served up to him on a warm plate, with viands well-cooked and served, in a first-class hotel: and this depresses me. I have asked Freya to encourage him when he comes tomorrow (she is so good with the young—at least with young men), and I hope she will.

Freya is a terrible old tyrant. I am horrified at the dictatorial way in which she expects the Pawsons to disorganise their lives for her convenience. She simply won't take No. On the other hand I do find that I can get on with her. Perhaps we are a match for each other: as Pamela Pawson says, it is a case of Greek meeting Greek. But however that may be, she is a real character, life-enhancing not life-diminishing, as BB would say, and I like being with her, though I wish James had come too, rather than staying in Athens to be shown round by the difficult daughter who has arrived to stay with the Pawsons. However, I look forward to having his company tomorrow.

On our walk today there was a sudden dramatic incident. There was a scream, a cloud of dust, a noise of centrifugal explosion; and looking back I saw poor old Freya flying through the air like a domestic fowl which has felt its tail-feathers nipped by a fox. Her elaborate headgear was in dissolution, her camera flying in one direction, her basket (I never understood why she needed to walk with a basket) in another. I picked her up and found that she had been stung in the back of the neck ('quite unprovoked', she insisted) by a hornet. Picking up the detached lens of her camera, I found one hornet, still reeling from her counter-attack; and lifting up the residue of her head-dress, I found another, deeply involved in the network. Fortunately, after my encounter with the wasps' nest at Chiefswood, I knew exactly what to do; and fortunately, when this incident occurred, we were just at the end of the wild part of our walk coming out on to a road. So I went to the first house (which happened to be an inn), explained the situation, and got some ammonia, which they happened to have (I think they must be used to such incidents in Poros). Anyway, all is now well: external application of ammonia and internal replenishment of *retsina* seem by now to have put the old girl on her feet again, and have made her regard me (for the time being at least) as a more efficient travelling companion than Derek!

I must now go to bed. Tomorrow James and Pamela & Deborah (the daughter) Pawson should arrive, and we should go to Troezen, the scene of Euripides' tragedy of *Hippolytus* (Do you remember it? You saw a version of it in the Divinity School at Oxford). I will try to find time to continue this letter after our return.

29.9.60 Pylos

I meant to continue this letter, and finish and post it, in Athens, but never had a minute. Now, reposing at Pylos, I can't get out of the habit of getting up at 5.30, so am seizing the hour between 6.0 & 7.0 a.m. to do it.

We duly went to Troezen. The country was most beautiful: a fertile plain between the hills and the sea in the Argolid, and the air scented with lemon-groves and *agnus casti*. The remains were nothing much, but we had a picnic in a most charming spot, by a spring in a gorge in the foothills. We took a boat across the bay from Poros and then walked inland. Freya was pretty trying. She simply insists, by silent pressure and constant objections to all alternatives, on having her own way. On this occasion she didn't get it in the end, and she was in a pretty bad temper in consequence, continually sniping and hinting how much better it would have been if we had all given way to her. She also tried to force us into an altogether impossible expedition the next day—impossible because it depended on finding boats and guides, where there was no likelihood of finding either, and we would almost certainly have been stranded on a remote shore in the Argolid and missed our essential engagements in Athens (including her own boat back to Venice)—but we simply made a solid front and refused to listen. I'm afraid she was furious. Still, she was a majestic sight, walking slowly, infinitely slowly—she exhausted us all by her solemn snail's pace— under her red parasol over the romantic Greek hills. I am all for her existence; but on the whole I would like her to travel with others, not with me.

On Saturday James and I set out early from Athens to Delphi. We spent a night there, and then crossed by the ferry from Itea to Aigion on the north coast of the Peloponnese. Since then we have been to the Frankish castle of Khloumoutsi, which I wanted to see, on the coast of Elis; to Olympia; and, after some misadventure and detours, to Pylos. I now withdraw all my earlier remarks about James. He has suddenly taken to Greece, and the conditions of seeing it: springs up to catch 6.0 a.m. 'buses by choice, is thoroughly energetic, eats goat's-entrails on skewers in street-corners without hesitation, and is altogether an ideal companion. We disagree on almost everything: where to go, how to get there, and where to stay when we have arrived. But we compromise happily and our days are very full. James seems to love Greece and is determined to come back.

Our first adventure was in pursuit of the castle of Khloumoutsi. No one could tell us where it was; the *Guide Bleu*, we have discovered, is thoroughly unreliable; our maps did not mark it. However, we decided that the best way was to go to Kyllini, a village on the easternmost tip of Elis, which seemed to be the nearest to it. We got by train to the junction for Kyllini, only to find that there was no connexion for some time. We tried to find a taxi, but the only taxi was away at a wedding. In the end we had to waste time waiting for the train, and so arrived at Kyllini inconveniently late in the afternoon. On arrival we found that Kyllini was the wrong town and that there was no taxi there either. We could walk to the castle—some six miles by a footpath along the sea—but it would be impossible to walk there and back in time to catch the last train away from Kyllini, and in Kyllini there was neither inn nor restaurant nor, it seemed, anything else: it was the deadest dead-end imaginable. However, since we had come there to see the castle, we decided to see it, *coûte que coûte*.[1] Perhaps, we reflected, we would find a taxi there (for we now discovered that there was a village actually at the castle, far larger and more accessible than Kyllini, though not mentioned in the *Guide Bleu* or marked on our maps). So we deposited our luggage at the station of Kyllini and set out by the footpath.

---

[1]  'Cost what it may'.

If only we hadn't been so pressed for time, it would have been a charming walk: it was along a rough, sandy path (sometimes very rough), parallel with the sea; and after two or three miles we could see the castle—a grim, tyrannical castle as Frankish castles in Greece always are—rising high up on its hill on the skyline. As we approached it, we suddenly came upon a gay party at an open-air tavern, who drew us in and insisted on our drinking *retsina* with them: they explained it was a marriage-party (the same marriage which had drained away all the taxis in the area): James said it reminded him of Camacho's marriage-party in *Don Quixote*.[1] Then we went off and saw the castle. By the time we had seen it the sun was setting, and we decided to hunt for a taxi to get back, by whatever route, to Kyllini and our luggage. But all efforts failed and only succeeded in holding us up: in the end we set off, perforce, by foot along the now hardly visible footpath. It was a sadly memorable walk. Before long it was dark and we could not see the footpath. Then it began to rain, in torrents. We had only our shirts. For an hour and a half, going flat out, we stumbled along the track, getting colder and wetter every minute, and finally arrived, like drowned and frozen rats, at that dead-end of human society, Kyllini. Of course it was too late to move further. We subsided in a peasant hovel, contented ourselves with some bread and tomato (there wasn't even *retsina* in Kyllini) and awaited the next day.

Next day we moved on, by infinitely slow stages (a train and three buses) to Olympia. All the time it poured with rain: our yesterday's clothes were still soaked in our rucksacks, our today's clothes (our only alternatives) were soaked on our backs. Secretly, I didn't want to go to Olympia at all: my memory of those quiet meadows with their graceful ruins in the plain of Elis was so pleasant to me that I had no wish to replace it by another image of a drenched and dreary landscape seen in an exhausted state through jaundiced eyes and rain-soaked spectacles. However, we plunged on, arrived there, sank into the grandest (but I'm afraid

---

[1]  The eventful wedding-party of Quiteria the fair and Camacho the rich, interrupted by the arrival of Quiteria's suitor Basilio, who wins her for himself.

*not* the nicest) hotel, and went straight to bed till they had dried our clothes. Then we had lunch. And then, happily, the miracle happened. The rain ceased, the sun shone, the landscape, fresh from the rain, was more beautiful than ever, and my image of Olympia was not damaged but rather improved by revisitation. James was delighted with it and forgave me for the adventures at Kyllini, which, in retrospect, I think he enjoyed: at least it has given him a good talking-point against me in our frequent debates about our future plans.

After Olympia we aimed at Pylos. We got, by train, to Kyparissia, but then the bus to Pylos failed us and we had to go on by train—a beautiful journey through Messinia, round Mount Ithome—to Kalamata, a dreary and squalid town where we spent the night. Next morning, at 6.30, we found a bus to Pylos. It was an adventurous journey. After half an hour, while we were going along a road with a deep gully on one side, a bus in front of us suddenly drove into the side and braked sharply. We did the same and just stopped behind it. Then there careered towards both of us, at high speed, from the opposite direction, a huge truck carrying a bulldozer which projected towards us. It passed us in a flash, but as it passed there was a fearful noise and everything was enveloped in clouds of dust. When all was over, we were intact, but looking forward I saw that the entire left-hand side of the bus in front of us had been simply shorn away by the bulldozer. The road was strewn with wreckage of every kind. We got out of the bus, sadly shaken. At first I hardly dared go to the bus in front. Every Greek bus I had been in had contained some 36 passengers sitting and as many standing, and I dreaded to see what was left of them. Miraculously, there had only been very few passengers and they had all sat in front. The bulldozer had only struck the bus near the rear, though with such force that it had ripped the whole side away, from the driver's seat to the tail. No one had even been hurt. But James and I could not help reflecting that if we had been only a few feet further forward, the blow would have struck not the tail of the front bus but the head of the rear bus, and we would both (since, for the sake of the view, we had nabbed the extreme front left-hand seats) have been decapitated. Shaken by this incident, we arrived at Pylos at 8.30 and consoled ourselves by heading for the most luxurious hotel, where we have now spent two very full and energetic days, visiting recently excavated Mycenaean tombs and palaces in the surrounding country.

And now the notes of the oboe, floating from our bedroom over the bay remind me that we are to sail to the island of Sphacteria, famous in the Peloponnesian War, in order to refresh those romantic solitudes with that enchanting noise. In the night it rained terribly: I never thought rain could fall so hard for so long; but now all is serene, and I look forward to sailing across the bay. We have been so energetic, and have got up so early, and have walked so far, up and down such hills, in such heat and rain, that we are enjoying these occasional relaxations. On such occasions we sometimes think that you would like to be with us; but generally, I must admit, we conclude that you would not. The early mornings, the crowded buses, the long waits, the walking, the bad, ill-cooked food, the smelling lavatories (we have now concluded that the only difference between expensive and cheap hotels in Greece is in the relative stench of the lavatories) would *not* appeal to you. But we have not forgotten you. Indeed James, who is becoming an archaeological enthusiast, has, with remarkable skill, made a most interesting discovery in the ruins of Olympia, which we are bringing back to you. I wonder where you are: at Oxford, at Cestyll[1] or at Chiefswood. Perhaps we shall find a letter when we get back to Athens. I hope so.

Incidentally the Pawsons are absolutely delighted with James whom they think quite charming. And James and I have been giving some serious thought to the drive at Chiefswood. Should we not cut down all those holly, thorn, rowan and crab-apple trees and plant instead a double row of those tall thin cypresses which look so beautiful in Greece? Is there any reason to suppose that they would not grow in Scotland? We can't

---

[1]  Cestyll House, Anglesey, home of Xandra's aunt, Violet Vivian (1879–1962), who had been Maid of Honour to Queen Alexandra 1901–25.

plant big trees, because we would have to set them back from the drive, and we don't own the land outside the drive; but wouldn't cypresses, planted in the drive, answer all problems? Do think of this.

Now I must stop. Already the oboe has stopped, and we must go. All my love, my darling, from

Hugh

⸺⸺

*Early in April 1961 Trevor-Roper flew to Israel to report on the opening of the Eichmann trial for the* Sunday Times. *Adolf Eichmann had been a crucial figure in the administration of Nazi genocide, responsible for rounding up hundreds of thousands of Jews and transporting them to death camps. At the end of the war he had escaped capture and fled to Argentina, where he had lived untroubled for ten years. But in 1960 he was kidnapped by Mossad agents and brought to Israel to face trial. The proceedings were conducted in Hebrew, with simultaneous translation into German for the benefit of the accused, and into English and French for the sake of the world's press. A bullet-proof glass screen protected Eichmann from assassination by the outraged relations of the dead.*

*This was a major international news event. Most British newspapers sent special correspondents to Jerusalem to cover the story. The* Daily Telegraph *was represented by Trevor-Roper's friend Freddie Birkenhead, who was accompanied by his wife and daughter (then in her first year as an Oxford undergraduate). Frank Giles (b. 1919), who, after stints as* The Times *correspondent in Rome and Paris, had recently become Foreign Editor of the* Sunday Times, *decided that his friend Trevor-Roper was the best man to cover such a story. Though Trevor-Roper was reluctant to be diverted from the writing of his book, he felt that he must accept the commission or forfeit his lucrative contract with the* Sunday Times.

## To James Howard-Johnston, 5 April 1961

King David Hotel, Jerusalem

My dearest James

O sleep it is a blessed thing
Beloved from Pole to Pole

says the Ancient Mariner;[1] and what a difference 8 hours of sleep (plus half a bottle of peculiarly disgusting 'Mount Carmel hock') can make! After them, and with the solid earth beneath my feet, I can look back with absolute equanimity on the horrors of the air yesterday. And yet even them I enjoyed for one moment, when I looked down and saw, an infinite distance below, the island of Crete and all Mount Ida thick in snow. My love of Greece grows parallel with my hatred of the air: increased by travelling there with you: ἦδε δ' ὁδὸς καὶ μᾶλλον ὁμοφροσύνησιν ἐνῆκεν.[2] I hope the earth feels solid beneath your feet too, and you can, or soon will, look back on the less satisfactory days of your past with equal equanimity. Please don't trouble yourself with it too much. Great quarrels, says my old Oracle Logan Pearsall Smith, are great emancipations,[3] and to quarrel with your past may be to emancipate yourself from it: only don't let the discarded husks, the broken, sticky eggshells of it, cling to you as unsavoury reminders of that otherwise forgotten state, but sit firmly on your new, somewhat higher bough (which is very firm, I assure you) and observe the outer world, in all its enchanting diversity, anew. I sometimes think that you pay too little attention to the outer world, and too much to yourself. In the past you looked at yourself only, and found that enough; now you do the same and find it far less satisfying and you lament your own past self-satisfaction and see in the outer world only associations which remind you of that now faded satisfaction. But the outer world has its independence: why should we see it only as an extension of ourselves (which is surely too selfish an attitude) and not ourselves as part of it! Besides, it is so interesting in its own right...

Here all the ghosts of Nuremberg are gathering. Telford Taylor, the American prosecutor at Nuremberg;[4] Lord Russell of Liverpool, the

---

[1]   Coleridge wrote: 'Oh sleep! It is a gentle thing | Beloved from pole to pole!'

[2]   'This journey has brought yet more harmony between us.' Homer, Odyssey 15.198.

[3]   Pearsall Smith's advice to young men: 'For souls in growth, great quarrels are great emancipators.'

[4]   Telford Taylor (1908–98) was a wartime US liaison officer at Bletchley Park responsible for the secure distribution of decoded Ultra intelligence to American commanders in the field; afterwards US prosecutor at the Nuremberg trials and a professor at Columbia Law School. Author of Sword and Swastika (1952), Nuremberg and Vietnam (1970), and other works.

British Judge-Advocate then;[1] and no doubt many others. Even Dr Servatius, Eichmann's German lawyer, learned his art defending other Nazis at Nuremberg.[2] I have spent the whole morning filling in forms, collecting earphones, signing declarations etc. My Jewish friends are not back from their Passover holidays. So I have a brief moment in which to write to you before going, later this afternoon, to inspect the court-room. There is nothing to do in Jerusalem, and owing to the air-delays yesterday I motored up from Tel-Aviv to Jerusalem in the dark and so was unable to see the farms and citrus-groves which are always the pleasantest sight (and sweetest smell) of the plain. But I have an excellent room in the hotel here, and can sit and write by the open window, through which the fresh mountain air and the smell of spring is wafted to me. If only the same breeze did not waft so many noises of traffic and the insufferably loud canned music from the grotesque YMCA building (half-skyscraper, half-mosque) opposite! And I have brought some books.

In particular I have brought the letters of Robert Burns. You know, I have never really taken to that compatriot of yours and his poems, or at least those of his poems which are most repeatedly uttered by kilted stockbrokers at commemorative Caledonian beanos (but *Holy Willie's Prayer*—that is another matter!).[3] But how I have taken to his letters! I have discovered a new Burns: a splendid character, whom I suppose I would never have discovered had I stayed within earshot of a Scottish accent! I wish you would learn to read. That is, to read some books quickly, others slowly, according to the type and merit of the work. Only thus can one be at home among books. But you will, you will.

[1]   Langley Russell, 2nd Baron Russell of Liverpool (1895–1981), published *The Trial of Adolf Eichmann* in 1962. As deputy judge advocate general, he had been responsible after 1945 for all war crime trials and courts martial held in the British-occupied zone of Germany, but had been forced to resign in 1954 after publishing his bestseller *The Scourge of the Swastika.*

[2]   Robert Servatius (1894–1983) had defended at Nuremberg, among others, Fritz Sauckel, Gauleiter of Thuringia and plenipotentiary for labour deployment, and Karl Brandt, Reich Commissioner for Health.

[3]   In 'Holy Willy's Prayer' (1785) Burns satirizes the hypocrisies of an elder of the kirk.

By the time you get this letter, you will have dined with the Cairns[1] & danced with the Neilsons, and I hope you will have enjoyed both, shedding rays of satisfaction both on those two households and into your own heart. And I hope you have written, or will write, to that Eton master who, alone of them all, taught you both to learn and to enjoy learning.[2] You can't believe what pleasure such a letter from a former pupil can give. Old D[3] had a phrase, learned I think from an antique Scottish Nanny, 'Always purr when you're pleased'. I think it is a very good phrase, and purring is a very pleasant noise to hear.

Do write and tell me that you are well, in mind and body. I am posting this letter at 4.0 p.m. today, Wednesday, 5th April; so you will see how long a letter takes to travel the vast difference between us, which however my constant thoughts of you attenuate even to nothing.

Best love from

Hugh

⎯⎯✕⎯⎯

## To James Howard-Johnston, 8 April 1961

King David Hotel, Jerusalem

My dearest James

I had meant to send you a gay, cheerful letter today, describing a visit to Beersheba; but how can I, since I have not in fact been to Beersheba but spent the whole day in bed, in the dark, in this grim hotel, with flaming eyes and throat and a grinding headache? Oh this wretched ailment

---

[1]  Francis Cairns (b. 1942) was in college at Eton at the same time as James. His father was a gentleman farmer at St Boswell's, near Melrose, and a cousin of the Buccleuchs.

[2]  John Roberts (1932–2005), who had just come down from Oriel, brought ancient history alive in class, and was subsequently head of classics. He edited the *Oxford Dictionary of the Classical World* (2005).

[3]  Unidentified. Possibly Robin Dundas.

which seizes upon me whenever I get cold! It has been horribly cold and wet and I was quite unprepared for it: after all, in wartime in these parts one changed into tropical dress on 20 April! The hotel bed is like rock, the bedclothes are too small and always slide off, there is no service (the hotel is a milling mass of elderly American Jewesses who, having killed off their husbands, are spending the insurance money on collective feminine jaunts to the Holy Land), and if there were it wouldn't make any difference as the food is uneatable. I have found an Italian restaurant which has opened just as I am confined to bed. And finally, having filled myself with aspirin and hoped to close my eyes in sleep, the canned music of the YMCA outside my window has started up. So I have given up and am writing instead this not, I'm afraid, very gay or cheerful letter.

I hope it finds you gay and cheerful all the same. Did Rawlinson's *Herodotus* come?[1] What are you doing? Do write and tell me. I think of you and hope you are happy. I also remember how you offered to drive me to Edinburgh. Of course it was absurd for anyone to drive 80 miles when there was a train, but I was very touched by your offer and greatly appreciate it.

I had tea the other day with a very interesting man, General Yigal Yadin.[2] He was commander-in-chief of the Israeli army in the 'War of Liberation' in 1948—i.e. the war against Egypt, Jordan & Syria who tried to destroy Israel when it was founded on the termination of the British Mandate. He was then 31. He is now professor of archaeology, and it was he who, by an extraordinary series of chances, was able to buy the first scrolls from a Christian priest who had smuggled them to America and bring them to Israel (they had been found by Beduin in Jordan). He also

---

[1]  T-R had sent his stepson the annotated English translation of *The History of Herodotus* (1858–60) compiled by George Rawlinson (1812–1902), Camden Professor of Ancient History at Oxford 1861–9.

[2]  Yigal Yadin (1917–84) had been described in *The Observer* of 19 February 1956: 'When he left the army in 1952, his standing in Israel as a soldier was so high, and his disinclination to be a party man so admired, that his admirers saw in him a kind of political Israeli Nasser. But his return to his excavations was quite decisive, and he remains outside politics, a youthful "elder statesman".' However, in 1976 Yadin founded a political party opposed to Israeli military control of the West Bank.

discovered two new lots, one lot a year ago, another a few days ago, in a cave 300 yards up a sheer rock face near the Dead Sea. He described the whole story, which was fascinating, and also showed me both lots of scrolls, which were also fascinating. They were mainly papyrus (and one wooden πίναξ[1]), written in Hebrew and Aramaic (one in Greek) and they included a series of military instructions from Bar Cochba himself, the leader of the last Jewish revolt against Rome, under Hadrian. (When it was suppressed, Jerusalem was destroyed and replaced by a Roman city Aelia Capotilina—Aelius being Hadrian's name: cf Pons Aelii, which is Newcastle-on-Tyne). It seems that just as the last Zealots, after the capture of Jerusalem by Titus in 70, retreated to caves around the Dead Sea (there is a famous description of this in Josephus) and there stood out till starved or massacred, so the followers of Bar Cochba did the same. Yigal Yadin says that there were 24 human skeletons—men, women and children—in his cave, and a Roman fort on top of the hill, 100 yards sheer above it: so presumably they were starved out.

I expect to be starved out in the cave too. I have sent a S.O.S. to the Birkenheads for relief, but the service here is such that I fear it may never reach them. In which case archaeologists far hence will discover my skeleton in room 208 of the King David Hotel, together, perhaps, with this half-finished scroll. 'If I forget thee, o Israel', said the original King David, 'let my right hand forget her cunning'.[2] I think I am as unlikely as the royal psalmist to forget this grim country. Last time I came here I picked up a strange disease, unidentifiable by the genial Dr Stewart,[3] and languished long in bed in Peck 9.[4] This time it looks as if I shall languish here and miss the trial which was the cause of my coming.

Yesterday I went to Galilee, and drank a bottle of Mount Carmel hock in Tiberias in order to fill the bottle, on my way back, with water from

---

[1]   Wooden writing tablet.

[2]   Psalm 137: 5 'If I forget thee, O Jersualem, let my right hand forget her cunning.'

[3]   Dr Martin Stewart (1920–2006) was College Doctor to Christ Church, partner in a medical practice at 27 Beaumont Street, Oxford, and Chief Medical Officer to Thames Valley Police.

[4]   T-R's Christ Church rooms were in Peckwater Quad.

the Jordan, for the baptism of my future step-grandchildren (You know it is far more efficacious theologically than Tweed or any other water: see *The Way of All Flesh*[1]). If you have to come to identify my corpse, you will find it in a bottle with a Carmel hock cork, labelled 'Jordan water. For baptismal purposes only'. Don't drink it: it is certainly, like everything else holy, crawling with the most fatal bacilli. Incidentally we stopped at Haifa on the way and there went to the original church of the Carmelite order, which was founded by the Crusaders (they fathered it on Elijah; the Church was built, like all Christian antiquities here, about 1850).[2] We were shown around by the most revolting cleric I have ever met. He had a top-speed sanctimonious gramophone-record which alternated with slick sales-talk, conducting a brisk sale in relics, bric-à-brac, rosaries ('that's what we like to hear ordered: got a large stock of them'), fragments of the True Cross, etc. etc. tastefully mounted in wooden frames with jolly, painted inscriptions, all the work of a very artistic lately deceased brother who had done an illuminated *crèche* too, with camels moving on a concealed electric tank and a tape-recorder playing Christmas carols.

My eyes droop, my nose runs, my head beats, and (or am I mistaken?) the canned music outside has died away. I shall try to sleep. Keep well and write to me.

My love to you all
Hugh

---

[1] Samuel Butler, *The Way of All Flesh* (1903), chapter 17: 'I have long preserved a phial of water from the Jordan for the christening of my first grandson, should it please God to grant me one...there is a sentiment attached to the waters of Jordan which not be despised. Small matters like this sometimes influence a child's whole future career.'
[2] The Stella Maris Carmelite Monastery stands on the slopes of Mount Carmel.

## To James Howard-Johnston, undated (probably 11 April 1961)

King David Hotel, Jerusalem

My dearest James

I had hoped to feel better today, but alas, am not, and must have a third day in bed and then go, *coûte que coûte*, well or ill, to the trial at 8.0 a.m. tomorrow. I feel very isolated here. All other special correspondents have 'stringers' they can rely on. A 'stringer' is a man who lives and works in a foreign country, without being a professional journalist, but receives a retainer from a newspaper to report to it if that country (which by definition is an unimportant country: in important countries a newspaper would have a permanent correspondent) suddenly becomes important or if his newspaper requires any help of any practical kind. The *Daily Telegraph* stringer does everything for Lord Birkenhead, the *News of the World* stringer for Lord Russell. But my stringer, who keeps a hotel at Lod, some 30 miles away, has done nothing: though instructed to meet me at the airport, he didn't turn up; and I haven't even met him. So I feel cut off from the world. I have written nine letters to Chiefswood but so far have received none. So altogether I feel pretty depressed.

But to complain is the sign of a feeble spirit. Let me not complain. Let me rather refresh myself by thinking not of Israel and its horrors—no doubt it is an admirable country, and I feel that I ought to admire it, and do admire it, but it is horrible too—but of all of you, and perhaps particularly of you because I feel that, for very different reasons, you also feel, temporarily, somewhat isolated (more isolated than you need be), in the world. I hope that, at the moment, this is not so. There is really no ground for it. You are not unique. To all of us there comes a moment when we destroy our past, or at least a large part of it, and turn to make new conquests in a different direction. The essential thing is to know what to destroy and what to preserve as the essential basis upon which this difficult manoeuvre can be executed and from which these new conquests can be made. Some people destroy too little: they are the 'professional Old Boys' who—in an extended sense—never leave school. Others destroy too much and then, having no basis for the orderly execution of these complex manoeuvres, flounder for a time in unseemly postures before discovering, by trial and error and the mere efflux of time, a new equilibrium. Such are the 'Angry Young Men', the socially-displaced, beard-wearing undergraduates. But I know that you are not a professional old boy or a Wykehamist (they are all professional old boys, except the 'rogue Wykehamists' who go to the other extreme) and I hope that we shall show enough of both understanding and affection to enable you to keep a continuous basis through this period, a plank-bridge over the gulf which for some (the Old Boys) does not exist, and in which others (the Angry Young Men) horribly flounder. If you have such a bridge, then you need not worry about yourself or your work. Of course you must *think* of both. No man does anything in the world who does not think of his own character and its improvement, or of his work and its value. But I ask you not to *worry* about either: that is, by continual, unproductive questioning to distract yourself from real progress. It is better to be idle—to let the character gather physical or structural strength through temporary repose (after which it can address itself to the same task with a better sense of proportion)—than to consume yourself in fretful, circular, destructive energy. I have learned never to censure idleness provided it is of this kind, not the idleness of dissipation or of habit. It can sometimes be the condition of later activity.

Today I am at last able to read, so I have been reading the letters of Sydney Smith. Do you know of him: the wittiest, most agreeable, most sociable, most sensible of Anglican clergyman (how the orthodox hated him!), 'the Smith of Smiths' as Macaulay called him,[1] the oracle—but no, that is too pompous a word, the not-too-holy Castalian stream that trickled musically through the great whig centre, Holland House?[2] I find

---

[1]  In a letter of 1826.
[2]  Water from the Castalian Spring, where visitors to Delphi ritually cleansed themselves, was used to sprinkle the temple of Apollo. Roman poets came to the spring for poetic inspiration.

them infinitely refreshing in my dreary state. I also find one sentence for you. 'It seems to me a long time since I heard from you', Sydney Smith writes to his brother, to whom he was devoted. 'Pray write to me, and if you are vexed, or uneasy, or dispirited, do not be too proud to say so'. So if you are similarly dispirited, do not be too proud to say so, at least to those who are devoted to you.

Oh this hotel! Nothing works, no-one answers the telephone or the bell, or, if they do, they do no more than promise: they never perform. Last night, after two days of fasting, I felt that I could eat something, so I ordered some soup and an omelette. I waited for an hour (I am used to waiting hours now) during which my appetite grew. Finally I rang up and asked whether my supper was coming. They had forgotten—and not only that, but the kitchen was closed and nothing could be produced. However, once again, let me not complain: let me rather count my blessings. What would my condition be but for the Birkenheads? They were away for the first two days of my illness, in the north, but they came back last night and at once things have improved: they ensure that I get what I want, or get it for me; and quite apart from these solid services, an English voice is musical in this hubbub of unintelligible Hebrew and far, far too intelligible judaised American.

Do write: a letter from anywhere (but especially from Chiefswood) would cheer me up. How was the dance? Are you going to Rosehill?[1] Are our neighbours at Huntlyburn[2] now in full blast, with feasts and flood-lighting, fanfares and fireworks, barbecues and champagne, and all (or not quite all) of the nobility and gentry (and all of the bores) of the neighbourhood exchanging slow, Theban witticisms in their flame-coloured dining-room? But I must learn to be less malicious. All love,

Hugh

---

[1]   The home at Moresby, near Whitehaven, of Miki Sekers (see p. 104). In 1959 he founded a theatre there, which hosted concerts by outstanding classical musicians.
[2]   Huntlyburn was a house on land immediately above Chiefswood.

# To James Howard-Johnston, 13–14 April 1961

King David Hotel, Jerusalem

My dearest James

It is depressing to be alone in a large, crowded, impersonal hotel in a squalid Oriental city, and to be confined to that city, and indeed ill most of the time, and to receive no letters from anyone: no, not one. Perhaps I shall hear from someone. If not, there is no point in anyone writing now: it won't reach me in time.

I had hoped to leave on 19 April but the *Sunday Times* wants me to stay till the 21ˢᵗ. This is a great nuisance—indeed a far greater nuisance than by mere loss of time, for I find that this hotel, which with all its faults is the best in Jerusalem, can't have me after the 18ᵗʰ; nor can any other in the whole city. So I am simply turned adrift with my notebook and a mountain of documents and a lot of dirty laundry and Sydney Smith's *Letters* and Thucydides and Lord Birkenhead's sweater which, as it has saved my life, I suppose I ought to hang up, as a votive offering, in the Church of the Dormition of the Virgin Mary. I do not know where I shall hide my head and (what is much more difficult) write my last article. Perhaps I shall find a *kibbutz*—that is, a collective farm. I have stayed in *kibbutzim* before: one can do anything if one must; but I don't relish it. And it will not be easy to send messages or catch aeroplanes from a *kibbutz*: one might as well try to speculate on the Stock Exchange from that mountain-bog in Skye.

I went this evening to a very moving ceremony. Today is 'Holocaust Day', the day of remembrance for the Jews murdered by the Nazis, and there is a service in the open air on Mount Herzl, just outside the city, with a majestic view over the hills of Judaea. (It is named after Theodore Herzl, the Austrian founder of Zionism, who is buried there). Several thousand people gathered there. There were the makings of a wonderful pageant, with the mountains and the darkening sky and the torchlight, but of course the Jews are no good at that. In their Central European dark clothes, and with their ragged discipline and croaking loud-speakers, they made everything aesthetically third-rate. And yet, in a sense, this made the whole affair more moving. I felt that other people would have done wonders with the stage-properties, but they would have lacked the terrible tragedy which made the whole ceremony, in this case, so real. They sang, in Hebrew, Psalm iii and other psalms, and then a rabbi read that strange chapter of Ezekiel about the wilderness of dead bones. I suddenly realised, as he was reading it—in Hebrew of course, but I had a crib—how incredibly apposite it was. In 1930 (say) that extraordinary chapter—it is chapter xxxvii—would have seemed mere gibberish: the valley of infinite dry bones which were reanimated by the voice of the prophet and responded to the voice of God saying 'O my people, I will open your graves and cause you to come out of your graves and bring you into the land of Israel…and shall put my spirit in you and ye shall live, and I shall place you in your own land'. But now they are an exact image of what happened in the 1940s: the mountains of charred bones in the extermination camp and the foundation of the state of Israel. Then there was a prayer of remembrance for the victims of Nazism. As it was being said, I was suddenly aware of a gentle, general murmuring noise, and realised that half of the thousands of people there were in tears: for after all, there can scarcely be a family of immigrants which did not lose half its members in the extermination-camps: there are under two million Jews in Israel and six million were exterminated. I found it very harrowing; and the thought that Eichmann, the man who calmly organised the whole system of extermination, was actually being tried in Jerusalem at that time, and that his lawyer was calmly arguing that he was entirely guiltless, all guilt (which was never his) having been washed away by a cash payment, made the whole episode particularly bizarre.

Eichmann is a miserable, dreary, empty, mean, rat-faced creature. He sits quite calmly in his bullet-proof, glass dock, and has apparently now convinced himself that he is quite guiltless and should and will get off altogether! It makes one utterly despair of Germans.

I love Jews in general and am filled with admiration for their achievements in Israel. I find the whole story of Zionism like a heroic fairy-tale.

But I'm afraid I find life in Israel, for myself, utterly repellent. I would never (after my first visit in 1954) have come back of my own free will, and I have no desire to come again. I suppose I feel as some sophisticated, pleasure-loving English gentleman or aristocrat might have felt in the 1630s towards New England: 'admirable, but not for me'.

I wish I were in Chiefswood, reading Homer with you in the evenings: preferably the *Iliad*. The evenings are very dull here. If there were decent food, one could dine; if there was anywhere comfortable to sit, one could read. But there is neither.

14.4.61

I got this far with this letter, and found that it was nearly 1.0 a.m.; so I stopped. Now it is Friday and I have waited for the Friday post; but it has brought nothing, and I suppose there will be no hope of receiving any letters now (since the Sabbath is upon us) till Sunday. I spent this morning in court. The court adjourned at noon till Monday, and we shall not hear till then (at earliest) whether it considers itself competent to hear the case against Eichmann. I think it will declare itself competent, and in that case we shall have a 7-hour speech from the Attorney-General, which will be the main item of next week. I have just been lunching with the Attorney-General. Officially he will not see any journalist, but there was a very unofficial private party: Lord Birkenhead & Telford Taylor were also there (perhaps we don't count as journalists), and the Adviser to the Prosecution and Legal Adviser to the Foreign Office. The Attorney-General, Dr Hausner, is a very able Polish Jew,[1] his adviser a Lithuanian with the unlikely name of Robinson but the great virtue of having read all of my writings, even the obscurest of them, on Germany.[2] I find I have a great name

---

[1]   Gideon Hausner (1915–90), Attorney General 1960–3, was formidable in his cross-examination of Eichmann; a cabinet minister under Golda Meir in 1974.

[2]   Jacob Robinson (1889–1977) was a law graduate of Warsaw University, served in the Russian army 1914–15, was a German prisoner-of-war 1915–18, ran a Hebrew secondary school in Lithuania 1919–22, practised as a lawyer in Kaunas, and was elected in 1923 to the Lithuanian parliament, where he led the Jewish faction and the Minorities bloc until the *coup d'état* of 1926, which led to the prohibition of Jewish representation in Lithuania in 1927. He became an international jurist before his flight from Lithuania to the USA in 1940. He was active in the prosecution of genocidal Nazis and in pressing for Holocaust reparations; legal counsel to Israel's delegation at the United Nations 1948–57.

in Israel. This is perhaps only fair, to compensate for my absolute obscurity in Germany, where nothing that I write is ever published, or known.

My dear James, I am writing all about myself. I am sorry. How are you? I do hope you are well, enjoying Chiefswood, enjoying whatever you are reading, enjoying Rosehill (if you went there), enjoying staying with the Morses[1] (if you stayed with them). I only wish I could hear from you. But if that pleasure is denied me I shall still hope to see you in Oxford on Saturday 22nd, when we can perhaps have lunch together. I am sending this letter direct to Oxford, as I realise that it will probably take all that time to reach you, and anyway, I have no idea where you are—at Chiefswood, or at Rosehill, or in the Lake District. I wish I were in any of these three places. Miki Sekers has sent me a telegram urging me to come to Rosehill for the week-end of 21st April; but alas, I shall be just too late.[2]

All love from

Hugh

PS. James Morris, who wrote that very highly praised book on Venice, is here. He is very nice, and protests that he was a pupil of mine. How awful that I should have totally forgotten a pupil, but even after he has told me I cannot recollect teaching him![3]

---

[1]  Jonathan Morse (b. 1942) was an Eton contemporary of James's: his sister Annabel (b. 1944) was at Cranborne Chase with Xenia. Their father was a physician at Tynemouth in Northumberland, but had a house in the Lake District.

[2]  (Sir) Nicholas ('Miki') Sekers (1910–72) left Hungary in 1937, and opened West Cumberland Silk Mills at Whitehaven. During the war his factory made parachute fabric, but afterwards used his flair for design and colour to supply fashion fabrics to Dior, Cardin, Givenchy, Molyneux, and other dress-makers favoured by Xandra. He supplied the silk for Chiefswood's dining-room. A trustee of Glyndebourne and supporter of the Mozart Players, London Philharmonic Orchestra, and Oxford's Meadow Players, he was well known to the T-Rs.

[3]  James Morris (b. 1926) was on the staff of The Guardian, for whom he reported on Eichmann's trial. Known as Jan Morris since 1972, she is a pre-eminent travel essayist, whose celebrated book on Venice was published in 1960. She recalled in 2013, 'he was quite right, I was never his pupil, but when I was an (ex-service) undergraduate at Christ Church I was once summoned before him, as Senior Censor, for some minor disdemeanour. He let me off kindly and humorously, and that's probably what I reminded him of.'

# To James Howard-Johnston, 15 April 1961

15 April 1961                                   King David Hotel, Jerusalem

My dearest James,

You see I cannot stop writing to you—αὐτὰρ ἐγὼ παρα σεῦ ὀλίγης οὐ
τυγχάνω αἰδοῦς[1]—but it has become a habit. Besides, I like writing to you;
and I have just had an experience which I should like to communicate,
and why not to you? It is so much easier, as well as more enjoyable, than
to start afresh to some other correspondent to whom I would first have to
explain why I am in Jerusalem, etc. etc.

There is in this city, as the representative of *Paris Soir*, a well-known French
novelist of Jewish origin, Joseph Kessel.[2] I know him because he came over
from Paris to see me some time ago, and got me to write a preface for his recent (and highly successful) book *Les Mains du Miracle*, about Felix Kersten,
Himmler's masseur. Well, in the court-room, while the Attorney-General
and Dr Servatius were disputing refined legal doctrines and Eichmann
was looking stonily through his glass spectacles at the glass case in which,
like some strange and horrible sea-monster, he is preserved, I bumped into
Kessel and he asked me if I would like to accompany him, on Friday evening—
i.e. at the beginning of the Sabbath (it runs from sunset on Friday to sunset on
Saturday)—to see some religious fanatics in operation. As I always enjoy seeing strange aspects of *la comédie humaine*, and have a particular taste for religious eccentricities, I naturally said yes; and so, at 6 o'clock, a very civilised
French Jew, who has lived here since 1936 and knows every inch of the place,
came to the hotel, and having borrowed a ritual cap (for one cannot go into a
synagogue uncovered), I accompanied him and Joseph Kessel to a part of
Jerusalem known as Mea Shearim, where live the sect of the Hasidim.

---

[1]  'But I don't get the least respect from you.' T-R is adapting Theognis, *Elegy and Iambus*,
I.253, where the poet rebukes a young man who has not reciprocated his solicitude.
[2]  Joseph Kessel (1898–1979) had been born in Argentina of Lithuanian ancestry. His
strenuous life as a First World War aviator, war reporter, travel journalist, and Second World
War resistance fighter provided the basis for most of his novels (but not *Belle du jour*, the story
that Buñuel adapted into a film). Elected to Académie Française 1962.

The Hasidim date, I think, from the 18th century. They are fundamental-
ists and the most orthodox of the orthodox. There are 8,000–10,000 of
them in Jerusalem, and they have lived there since the beginning of this
century. Most of them come from Rumania. They refuse to speak Hebrew:
that would be to contaminate by human uses the language of God; they
speak only Yiddish. (Yiddish is the *lingua franca* of the East European Jews:
a kind of debased, judaised German which however, when written, is written in Hebrew characters). And they live in fortress-like blocks, with only
one outer door to the whole block, and internal courtyards, rather like
colleges. Each block is crystallised around a particular rabbi, who has despotic powers over his congregation and is abjectly revered by them. The
Hasidim are generally artisans by trade. They refuse military service or
other profane activities. Outside their trade they only pray.

As we went through these strange, elongated colleges, I noticed that
there were no men or boys: only the feminine sex seemed to exist. But our
guide, who is called M. Rechev, explained that the male sex would by now
all be in the synagogue. So we went to a synagogue. As we approached it,
a strange noise was issuing from it, and then, as we came nearer, I could
see, through the windows, wildly moving shadows, enlarged by candle-
light. We went in, and the sight was stranger still. We seemed to have
come into a madhouse, and my first impulse was to turn and flee. But
M. Rechev told me to stay with him and I stayed.

The synagogue was like a lower-class restaurant. There were long tables
placed in all directions, and men and boys of all ages, from 3 to 90 or thereabouts, about a hundred of them, were crowded around the tables, some sitting at them, others standing between them, wherever there was room. A
few of them were wearing European clothes and black hats, but most of them
were in white robes with zebra-striped scarves and white hoods over their
heads. Others had caftans (wide, flat, round brown fur hats). All of them had
long ringlets hanging down in front of their ears. But all of them looked very
clean, both in person and in their clothes, and the synagogue was very clean
too: scrubbed tables, whitewashed walls. But what made the whole spectacle
so bizarre was that everyone there was not only making strange, discordant,

repetitive nasal noises (that, after all, happens in every popish church), but also making the most violent gestures. Whether standing or sitting, they were bobbing furiously, bowing up and down with the whole body, throwing themselves from side to side, and making strange faces. One man beside me stood facing the bare wall and for the whole time we were there he was in constant sharp electrical motion, using his bottom as a hinge: now fully erect, now with his nose touching the floor and his bottom in the air. As most of them had their eyes shut, and no one cared in which direction he faced, and there was no attempt to synchronise either the movements or the noise, the whole performance was wild and disorderly in the extreme. I wondered whether we also ought to compete; but one of the worshippers pressed me to take his seat at a table, which I did, and thrust a Hebrew prayer book into my hand, so I took it and concentrated, with grave, Anglican decorum, on the Holy Writ. They were singing a psalm. Then, quite suddenly, they all broke, of one accord, into wild shouts and screams. The whole synagogue shook; and M. Rechev explained to me that they had come to the verse about the voice of the Lord which shakes the mountains and breaks the great trees, even the cedars of Lebanon.[1] By the great noise they were making, they were representing this great and terrible Voice of the Lord. He also explained to me that the violent movement of the body was in obedience to another divine injunction, that we should praise the Lord with all our limbs and body. After the voice of the Lord had subsided, we all turned to the door of the synagogue to greet the Sabbath which was understood to be 'coming in', and when it was 'in' there was first a great serenity and then wild cries of rejoicing. From then on, said M. Rechev, they would continue to keep up the bobbing and nasal noises all through the night, 'keeping the Sabbath alive'.

We went out and dined. At 11 o'clock we returned to the same synagogue. They were still at it, 'keeping the Sabbath alive', although many of them had passed out with the effort and were lying prostrate and asleep on benches or in corners. Even among the survivors, the noise and the movements had become somewhat languid. Then, suddenly, there was a pause. In front of

---

[1]  Psalm 29: 5, although T-R slightly misremembers it.

the rabbi there was a large loaf, which he cut up and distributed. After that a meal was brought in to him, course by course. He ate as much as he wanted of each course, and then there was a wild scramble as all the congregation competed for the scraps which had been consecrated by the touch of the holy man. Between each course the noise and the movement was resumed. At the end of the rabbi's meal, wine was distributed. Then the old familiar noise was resumed and doubtless continued long after we had gone.

It was an extraordinary experience: a throw-back, past christianity, past modern Judaism, to the world out of which christianity was formed: the world of the Old Testament or at least the background of the New. The disciples crowding to touch the hem of Christ's garment; the last supper; all were there. I tried to envisage our sedate Anglicanism, our beautiful, exquisite, lyrical singing of the psalms, as a derivative (which it is) of those primitive goings-on, but it was very difficult. Even our most ridiculous atavisms, even the most recondite absurdities of Dr Mascall (though sillier, since they are deliberately excogitated while these have been merely preserved) can hardly compete with them.

How extraordinary it is that the Jews, in the full light and freedom of the 20[1] century,[1] should still preserve these tribal superstitions, while the Greeks, in the darkness of their earliest antiquity, should have been so free from them! How little of religion there is in Homer! I have cast my mind over Iliad and Odyssey, over all 48 books of them, and (although no doubt I have forgotten much) I can only remember three clergymen; and even they are not noticeably devout. First, of course, there is the first person who enters the stage in the Iliad, the Revd Chryses, vicar of the parish of Chryse, who starts all the trouble by mobilising his patron and persuading him to intervene in his own domestic troubles (which have nothing whatever to do with religion); thus confirming the wise observation of our present Prime Minister's old Nanny,[2] as quoted by him at a

---

[1]   T-R echoes Gibbon's *A Vindication of...the Decline and Fall* (1779): 'the full light and freedom of the eighteenth century'. T-R wrote the preface to an edition of that work in 1961.
[2]   In old age Macmillan said that his nanny, Mrs Caroline Last, had been 'the true centre of life' during his childhood.

Cabinet meeting, that 'whenever there is a spot of trouble in the world, if only you will look deep enough, you will always find a clergyman at the bottom of it'. Then there is our old friend whose name I have forgotten, the epicurean incumbent of Ismaros, who is only remembered because of his particularly choice cellar, and his refusal to part with the key of it except to his safely teetotal housekeeper. And finally, I recall some rather primitive lower, unbeneficed clergy—I expect it was a theological college, like Cuddesdon—at Dodona, who are only mentioned because of their unhygienic habits of sleeping on the ground and not washing their feet: ἀνιπτίποδες, χαμαιεῦναι.[1] Perhaps I shall remember others later, but on the whole I think we can take these three as typical representatives of the Homeric Established Church: and a very typical Established Church too.

I must stop. This is positively my last letter to you; at least from Jerusalem. It takes two to keep up a correspondence.

All love from

Hugh

---

*'There is no better way of learning about a subject than by supervising a sympathetic and stimulating research student,' Trevor-Roper observed of Felix Raab, whom he described as 'my pupil and friend'. Raab, the son of Jewish Australians who had fled Austria after the Anschluss, was a graduate of Melbourne University, who had come to Oxford to work on the reception of the thought of Machiavelli in England. Trevor-Roper warmed to this young man, whom he described as one of his best graduate students. 'Whenever he appeared at my door—a heavy, square frame, slightly stooping, black-bearded, with a genial glint in his large, bulging eyes—my spirits would rise.' A voluble raconteur, Raab recounted with gusto an early encounter with his supervisor, when the two men met to discuss a draft which Raab had submitted. They were seated facing one another across a table. Trevor-Roper extracted the draft from a folder and pushed it across the table with the nail of his middle finger, commenting, 'My dear Raab, it won't do, you know.' Raab claimed that he pushed it back, declaring in his guttural Austrian-Australian accent, 'It bloody well will!'*

[1] 'With unwashed feet and sleeping on the ground'. Homer, *Iliad* 16.234.

*Though a well-organized scholar Raab was also something of a free spirit, who had fi-
nanced his study of history by what Trevor-Roper would later describe as 'an active, wandering, and enjoyable life as a stage-electrician, bricklayer, odd-job man'. Intermittently
Raab escaped to remote regions of Europe, where he hiked along wild and lonely trails. In
September 1962, having finished his thesis, and before the start of the academic year, he left
for Calabria. Trevor-Roper sent this letter poste restante to Reggio di Calabria, in accord-
ance with Raab's direction, but it was returned unclaimed. While walking on Monte Pollino,
Raab had been surprised by bad weather and had fallen to his death in a ravine. It would be a
month before his body was found. He was posthumously awarded a D.Phil. for his thesis; two
years later it was published, with an elegiac foreword by Trevor-Roper, as* The English Face
of Machiavelli.

## To Felix Raab, undated (September 1962)

Chiefswood, Melrose

My dear Raab

Thank you very much for your letter. Those kind words gave me the
greatest pleasure, though really I don't think I deserve them: I have done
nothing, and am conscious of having done nothing, except of having had
a very good research student! And I am sure that the examiners will think
so too, and that you can have a complete holiday in Calabria without
thought of that future. Don't hurry back: the Board *can't* appoint the
examiners till the Thursday of the second week of term, and so you can't
conceivably be needed for any purpose connected with your thesis for at
least ten days after that: the examiners have to receive the request from
the Board, accept it, then receive the thesis, then read it, before they can
need to communicate with you. So spend as long as you like in Calabria,
and enjoy it.

I am very glad to hear the good news about your parents' finances and
the relief it gives to you. I hope it may enable you to return to Europe.
Anyway we can discuss that, and Greece too, when you are back.

The subject you suggest—the century of dying religion—is a fascinating but enormous subject. I think you would find it changing in your

hands as you worked on it; but you have a strong, clarifying mind and could, I think, tackle a subject whose vastity and formlessness would overwhelm others. I quite agree that there are infinite varieties of secularism. There was also a 'third force', which was perhaps more important than straight 'secularism': I mean, a kind—or rather many kinds—of religious solvents of religion.[1] Socinianism is the most obvious form, but there are others. I think that there are differences from country to country. In Protestant countries, where there was relative freedom for sects, I think that secularism came in often in this way, but in Catholic countries, where sectarianism was crushed out—this seems to me one of the great social consequences of the Counter-Reformation—pure secularism seems to me to make a much more frontal attack. In England, religion is undermined by Socinians, Quakers, mystics; in France it is challenged by *libertins*.

Do you know Gottfried Arnold's *Unparteyische Kirchen—Kitzengeshicthe?*[2] (I quote from memory, writing in bed, with only one eye in use, which may account for calligraphic uncertainties and linear lapses). It was published towards the end of the 17th century, and had a great influence on, among others, Goethe (see *Dichtung u. Wahrheit*):[3] and that alone—in my eyes—is a great recommendation.

Do you realise how fortunate you are to read German?[4] It is becoming—to judge from most of my pupils—an extinct language in England. And yet what wonderful books were written in it in the *Goethezeit!*[5] Do you know Voigt's *die Wiederbelebung des klassischen Alterthums:*[6] it is a

---

[1]  T-R explored these themes in his essay 'The Religious Origins of the Enlightenment', first published in the collection *Religion, the Reformation and Social Change* (1967).

[2]  Gottfried Arnold (1666–1714), a Lutheran professor of church history, whose *Unparteyische Kirchen- und Ketzer-historie* treated heresy with impartiality.

[3]  Goethe's autobiography of his youth, *Aus meinem Leben: Dichtung und Wahrheit* (*From my Life: Poetry and Truth*' 1811–33).

[4]  T-R had ambivalent feelings towards German culture: he disliked the language, but loved much of the literature.

[5]  The Age of Goethe, i.e. 1770–1830.

[6]  Georg Voigt (1827–91), German historian, author of *Wiederbelebung des klassischen Alterthums oder das erste Jahrhundert des Humanismus* ('Revival of Classical Antiquity or the First Century of Humanism', 1859).

marvellous book, never translated. And—though of course much later—Gregorovius's *Wanderjahre in Italien?*[1] But I may be prejudiced in favour of Gregorovius: I taught myself German as an undergraduate, reading his *Geschichte der Stadt Rom im Mittelalter.*[2]

I knew Norman Douglas quite well: at his best he is a marvellous writer.[3] He hated D. H. Lawrence—precisely because of his meanness—see his (rare) pamphlet on D. H. Lawrence and Magnus.[4]

yours sincerely

Hugh Trevor-Roper

—⊗—

In 1963 Trevor-Roper visited Portugal on behalf of the Sunday Times. *Like Spain, Portugal was isolated from the rest of Europe, still ruled, as it had been since the early 1930s, by a right-wing dictator, Dr António de Oliveira Salazar (1888–1970).*

## To James Howard-Johnston, 5–7 April 1963

Lis Hotel, Avenida da Liberdade 180, Lisboa 2

My dearest James

I have often thought of you and wondered how you fared on your expedition to the Dordogne. Where did you go; how did you enjoy it? I have

---

[1]  Ferdinand Gregorovius (1821–91), German historian. His *Wanderjahre in Italien* (1856–77) is an account of the walks he took through Italy in the 1850s.

[2]  Gregorovius' *Die Geschichte der Stadt Rom im Mittelalter* (*History of Rome in the Middle Ages*, 8 volumes, 1859–72), a classic of medieval and early Renaissance history. T-R read this huge work in his first year as an undergraduate, while he was still studying classics.

[3]  Norman Douglas (1868–1952), novelist, travel writer, and reprobate, whom T-R had visited in Capri during the Christmas vacation of 1949–50 and for whom he instigated a Royal Literary Fund grant. It seems likely that Raab had been reading Douglas's *Old Calabria* (1915), at T-R's recommendation.

[4]  *D. H. Lawrence and Maurice Magnus: A Plea for Better Manners* (1924). Lawrence had based a character on Douglas in his novel *Aaron's Rod*, published in 1922, and in that same year had written a merciless memoir of Maurice Magnus, an American tuft-hunter and ne'er-do-well, who had taken poison some years earlier.

envisaged an oddly assorted trio, you, McCreery[1] and the Filipino, two white and tall, one black and short, arguing volubly and inconclusively about philosophy, literature, life on the calvaried hilltops and prehistoric caves of that ancient region. Do let me know how it went: that writing-paper which I pressed upon you was a kind of blackmail. Admittedly, being blackmail, it deserved not to succeed.

I am not enjoying Portugal, I'm afraid. I could enjoy it, in theory: there are things that I like about it. The fish, for instance. What delicious lam-preys there are, what rich marine-soups, what variety of molluscs! And when shall I ever enjoy such a magnificent squid-pie as was produced last Sunday, when I went to Sintra to lunch with an old friend whom I was delighted to find, at 83, as gay and well-informed and outrageous as ever? He is Dr José d'Almada, once financial adviser to the Portuguese ministry of Overseas [Development], a man who almost knew Cecil Rhodes and certainly knew everyone, English or Portuguese, who was involved in the great imperialist politics of Africa after Rhodes.[2] He is the best of my sources, and the most entertaining: I had feared he might be dead, or gaga; but he is far from either, and I go regularly to lunch with him—his lunches are always delicious—both at his home in Lisbon and in his beautiful villa at Sintra where he has made a wonderful garden of African flowers. He has a house in Madeira too, which he wants to sell, preferably to an Englishman, because the English, he says, take trouble over gardens and the garden is his great pride: would not Oxford university like it, a place in which dons could write books? Alas, I had to explain, dons cannot afford to keep, or travel to, houses in Madeira.

But alas, for all this, and for all the beauties of Portugal, which I admit are many, I feel a prisoner here. I have to write my article, and to write it I

---

[1]   Charles McCreery (b. 1942), James's Eton contemporary, was a gifted pianist reading philosophy and psychology at New College, Oxford. Subsequently McCreery held posts at Trinity College, Cambridge and was Lecturer in Experimental Psychology at Magdalen College, Oxford; researched hallucinatory states, out-of-body experiences, extra-sensory perception, and proposed a theory linking psychosis to sleep and dreams; composer, and Director at St Maur Music, Oxford.
[2]   José d'Almada (b. 1879?), of Banco Nacional Ultramarino (the National Overseas Bank).

must stay in Lisbon, talking to people, and reading papers and documents, and therefore all the beauties are unvisitable. The people I have to dance attendance on are rather dull too. I wish I were less conscientious: I should then write a merry old article based entirely on the rich gossip of Dr d'Almada and spend the rest of my time eating lampreys and lobsters in some romantic *pousada*[1] by the sea in Algarve, the southernmost tropical province of Portugal. But somehow I cannot do this. And then, I must admit, Portuguese politics, or rather the political structure of Portugal (for politics are not allowed), does fascinate me. This strange dictator, half chartered-accountant, half-priest, who lives like a hermit (but likes the smell of millionaires around him) and poses as a philosopher (whereas I think he is really only a humbug), is something unique in this century, or in any other outside Spain or Portugal. I suppose Philip II was rather like him;[2] but at least Philip II, when he caned the Pope, did it as the most powerful monarch of Christendom, on whom all the hopes of the Church depended; while Salazar shows no sign of realising that Portugal, this miniscule Tibet, which for 35 years he has isolated from all progress, is really rather small and very poor. Nevertheless, the devout Catholic statesman has just kidnapped all the black priests in Angola and carted them off to Lisbon, from which he will not let them out, and has pushed the Bishop of Oporto out of Portugal and for five years has never let him in again: if he appears at the frontier, he is turned back by the police. It is all very mortifying for the Pope…

Today, feeling generally depressed by life in Lisbon, and knowing that at the week-end I would anyway find no one there, I decided to escape. I felt the need of fresh air: I longed to be in rural solitude, among the woods (Portugal is richly wooded) and by the sound of running water. So I consulted a reliable friend, who advised me to go to Abrantes, about 100 miles up the Tagus. But alas, there is no such thing as a 'reliable' Portuguese. The Portuguese, like the Persians, believe in telling you what they think

---

[1] 'Inn'.
[2] Philip II (1527–98), the rigidly minded King of Spain, led a reclusive existence at his palace near Madrid.

you will like to hear, quite regardless of the truth. I am constantly being reminded of this. No less than four separate Portuguese passengers on a train assured me that I was on the right train this morning—fortunately without convincing me, for in fact it was going in the opposite direction. And this is a regular experience. As for Abrantes, when I arrived here, after a journey of infinite tedium (Portuguese trains are incredibly slow), expecting a delightful rural *pousada* in some old castle, shaded by euca-lyptus trees and refreshed by a running stream, I found myself in a ghastly modern road-house situated in the bend of a road, with lorries in low gear perpetually encircling it, no garden at all, disgusting food, no service, and canned music resounding through the whole building. Of course I was furious, but to no effect. Misinformed twice in succession about (a) the time and (b) the route of the buses, I have spent the whole afternoon sit-ting, steaming, in the front hall for the means of escape which never came. Now I am condemned to spend the night in it. My temper, as you can imagine, is very bad, and my confidence utterly shaken. The same reliable friend who recommended it has offered to take me to his house in the North next week; but now I wonder what the house will be like. Shall I run out? But if so, how else shall I spend my time, or get through the hor-rors of Holy Week? Admittedly they are not so horrible here as in Spain: Dr Salazar sees to that: in his attitude of mind he is really a *protestant* cler-gyman. He would do well in the Kirk of Scotland. I can see him preaching in Mertoun Kirk if Dr Sawyer happened to be away.[1] He would *read* his sermon, in a toneless voice (he is not to be confused with the Rev. Boaner-ges Stormheaven who was an anticipatory Wee Free[2]). Incidentally, he was brought up in a seminary to be a priest (like Stalin); but I understand that he doesn't like this to be widely known. He makes all the R.C. priests here dress like protestant clergymen: no nighties or birettas; and he is very strict about processions. There are no monks or nuns: all their mon-asteries have been turned into army barracks.

---

[1]    Mertoun kirk was a small, plain 17th-century building close to Dryburgh Abbey.
[2]    A fire-and-brimstone Calvinist preacher in Scott's *The Heart of Midlothian*.

You see my mind always comes back to Dr Salazar. One simply can't avoid him. Every aspect of Portuguese life brings him back, each time in a slightly different form, sometimes as an old family solicitor, sometimes as a domineering nanny, sometimes as a puritan minister: but always certain characteristics are constant: puritanism, old-fashionedness, strictness. Every now and then he tries to sweeten his public image, but I'm afraid it hasn't been very successful. Some years ago the millionaires around the throne thought that something had better be done, so they hired a female French novelist to come and spend her holidays with him and say how nice and cosy he was. She did, but somehow no one took her seriously.[1] Recently he has abandoned these amateur tactics for a more streamlined method, and has hired a high-pressure American public relations business, Messrs Selvage and Lee Inc., of New York, to make him appear imaginative, progressive, liberal etc. But I'm afraid this hasn't been very effective either. I wonder if Selvage and Lee were started by Ivy Lee who made his fortune by converting the public image of John D. Rockefeller from the hideous reality into that of a kindly old golfer only interested in giving sweets to children and millions to charity.[2] One would have thought that anyone who could sweeten Rockefeller could sweeten Salazar, but evidently this is not so, or all the work is undone again by a wicked conspiracy of Afro-Asians, liberals, communists, atheists, protestants, etc. (to which must now be added admirals, generals, cardinals and pirate captains on the high seas).

I started, a few days ago, to take the Portuguese language seriously. Since I read it easily, I find it maddening and frustrating that I cannot speak or understand it except on the most elementary level. So I took a firm resolution and (since the great problem is the pronunciation, which cannot be deduced from the spelling) borrowed a gramophone and a series of Linguaphone records from the British Institute. I was getting on

---

[1]   Christine Garnier was the *nom de plume* used by Raymonde Cagin (1915–87) for such novels as *Fetish*, *Elsa de Berlin*, and *La Fête des sacrifices* as well as for *Salazar: An Intimate Portrait* (1952).

[2]   Ivy Lee (1877–1934), uncle of William S. Burroughs. The firm of Selvage and Lee was founded in 1938.

beautifully, saying everything sideways through the nose and skilfully silencing half the vowels and half the consonants in the approved manner, when I dined last night with Virginia Rau, a Portuguese historian.[1] She threw up her hands in horror and ordered me to stop at once on the grounds that (a) no foreigner has ever been able to speak Portuguese well anyway, and (b) the only result will be to ruin my Spanish. She has commanded me to return the gramophone and the records of the British Institute and to renounce for ever the folly, or vanity, of seeking to speak the language. So you see how frustrating my life is.

I long to be at Chiefswood. As I struggle with these successive frustrations, as I painfully scale, or gingerly de-scale, the streets of Lisbon (which have an average gradient of 1 in 3 and are paved with polished stones guaranteed to pitch any foreigner on to his nose), I always hear the music of that stream and see before me, like a mirage above the burning desert, the image of those woods now coming I suppose—not furiously, all at once, as here, but gently, slowly, lovingly—into flower. Are you enjoying it? How are our new trees? Has anything survived that winter? How is the French boy? I fear he will be a disastrous influence on Peter.[2] Have you had any gossipy, *bavard*,[3] self-exposing letters from Xenia[4] in France? Did you turn off the heating at 8 St Aldates? Is Chiefswood as beautiful as I think it must be?

Ille terrarum mihi praeter omnes
Angulus ridet, ubi non Hymetto

[1]  Virginia Rau (1907–73), who held a chair at Lisbon University, was an economic and maritime historian of late medieval and early modern Portugal.

[2]  James's younger brother (b. 1950), who founded Howard-Johnston Cars Ltd., an Edinburgh used car retailer, in 1969.

[3]  Chattering.

[4]  James's sister (b. 1944). She was an undergraduate at St Anne's, Oxford, before studying Russian politics at the London School of Economics (LSE), as a pupil of Leonard Schapiro. As Xenia Dennen, she co-founded the Keston Institute in 1969, and in 1973 launched the academic journal *Religion in Communist Lands*, which she edited until 1981. She was the Keston Institute's Moscow representative during the 1990s, and became chairman of the institute in 2002. A contributor to numerous specialist journals, she is associated with openDemocracy and with Gresham College in the City of London.

Mella decedunt, viridique certat
baca Venafro…
(*baca*, in this case, of course, is the rowan!).[1]

Love from
Hugh

6 April 1963
PS. This letter is unposted 24 hours since I wrote it, so I might as well add a little and bring it up to date: especially as this means that I can end it more cheerfully. This morning I fled from that ghastly road-house: but whither (I asked) should I flee? Lacking all counsel, and having no faith left in anyone besides myself, I decided to flee towards Lisbon. At first I thought I would stop in Santarém; so I took a bus to Santarém. (Buses are *even* slower than trains in Portugal, but they are gayer and I much prefer them. The difficulty is that one cannot find out anything about them. Tourist agencies refuse to admit their existence, as they have their own tourist-buses which take groups of gaping foreigners on set runs to Fátima, where three children had a vision of the Virgin Mary in 1917 and which now coins hard currency as the Portuguese Lourdes. No oral information in Portugal is reliable; and so far I have been unable to find any printed timetables). But on arrival, I thought that Santarém would not do, and finding that my bus was going on to Lisbon, I stayed in it. Then, after five hours in the bus (during which we had covered 50 miles, so you will be able to calculate the average speed), I suddenly saw that we were in Vila Franca de Xira, a place which had caught my fancy last time: for it is in the flat, watery pastures of the Tagus and is populated almost entirely by bulls, which roam in great herds, awaiting their fate either in the bull-ring or in butchery. So I at once pulled the communicating-cord, and got out, and found a taxi, and told the taxi-driver to take me to an inn that I had heard of, in the centre of the bull-pastures. Happily I found a room there. It is a charming place—has all the atmosphere that was lacking in that dreadful roadhouse.

---

[1] 'That corner of the earth smiles for me above all others, where the honey is not inferior to Hymettus; and the olive rivals that of green Venafrum.' Horace, *Odes* 2.6.13–16.

When I arrived, it was too late for lunch: it was four o'clock, so I had missed the enjoyable mid-day snack; but what of that? At once I went for a walk through the pastures of the Tagus. For three hours I walked, along a straight path, with bulls to the right of me, bulls to the left of me (and wire fencing, I hasten to add, between us). Here were young, energetic bullocks trotting to and fro to use up their spirits; here were elderly, senatorial bulls, with inexpressibly gentle faces, dozing recumbent in the long grass. I never met anything except an occasional ox-cart and a herd (if that is the right word) of horses and mules, all with bells round their necks, being driven along by two horsemen with a dog. And the evening air was chill and clear and all the fields yellow in the declining sun. What a wonderful change from last night! That long walk, that universal calm, was a sovereign remedy to disentangle the perplexed and soothe the troubled mind. And when I came back to the inn, what a delicious meal was put before me for dinner! I won't say that it harmonised perfectly with the strong red port which accompanied it; but what of that? I enjoyed them both, in separate compartments of my palate. Tonight I shall sleep, I think, well; and tomorrow I shall go back to Lisbon and begin again, I suppose, that dreary routine of waiting on the great.

Or shall I? Hang it, I am sick of the little great of Lisbon. They always speak to me, from the smallness of their own minds, as if I knew nothing but what they could tell me and could not see through that. In fact I can always predict exactly what they will say, so it is a waste of time to let them say it. I really think I have enough to write my article now. Perhaps I will write it tomorrow. On Tuesday I lunch again with Dr d'Almada: he will dot my i's and cross my t's more reliably than any of these twopenny law-professors of Coimbra who succeed each other, in dreary, monotonous succession, as Dr Salazar's ministers of state!

H

PPS 7 April 1963

Have now reached Lisbon. Drowned rat. It's a great mistake to go anywhere till the spring has *really* come. Thank God for a bath and a roof!

⁓

*In January 1964 Frank Giles, Foreign Editor of the* Sunday Times, *asked Trevor-Roper to do 'one of your major pieces in depth' on the war crimes trials which had just opened in Frankfurt. In 1947 the most senior officials responsible for the Auschwitz extermination camp had been tried under Allied jurisdiction, as a result of which twenty-three of the defendants had been sentenced to death. Now their subordinates were being put on trial, under the jurisdiction of the Federal Republic. Trevor-Roper flew to Frankfurt at the end of February. This time the accused were not the bureaucrats or commanders who had ordered murder, but the torturers and murderers who had pushed mothers and children alive into furnaces.*

## To James Howard-Johnston, 29 February 1964

Hotel Frankfurter Hof, Frankfurt am Main

My dearest James—

It is Saturday night: I have a moment in which to breathe; I am alone; why should I not write to you?

Did Mummy get off all right on Friday? I hope so. I wish I could have stayed to see her off. I hope she got my telegram and will report safe arrival at Hever.[1]

Ever since I arrived here I have been—until today—stuck in the court house. It is a fascinating but horrible trial. At Nuremberg and in Jerusalem the prisoners were far away, separate from the observers: Eichmann doubly separated, behind bullet-proof glass. Here they sit among us, some of them free, on bail. I find myself next to two SS dentists accused of selecting victims for the gas-chambers, supervising the gassing of them, and extracting the gold teeth from the corpses.[2] Both are hideous; but so are most of the defendants: their faces are inhuman, empty with a truly German emptiness. The crimes with which they are charged are revolting: sadistic killing of the most loathsome kind; and yet they all, in true

---

[1]  Hever Castle was the home in Kent of Xandra's youngest sister 'Rene': Irene (1919–2001), wife of Gavin Astor, later 2nd Baron Astor of Hever (1918–84), co-chief proprietor of *The Times* 1962–6.
[2]  Willy Frank (1903–89), chief SS dentist at Auschwitz-Birkenau, was sentenced to seven years, but his deputy Willy Schatz (1903–76) was acquitted.

German fashion, knew absolutely nothing—'can't remember' whether they murdered people or not, or, if they did, murdered 'only Jews'; and then the tears stream down their noses as they reflect on the many unrewarded kindnesses which they performed for those ungrateful prisoners and give evidence of their real softness of heart—how one of them regarded himself as 'the Angel of Auschwitz' (he is accused of killing 119 Polish boys by injecting carbolic acid into their hearts), and how another wept for a day when his cat was run over... And then one goes out of the court-house and finds oneself standing next to one of these creatures in the lavatory, or sitting next to them in the restaurant. One of the nastiest of them is Dr Capesius who made enough out of the prisoners—gassing 1200 children at once, etc. etc.—to set up on his own as a chemist afterwards and now has six assistants and a turnover of £30,000 p.a. from his chemist's shop in Goeppingen and his beauty-parlour in Reutlingen.[1] Friday was a dramatic day, when a survivor from Auschwitz gave evidence against one of the defendants (he had shot a woman prisoner for recognising her brother when he was unloaded from a train at Auschwitz, developed a particular method of killing people with his hands, driven others against electric wires, pushed 4000 into gas-chambers etc. etc.). At a certain moment the defendant's lawyer challenged the witness to identify his client. As twenty years had passed and the witness was a '70% invalid' owing to his experiences in Auschwitz, I was afraid he would fail, especially as the defendants sit among the press, lawyers, etc. in the body of the court-room. But he walked slowly round the room peering through his thick glasses and then spotted him correctly at once. I think everyone in court (except the defendants) was as relieved as I was when he got him right.

After all this I was, as you can imagine, glad of a rest today, Saturday. First of all, I slept late. (The court opens at 8.30 which means that, when it

[1]  Victor Capesius (1907–85) was a major in the Waffen-SS. As pharmacist at Dachau 1943–4 and Auschwitz 1944–5 he was in charge of chemicals such as phenol and Zyklon B used to exterminate Jews. At the Frankfurt trial he was sentenced to nine years, but served only three.

sits, I have to get up at 6.45). Then I went to the Goethe Museum in the house in which Goethe was born. It is an excellent museum in his father's house, a large town-house built around a courtyard, full of pictures by Fuseli, and Angelica Kauffmann, views of Rome by Piranesi and Volpato, busts of Winckelmann, Schiller, Herder etc. I *love* Goethe more and more. There is a Goethe Museum in Weimar, now in East Germany, which I have visited too: it has more things in it, because Goethe himself lived there and left all his possessions there; but the communists, though they arrange everything with a kind of antiseptic thoroughness, kill it all by presenting it as propaganda; and there is something disgusting about the attempt to make Goethe a marxist-leninist. I really enjoyed the Frankfurt Goethe-museum far more and spent most of the morning there, forgetting about the horrors of Auschwitz very happily.

Then, this afternoon, I had a sudden idea. I remembered that a German friend had told me that Willy Johannmeyer now lived at Frankfurt.[1] Johannmeyer was the German officer whom Robert Maxwell of the Pergamon Press failed to 'break',[2] but whom, after a long struggle, I forced or persuaded to admit that he had Hitler's will buried in his back-garden at Iserlohn. I am sure that I have told you the story, probably often. Anyway, he was not a Nazi and he was the only person whom I interrogated in 1945 whom I liked and would ever want to see again. So I looked him up in the telephone-book, found his name, and telephoned. A feminine voice answered. Could I speak, I asked, to Herr Willy Johannmeyer? What name she asked. Trevor-Roper, I replied, preparing myself for the inevitable expostulation, demands for repetition, spelling, etc. 'Ah, Herr Trevor-Roper', the feminine voice replied at once, faultlessly and with excitement, 'I will get him at once'. It was as if I were a familiar friend, whom they saw

---

[1]  Willi Johannmeyer (1915–70), an army adjutant in Hitler's bunker during the fall of Berlin. While seeking Hitler's will T-R had interrogated Johannmeyer over several days. Ultimately Johannmeyer revealed that he had buried the document in a glass bottle in his back garden.
[2]  Robert Maxwell (1923–91), future Labour MP and founder of the Pergamon Press, which bought the British Printing Corporation (1981) and Mirror Group Newspapers (1984). Johannmeyer withstood interrogation by Maxwell, but yielded to T-R's patient, logical questioning.

regularly, not the unnamed English officer whom she had never seen and whom her husband (if she was Mrs Johannmeyer) had last seen 19 years ago in somewhat strained circumstances: so I suppose he must dine out on his side of the story as I do on mine. Anyway, he then came to the telephone, absolutely delighted that I had rung up, and I am going to have tea with them tomorrow. It was very refreshing to feel that, in spite of the strained circumstances, he evidently regarded me as a friend and pre-served that feeling for 19 years.

So you see that I have enjoyed the whole day, and it is in order to make it enjoyable to the last minute that I now finish it by writing to you instead of by reading (as I suppose I ought to be doing) documents about Ausch-witz; to which however I shall have to return tomorrow if I am going to get my article written in time. For I must stay here until Monday in order to attend what may be another dramatic session, and must fly back on Tuesday, with my article already written in my hand, and give it that morning to the *Sunday Times*. Then, still on Tuesday, I shall return to Oxford. I hope all is going well there and that the material basis of life—by which I mainly mean the hot water supply—is not breaking down in the absence of the habitual, earthbound, troglodyte stoker who herewith, across the intervening desert air, sends you his love, *viz:*

Hugh

—∞—

*Trevor-Roper spent the last three months of 1964 as a Senior Research Fellow attached to the William Andrews Clark Memorial Library in Los Angeles, which housed a fine collection of seventeenth-century English books. It offered a substantial stipend, and a chance to give Xandra a holiday.*

## To James Howard-Johnston, 6 January 1965

The Carlton House, Madison Avenue, New York 21

My dearest James

We have now left California and are in New York. It is now my turn to be ill, and I am feeling very low. After a day in the dark, I have got up to eat some supper while Mummy has gone off to a theatre and a party; so let me cheer myself up by writing to you. We have had your letter from Hever and are so glad you enjoyed being there. We have also had a letter from Rene, and clearly they greatly enjoyed having you: it is full of your praises. I suppose you are now back in Oxford after your visit to that Welsh town which you have all persuaded yourselves is in Devonshire.[1] I hope you enjoyed being there too.

We left California on New Year's Eve. I was glad to leave it. It is an unreal place, with an unreal climate, and although we had many a gay evening with the film-stars in Beverly Hills, I felt that I never penetrated the university. We flew direct to Philadelphia. Mummy always lamented, and still laments, that owing to my unreasonable desire to do some work, we never 'got about' in the West: i.e. we only covered the coast from Canada to Los Angeles, and did not penetrate inland to the Yosemite National Park and the Grand Canyon. Considering that the 2000 tourists who went to the former of these attractions at Christmas were trapped by tempests, avalanches and floods, I think we were well away from it. As for the Grand Canyon, I'm afraid I can't arouse enthusiasm for the hideous excrescences and monstrosities of Nature. I love not 'antres vast and deserts idle',[2] but gentle hills and woods and streams, *loca pastorum deserta atque otia dia*,[3] such as beckon me from the Alps, or from Skye, to

---

[1] James had been staying with Rosalind Toynbee at a cottage at Clovelly, to T-R a Welsh-sounding name.

[2] *Othello* I.iii.154.

[3] 'Through the deserted haunts of shepherds, and the divine places of their rest.' Lucretius, *De rerum natura*.

my native Northumberland or adopted Borders. So I felt that I could dispense with the Grand Canyon, or at least be satisfied with the glimpse that we had, through parting clouds, from 37,000 feet up in the air: a grim wilderness of pink rock which the clouds mercifully enclosed again from my shuddering view.

But why, you may ask, did we fly to Philadelphia? I will tell you. You may have observed that I am fascinated by the sociology of religion. (Yes, I have read Dodds' *The Greeks and the Irrational*, and think it an excellent book: I forgive Dodds all his personal disagreeableness for that).[1] Well, Pennsylvania—or rather Lancaster county, Pennsylvania—is the home of a particularly interesting religious sect; and since we happened to be invited by some newly acquired American friends to stay in that county, the chance seemed too good to miss. Our friends promised, if we should spend New Year with them, to introduce us to this sect; and they were as good as their word.

First, our friends. They are called Mann, and are a thriving and long-lived family. Shortly before leaving California we heard that Mrs Mann had to go to hospital for an operation; but we were told that we were still to come: the only change would be that we were now to stay with the previous generation. We found our hosts a perfectly charming and amazingly vigorous couple, both aged 75. We soon discovered that Mr Mann's parents were also still thriving, at 101 and 98 (Mrs Mann's father had unhappily passed away recently at 102). Five generations of the family flourish side by side in Lancaster county, most of them farming and selling tobacco, which is grown there. And among the farmers whose tobacco-crops they buy up are the members of the esoteric local sect which I went to see. This sect is called the Amish (pronounced as the last two syllables of 'school-ma'amish'). I once sent you, from Jerusalem, an account of the Hasidic devotees there. Allow me now to give you an account of the Pennsylvanian Amish.

[1]  Eric Robertson [E. R.] Dodds (1893–1979), Regius Professor of Greek 1936–60, had been elected an Honorary Student of Christ Church in 1962. T-R found him tense and austere, but acknowledged his scholarly stature.

The Amish are a branch of the Swiss Anabaptists or Mennonites. Mennonites anyway interest me *per se* (and I paid heavily for my interest, attending a Mennonite service last Sunday); but the Amish are far more interesting. They are the Wee Frees of the Mennonite Church. About 1690 certain extreme Mennonites in the Swiss valleys decided that the Mennonite establishment was being corrupted by the lax principles, liberal ideas and technical novelties of the World (just as the Wee Frees also thought about the Kirk of Scotland), and resolved to halt this process of decay. Under their leader Jacob Amann, they declared war on education and progress as the ruin of rural industry and morality; they seceded from the Mennonites; they set about protecting the purity of their doctrine and discipline by formidable powers of excommunication; and having been pushed about the Alps and the Upper Rhine for some time, they migrated, in 1727, to America. There, for over 200 years, by various elaborate devices, they have kept their society static and their faith pure, or almost pure.

It is an extraordinary society. It is rural, self-enclosed, uncompromising. To the Amish the spirit of modernity is represented by the motor-car, and the motor-car is absolutely expelled from their world. They travel in horse-drawn buggies of an archaic type, with iron wheel-rims (tyres are taboo as modern). There is no electricity in their houses, no telephone. No motor traction may be used on their farms. Education for them ceases at 14: only thus, they think, can habits of real industry be acquired. They are extremely industrious. Industry (without industrialism) is their religion. They are also extremely devout. They have no churches. They meet for long services in each other's barns. Since they rely on buggy-transport, they live close to each other. They speak German among themselves and use German works of devotion. They have no other literature. They join their church voluntarily by baptism at 18; but those who have arrived at that age are already so dependent on the community that few refuse full membership. They make no converts, and what they lose by desertion to the Mennonites (or to the 'Beachy-Amish', a lax sect which has compromised with the motor-car) they make up by natural increase, for their families are large. Their priests and bishops are unpaid, farmers like the rest, chosen by lot; but they have despotic social power, exercised to protect this jealously guarded way of life, and symbolised especially by the power of excommunication which leads to *Meidung*, or 'shunning'. At every point, Amish society is jealously guarded against the infectious touch of the world. The Amish wear special clothes and have hundreds of taboos. Beards are obligatory for married men, buttons taboo for all. There are also numerous sophistications, the badges of sub-sects. Certain sects have blue tops to their buggies; others yellow. There are the 'Bean-soup Amish' and the 'One-suspendered Amish'. But these are minor differences. The essential taboos do not distinguish one kind of Amish from another. They distinguish, and protect, the Amish from the World.

'A fossil society!' you exclaim. But no. The extraordinary thing is that it is not. The Amish are positively expanding without tractors or electricity; they are excellent farmers. Their farms, easily recognised by the white colour, the windmill, the buggy, and the absence of tractors or wires of any kind, are tidy and prosperous. They work like mad, refusing all dependence on the state or society, all forms of insurance or public assistance. And the system is preserved, as it has been preserved for two centuries, by immense moral conviction. Without such conviction, obviously, it would crumble in an instant. Even if one generation had accepted it merely because they were imprisoned in it, how could they perpetuate it, fight against local, state and federal authorities to prevent the education of their children, preserve their children from the corruption of the motor-car etc, if they were not inspired by a positive conviction that the hard-working, pre-industrial, rural, Amish way of life is demonstrably better than the lazy, industrial, affluent society which so visibly surrounds it?

On New Year's Day we penetrated an Amish house. I got an introduction from a local journalist in exchange for an interview given by me to the Press. At first the Amish farmer was suspicious, but gradually he thawed. The farm was spotlessly clean, and everything in it was archaic in style. He told me of the great battle against education, which the

Amish have now won, and the great battle against insurance which is still being waged. When we left his house we motored through Amishland. It was like a distant country which modernity had not yet reached. Everywhere white farms with windmills, naked but spick-and-span; and everywhere on the roads we met or passed spanking buggies: closed buggies for married men, open buggies for bachelors and courting couples, all in Amish dress, whisking this way and that, confidently, as if this were the most elegant, most practical, most up-to-date method of travel in the 20th century. Next day we visited another Amish farm, with a friend who had the *entrée*. It too was spotless. The family was charming. Then we went to an Amish coach-factory: a long shed filled with buggies in process of manufacture, buggies in for repair, as vigorous and thriving as City Motors in Oxford. The great difficulty, we were told, is the lack of land. The Amish, relying on buggy-transport, have to live close together. They have large families. But to preserve their large families from the corruption of the world, it is necessary that they work on farms, and how can farms be bought for so many when prices are so high and the Amish, for all their economy, only make modest rural profits? There are at present Amish settlements in Iowa and Indiana as well as in Pennsylvania; but already they are looking further afield. They are prospecting in Mexico. As the superfluous daughters of the Amish make excellent maids in 'English' houses (such corrupting contact with unbelievers used to be forbidden but is now allowed by the clergy as a necessary concession), Mummy would like to settle some in the Borders, but somehow I doubt whether a return to Europe would be a success.

Enough of the Amish. They seem very remote here in New York, where very few people seem even to have heard of them. Even our 75-year old host and hostess in Lancaster, who had lived among them all their lives, had never been into an Amish house until we took them in. The New York world, when we meet them, are more interested in the Warren Report than in those quaint survivals from 17th century Switzerland. So yesterday I both lunched out and dined out on that subject. Little did I think, when I wrote my first article for the *Sunday Times*, that it would cause such a stir.[1] The BBC keeps ringing up from London asking whether I will broadcast on the subject when I return. Perhaps I will. The *Sunday Times* man in Washington, Henry Brandon, is furious.[2] When the *Warren Report* was published, he wrote an article in the *S.T.* saying that all controversy would now stop. I see his point now. He is a tremendous toady of the Washington establishment. Did you see his cross letter in the *Sunday Times*?[3] It is sad that his authoritative, not to say dogmatic answers, derived from 'those closest to the Warren Commission' and 'those who drafted the Report' are sometimes diametrically opposite to the answers which the *Observer's* Washington correspondent ascribes to the same sources.

Was Sparrow vitriolic?[4] I didn't think so. But perhaps I know him too well and know that he means no vitriol.[5] People sometimes think I am too, which

[1] The Warren Commission's Report on its investigation into the assassination of President John F. Kennedy, published soon after the T-Rs' arrival in California, provided a subject for general discussion. Informed American opinion accepted the Warren Commission's findings, but T-R was sceptical. In assessing the Commission's conduct of its investigation, he drew on his own investigation into Hitler's death. After studying the 26 volumes and 20,000 pages of evidence collected (but, he felt, inadequately analysed) by the Warren Commission, he concluded that it had been negligent. On 13 December 1964, three weeks before this letter was written, T-R's full-page article 'Kennedy Murder Inquiry is Suspect' appeared in the *Sunday Times*.

[2] Henry Brandon (1916–93) was born in Prague and, as a graduate of the universities of Prague and Lausanne, followed the exiled Beneš government to England in 1938. As Washington correspondent of the *Sunday Times* 1950–83, he cultivated a superb range of contacts and had privileged access to confidential information.

[3] Henry Brandon, 'Examining the Warren Report', *Sunday Times*, 27 December 1964, p. 12, accused T-R of 'character assassination of the Warren Commission', but conceded that 'doubts have arisen from the bungling of the Dallas police'.

[4] On 20 December, a week after publication of T-R's article, the *Sunday Times* had carried a response from John Sparrow, who had been a Chancery barrister before his election in 1952 as Warden of All Souls. T-R's analysis of the Warren Report, Sparrow told *Sunday Times* readers, was 'a travesty, so marred by bias and blotted with inaccuracies that it is hard to believe that it was written by so honest and intelligent a man as he is. It is deplorable that such a document should carry the authority of the Professor's name.' Sparrow argued that T-R had misinterpreted the evidence, and suggested that he had relied dangerously on innunendo. 'Nothing is easier than to create an atmosphere of suspicion, nothing—so long as the crackpots and credulous abound—more difficult to dispel.'

[5] On 3 January 1965 (three days before this letter was written), the *Sunday Times* had printed T-R's riposte to Sparrow entitled 'How was the President Shot?' He admitted mistakes, but insisted that 'vital questions' remained unanswered and recalled that he had 'explicitly stated that I distrust conspiratorial solutions'. On 20 January, Sparrow's second piece, entitled 'Making Mysteries about Oswald', would appear in the *Sunday Times*. It so incensed T-R that he threatened to sever contact. Amity between the two men was soon restored, however. 'I never forgive but I often forget,' joked T-R.

always astonishes me, as I mean only balm and honey. Anyway, he was right about the paper-bag, so I must capitulate on that point. But he hasn't read the 26 volumes of testimony, which are fascinating. I luckily have. Two rich ladies from Beverly Hills came to my door in Los Angeles, with obedient husbands, like porters, behind them, carrying *two* sets of the precious volumes. They have given me dining-out material for weeks. Tonight, perforce, I dine in, and you see the consequence: I discharge it all on you.

Looking forward to seeing you soon

Love from Hugh

*Valerie Pearl (b. 1926) was one of Trevor-Roper's closest confidants, to whom he wrote long letters, spiced with academic gossip. A historian of the English Civil Wars, she was a Lecturer at Somerville College, Oxford, between 1965 and 1968. She then moved to University College London, as Reader and later Professor in London History. She was co-editor (with Hugh Lloyd-Jones and Blair Worden) of the Festschrift in Trevor-Roper's honour,* History and Imagination *(1981). That same year she was appointed as the second President of New Hall, and thus served as head of a Cambridge college in the same decade as Trevor-Roper.*

## To Valerie Pearl, 12 September 1965

Chiefswood, Melrose

Dear Valerie

I returned from Vienna two days ago and found your letter. The Photostat from the BM[1] came next day. Your influence in that citadel of learning is clearly immense and I fear I may well exploit it in future. Thank you so much for exerting it for me.

Now about the Hartlib MSS.[2] I'm afraid I don't know where they are at present but I can and will find out. They have an odd history. Having been

---

[1]   The British Museum.

[2]   The utopian social reformer Samuel Hartlib (1600?–1662), whose voluminous archive, now in the Hartlib Centre at the University of Sheffield, is an invaluable record of the European intellectual community of his time.

lost for many years they were re-discovered in a solicitor's office in (I think) Chester during the war, and it was decided, by the solicitor I think, that they had been deposited there by the Delamere family—i.e. the Booths of Booth's Rising—in the last century.[1] The present Lord Delamere lives in Rhodesia but he is agreed to be the owner. He allowed Turnbull to use them, and Turnbull kept them in his house.[2] There are about six crates of them. I last saw them in the house in Prestatyn, N. Wales, to which Turnbull had retired. I have transcripts of some of them, but only such as interested me at the time. Turnbull is now dead, but G. R. Armytage, his successor as Professor of Education at Sheffield,[3] got hold of the papers and said that he was going to publish the *Ephemerides*, which are a mine of information about Hartlib's contacts. I urged the Clarendon Press to undertake this but between the dilatory bureaucracy of the Press and the uncertainties of Armytage, the project seems to have lapsed. But my excellent Kenya-Indian friend Pyranali Rattansi[4] (do you know him?) wrote to me recently that a colleague of his at Leeds[5] was now editing the *Ephemerides*. Rattansi is at the moment in Kenya and his letter is at Oxford; but when I am back in Oxford—to which I may be returning *via* China (I have just been invited there for next Saturday: I am not sure if I can possibly make such a detour at such notice. But it is tempting!)[6]—I will look

[1]   The rebellion, a prelude to the restoration of the Stuart monarchy, led by Sir George Booth in 1659. The papers were in fact found in 1933.

[2]   Lord Delamere actually lived in Kenya. George Turnbull (1879–1961), Professor of Education at Sheffield University 1922–54, pioneered the study of Hartlib, on whom T-R wrote an essay which appeared in *Encounter* in February 1960 and reappeared as 'Three Foreigners: The Philosophers of the Puritan Revolution' in *Religion, the Reformation and Social Change*.

[3]   Correctly, Harry Green Armytage (1915–98), Professor of Education at Sheffield 1954–82, author of *A Social History of Engineering* (1961), a history of English utopianism, and other works.

[4]   'Piyo' Rattansi, Professor of the History and Philosophy of Science at University College London, from 1996.

[5]   Charles Webster, Fellow of Corpus Christi College, Oxford, and Reader in the History of Medicine (1972–88) and Fellow of All Souls 1988–2004, edited, not the *Ephemerides*, but extracts from Hartlib's writings on education (*Samuel Hartlib and the Advancement of Learning*, 1970). Hartlib is a central figure in Webster's *The Great Instauration* (1975).

[6]   He did go, as part of a group sent by the Society for Anglo-Chinese Understanding, taking the place of Maurice Bowra, who had been advised by his doctor not to undertake such a strenuous trip.

into the matter and let you know. Turnbull had made an index to the *Ephemerides*; so if there is any reference to Dillingham, it should be easy to trace it.[1]

Nothing in Christopher's book now surprises me.[2] I am totally disillusioned by it and ask myself seriously what has happened to him. I believe he has simply galloped through a mass of often worthless secondary sources picking out whatever snippets—unverified and often misquoted—seem to the eye of faith to support his predetermined conclusions. Does this seem too strong? It is not. I can document it again and again. I have just read through the whole of Ralegh's *History of the World* and Camden's *Annals*, and I find Christopher's generalisations totally irresponsible. Also he misquotes wildly. Look, for instance, at the reference given in note 17 on p. 211 and see how it compares to Christopher's quotation. I have now reached, in respect of him, the same position I long ago reached in respect of Stone:[3] I can believe nothing that he says on trust. And yet what a good book *Economic Problems of the Church* is![4]

I get more and more sceptical, I'm afraid, about the academic world in general and about the *possibility* of intellectual honesty. I have just—thanks to the first photostat which you procured for me—completed a brief study of a historiographical problem involving George Buchanan.[5] My conclusion is that Buchanan *knew* that his views about the ancient Scottish constitution were all rubbish by 1572, and that, thereafter, he drew in his horns and attenuated his references to it; and yet, since he was determined to

---

[1]   Valerie Pearl was interested in the Civil War journalist John Dillingham's relations with Oliver Cromwell's cousin Oliver St John.
[2]   T-R subjected the volume of Christopher Hill's Ford Lectures, *Intellectual Origins of the English Revolution* (1965), to a critical review in the journal *History and Theory*.
[3]   Lawrence Stone (1919–99) had been an undergraduate pupil of T-R's at Christ Church, and then a don at Wadham, before leaving for Princeton where he was Dodge Professor of History 1963–90. In the early 1950s there had been an acrimonious public exchange between the two men in the pages of the *Economic History Review*, and thereafter they were regarded as enemies.
[4]   Hill's *Economic Problems of the Church* had been published in 1956.
[5]   George Buchanan (1506–82), scholar, poet, and political theorist, was tutor to King James VI of Scotland. Buchanan's account of the ancient Scottish constitution was dissected by T-R in a 1966 article in the *English Historical Review* and in T-R's posthumous *The Invention of Scotland* (2008).

keep to his conclusions, he could not jettison their basis and so he regurgitated the whole sea of rubbish again in 1582. Just when I had finished this, I received a letter from Gertrude Himmelfarb[1] who has written a fascinating article—part of a forthcoming biography—on Bentham's *Panopticon*. Do read it: it is in *Ideas in History: Essays in Honour of Louis Gottschalk* (Duke Univ Press 1963). The article convinces me that the doctrinaires of the bourgeois 'liberal' revolution were no less inhuman than those of the proletarian revolution. In her letter she described the reaction of her Benthamite friends to her article. It is exactly the same as I presume Buchanan's to have been: they have altered their texts to meet the shock of the facts, but have left the conclusions untouched. Perhaps we all do this. As Miss Himmelfarb says 'it's a familiar enough experience—I know you have encountered it again and again—and yet it never ceases to surprise and shock'. It surprises and shocks me in Christopher's book.

I didn't greatly enjoy Vienna. The congress was much too large to be of any value, though of course one meets friends; but to reach every friend one runs the gauntlet of a dozen bores. I enjoyed meeting Fritz Fischer of Hamburg, who has convulsed the German Establishment by blowing up the official orthodoxy about 1914.[2] His stories of German academic life leave anything we can describe nowhere. Apparently there are about five old men    Gerhard Ritter,[3] Percy Schramm,[4] etc—who have absolute control over all historical teaching and can, in effect, block any appointment anywhere. No one can be appointed to the humblest position in any

---

[1]    Gertrude Himmelfarb Kristol (b. 1922), an American historian of Victorian virtues and ideas. Her letter of 25 August 1965 described how 'respectable "liberal" historians and philosophers' had responded to her essay: 'they were properly appalled by the Panopticon, impressed by its importance in Bentham's life and thought, and yet entirely unwilling to amend their conventional view of Bentham, Benthamism, or "Benthamite reforms".'

[2]    Fritz Fischer (1908–99) argued in *Griff nach der Weltmacht: Die Kriegzielpolitik des kaiserlichen Deutschland 1914–1918* (1961: published in English as *Germany's Aims in the First World War*) that Germany had deliberately instigated a European war in 1914 in an attempt to become a world power.

[3]    Gerhard Ritter (1888–1967), Professor of History at Freiburg 1925–56, was a conservative and monarchist who issued furious rebuttals of Fischer's book.

[4]    The medievalist Percy Schramm (1894–1970), Professor of History at Göttingen 1929–63, was official wartime historian of the Wehrmacht and wrote a contentious introduction to a German edition of Hitler's *Table-Talk*.

university except by a 2/3 majority of the whole Faculty—i.e. of all established teachers in *all* subjects—so of course the non-experts simply bow to the authority of the established oracles. I suppose Powicke *nearly* attained that position with us: nearly but not quite. There are times when I thank God for the Oxford and Cambridge college system.

There was one enjoyable episode at the congress. Do you know about Robert Peters?[1] He is a roving imposter—a twice-defrocked parson who has been in gaol in England for bigamy, in Canada for gross moral turpitude, and who awards himself bogus degrees in order to obtain academic appointments. He evidently has a psychological craving for academic and clerical status and functions. He even (on the strength of the usual forged documents and plausible tales) got into Oxford, to Magdalen, a few years ago; but he was unwise enough to enlist my aid against the bishop of Oxford who, he said, was persecuting him; and so I started investigations which led to his precipitate flight via Dublin to Canada. Well, at Vienna I was dozing through a series of grave statements about heresy in the 17th century, when I suddenly heard the French president of the session call on 'M. le professeur Peters de l'Université de Manchester', and there, sure enough, I saw my old friend, seeking to attract the notice of possible patrons by making a learned 'intervention'. I'm afraid he was put out by finding me there and fled the next day. But he contrived to get to all the functions, and although he was pretty cautious at the British ambassador's reception—especially when he discovered that the girl to whom he was making doubtless improper advances was my stepdaughter—he was uninhibited at the reception given by the Cardinal Archbishop and offered his services to several obscure Catholic universities in America. I enjoyed writing a grave letter to Ernest Jacob asking how Peters got through the careful mesh which is intended to confine participation to *bona fide* historians. I surprised Jacob in the act of reading my letter.

---

[1]  T-R first encountered the fraudster Robert Peters, né Parkins (b. 1918), in 1958, and kept a dossier on him, which was compiled from accounts supplied by correspondents around the world. Peters's activities entertained T-R by exposing the gullibility of academic and religious institutions.

His hands were trembling so hard that he couldn't get it back into its envelope. 'It shall be investigated!' he cried. 'It *shall* be investigated!'

I must stop and sleep on the delicate question: shall I, or shall I not, make this sudden wild dash to China?

yours ever<br>Hugh

⸻⸙⸻

*In the mid-1960s Trevor-Roper wrote a long essay on the rampant persecution of witches, the witch-craze of the sixteenth and seventeenth centuries, which he subsequently published as a short book in 1970. At this time he befriended Alan Macfarlane (b. 1941, at Shillong in India), an Oxford graduate student analysing witchcraft prosecutions in Essex during the early modern period. Macfarlane was amazed to receive long letters from the Regius Professor, who encouraged him, gave him dinner, invited him to Chiefswood, corrected his prose, and helped him to find temporary teaching work. Macfarlane was interested in anthropology, in which he would eventually make his career. During their discussions of witchcraft, Trevor-Roper was slow to realize the gulf between their two approaches. At the heart of these was a radically different attitude towards witch-beliefs. As a rationalist, Trevor-Roper regarded them as nonsense; as an anthropologist, Macfarlane treated them with respect. Their relations soured after Trevor-Roper belittled Macfarlane's criticisms of his witch-craze essay as 'those pernickety little arrows of yours which come whizzing out of your piddling little county of Essex', and dismissed the credulities of 'your pig-bound peasants'. He subsequently explained that those remarks had been offered only in a humorous and genial spirit.*

*The following letter (which in passing teases Macfarlane about his birthplace under the Raj) is partly a response to Macfarlane's request for guidance about the submission and examination of doctoral theses.*

## To Alan Macfarlane, 22 January 1967

8 St Aldates Oxford

My dear Alan

Thank you very much for your letter. I am so glad that your thesis is finished. I agree with you and Francis Hutchinson about witchcraft—in fact

I nearly used Francis Hutchinson's phrase as an epigraph to my essay, which is also now in proof.[1] It is a depressing subject; and yet if the 'horror' depresses, the 'difficulty' attracts. I am so glad to have tackled it. I hope I have said something new about it. I am sure you have, and I shall be interested to see whether your well-timed thesis has blown up my airy generalisations. I hope not. I assure you that it is no very admirable quality that takes me into these tangled thickets. As Dr Johnson retorted to Boswell, who credited him with 'courage' for going 'sliding in Ch Ch meadow' when he should have been waiting on his tutor in Pembroke College, 'Courage? No sir: stark insensibility'.[2]

You ask how long examiners like to read a thesis. I think that a month is a fair allowance. They are seldom free to read it when it first arrives—theses *tend* to be presented in term—and so they have to wait and find time. Then they generally need to do some checking. Then they have to find a date for *viva* convenient to them both. However, they are usually reasonable people and if you have a particular time-table problem, say so in our submission to the Registry. The Board is thoroughly accustomed to applications, especially by Indians, for 'late submission' (so that they can scribble to the last minute) *and* 'early viva' (so that they can catch an available dhow or catamaran back to Bombay or Madras). This can be very inconvenient—especially when they time it, as they sometimes do, so that the examiners would have to do everything between Christmas and the New Year. However, the Board tries to co-operate, only insisting that its approval of such courses is subject to the convenience of the examiners, whom we never commit to an unreasonable time-table. It is always convenient to the Board if a supervisor suggests examiners. We don't *necessarily* appoint the suggested examiners but we generally do, and suggestions are always a help; so you will probably discuss possible examiners with Keith Thomas.[3]

---

[1]  Francis Hutchinson (1660–1739), Bishop of Down and Connor, wrote: 'As the very nature of the Subject carries both Horror and Difficulty, polite Men, and great Lovers of Ease, will turn away their Thought from it with Disdain' (*Historical Essay Concerning Witchcraft* (1718), p. vii).

[2]  This was Johnson's retort to Boswell's comment: 'That, Sir, was great fortitude of mind.'

[3]  Macfarlane's supervisor was (Sir) Keith Thomas (b. 1933), Fellow of St John's College, Oxford, 1957–86, Professor of Modern History 1986, President of Corpus Christi College 1986–2000. Witchcraft is a major subject of Thomas's *Religion and the Decline of Magic* (1971).

As for 'jargon' the rules—it seems to me—are very simple. First, one must distinguish between 'terms of art' and 'jargon'. At least I make this artificial distinction. 'Terms of art' are agreed, exact definitions, necessary to the discussion of an esoteric subject. The terms you mention ('agnatic', 'affinal', 'matrilinear', 'sibling') are such terms and there is nothing wrong with them at all, or with any other such terms. I simply think (a) that the terms should be 'agreed' between writer and reader explicitly if they are unusual terms, and (b) that they should be respectable, properly constructed, euphonious terms, as simple as possible, not fanciful neologisms or grotesque hybrids. 'Jargon' is (to me) something quite different; the use of pompous *clichés*, or second-hand conglomerations of words stuck together in habitual postures, when it is perfectly possible to use a clean, simple word or phrase. Thus where you or I would naturally say 'enter' or 'go', your Jargonaut, when in full sail, would just as naturally say 'effect an entry' or 'proceed', as if it were better English, and raised his social or professional status to say so. I'm afraid that many writers really do seem to think that this kind of long-windedness is necessary to their status, just as ratcatchers now, in our status-bound society, call themselves 'rodent operatives' and dentists 'dental surgeons', etc. etc.—and graduates 'postgraduates': a revolting word which I refuse even to use, but which I have tried in vain to exclude from the vocabulary of the university.

In 'jargon' I also include metaphors which are not *sensed* as metaphors: i.e. metaphors which are so dulled by use that they create no vivid comparable image but only elongate the phrase. I make it a rule never to use a metaphor unless, with my mind's eye, I *see* the action or object from which I draw the image. I have just seen the Jargonauts, sailing in the good ship Jargo, which however, for them, has a certain florid Hindu *décor* and tramples down the waves like its kindred vessel the Juggernaut, and uttering horrible, polysyllabical, prosy meaningless noises as they plough through the inky Black Sea towards the Gold Fleece of journalistic success. What is the point of a metaphor if it is not really a metaphor at all—if it creates no image in the mind of the reader (because there has been none in the mind of the writer), but is merely a means of taking longer to say something? It is for this reason that I hate mixed metaphors. A mixed metaphor is *proof* that the writer has not seen the images; for if he had, the two images would have cancelled each other out in absurdity. For instance, if I were to say that some scholar of whom my opinion was low (I fear there are some) was a poor fish, not worth powder and shot, it would be self-evident that I had not seen him as a fish at all: the phrase would have been, to me, mere jargon.

Why do I feel so strongly, indeed passionately about this? Even as I write, I feel myself to be somewhat absurd. But I have my reasons. It is not merely that the English language—all language—is to me something beautiful which deserves to be treated well: it is also a moral question. Clear language is the expression of clear thought and muddy language is the slime which obscures thought, concealing the slovenliness, the crookedness of slovenly, crooked minds and excusing the indolence of indolent minds. Indeed, it can be worse than that: it can excuse cruelty, vice, crime, anything. All the great crimes of our time have been palliated, perhaps made possible by jargon. The use of phrases like 'liquidate' by the Bolsheviks, or 'pass on', or 'send to the East' by the Nazis, instead of 'kill', 'send to the gas chambers', made it possible for a whole bureaucracy to organise and carry out mass murder without even admitting to themselves what they were doing. Slipshod language, opaque meaningless metaphors, not only excuse the mind from the rigours of thought, they protect the conscience from the sense of responsibility. I feel morally revolted by totalitarian (or other) double-talk—that is what really maddened me in China—and since double-talk is impossible if language is used exactly and clearly, this is to me a compelling reason for insisting on exact, clear language.

And yet, I do not want language to be purely dry, neuter, antiseptic. It is too noble a thing for that. It is capable of warmth, light, subtlety, power. I want it to realise these capacities. But even in realising them, it must not slip into jargon. Fortunately, the safeguards are already there. Thanks to metaphors, images, language can move in more than one dimension, and living metaphors, since they reinforce and vivify the intended meaning, cannot by definition obscure it. Only dead metaphors can do that. They are the unfailing resource of cant and hypocrisy.

Do you doubt my comforting equation? Then try reading some 17th century sermons, preferably Scotch. They never let one down. Try the letters of Samuel Rutherford.[1] There is a metaphor in every sentence, and every one is stone-dead. He never draws his images from the peel-tower or the yew tree, the oatmeal or the salt beef, the gannet or the grouse: it is always from the fish-pools of Hebron, the cedar and the cypress, the gourd and the hyssop, the flamingo and the quail. And the whole work, of which edition after edition seemed edifying to generation after generation of your compatriots, is nothing but nauseating cant from beginning to end.

If, as an anthropologist, you are faced with 'whole sentences which appear to mean nothing', don't despair; they probably do mean nothing and can therefore be ignored. Life is short, and those who will not take the trouble to write clearly cannot properly expect to be read.

Do please call on me. Tuesday is a bad day for entertaining you, as it is our servantless day, and Xandra hates cooking; also it is the day when we have a 'business lunch' at Oriel and guests aren't allowed. But I would give you a very dull dinner in college to show you what you have escaped. Otherwise take a chance and telephone me: I am likely to be in Oxford on Tuesdays.

yours ever

Hugh Trevor-Roper

P.S. Have you ever read George Orwell's essay 'Politics and the English Language' which is published in his volume of essays *Shooting an Elephant and Other Essays*? It says everything that I believe on this subject.

---

[1]  Samuel Rutherford (1600?–61), 'one of the most perfervid of Scotsmen', as the *Dictionary of National Biography* called him, Church of Scotland minister and militant theorist of the Scottish Covenanters, author of *Lex, Rex, or The Law and the Prince* (1644), a vindication of the armed resistance to Charles I. He was Professor of Divinity at St Andrews from 1639 until the Restoration in 1660, when he was deprived of his offices and put under house arrest, and *Lex, Rex* was burnt.

*(Dame) Frances Yates (1899–1981), Reader in the History of the Renaissance at the War-*
*burg Institute 1956–67, published* The Valois Tapestries *in 1959 and* Giordano Bruno
and the Hermetic Tradition *in 1964. To read the latter book, Trevor-Roper declared in*
*a review in the* New Statesman, *was to begin 'an intellectual adventure'. At the time of*
*the book's publication, Frances Yates's name was barely known. Already 65 years old, she*
*emerged diffidently from the relative obscurity of the Warburg Institute, with which she*
*had been associated since the war. She was unmarried, and lived quietly in Surrey with her*
*sister. Her homely appearance belied her intellectual power. 'She was so liberal in her com-*
*munication, so eager and friendly in discussion, and spoke with such open charm, and*
*with such a gleam in her eye,' Trevor-Roper wrote after her death in 1981, 'that I often saw*
*her not as the formidably erudite scholar which she was, but as a benevolent, matronly*
*lady, over-generous in her distribution, in a village sweet-shop.' He was one of her earliest*
*and most steadfast supporters. Some thought his enthusiasm for her work eccentric; others*
*that it did him credit. In the following letter he urges her to employ the services of his own*
*literary agent, A. D. Peters.*

## To Frances Yates, 2 November 1967

History Faculty Library

Dear Miss Yates

I am so glad you enjoyed the J. Walter Thompson seminar,[1] in spite of the
preliminary muddles. So did I. And I specially enjoyed your paper. But
then I enjoy everything you write: I regard you as one of the few people
who really make the complexity of the intellectual climate of the past
vivid and intelligible. I would like to see the Collected Works of Frances
Yates in every library.

I have already spoken to Margaret Stephens at A. D. Peters (Peters himself is in America at present). I have explained your position and your
eminence, and Miss Stephens is delighted, and I am sure you will, at the
same time, both gain financially and shed a lot of trouble. I used to deal
directly with Macmillan. Then I put myself in the hands of Peters. My relations with Macmillan remain excellent, and I am spared all bargaining.

---

[1]    On magic (held on 29 October in London).

I think—indeed, am sure—that everything you write is important, and anthologising publishers and reprint companies will certainly want to use it. Such companies, especially in America, reckon that authors are a vain class who are so glad to be in print that they will grant the right to reprint with heedless delight. But these companies operate for profit, and as the labourer is worthy of his hire, they should (and will) pay. Whenever I get any such request, I just send it to Peters. He knows what to ask.

I will certainly visit you at your institute—after due warning given. It was a great pleasure to meet you and I hope we shall meet again soon.

> yours sincerely
> Hugh Trevor-Roper

## To Gerald Brenan, 11 March 1968

8 St Aldates, Oxford

My dear Gerald

Your sad news, alas, was not unexpected after your last letter.[1] I felt very unsympathetic, not writing to you about it before; but I followed your instructions. I'm afraid you have had a very grim time and will feel very isolated now; but I hope that you are better and that you have friends to see and books to read (and write) to distract and stimulate you. I hope that one day I may visit you again—I always intend to return to Spain—but meanwhile can I send you a book? It is a book which was published three years ago, but possibly you have not yet read it: Frances Yates' *Giordano Bruno*. It is one of the books—I think it is *the* book—which has

---

[1]  Brenan's wife, the American poet and novelist Gamel Woolsey (1895–1968), had recently died of cancer.

most excited me in the last few years. It opens a new window on the whole intellectual history of the 16th century. If you don't know it, do tell me, and I will post it to you: I feel sure that you would be as interested in it as I was, and am. In fact, I don't think that I could have written my essay on witches if I had not read—irrelevant though it seems—Miss Yates on Giordano Bruno.[1]

Do you know her other work? She is a wonderful woman. She has written nothing which is not fascinating, and she writes on such different subjects (but always within the field of intellectual history). She is one of the Warburg Institute scholars, who knows all about the symbolism of the Renaissance and can extract hidden, but convincing significance from arcane emblems. She wrote a marvellous study of the Valois Tapestries re-creating, from their symbolism, 'a lost moment of history', an attempt, which failed, by Catherine de Medicis and William of Orange to settle the Netherlands on an 'Erasmian' basis. She has also written on Paolo Sarpi[2] and on John Florio[3] and—another wonderful work—on the French academies of the 16th century, the world of Baïf and Ronsard[4] and *Love's Labours Lost*. Now she works mainly on neo-platonism and that 'hermetic core of Renaissance platonism' out of which—as she more than anyone else has shown—the new science of the 17th century was born. A few months ago I heard her read a wonderful paper on John Dee, which brings out her argument with perfect clarity. Of course she is not alone in bringing out these ideas—in fact I first got interested in the subject by reading (on the recommendation of Bernard Berenson) a German book

---

[1]  T-R's article 'Frances Yates, Historian', in *The Listener* (18 January 1973) begins: 'If I were asked whom, among living English historians, I most admire, I should have no difficulty in answering the question. There are many historians whose work I would always read for their insight, their power, their technical virtuosity or their style. But Frances Yates has a gift which transcends all these. It is the power not merely to answer old problems but to discover new, not merely to fill in details, but to reveal a new dimension which alters the whole context.'

[2]  Paolo Sarpi (1552–1623), Venetian theologian, anti-papal pamphleteer, and historian of the Council of Trent, who was described by Sir Henry Wotton as 'a true Protestant in a monk's habit'.

[3]  The linguist and lexicographer John Florio (1553–1625) was Giordano Bruno's friend, and son of a Franciscan friar who became pastor of the Italian Protestants in London.

[4]  The poets Jean-Antoine de Baïf (1532–99) and Pierre de Ronsard (1524–85).

by Moritz Carrière, written a century ago—but she does it better than anyone else.[1]

Like you, I love the 4$^{th}$ and 5$^{th}$ centuries AD, and especially St Augustine (I have read his *Confessions* three times) and St Jerome. St Jerome's letters are wonderfully comic: I particularly like the one in which he urges one of his devout ladies to use her squealing infant to convert her obstinate old pagan father: 'cum avum viderit, in pectus eius transiliat, e collo pendeat, nolenti *alleluia* decantet';[2] and all those scenes of Roman high life: great ladies with their trains of eunuchs and tame, avaricious, dependent clergy. Also St Jerome's *gourmandise* which struggles with his Puritanism, his love of literature which struggles with his hatred of music, etc. It is very odd that Erasmus liked him. But I have not read the Vulgate—perhaps I must.

I think that Peter Brown's book on St Augustine is excellent.[3] I selected it as my book of last year for the *Sunday Times* and I am trying to get a literary prize for it from the Arts Council. It is—apart from being scholarly and intelligent—so well written; and so few scholars even try to write well in England now. (In America, of course, they are worse).

I shall venture to defend Gibbon to you. I don't find him smug. It seems to me that, behind the genuine belief in progress (far less smug than in, say, Macaulay), there is always, in Gibbon, a subtlety, a sensitivity, occasionally a melancholy, which is totally absent from (say) Voltaire. I suppose I have, by now, got so used to the formal style that I hardly notice it, and I enjoy all the more the urbanity, the irony, the humanity, which underlies it. Also I love the marvellous precision of his language, the exact choice of words in order to convey such delicate shades and ambiguities

---

[1]  Moritz Carrière (1817–95), a professor at the University of Munich, wrote an essay on Oliver Cromwell which expressed his own political credo in favour of German unification. Berenson admired his *Aesthetik* (1859) and *Die Kunst im Zusammenhang der Kulturentwicklung and der Ideale der Menschheit* (1877).

[2]  From letter 60 of Jerome: 'when he sees his grandfather, let him jump into his lap, hang on his neck, and sing *Alleluia* into his unwilling ear.'

[3]  Peter Brown (b. 1935) had been acclaimed for his first book, *Augustine of Hippo* (1967). In the *Sunday Times* of 3 December 1967 T-R had written: 'Mr Brown is an impeccable scholar but also a vivid biographer and a delightful writer'. He added that the book brought to life 'a personality of infinite complexity who dominated a dramatic era in the last agony of the Western Roman Empire'.

of meaning. I think I would rather be thought to write like Gibbon than any other writer of English (because nobody could write like Sir Thomas Browne or Doughty[1]); but then I recall a remark made to me, in 1940, by Frank Pakenham. He said, 'I have been reading your book on Archbishop Laud. It reminded me of Gibbon...' and then, just as I was inwardly purring at this undeserved compliment, 'I mean, it made my gorge rise!'

I haven't read Schonfield's *Jesus as Messiah*.[2] I will do so. I admire Guignebert;[3] but Loisy[4] has been destroyed for me by a *devastating* biography of him—very scholarly and exact—by a disillusioned disciple, which I read in Paris a few years ago.[5] It *proves* that Loisy was a most disreputable hypocrite, and I can never respect him again. I'm afraid that my respect for Renan[6] has shrunk too, after reading some of his purely social opinions. Do you know the writings of Gershom Scholem, of Jerusalem?[7]

[1]    Charles Montagu [C. M.] Doughty (1843–1926), poet, writer, and traveller. T-R greatly admired the inventive prose of Doughty's two-volume *Travels in Arabia Deserta* (1882). In a long appreciation of Doughty in his *Wartime Journals*, T-R had written, 'Doughty is neither baroque (his personality was too complete) nor classical (his style is too elaborate); he is unique, a law unto himself in literature.'

[2]    Hugh Schonfield (1901–88) was a Hebrew Christian, campaigner for world peace, and prolific historian of the early Christian religion and church. He published a historical biography of Jesus in 1939. The quest for the historical Jesus was one of many subjects outside T-R's chief areas of study in which he engaged in controversy.

[3]    Charles Guignebert (1867–1939), Professor of the History of Christianity at the Sorbonne from 1919, was a pupil of Ernest Renan and a follower of Alfred Loisy (see the next note). He wrote the first French biography of Jesus Christ from a strict historical standpoint (published in 1933). His other books included *Modernisme et tradition catholique en France* (1907) and *Le Monde juif vers le temps de Jésus* (1935).

[4]    Alfred Loisy (1857–1940) was a French Catholic priest and theologian who challenged the historical value of the Old and New Testaments. Five of his books were placed on the Index in 1903 and he was excommunicated in 1908. Professor of Church History at the Collège de France 1909–32.

[5]    *Alfred Loisy: sa vie, son œuvre* by Albert Houtin (1867–1926) and Félix Sartiaux (1876–1944), which was not published until 1960, depicted its subject as a faithless priest who remained in the Church from ambition rather than sincerity.

[6]    The French philosopher, philologist, and orientalist Ernest Renan (1823–92), an unfrocked seminarist who was briefly Professor of Hebrew at the Collège de France (1861–2), published his controversial *Vie de Jésus* in 1863. His robust views on national identity were unpalatable to 20th-century opinion.

[7]    Gershom (Gerhard) Scholem (1897–1982) was born in Berlin, but migrated to Palestine, where he was Professor of Jewish Mysticism at the Hebrew University of Jerusalem, 1933–65. He was an intimate friend of Walter Benjamin, and an influence on Borges, Derrida, and Eco: Jürgen Habermas spoke at his funeral. T-R may have encountered him through Scholem's opposition to the execution of Eichmann and as a result of their shared objections to Hannah Arendt's book *Eichmann in Jerusalem* (1963).

He writes about Jewish intellectual traditions—e.g. Messianism—and I have greatly enjoyed his works. The foundation of the state of Israel may have convulsed the Middle East but it has certainly done a lot for Christian scholarship: the Jews are no longer either assimilated as Christians or stuck in the Jewish ghetto: they have contrived, thanks to Israeli national consciousness, to look, with gentile objectivity, at their Jewish selves.

You are far too flattering about my book *Religion, the Reformation and Social Change*: but I love flattery (I suppose all writers do) and flattery from you is indeed intoxicating. Ever since I read *The Spanish Labyrinth*, I have looked upon you as my ideal historian—you *see* the past in the present, and the present in the past, imaginatively, and yet with corrective scholarship, and you express it in perfect prose—and I would rather write for you than anyone else. But I share one weakness with you. I too 'find so many people and periods interest me that I am unable to choose, but go continually from one thing to another'. I used, in my *marxisant* phase, to think I was interested in economic history; but then I realised that the only thing which raises humanity above the other animals, and makes its history worth studying, is its independence of mere conditioning economic, sociological or ecological facts: i.e. intellectual history, literature, philosophy. For this reason I am glad now that I was trained as a classical scholar: I find more pleasure in good literature than in dull (even if true) history!

I meant to tell you about Formosa, but it is late, and I will spare you.[1] In a fortnight I am supposed to be going to America, but I think that I shall run out and go to Europe instead.

Do write again: I love your letters, and I long to hear of you, and from you. Do keep well. I wish I could see you.

yours ever<br>
Hugh

---

[1] In 1967 T-R had accepted an invitation to visit Formosa (Taiwan), which impressed him as 'confident and prosperous, investing in itself both materially and spiritually'.

*In the early spring of 1968 Trevor-Roper spent a fortnight walking in Greece. In Athens, he caught an early morning bus for an eight-hour journey to reach the rugged and mountainous region of Epirus, in the north-west of the country bordering Albania, with a coastline on the Ionian Sea. He spent the next week walking, often rising early and returning to his room aching and weary.*

## To James Howard-Johnston, 4 April 1968

Hotel Palladion, Ioannina, Greece

My dear James

I hope you enjoyed Stubel am Arlberg. I wish you were here. The Greek country, as you know, is beautiful, inexpressibly beautiful, but Greek towns are squalid and depressing; so I would like company. But alas, how few of my friends share my tastes: I don't think I can imagine any, of those whose conversation I enjoy, enjoying my company on these occasions, any more than I would enjoy Portofino with Isaiah Berlin or sliding down uniform slopes of inert, lifeless snow with you (and an attendant party). So I must not complain, but instead spend my evening, while I dine in an animated Greek restaurant, writing to you.

I spent four days with the Pawsons in Athens. They were full of enquiries for you. Most of the time I spent in the Gennadeion Library, but we also went, on Sunday, to Corinth (which I have somehow hitherto skipped) and climbed the Acrocorinth. It was a marvellous day: not very clear, but cloudless; the air on top fresh and cool; and one looked down the Nemean valley towards Mycenae, and along the Gulf of Corinth, and the white snow-bound tops of Cyllene on one side of the gulf and Parnassus on the other rode upon the haze.

Then, on Tuesday, I left for Epirus: a part of Greece which I don't know at all. I wanted to visit Arta, as the capital of the medieval despotate; and Yannina, as the capital of that wonderful old rogue Ali Pasha, the philhellenic Albanian who ruled over most of Albania and most of Greece, as an almost independent prince, and was visited by Byron (isn't it odd that *both* the great independent pashas of that time, Ali Pasha in Greece and

Mehemet Ali in Egypt, were Albanians—as were the great Turkish Grand Viziers, the Köprülü dynasty in the 17th century?); and Dodona, which has always fascinated me—it is partly the name, I think, and partly the mystery of those three cryptic lines in Homer

Ζεῦ ἄνα, Δωδωναῖε, Πελασγικέ, τηλόθι ναίων,
Δωδώνης μεδέων δυσχειμέρου, ἔνθα τε Σέλλοι
σοὶ ναίουσ' ὑποφῆται, ἀνιπτίποδες, χαμαιεῦναι[1]

Anyway, I have now visited them all, not without dust and heat. Only one day have I risen later than 5.0 a.m., and today I feel totally incapable, by sheer cramp, fatigue, exhaustion, of doing anything further. The final touch was given by my expedition to Dodona, which was today.

It began at 5.0, when that infallible internal clock, whose working you had an opportunity to admire in Ierakio, woke me up to catch the bus to Tyria, from which I was to disembark at a certain point and walk to Dodona. I arrived at Dodona before the amphitheatre—a great amphitheatre, like that of Epidaurus, built by King Pyrrhus—was open; so I decided to fill in the time by climbing Mount Tomaros, a huge, snow-clad mountain which forms the background to the stage of the amphitheatre. I climbed up to the snow-line: a hard, but a wonderful climb. How I love the solitude of mountains, when not deadened by lifeless snow: the solitude and the silence, that silence of Nature which is broken only by slender, occasional sounds: the noise of beasts, or their bells; the Gregorian chant of distant donkeys, the swish of a fugitive lizard, the rock-cuckoo and the humble bee! The sweat burnt off me in the sun as I walked, but I noticed nothing of it at the time. Dodona, like all Greek oracles, is in a heavenly place. There is an old, disused church there, surrounded by a grove of ilex trees, some of them huge and gnarled, like Sir Walter Scott's oaks at Chiefswood: the descendants, I suppose, of the old oracular Pelasgian oak-trees—for I presume that they were really ilex. When I returned to the village, I sat for a little at the rustic café, drinking

[1] 'O Zeus above, Dodonian, Pelasgian Zeus, living far away and ruling over wintry Dodona, where your prophets the Selli live, with unwashed feet and sleeping on the ground.' *Iliad* 16.234.

wine to restore my strength (the wine of this area is fizzy and sweet but very drinkable), and then I set out to my cross-roads—a long and weary up-hill climb—to pick up the bus from Tyria which should pass, I had been told, at 1.0 p.m.

I waited: it did not pass. At 2.30 I began to feel sick and faint. Was it sunstroke? I asked myself. I looked around: there was no leaf of cover beneath the cloudless sky. Or was it merely inanition, for of course I had had no time for breakfast? But where would I find, on that scorched and empty hillside, so much as a locust or a drop of wild honey to sustain me? I draped my jersey over my head, as protection from the sun, and waited helplessly. Finally, at about 3.0, a car passed, and I stopped it. It was an American couple, and they took me to the main road, where I found a bus to Yannina. I can now barely move, but I do not mind. Tomorrow, I shall bob up, though perhaps not at 5 a.m., and I feel that, by this visit to Dodona, my journey has been justified.

Where do I go now? I do not know. Last night I had two dreams. In one, I dreamed that I had rashly confessed, *inter pocula*,[1] to someone—perhaps you—that for the past 30 years I had been a Russian agent, and I was much exercised about how to prevent this fact from coming out (you will recognise one source of this dream; another, I suspect, was *Silas Marner*, which accompanies me as my bedside book: I am greatly enjoying it). The second dream has a good precedent: I dreamed that a man came and said to me, come over to us in Macedonia.[2] Almost I had decided to do it: to walk over Pindus and to visit Kastoriá, Kosaini, Siatista. But tonight I have thought better of such a mad project. Pindus is deep in snow; time is short; I am already crippled with walking; and anyway, it is a mistake to overcrowd experience: I am content, now, with Epirus. So I shall go back, one way or another, to Athens; and if I can resist the blandishments of the Pawsons, who want me to stay and accompany them to the celebrations at Missolonghi next week-end—the anniversary alike of the famous

---

[1] 'In my cups'.
[2] Acts 16: 9: 'And a vision appeared to Paul in the night. There stood a man of Macedonia, and prayed him, saying, Come over unto Macedonia, and help us.'

'Exodus of Missolonghi' and of the death of Byron[1]—I shall return, in the course of the week, to Chiefswood.

And you, where are you? At Chiefswood? Alas I fear not. At Oxford? If so, may I exploit you? Would you call at the History Faculty Library (or telephone, 43395) and ask them to forward mail to Chiefswood, to which I shall try to fly direct? And if you should see the Warden of All Souls, perhaps you would give him two messages, of no importance, except to twist the old wretch's tail.

First, you might suggest that I am about to write a letter to the *Times Lit. Suppl.* which, *with great economy of language* (emphasise this point, maliciously), will surgically destroy *both* him *and* Mark Lane.[2] I'm not sure that I shall really do this. The temptation is strong and the words chatter behind my teeth, crying to be released; but like Hitler, I don't like *Zweifrontenkrieg*,[3] and I am already rather deeply engaged with Rolf Hochhuth (I am asking Randolph Churchill if the Churchill Fund will guarantee my costs if I go into an action which might escalate hugely).[4] But there is no harm in thinking aloud in the Warden's ear.

---

[1]  Byron died on 19 April 1824. Two years later the planned escape of the besieged inhabitants of Missolonghi (now Messalonghi) was betrayed by a spy, and the Greek fugitives were massacred by the Turks. Byron died in the town and is commemorated by a cenotaph there.

[2]  In November 1963 T-R had dined with Mark Lane (b. 1927), a New York lawyer whose request to represent Oswald's interests before the Warren Commission had been denied. Lane subsequently published a close critique of the Warren Report entitled *Rush to Judgment* (1966), to which T-R contributed an introduction. But Lane's claim in a *Playboy* interview that T-R had received private encouragement from Robert Kennedy, the President's brother, had irritated him. This story, which originated in indiscreet and muddled remarks by Xandra, was untrue; but T-R could not expose the *canard* without making her seem ridiculous.

[3]  'War on two fronts'.

[4]  The case arose from the aborted attempt by Kenneth Tynan (1927–80) to mount a play *Soldiers*, by the German dramatist Rolf Hochhuth (b. 1931), at the National Theatre. Hochhuth's script revived a mischievous tale, circulated by both Goebbels and Stalin, that Winston Churchill had been responsible for the death of the Polish leader General Władysław Sikorski in an aircraft crash at Gibraltar in 1943. During the course of exchanges in the correspondence pages of *Der Spiegel*, Hochhuth alleged that T-R had opposed *Soldiers* under orders from the British Secret Service, had chosen to be 'a patriot rather than a scholar', had 'piled falsehood upon falsehood' on the instructions of his Whitehall masters, and would doubtless be rewarded with a knighthood for having 'sacrificed to his country his integrity as a historian'. T-R sued *Der Spiegel*, which eventually paid him £6,000 in damages and costs. He gave this money to a needy graduate student.

Secondly, you might tell him that, once again, I am in bad with his colleague the Cornish doctor, *alias* Dr. A. L. Rowse, who has written a hysterical letter of denunciation to the *New York Review*.[1] Poor old Rowse: I fear he has never really transcended his social origins. That tongue which shoots out with such chameleon agility towards a ducal posterior, never uncoils, in our little republic of letters, except to discharge the hoardings of a parish scold. I have written a grave, Aesopian reply which, I fear, will be oil not on the wound but on the flames. But it is quite useless to try to appease Rowse, as I know by experience: he takes everything for granted and is furious that the soft answer is not more abject in tone, more total in its surrender. Often I think of devastating replies to make to his virulent abuse; but I can never utter them. I think of him as a mental case, that must be pitied and treated gently. But then the olive-branch is no sooner extended than it is snatched from one's hand and swatted in one's face. So—especially since he is in fact a grinding bore and has nothing to say and can't write—in the end I just push him out of mind, till he forces himself back, to some tune, with another outburst.

My more serious battle is on the Hochhuth front. My lawyer tells me that, once engaged, it would be quite impossible to retreat, short of victory; and although the enemy might surrender at once—for he is clear that they cannot win—they might persevere to the end. Hochhuth is a fanatic, and *Der Spiegel* may well hold the view of my colleague A. J. P. Taylor, that all publicity is good publicity; so that I might be forced to prove, in court, not only the libel, which is clear enough, but also that no justification is valid, since, on the facts, Hochhuth has no case. This would mean defending a public cause at my private expense; and as the expense would be huge, I naturally shrink. But I will see what Randolph has replied to my letter.

I must now stop, and creep or stagger back to my hotel. I hope I shall see you soon and that the thesis runs fluently from the pen. Damn theses

---

[1]  See p. 151.

(I have two waiting on my table to read); but they have now become part of the academic rat-race, from which now there is no escape!

Love from

Hugh

⸎

*During the late 1930s and early 1940s the testy historian A. L. Rowse thought of Trevor-Roper as his protégé, but their relations had subsequently deteriorated. A review by Trevor-Roper of a biography of Gibbon in the* New York Review of Books *in December 1967 provoked a letter of objection from Rowse. 'No doubt Trevor-Roper felt that he could have written the book better,' Rowse snapped. 'Then why does he not do it, instead of so much "smart-alec" journalism…? We can all perceive, and enjoy, Trevor-Roper's self-identification with Gibbon. The only difference is that Gibbon wrote* The Decline and Fall. *And, what, pray, has Trevor-Roper to show for it at a comparable age?'*

*'I admire Gibbon and obviously know more about him than Dr Rowse,' replied Trevor-Roper, in a retort published beneath Rowse's tirade, 'but it has never occurred to me to identify myself with him, any more than Dr Rowse (I presume) would identify himself with Shakespeare or Queen Elizabeth; so I shall charitably overlook the good doctor's concluding irrelevancies.'[1]*

*Following their public exchange in the* New York Review of Books, *Trevor-Roper wrote privately to Rowse, to suggest that it might have been better for him to have addressed his letter from 'the Californian institution from which you wrote', rather than 'your summer cottage' at All Souls. This produced a predictable eruption. 'You must know by now how generally detested you have made yourself,' Rowse fulminated. He excoriated Hugh's letter as impertinent, offensive, and incorrect. 'Why are you so nasty to people?'*

---

[1]   *New York Review of Books,* issue dated 25 April 1968 but published earlier.

## To A. L. Rowse, 12 April 1968

Good Friday (dies humilitatis) 1968                                          Oriel

My dear Rowse,

What a genius you have for what the lawyers call, in their specialised language, 'vulgar abuse'! I assumed that you wrote to the NYR from America because you used the writing-paper of a Californian institution;[1] and I thought that it would have been better to leave the letter-head unchanged because, by changing the address to All Souls College, you might—no doubt mistakenly—be interpreted as venting a local grievance. However, now that you are at your real country cottage,[2] I hope that the sweet air of your native county and your own house (which I believe is beautiful) will calm your ruffled spirit.

It is hard work offering you periodical olive-branches, when they are invariably snatched up and swatted in one's face. However, I shall not take the insults too seriously. As for the substance of your letter, I suppose it is true that I am 'naturally obtuse' and 'don't mind'. I have too many close and real friends to mind about distant and imagined detestation.

yours sincerely
Hugh Trevor-Roper

―❧―

*In 1967* The Spectator *had published, under the pseudonym Mercurius Oxoniensis, the first of the letters Trevor-Roper wrote in the manner of the seventeenth-century scholar and author of* Brief Lives, *John Aubrey: a 'brief life' of the Christ Church eccentric R. H. Dundas. Trevor-Roper disclaimed authorship, speculating that, if not a genuine Aubrey, it might have been written by his Christ Church colleague, the novelist J. I. M. Stewart. The*

---

[1]   The Huntingdon Library at Pasadena.
[2]   Rowse had leased Trenarren House, in a sheltered valley overlooking St Austell Bay, since 1953.

*Editor of* The Spectator, *Nigel Lawson, who had become friendly with Trevor-Roper in his undergraduate days at Christ Church in the 1950s, protected his anonymity. Now Trevor-Roper began to circulate to a few confidants his 'transcript' of a document which he claimed to have found in the Bodleian. This fanciful document purported to be another unpublished Aubrey manuscript, a 'brief life' of 'Dr A.L.R. of Old-soules' college'.*

## To Wallace Notestein, 19 June 1968

Savile Club, 69 Brook Street

Dear Wallace

Our greetings to you both, and I hope that you are both well, and that Student Power has not come to Yale. We have a few rumblings here, but I tell my timid friends about the fate of those transient radicals of the 17<sup>th</sup> century, like the Levellers and Harrington's *rota*: as Aubrey wrote, 'upon the unexpected turn upon Gen. Monk's coming in, all those airy models vanished.'[1]

Talking of Aubrey, whom I know you enjoy, I think I should communicate to you a little discovery that I recently made in Bodley. It is a hitherto unknown, or at least unpublished, 'Brief Life' of Aubrey, which has long nestled unobserved among his MSS there. It was evidently designed for a second edition of Wood's *Athenae*, but must have been overlooked. I have made a transcript of it, which I enclose. Don't return it; I have a copy; but if you think that scholars would welcome its publication, perhaps you would send it to the *American Historical Review* or some such learned journal.

Keep well. Xandra joins me in sending our love to you both.

yours ever

Hugh Trevor-Roper

---

[1] The Rota Club, whose meetings Aubrey and Samuel Pepys attended, met in the winter of 1659–60, when the Commonwealth was collapsing, to debate schemes to provide a durable republican government, which had been first propounded in James Harrington's *The Commonwealth of Oceana* (1656).

Copia Vera

## Bodl MS. Aubrey (unnumbered)

Dr. A.L.R. of Old-soules' college (*Mem*: forget not the D$^r$) is a very egregious person. He was born *anno* 1903, in Cornwall, of poore but honest parents, as himself would often boast, at least before the late warre, when 'twas seldom that such came to the university. But that being now common, he haz sophisticated his pedigree, and putts it about that *re vera*[1] he is a bye-blow of a Cornish nobleman; hinting darkly at the Lord St. Levan, at whose castle, St. Michael's Mount (a romancy seat), his mother was once a serving wench. So now, it seems that only one of his parents was poor, and she not honest.

Coming as a poor scholler to Ch: Ch: Oxon, he was at first abashed by the aristocraticall splendour of that place. But the Lord David Cecil, a fellow collegian, taking him by the hand and teaching him the rudiments of gentility, he soon became vastly pleased both with it and with him, at least for a time. For afterwards, his Lordship being advanced to the Companionship of Honour, our Les (who is jealous of publick titles) was mightily miffed and forbore his company; and Ch: Ch: not electing him to a Studentship (but preferring one Myres, the same that was afterwards Bodley's librarian),[2] he has huffed and sulked and took his name off the college books; nor could he be prevailed upon to enter that college, or converse with any in it, for forty years.

In Old-soules' college, of which he was elected fellow, he was at first *in deliciis*. At that time many great men (as His Grace archbishop Lang, my lord marquis of Lothian, my lord viscount Halifax, my Lord Brand, Sir J. Simon, M$^r$ Geoffrey Dawson *et al.*) would come thither often to dine and to machinate over their port. Our Les, having now tasted grandeur, must needs barge in among them and tell them their business (which indeed they needed telling, though not by him); and they, though not heeding him, yet being old men and pleased with academicall freedom,

---

[1] 'In truth'.
[2] The archaeologist Nowell [J. N. L.] Myres (1902–89) was elected a Student of Christ Church in 1928, and was appointed Librarian in 1938. After serving as head of the fruit and vegetables division of the wartime Ministry of Food, he was Bodley's Librarian 1947–65.

would humour him; which he, not having learned their nice language, mistook for docility, and so thought himself an oracle, fit to be a legislator of the nation. *Anno* 1936 he stood as a parliament-man, for a Cornish borough. He was then a hot Labour Party man and preached root and branch doctrines.[1] But the lower sort not relishing these airy notions from gaffer Rowse's queer boy (as they called him), voted rather for the squire; which our doctor has never forgiven them, writing of them opprobriously ever after as 'the idiot people', 'apes' and what not? 'Tis said that during this election the enemy party caused to be printed and dispersed among the electors a rash pamphlet he had writt (but for another auditory) recommending free use of Venus between, if not within, the sexes. This lost him the votes of the godly or Methodist party, which swarm in that county, without gaining the orthodox or prelaticall.

During the great warre of '39 to '45 our doctor did not exert himself but stayed snugly in Old-soules' college, writing and telling all men how rich he was becoming and how familiarly he was used by great persons; which was very taedious and hath emptied many a common-room, then and since.

He is vastly pleased with his own genius, which 'tis dangerous to question, even in jest: *experto crede.*[2] No flattery too crude or gross for unrefined appetites. 'Tis pity to see such folly in a learned man, for he had formerly a little talent, tho' long since evanished. His *Tudor Cornwall* admired by antiquaries. His last solid work *The England of Elizabeth*, 8vo, 1950. Since then a sad decline: slipslop, plagiarisme, etc. His poems…but 'tis best to bury them in silence. Those who have never been admitted to converse with the Muses should not trouble them with their solicitations.

After the warre he thought again of serving his country; but as he had now done with vulgar elections, being inward with duchesses and other great ladies, he fancied himself rather in the upper house, with peers and bishops, than in the commons' chamber with mere knights and burgesses.

---

[1] In Aubrey's time the phrase 'root and branch', meaning fundamentally radical, acquired resonance from the 'Root and Branch Petition', the demand for the abolition (rather than mere reform) of episcopacy which was submitted to the Long Parliament.

[2] 'Believe one who speaks from experience'.

So he writt several long letters to Major Attlee, then Prime Minister, angling for a viscounty or barony. 'Twas in the publick interest, he said, that their lordships should be penetrated by some procreative spirits who could impregnate 'em with philosophy. The Major found these letters vastly diverting and would carry them in his pocket to dinner-parties, to make his friends merry. But he never took the hint, nor any of his successors neither, so the poor doctor is still without a title of honour, which much distresses him.

But the court is the true fountain of honour and there he still had hopes. 'Tis said he had given private lessons to our present Queen, as princess, in Buckingham Palace (*quaere*, how procured?), which must have borne hard on the poor child. Certainly, her Majesty the now Queen Mother took him up, as others of his kind (but this *inter nos*[1]), and her name dropt often from his lips. But when her Majesty that is now came to the throne, she pluckt up her courage and, like her ancestor King James, repudiated her old pedagogue, just as he was glorying immoderately in the new Elizabethan age, and himself its harbinger. *Vide* her Majesty's nipping rebuke on that subject, which she thought it prudent to utter at a safe distance, in Tasmania, among the Antipodes.

Bruised by this fall, the poor doctor now turned to a rustic life. Having by now made a pretty penny by exhibiting himself in the Ladies' Journals, he bought a delicate fair house by the sea in Cornwall and there set up as a squire. It pleased him to insult thus over the peasantry who would not have him as their burgess. And yet methinks he loves that country too, if only the idiot people were purged out of it: for them he cannot abide. In term-time he stayed still at Old-soules' college, scribbling and courting the Fellows: for he had designs on the Wardenship. He also had designs of another kind on the Junior Fellows, and courted them; but they, so farre as 'tis knowne, resisted him *seu venerem seu vota petenti*.[2] So he missed the Wardenship too, the Fellows preferring one Sparrow; whereat the doctor

---

[1] 'Between ourselves'.
[2] 'Whether he sought their love or their votes'.

once again took huff, printed no more *encomia* of the college and its cozy home life (see his epistle to the reader in *The England of Elizabeth*), and thereafter deigned not to speak to any Fellow who, on that occasion, had voted against him.

He has a thin, exile voice, but harsh like a corncrake: no witt nor warmth to soften it; and very shrill when at boasting or abuse (its usual office). But he can purr if stroked and wheedled. In his young days he had a lean hatchet face and a wild black forelock, very ferocious: when he screamed revolution, 'twould make a good subject's backbone curdle. But now that he is plump and pawky and does but cockadoodle about his genius, his ducats and his duchesses, and despise the rest of us as not worthy of him, none minds him.

[Endorsed] To my good friend M^r Antony Wood, of Merton coll., for his *Athenae Oxonienses*, <u>ed. Altera</u>, these.

⸙

By the mid-1960s, Trevor-Roper had discarded the major study of the Civil Wars on which he had begun concerted work in 1957: it survived in drafts, but was never published. In his letters Wallace Notestein, who would have known little if anything of the attempt at the book, urged him onwards. 'I believe that you are on your way to great eminence as an historian,' Notestein predicted in March 1968. In the same letter he identified one of the distractions that prevented Trevor-Roper from devoting sufficient time to books. 'I wish you did not have to spend energy on journalism. I cannot say that I find fault with you. But you cannot ride two horses indefinitely and you may be one of the greatest of English historians.' A few months later Notestein reiterated his hope that Trevor-Roper could devote all his time to history. 'The trouble with controversies is they will take your mind away from history. Historians need leisure and quiet almost as much as poets.' The following letter was Trevor-Roper's response. A few weeks later, Notestein again urged that 'the great book on Cromwell' should be done. It was understandable that Notestein, now 90, should be contemplating futurity (he died during the following year). 'It will be a sin against the gods if you go down to the shades without four or five volumes in which you let yourself go about the whole Cromwellian crowd and the people in London and the country.' He warned: 'I shall haunt you from Hades.'

## To Wallace Notestein, 21 July 1968

Chiefswood, Melrose

My dear Wallace,

Don't worry about poor old Rowse. I have forgotten all about him now. I shall not risk seeing him now till next May; for by now he will be in Cornwall, in that delicate fair house by the sea, living in a dream world of his own; and soon he will be off, lecturing his way from woman's club to woman's club, till he arrives, bubbling with self-importance and bulging with dollars, at Pasadena.[1] What a life! I cannot but admire his stamina, and his mobility. I am so dependent on my books—my own books, with their indexes and marginalia—that I could not live and work in two separate places. I find Oxford and Melrose quite far enough apart. Anyway, I now feel free of him. He boasts, to Denis Mack Smith,[2] that he 'sees to it' that I shall never be invited to America, and I see to it that we do not meet in Oxford. We only met once last term, in a tailor's shop, where I found him, in typically narcissistic posture, admiring himself in a glass. I have never seen him in Bodley, or at any university function. He plays no part in the university at all.

How right you are about the Swedes! They were just as bad in World War II. I regard all Scandinavians as bores, but the Swedes are such *smug* bores. Actually, as bores, I believe the Norwegians pip them to the post; but, though terribly stupid, they are more honest, and nicer, than the Swedes. An American, whom I met in Norway, and with whom I deplored our common fate, said to me, 'there is nothing more boring than a dull Swede,—except a gay Norwegian'. I suppose it is the climate that makes them so gloomy and mad. What can one say for countries whose great cultural figures are, respectively, Ibsen, Strindberg and Kierkegaard? The

---

[1]   Rowse bragged of the money that he made by regular lecture tours of the USA.

[2]   Denis Mack Smith (b. 1920), Fellow of Peterhouse 1947–62, of All Souls 1962–87, and of Wolfson, Oxford, 1987–2000; historian of modern Italy.

Finns, I think, are the maddest of the lot. I have not read their great epic, the Kalevala. I doubt if it is very sparkling or jolly.

I am very touched by your kind remarks. You have more faith in me than I have in myself. I love flattery, but don't believe it! The trouble is, I am too interested in too many things; and I write so slowly, so painfully slowly, that by the time I have written a chapter, I have got interested in something else. And then, there are the delights of idleness: of walking in the country, of scratching the noses of horses, or the backs of pigs; of planting and lifting and cutting trees (I *love* trees); of enjoying—though I have to travel great distances to enjoy it—a mute but protracted marriage of minds with that most enchanting of creatures, the Asiatic water-buffalo. Nor must I omit those other indolent delights of tickling woodlice, or organising snail-races, or tempting the shy, engaging badger into dialogue; or the pleasures of convivial, social life: of slow, monosyllabic conversation, over beer and cheese and pickled onions, in rural inns, or—alternatively—of gay, sparkling dinners in glittering palaces, where (like Rowse) I can listen, with guilty pleasure, to the inane but comforting flattery of jewelled duchesses. And then, perhaps most seductive of all, there is that pleasure of total vacancy.

It is all, I fear, very reprehensible. No doubt I should be proof against such worldly seduction. I ought to sit, night and day, in the Bodleian Library or the Public Record Office, 'with learned dust besprent',[1] like old Prynne[2] in his chambers, wearing an eye-shade over my nose, and munching a periodic dry bun, in order, by my copying of earlier copyists, to earn a place in some future *Dunciad*. Then, no doubt, I would have my immediate reward. I would be cited with respect in my colleagues' footnotes. I would be a Fellow of the British Academy.[3] I would glitter with honorary doctorates—D. Litt. (Boulder, Colorado), D.D. (Wabash); I would be heard, with yawning respect, at learned congresses. I would be

---

[1]  Alexander Pope's *The Dunciad* mocks an antiquary who is 'with learned dust besprent'.
[2]  William Prynne (1600–69), lawyer and antiquary, who produced an unending stream of Puritan and parliamentarian polemic.
[3]  T-R was elected a fellow in 1969.

a Corresponding Member of the Academy of Sciences in Ruanda, or San Salvador...The trouble is, I don't find myself tempted. I can't take the academical honours system (or indeed any other honours system) seriously. I fear I am incorrigible.

No, not quite incorrigible. I do take the advice of my friends seriously. I don't care a hang for reviews in the professional learned journals. I don't even read reviews of my own work—unless they happen to come to me. But for certain people (not all of them academics) I have the greatest respect, and their opinion, their praise or censure, means a great deal to me. You are one of that select band (Gerald Brenan, that incomparable non-academic scholar and ever-fresh writer, is another). Whatever you say, or he says, I take seriously; and your sage advice, so delicately offered, will be followed.

Just after receiving your letter, with that sage advice, I found myself reading the slightly earlier letters of the late Hugo Grotius.[1] (He is my new historical hero, and I am reading my way straight through the seven stout quarto volumes of his correspondence). There I found a splendid letter from Jacques-Auguste de Thou[2] to Grotius, of 15 May 1615, which reminded me (somewhat wryly) of our correspondence. 'There is one thing that grieves me', says the venerable de Thou, 'and that is, that you spend too much of your time in controversy. I beg you to leave that arena, and get on with your great *History*, to which we are all looking forward. I am now old and tired, dispirited by the ingratitude and envy of this degenerate age. I have now stopped writing; but I hand on the torch to those who will continue the work...' To this paternal letter Grotius replies with proper humility. He defends his controversial writings: he has, he says, been fighting the battles of truth. But now he is grateful for his mentor's advice. 'Persuaded by your authority, and yielding to my own inclinations, from

---

[1]  Hugo Grotius (1583–1645), Dutch statesman and scholar, whose motto was *Ruit hora* ('Time is running away'). T-R's lecture on him was published in *From Counter-Reformation to Glorious Revolution*.

[2]  Jacques-Auguste de Thou (1553–1617), French poet, historian, bibliophile, and memoir writer, who conducted extensive correspondence with scholars across Europe.

now on I am resolved to shun all unnecessary controversies. I am going to finish my *History*...'

A fine moral tale, a noble example, I said to myself, as I put your letter into the volume to mark the place. But unfortunately, I must add, my eye moved on to the next letter: a letter which Grotius wrote on the very same day on which he penned these pious phases to de Thou. It is a letter to the Danish preacher Walaeus.[1] 'In spite of the many distractions which distract me', writes the newly reformed philosopher, 'I could not resist the temptation to read Socinus' book *de Jesu Servatore*...When I saw that nobody had answered his rotten arguments, I thought it my duty to enter the fray. In great battles, even a skirmisher is of use...'[2]

I forbear to draw any moral from this story; but at least you will see that I am hard at work, reading. I wish I were writing; but my pen moves so reluctantly: ink is treacle in my nib; but I will, I will.

I am so glad you approve of Rabb. I have not seen his book on Sandys—only two articles; but I hope to read it soon.[3] Sandys is of great interest to me as an intellectual figure—his *Speculum Europae* makes him, in some sense, a precursor of Grotius.[4] A charming and brilliant Italian, Gaetano Cozzi, has done some work on this side of Sandys: I have put him in touch with Rabb, and they are now busily exchanging off-prints.[5] Even if

---

[1]  Antonius Walaeus (1573–1639) was a Dutch (rather than Danish) Calvinist preacher, theologian, and philosopher.

[2]  *De Jesu Christo Servatore*, published in 1594, was the most influential work of the Italian theologian Faustus Socinus (1539–1604), leader of the anti-Trinitarian or Socinian movement, which T-R saw as a precursor of the Enlightenment and which he explored in essays republished in his collections *Historical Essays*; *Religion, the Reformation and Social Change*; and *Catholics, Anglicans and Puritans*.

[3]  T-R was mistaken in supposing that Rabb's biography of Sandys, *Jacobean Gentleman*, had already been published.

[4]  T-R was interested in Sandys's place in the ecumenical movement which strove to reunite Catholicism and Protestantism. *Speculum Europae* was first published in 1605 as *A Relation of the State to Religion*.

[5]  Gaetano Cozzi (1922–2001) was confined to a wheelchair for life after an accident during his military service. He emerged in the 1950s as a distinguished historian of early modern Venice, and in the 1970s became founding Professor of History in the expanding University of Venice.

I don't write much, I feel I have my uses as the lubricant of the Republic of Letters.

Best wishes to you both from Xandra and

yours ever

Hugh Trevor-Roper

—⦿⦿⦿—

*Trevor-Roper was not enamoured of Borders society, but he sometimes submitted to Xandra's pleasure in visiting her friends with great Scottish houses.*

## To James Howard-Johnston, 23 August 1968

Chiefswood, Melrose

My dear James

I long to write to you, but I seldom do. Always, as I sit at my desk, I see in front of me that mound of paper. Those boring letters to answer. Those bills to pay. Those forms to fill in. Those theses to examine. Those books to review. And then, when I have begun to cope with the easiest and least important of these problems, come the interruptions. The telephone. The gardener. The need to fetch a cheese from Melrose. The Sheriff. Two impertinent small boys spotted tickling for trout in the stream, immediately in front of the house. A flock of sheep which have broken into the garden. The Duchess of Argyll.[1] So what do I do?

---

[1]    Mathilda Coster Mortimer (1925–97) had married in 1948 Clemens Heller, Professor of Human Sciences at Paris University, co-founder of the Salzburg Global Seminar and co-founder in 1963 with Fernand Braudel of La Fondation Maison des Sciences de l'Homme, where he succeeded Braudel as Director. In the spring of 1963 the T-Rs had rented the Paris apartment, at 6 rue du Tournon, which Madame Heller had inherited from her grandmother. 'At present our flat is rather convulsed, as the owner (who is really rather dreadful) is here, occupying part of it herself and the whole of it uninhabitable by noise, telephoning, workmen, femmes-de-ménage, secretaries, etc,' T-R reported on 8 February 1963 to James. 'We hope to get the rent, which is high, reduced on account of this, but I am not too optimistic: Fernand Braudel describes her as *très riche—et très avare!*' Having divorced Heller in 1961, she married, in 1963, the 11th Duke of Argyll, and set up as chatelaine at Inveraray Castle. She took an eager delight in the company of the intelligentsia, sent T-R zestful but artless letters, and began publishing articles on political philosophy.

To escape from it all, I saunter out into the woods, idly to tie up wild honeysuckle, or trim a weeping beech, or commune with a tawny owl which has made its nest there and braves the daylight, or watch the roe-deer which trip elegantly past me, or tickle a woodlouse, or an earwig (I love earwigs: primeval creatures, living fossils, like antique servitors in a Greek chorus, or gardeners in Shakespeare's plays—I am thinking of the garden scene in *Richard II*—or old Scotch retainers in Sir Walter Scott). And so the day passes, and I have done nothing. The mound rises. A smell of decomposition issues from the nethermost papers. And still I have not written to you.

What can I tell you? We have been here almost continuously, although I went to Oxford for a week at the beginning of August, to fix the graduate quota, and we have just taken a jaunt to the West. Little by little, I am discovering this strange northern peninsula. It all began with Mummy's *bête noire*, the D. of A. Mummy, as you know, was prepared to suspend her animosity in exchange for a sight of Inveraray, and it happened that the Duchess, who, now that she is a Duchess, reckons on capturing the intellectual world from above, instead of painfully creeping into it from beneath, invited us for two nights for a domestic concert. So we went, via Galloway, and spending the first night at Lochinch, near Stranraer (another socially suitable address). I must confess that I was really rather taken with the Western Highlands. Perhaps I should examine them further. There is something wonderfully seductive (in fine weather) in those placid, mild, romantic lagoons and islands into which, as into a neglected dustbin, we practical Saxons have driven the impractical Celts. But to live there... I must admit that my heart shrinks at the thought, especially after the Inveraray concert, to which the natives came, in kilts and trews, with sandy hair and pink, freckled faces. Their talk was of bullocks.[1] One lady in a blue dress came up to me: 'Are you *Hugh* Trevor-Roper?' she asked. Yes, I replied, my heart sinking as I awaited the unctuous litany of

---

[1]  'His talk is of bullocks.' Johnson's put-down of his old friend John Taylor, a country clergyman.

insufficiently sophisticated praise for the less valued of my works. Then she said, 'I once bought half a horse from you'.

I wonder when you will come here. We will try—if he is at home—to lure Steven Runciman over for you. Moses Finley, who is at Edinburgh for the Festival (I discovered this thanks to a letter he had written to the *Scotsman*), is coming to lunch next Wednesday (28 Aug). Sidney Watson is coming to stay next week.[1] And then, on Sunday, there is a slight social quandary. My pupil Alan Clark wrote tentatively to ask if they could stay on their way north to Banff. I had to tell him that, alas, he was permanently in the dog-house as far as Chiefswood (or 8 St Aldates) was concerned, and have got him rooms at the George and Abbotsford[2]...But come before 17 Sept when I have to go south for four days. At least, I am booked to do so, but recent events may convulse my programme. I am to go south (a) to attend an Anglo-Czechoslovak historical congress; (b) to examine a D. Phil. candidate who needs to be examined then because he is off to Prague on 21 Sept;[3] (c) to appear on television with a Russian. I strongly suspect that no Czechoslovak historians, & no Russians, will be in London, and that the D.Phil. candidate will not in fact be leaving for Prague so soon.

Have you read any newspapers since you left England? If not, you will find, on your return, that the world is in convulsion. I alone, with irrepressible confidence, see nothing but good ahead. I see all those dreadful old Stalinists in eastern Europe—Brezhnev, Ulbricht, Gomulka, Kadar—banded together in a panic attempt to put out the fire in their neighbour's house, lest it spread to their own;[4] and I see it, thanks to their clumsy

---

[1]  Sidney Watson (1903–91), Director of Music at Eton 1946–55, Organist, Choir-Master, and Music Lecturer at Christ Church 1955–70, Conductor of the Oxford Bach Choir 1955–70.

[2]  The George and Abbotsford is a hotel standing on the High Street in Melrose opposite the monastery ruins.

[3]  Robert Evans (b. 1943), who would become a specialist in the history of Habsburg Europe and eventually one of T-R's successors as Regius Professor of Modern History at Oxford (1997–2011). The thesis that T-R examined was turned by Evans into his first book, *Rudolf II and his World: A Study in Intellectual History 1576–1612* (1973).

[4]  Leonid Brezhnev (1906–82), General Secretary of the Communist Party of the Soviet Union 1964–82; Walter Ulbricht (1893–1973), *de facto* Communist leader of East Germany 1950–71 and East German head of state 1960–73; Władysław Gomułka (1905–82), *de facto* Communist leader of Poland 1945–8 and 1956–70; János Kádár (1912–89), Communist leader of Hungary 1956–88.

intervention, actually spreading the faster. How delightful to have the flames suddenly crackling under them in Moscow and Berlin, Warsaw and Budapest! Here the great problem is what will happen to the Edinburgh Festival which has invested heavily in Russia: the USSR State Orchestra, Rostropovich, Oistrakh, Richter.[1] I suspect that all will be forbidden to come, or summoned home, to escape the humiliation of silent, disapproving audiences and inconvenient questions.

Meanwhile, when there are no earwigs to distract me, I read. I have been reading the entire correspondence of Grotius. Then I shall move on to Casaubon, Paolo Sarpi, de Thou, Lingelsheim.[2] Nobody reads original sources now: they only read at second hand: or they read manuscript statistics. There are too many works of up-to-date scholarship, and we all have to read them. But I am for the pure, original fountain.[3]

I nearly flew to Formosa today, but sense prevailed. They offered me a D.Litt. of the China Academy. That would have been something with which to overtrump Steven Runciman in the game of academic one-upmanship. But really the only degree I want is D.D.[4] He has one—but it is only of Wabash. I don't think that is quite good enough. All the same, I would have liked—but for the thought of that long air-journey—to be D.Litt. (Taipei).

I fear that I may be in for trouble. Nigel Lawson—who has turned the *Spectator* into a good paper—is an importunate widow.[5] He persecutes

---

[1]   At the Soviet State Symphony Orchestra's *début* at the Proms on 21 August 1968, on the day that the Soviet army invaded Czechoslovakia and occupied Prague with tanks, there was barracking and slogan-shouting from sections of the audience. After the cellist Mstislav Rostropovich (1927–2007) played Antonín Dvořak's cello concerto, he held aloft the conductor's score of the Dvořak piece to demonstrate his sympathies with the composer's homeland, Czechoslovakia and the city of Prague—and was roundly cheered. Four days later the Orchestra performed a concert of Russian music at the Edinburgh Festival, said to have been remarkable for its intensity. The violinist David Oistrakh (1908–74) often partnered his fellow Ukrainian, the pianist Sviatoslav Richter (1915–97).

[2]   Isaac Casaubon (1559–1614), classicist and philologist, figures in T-R's *Europe's Physician*; Georg Lingelsheim (1556–1636), humanist and historian.

[3]   T-R spent months reading the Grotius manuscripts, only to lose all his notes on a visit to the British Museum manuscripts room.

[4]   T-R eventually triumphed on this front when he contrived to be awarded a doctorate of divinity from the University of the South in Tennessee in 1980.

[5]   Nigel Lawson (b. 1932), later Lord Lawson of Blaby, was editor of *The Spectator* 1966–70 and Chancellor of the Exchequer 1983–9. The importunate widow in Luke 18: 1–8 beseeches justice against her adversaries.

me, and I resist, like a good old protestant martyr in the days of Bloody Mary. But in the end I yield—and always I find that I have yielded at the wrong moment: the moment is determined by time and human frailty, not the particular issue involved. So I have written a review of the last volume of Harold Nicolson's diary. I fear that I shall have black looks in the Beefsteak;[1] and what will happen if Charles, the waiter (against whose decision there is no appeal), places me next to Nigel or Ben Nicolson, I shudder to think.[2]

Could you find me, while in Oxford, some 17th century paper and some 17th century ink? I have had a bright idea, to enliven the dull round of scholarship. I want to insert an extra, hitherto unnoticed page into the Aubrey MSS. It will read thus:

'Twas a pretty trick to father those exquisite pieces on one W. Shakespeare of Stratford, a poor country clown who cd. neither reade nor write. Mr Bushell tells me that his Lord (the great Lord Chancellour Bacon) knew something of it, but wd. never speak out, tho' often asked. Sometimes his Lordship wd. look slyly but say nothing. Sometimes he wd. say, Go aske my Lord of Pembroke, who (he wd. hint) had a hand in the business. Sometimes, when Mr. Bushell

---

[1]   T-R had been elected to the Beefsteak in 1966, and soon afterwards resigned from the Garrick to which he had been elected as recently as 1965. He was elected to the Athenaeum in 1978 as a Rule II (distinguished) member, but resigned in 1988. He had been elected to the more raffish Savile Club early in the war.

[2]   Nigel Nicolson (1917–2004), co-founder of the publishers Weidenfeld & Nicolson and former MP for Bournemouth, and his brother and fellow Beefsteak member Benedict Nicolson (1914–78), editor of the *Burlington Magazine*, both resented T-R's review in *The Spectator* of Nigel's edition of the third volume of their father's diaries and letters. T-R described Harold Nicolson as 'a prolific and felicitous, if sometimes feline writer, sensitive and humane by nature, expensively educated' before indicting the diarist as snobbish, politically obtuse, and smug. 'Not a single heretical thought, not a single arresting phrase, not a single profound judgment…That graceful ivory tower, hermetically sealed with protective egotism, is inwardly hollow. Its chambers reverberate only with an elegantly articulated but complacent purr. The spirit within it—that fastidious patrician of life and letters, who claimed special privileges for himself and his friends because of their superior sophistication—is trivial.' In 1957, while reviewing T-R's *Historical Essays* in *The Observer*, Harold Nicolson had challenged the use of the term 'essays' to describe a book largely composed of recycled book reviews, regretted an 'absence of even average human compassion', and concluded, 'Among the strings of his lute there is a wire of hate which is apt to twang suddenly with the rasp of a banjo.'

pressed him, he wd answer, Who, but my Lord of Oxford? meaning Edward de Vere, him that let flee the great Fart.[1]

I like to think of a devout American D.Phil. student discovering this and sending it in triumph to the *Times Lit. Supplement*; and the rage of Dr. Rowse.[2]

We went the other day to *Hamlet*, in Edinburgh. Tom Courtenay is Hamlet, and very good: we both thought he was better than Gielgud. The *Times* had a monstrous, snooty, spiteful review; but I hope that Tom Courtenay adopts my Olympian practice of not even reading reviews of his work.[3]

I am trying not to think of Shakespeare lest I go mad. The trouble is that almost everything I take up is something that sends people mad: Shakespeare, witches, and now...But I shall not say. δειδιόμαι Τρῶας καὶ Τρωάδας ἑλκεσιπέπλους: that is, you.[4]

It is past midnight. I must go to bed. Come soon.

Love from

Hugh

---

[1]  Aubrey has a life of Thomas Bushell, a confidence trickster, whose mining projects ruined his investors, and who was 'one of the Gentlemen that wayted on the Lord Chancellour Bacon'. In Aubrey's account of Edward de Vere, 'This earle of Oxford, making of his low obeisance to queen Elizabeth, happened to let a Fart, at which he was so abashed...that he went to Travell 7 yeares. On his returne the Queen welcomed him home, and sayd "My lord, I had forgott the Fart".'

[2]  Rowse regarded himself as an expert on Shakespeare. In 'The Myth of Shakespeare's Sonnets' (*Oxford Magazine*, 23 January 1964), T-R had mocked Rowse's dogmatism on the subject. T-R himself looked closely into the question of the authorship of Shakespeare's plays. Though he concluded, not without reluctance, that unorthodox theories on the matter lacked substance, he enjoyed teasing scholars who declined to confront them.

[3]  Irving Wardle reviewed the play in *The Times* of 20 August: 'The production is a curious mixture of stiff classical behaviour, almost suggesting a school play, and ludicrous strokes of invention...At the centre of these spiritless proceedings is Tom Courtenay's Hamlet. What he presents is an urchin Prince, his triangular face set in an impassive mask, delivering the lines with deadpan eccentricity; sometimes running sentences together, sometimes chopping the sense in half, and rarely communicating anything but boredom...A pygmy performance in a starved production.'

[4]  'I fear [the pleas of] Trojan men and women with trailing robes.' *Iliad* 6.441 (though T-R has altered or misremembered the first word). Homer's Hector is resisting attempts to

## To James Howard-Johnston, 15 September 1968

Chiefswood, Melrose

My dear James

I must resist the temptation to write you a 'vast' letter: I shall respect your Alexandrine views. I write, functionally, to confirm that I shall dine in Ch. Ch. on Wednesday and look forward to seeing you there. I have written to Hugh Lloyd-Jones.[1] Will you see that I am put down for dinner, and persuade him to come, and the chef to prepare a delicious, neat, Attick repast? I hope my next journey south, which will be thus rewarded, will be more enjoyable than the last, which is just over.

I am writing in bed. It is early. All my bodily processes are disconcerted, and sleep is impossible. But dawn is breaking, cool and clean, and everything looks fresh, pure and purgative after that nightmare interlude. I flew down on Friday, back on Saturday, i.e. yesterday. I spent four hours of yesterday in London airport. One hour was spent in an aeroplane, waiting to take off. We did not take off, as the instruments failed. We were trundled out again, into the bus, back to the waiting-room. After an hour, another plane was found. We embussed; we emplaned. Then we spent another hour, cooped in the plane, on the ground, with engines running.

---

dissuade him from entering battle: T-R fears that James, if T-R tells him of the project which he is 'now' pursuing, will try to dissuade him from it. Perhaps the undisclosed subject 'that sends people mad' is espionage, for T-R's *The Philby Affair* was about to appear. If so he evidently feared his stepson's reaction to the publication, for James had long urged his stepfather to complete his *magnum opus* on the English Civil Wars rather than embark on fresh controversies. T-R had his own reproaches for James, who had inhibitions in completing written work. In a letter of 30 April 1967 T-R urged his stepson to 'take risks', by which 'knowledge is advanced', rather than take shelter in 'perfectionism'. The letter continued: 'I know that you will return some of this criticism on me. You sometimes do, and in terms far more wounding than any which (I hope) I have used to you. But I will gladly accept your *tu quoque* [you also] from you, so long as you will admit that a retort does not necessarily refute an argument. Whatever my own failings, I should like you to succeed.'

[1]  (Sir) Hugh Lloyd-Jones (1922–2009), Regius Professor of Greek at Oxford and Student of Christ Church 1960–89.

Outside the rain fell in sheets. There was a thunderstorm. Visibility was nil. Then we rose into it. We were strapped in and forbidden to smoke throughout. I had been pinioned, in the bus, by a querulous and half-hysterical old Australian woman, who forced me to take charge of her, dictated where I should sit, forced me into the most uncomfortable seat in the plane (foremost of all, back to engine, so that I sat tipped forward by the rising bow of the plane), and wailed to me during the whole flight, while the child facing me was sick over the table between us.

And why did I go, anyway, on this dreadful journey? Because Nigel Nicolson wanted a confrontation and I thought it wrong to refuse. But the confrontation, I fear, was not a success. The 'discussion' was no discussion. When I was brought into the studio, I saw a hired claque of 100 morons, who were then addressed by a slick, vulgar professional funny-man, who told them that they were paid to intervene in the programme with noises of all kinds. I then found that our 'discussion' was to last only 6½ minutes, sandwiched between a pop-singer and a spoof bicycle-race. There were other items too. Colin Davis, the conductor,[1] had been brought—no doubt equally under false pretences—to appear between equally grotesque interludes. This, I was afterwards told, is the new policy of the BBC. It is the way in which they will keep up with the Frost Revolution.[2] It makes the ordinary viewer sample culture unawares... of course it does no such thing, as I vainly told them: if you mix trivial and serious things, you merely trivialise the serious. But my protests had no effect. The producers of such things are themselves, inevitably, trivialised and can entertain no such argument. Anyway, the programme was now to begin. The pop-singer was at the ready. And it was live: there could be no delay. I looked round for Nigel Nicolson, whose summons I had obeyed. He was nowhere to be seen. I only saw Frank Longford, wandering like a lost soul upon the Stygian bank. He too was to come somewhere in the programme.

[1]  (Sir) Colin Davis (1927–2013), then Chief Conductor of the BBC Symphony Orchestra; Musical Director of the Royal Opera House, Covent Garden, 1971–6.
[2]  *The Frost Report* was a satirical television programme—fronted by (Sir) David Frost (1939–2013)—which ran for 28 episodes in 1966–7.

As the pop-singer sang, the producer came quietly to me. It looked, he said, as if Nicolson would not be there, so I would have to be alone. I was secretly rather relieved. I thought that at least, in that case, I and not the producer would be in control, and I prepared a brief and, as I thought, dignified plan. I would explain the two worlds in which a public man lived, the two distinct *personae* which he showed to the outer and the inner world, and thus explain the different views held by his domestic editor and the reader. Then the pop-singer ceased. At that moment a side-door opened, and Nigel Nicolson appeared, breathless. As he passed me, he whispered, 'I will explain afterwards'. Then he sat beside me in a gilt chair and the producer took command.

I of course, by now, realised what we were in for. Nicolson, just arrived, and anyway, I suspect, unfamiliar with the system, did not. He expected a long serious discussion. He had brought his documents. What he thought of the *claque* I don't know. Perhaps he assumed that they were technicians, or survivors from a previous programme. Perhaps, in his haste, he did not notice them. After the producer had invited him to speak, he began a long statement. I then began to speak. But the 6½ minutes were now up. There was a sign; the *claque* broke into noise to indicate transition; and the spoof bicycle-race began.

Nicolson looked at me. He was black in the face with bewildered rage. 'What is all this?' he asked. I could only reply, 'I'm afraid it is not the kind of programme that you or I expected'. He began to make a scene. The producer protested: 'I am no more able to control the programme than you', he cried. But to appease Nicolson—I did not need appeasement, for I realised that *nothing* could save *anything* out of such a performance—he said that the matter would be remedied afterwards. So we sat through the rest of the degrading programme and then, at the end, a brief discussion was recorded, to be put on, we were told, as part two, next week…Of course it will not be: it was mere window-dressing, to appease the enraged Nicolson. Nor do I want it to be: I do not want to appear at all in such a programme, ever.

I had a long conversation with Nicolson afterwards. He is rather like his father in that he has no real sense of the outer world. He showed this when he was MP for Bournemouth, the safest of tory seats, and was evicted by the constituency for his too liberal views.[1] His views did him credit, but he played his cards with incredible lack of finesse and lost his seat quite unnecessarily, while Edward Boyle, on the same issue, though more open in his views (being a minister), kept his easily. I felt sorry for him, for he realises that, by publishing his father's diaries, and by his selection of the material, he is widely regarded as having damaged his father's reputation; which is certainly true. And yet, against this background, he made a remark which seemed to me extraordinary.

As we were going back to the West End together, he asked if I would advise him on a particular problem. Going through his mother's papers, he had found a diary of hers describing, blow by blow, a Lesbian elopement. It seems that Vita Sackville-West—'old Ry-vita' as Maurice Bowra called her: and she was indeed a tough old biscuit—after she was married to Harold Nicolson, ran away with another woman, who had been married for two days, but had found that two days of heterosexuality were enough. They fled together to France and had a blissful honeymoon there until Harold Nicolson arrived in an aeroplane and reclaimed his wife for more conventional domesticity. Nigel Nicolson's question to me was, should he publish this diary? I said, firmly, no. He protested that it was very interesting, very moving. I said that this was no doubt so, but that if he was pained by the reaction to the publication of his father's diaries, he would find the reaction to such a publication even more painful. He said that he didn't mind what 'that sort of people' said. I'm afraid that, like his father, he despises the vulgar herd: indeed, his chief complaint of me was that I criticised his father's *élitism* from within the mandarinate. I could not persuade him that I don't really belong to, or believe in, the mandarinate.

After that Xenia dined with me and then, from 10.0 p.m. till midnight, I saw, with my lawyer, one Carlos Thompson[2] who has written a book

---

[1]   Nicolson was deselected by the Bournemouth Conservative Association after voting to abolish capital punishment, abstaining in the vote of confidence in the government's handling of the Suez crisis, and supporting the Wolfenden committee's recommendations on the decriminalization of male homosexuality.

[2]   Carlos Thompson was the stage name and *nom de plume* of Juan-Carlos Mundin-Schaffler (1923–90), an Argentinian-born actor and television producer whose career was mostly

exposing the wickedness of R. Hochhuth, K. Tynan & co.[1] I have no doubt
that his conclusions are right, but I shall not feel sufficiently confident of
his scholarship to regard him as a safe and usable ally till I see his book,
which he has promised to send.

I am looking forward to examining Robert Evans on Wednesday.
John Elliott described him as the cleverest man he had ever taught.[2] I
think his thesis fascinating: it is the most interesting work that I have
read for a long time. How seldom can one say that of a thesis! But a
thesis *can* be a book and a good book too, if one writes it as such, aware
of the outside world. I hope you are enjoying yours. Things written
with pleasure are read with pleasure; and one can always obey, and
yet triumph, over the rules.

I am also looking forward to the Anglo-Czech conference. I wonder if
any conversation will be possible.

I hope you saw your friends in London. I look forward to seeing you again.
We loved having you at home. We loved Annunziata too: a paragon among
Mummy's catalogue of female guests.[3] I will stop now before the crunch of

spent in Europe. At the time of the National Theatre row over *Soldiers* he acted as an intermediary between his friend Laurence Olivier and Hochhuth, but later he became the latter's
trenchant critic. He married Rex Harrison's ex-wife Lilli Palmer, but had boyfriends, and shot
himself in Buenos Aires.

[1]   T-R reviewed Thompson's *The Assassination of Winston Churchill* (1969) in the *Sunday Times*
(11 May 1969) under the headline 'The Sikorski Case' and in Robert Blake's name, because T-R had
been advised that his lawsuit might be compromised if it appeared under his own. The review ridiculed *Soldiers* as a 'drivelling farrago of nonsense' and as an act of character assassination by Hochhuth abetted by Kenneth Tynan and David Irving (b. 1938). Tynan he dismissed
as 'the very type of "Trendy-lefty", the avant garde nihilist conforming rigorously to pattern',
and Hochhuth as 'one of those pontifical teutonic froth-blowers whose addiction to pretentious prolixity is all too familiar... Let us leave him wringing his hands on a Swiss mountain,
far above mere facts, his head in a swirling Alpine cloud of mystical piffle.' But Irving, as a
historian with potential abilities, he judged 'the most puzzling figure of the three'.

[2]   (Sir) John [J. H.] Elliott (b. 1930) was Evans's supervisor. A historian of Spain and the
Americas, he then held a chair at King's College London, and was Regius Professor of Modern
History at Oxford 1990–7. He and Michael Howard were the two younger men whom T-R
trusted in 1961 to read and criticize his unfinished history of the Civil War period.

[3]   Lady Annunziata Asquith (b. 1948), eldest daughter of 'Trim', 2nd Earl of Oxford and
Asquith, was at this time stepping out with James H-J. As she was a Roman Catholic, T-R had to
suspend 'my strong, invincible, protestant prejudices—no, rational convictions'.

gravel announces the arrival of Xenia off the night-train, and before this letter can be described as 'vast'. Vastity, I think, begins on p. 10, so I am safe.[1]

Love

Hugh

—∞∞∞—

*Trevor-Roper had worked alongside H. A. R. 'Kim' Philby (1911–88) in MI6 during the war. He liked Philby and admired his abilities. In 1951 Philby was forced to resign from MI6, following the revelation that his associates Guy Burgess and Donald Maclean had been spying for the Soviet Union, but he managed to avoid arrest. In 1955 he was named as the 'Third Man' in the House of Commons, but cleared by the Foreign Secretary, Harold Macmillan. Soon afterwards Philby was re-hired by his former employers on a covert freelance basis, as Trevor-Roper's friend Dick White was appalled to discover when he took over as its chief ('C') in 1956. In March 1957 Trevor-Roper spent some days touring the remote northern part of Iran with Philby. Six years later Philby fled to Moscow from Beirut, where the Foreign Office had arranged for him to work as The Observer's correspondent. In 1968, in response to Philby's memoir My Silent War, Trevor-Roper published an essay about him in Encounter, which was later expanded into a small volume. Philby sent congratulations (dated 30 April 1968) from a postbox address in Moscow. 'My dear T-R,' the letter began, 'I am delighted to see from your photograph in Le Figaro of April 1 that you seem to be growing younger with the passing years.' The letter continued in the same friendly tone, and ended with a sentimental postscript. 'I am grateful for the chance that enabled us to fight together, for a time at least, on the same side.'*

*It seems probable that Trevor-Roper consulted White about this response, which may never have been sent. The letter was typed, unlike Trevor-Roper's other personal correspondence, which was almost always handwritten. Perhaps this was so that a carbon copy could be made.*

## To 'Kim' Philby, 21 September 1968

Chiefswood, Melrose

My dear Kim,

Ought I to answer your letter of 30 April? Perhaps not. But I hate to leave letters unanswered (though I often take a long time to answer them).

---

[1]   This letter covers six sides of paper.

I must admit that I enjoy hearing from you, even across the vast inter-mediate gulf which now separates us: a gulf now, alas, not merely phys-ical. I always enjoyed your company, always look back on it with pleasure, and I appreciate your remark that you would enjoy a long discussion with me now. But if we had few serious discussions in the past, how could we possibly have any in the future? Discussion needs common ground on which to stand, how deep down soever it may lie; and where could we find such ground now? Probe as I may in search of it, the solid rock which I once imagined proves but a continuation of the spongy quagmire of double-spoken words; and in that quagmire we would surely founder.

You justify the treachery, the hypocrisy, the purges of the Stalinist period as a mere temporary phase, a necessary form of Caesarian sur-gery without which the next stage of progress cannot begin. I'm afraid I cannot accept such apocalyptic reasoning, nor could I find any basis for discussion with anyone who could seriously argue that Chamberlain-ism was an immutable, permanent 'evil', justifying total repudiation, while Stalinism was a temporary necessity, deserving permanent, un-qualified support.

You note that I 'abhor treason'; but 'what is treason?' you gaily ask, and, like jesting Pilate, do not wait for an answer. I would agree with you, I think, in rejecting conventional definitions. To serve a foreign power, even to spy for a foreign power, does not seem to me necessarily treason. It depends on the foreign power, and the conditions of service. At most, it is mere political treason. But to serve unconditionally, to equate truth with the reason of state of any power, that to me is treason of the mind; and to make this surrender to a form of power that is cynical, inhuman, murderous, that to me is treason of the heart also.

Since you are now a public figure, you will not expect to be immune from public criticism, and I send you, in return for your letter, an essay in which I have sought to correct some of your public critics.[1] As you will

---

[1]  Probably his review of Philby's memoirs and related books, which had appeared in the *New York Review of Books* on 9 May 1968.

see, if you read it, on a superficial level we often agree, and where we disagree, on that level, we could argue; but at a profounder level I could no more argue with you than with an unrepentant French agent of Himmler, who also regarded the murder of a few millions as the necessary surgery which would make possible a new millennium. I regret this, because I like to recall, and would like to resume, our old convivial conversations, whether over my claret (now happily matured) or your Georgian champagne.[1]

I agree with you about long-term psychology (I use the term 'schizophrenia' as a metaphor only),[2] but I think you are wrong in your evaluation of D.G.W.[3]

yours ever

Hugh

※

The year 1968 was one of upheaval. Protests against the Vietnam War radicalized students in Britain as in America, while French students challenged the authorities in Paris. There was much talk of revolution. Trevor-Roper took an ironical view of those 'trendy-lefty' dons who tried to conciliate student radicals. He mocked them in the letters of Mercurius Oxoniensis. His attitude was stiffened by his experience of giving the annual Oration at the London School of Economics in 1968. The following letter describes the episode to his stepson (then in America doing graduate work in the library at Dumbarton Oaks, Georgetown).

---

[1]  Philby (in his letter of 30 April) had promised to toast T-R 'with deep sincerity, in one of my May Day glasses of champagne'.
[2]  Philby's letter had pooh-poohed suggestions that he was psychologically abnormal.
[3]  The letter had denigrated Dick White as 'ineffective'.

## To James Howard-Johnston, 17 December 1968

Chiefswood, Melrose

Dearest James

We were glad to hear your voice (*faute de lettres*),[1] and although we are sad that you can't come home for Christmas, I must admit that I think you are right to stay and settle down and work. I know how difficult it is to work when transplanted, and re-transplantation makes it more difficult still. So I can only hope that you are now less depressed and will have a good Christmas, in warm and civilised company. Americans, I find, are always warm—like their houses, they are sometimes too warm; but sometimes, alas, they are not civilised. But then, I quickly ask, are we? And are not we, and our houses, perhaps too cold?

Chiefswood is icy. If you detect a certain angularity in my writing, it is because, though the heating is on and I am crouched over my wood-fire, my hand can hardly hold the pen. I motored up today alone, and am here, at present, alone: Mummy is arriving regally, when all has been organised, by train; but I must not begrudge her this last luxury, for it is the last time: never again shall we travel up and down so conveniently: the train-service ceases on 6 Jan. As I motored north, the climate gradually changed. After the sodden Midlands, Yorkshire smiled in the sun. Then Durham was hidden in mist. Then Northumberland, my own, my native land[2]—how beautiful it was! The air was dry and clear and the sun shone weakly on

The new soft-fallen mask
Of snow upon the mountains and the moors;[3]

the bare trees glistened with powdered snow. The only thing that I have against that enchanting county, to which I am so devoted, is that the food

---

[1]  In a telephone call instead of a letter. T-R often complained about his stepson's reluctance to write letters.

[2]  From 'My Native Land' by Sir Walter Scott.

[3]  From 'Bright Star, would I were stedfast' by John Keats.

and conversation are so thin. Especially, I thought today (for I had no need of conversation), the food. By setting out from Oxford at 7.0 a.m. I was in Northumberland at lunch-time, and having made such progress, and having no dinner to look forward to (and having breakfasted at 6.0), I would have relished a liberal and elegant lunch. But I pass over such material things. Once I crossed the Border, I was back in fog; and this time it was cold, piercing fog; and nowhere is it so cold and piercing as in the kitchen of Chiefswood, where I have just scrambled myself an egg. I hope to have the place warmer before Mummy arrives.

I enclose a further letter from our new Oxford writer, Mercurius Oxoniensis. There is much speculation about his identity.[1] The law tutor at Oriel (a with-it R.C. who wears red shirts and a pointed goat-beard) told me that he thought he was Auberon Waugh, although he had some doubts whether A.W. would use the adjective 'Sotadean'.[2] Bond, the Pembroke Mods tutor, whom I found placed next to me on a guest-night in Oriel, assured me that it was someone in Christ Church: who else, he asked, would use the pseudonym *Mercury*?[3] He suspected Hugh Lloyd-Jones. In his speech at the Censors' dinner (the only good speech), Robert Blake allowed himself some speculations on the same topic. He concluded that Mercurius was not Lord Franks[4] but the Registrar.[5] But this latest letter

[1]   T-R never publicly admitted that he had written the *Mercurius* letters, and when confronted by Kenneth Turpin, the Provost of Oriel, denied it outright. In 1974 he complained to a director of Sotheby's that an entry in an auction catalogue attributed the letters to him: by doing so, he claimed, they were 'tainting the stream of bibliographical science'. Sotheby's apologized and issued a formal correction.

[2]   The adjective Sotadean refers to Sotades, a Greek versifier who lived in Alexandria in the third century BC and wrote licentious, pederastic verses. Auberon Waugh (1939–2001), son of T-R's arch-enemy Evelyn, who briefly read PPE at Christ Church, was a prolific magazine and newspaper columnist, renowned for his gossip, mischief-making, and invective.

[3]   Godfrey Bond (1925–97), Fellow and Lecturer in Classics, Pembroke College, Oxford, 1950–92 and Public Orator of the University 1980–92. There is a statue of Mercury in the middle of Tom Quad, a Christ Church landmark.

[4]   Oliver Franks, Baron Franks (1905–92), philosopher, mandarin, and banker, was Provost of the Queen's College, Oxford, before his appointment as British Ambassador to the USA in 1948. In 1960 T-R ran Harold Macmillan's successful campaign against Franks's candidature to become Chancellor of Oxford University. Franks was Provost of Worcester College, Oxford, 1962–76.

[5]   Sir Folliott Sandford (1906–86), Registrar of Oxford University 1958–72.

suggests that he is a college tutor, with no love for professors in general, or for the Regius Professor of History in particular. Perhaps future letters (if any) will enable us to narrow the field and identify him clearly as (say) Felix Markham, or Griffith of Jesus, or Father Green of Lincoln College.[1]

But I must tell you (while waiting hopefully for news from and of you) about my most recent experience: my confrontation with Student Power. It happened ten days ago at that hotbed of English—or rather *émigré* American—Maoism, the LSE.

Last summer the director of LSE, Dr Walter Adams, called personally on me and invited me to give the annual 'Oration' on 5 December.[2] He invited me in so flattering a manner, and his personal presence so reinforced his invitation, that I accepted. I decided—especially after reading the idiotic speech which the Minister of Education[3] made in June to a conference of Local Education Authorities: a speech in which he stated that 'society' would not tolerate such subjects as history in education—to lecture on 'history and sociology'. Then, at the time of the great, abortive 'Demo' of 27 October, the LSE was 'occupied' and became, once again, as at the time of Dr Adams' appointment, the centre of student belligerency. I thereupon decided to give the enemy no advance hint of what I was going to say, and I entitled my lecture simply 'The Past and the Present'.[4] But the substance remained the same.

Two days before the lecture, I received a letter from Dr Adams giving me the administrative details. Xandra, Xenia[5] and I were to come to his

---

[1]  Felix Markham (1908–92), Fellow of Hertford College since 1931, biographer of Napoleon and of other Bonapartes; John Griffith (1913–91), Fellow and Tutor in Classics at Jesus College until 1980, and the university's Public Orator; Vivian [V. H. H.] Green (1915–2005), Chaplain of Lincoln College, Oxford, 1951–69, Fellow and Tutor in History 1951–83, Rector of Lincoln 1983–7, one of the models for John le Carré's character George Smiley.

[2]  (Sir) Walter Adams (1906–75), Director of the London School of Economics 1967–74, was the former Principal of the University College of Rhodesia, who had been decried by some students as a 'lackey' of Ian Smith's minority-rule government. Throughout his subsequent career in university administration he preferred compromise to conflict.

[3]  Edward ('Ted') Short (1912–2012), later Baron Glenamara, was Secretary of State for Education and Science 1968–70 and Deputy Leader of the Labour Party 1972–6.

[4]  The lecture was published as a pamphlet, and as an essay in the journal *Past and Present* in 1969.

[5]  Trevor-Roper's stepdaughter Xenia Howard-Johnston was then at LSE researching a thesis on Pushkin.

office at 4.0. We would have tea. Then I would lecture at 5.0. Lord Robbins, as chairman of the governors, would be in the chair.[1] Xandra and Xenia would sit, with the other guests, in the front row. Then we would go to a concert and so to dinner. There was no hint, in this letter, of any conceivable trouble.

That same night the first hint came. Xenia rang up. She reported that LSE was plastered with notices denouncing me; that the radicals had resolved to 'occupy' the theatre and to exclude governors and invited guests from their seats; and that I would not be allowed to speak. The ostensible complaint against me was that I had published impermissible views on the present Greek *régime*;[2] but it was clear that the real purpose of the exercise was to attack the governors for being governors—LSE should, of course, be a self-governing radical commune—and this Oration, being an occasion when the governors were in evidence, was the right moment at which to strike. I was, in a sense, incidental. I was objectionable as an orator chosen by the governors. It was convenient that evidence of a different kind, in an irrelevant field, could be dug out. I have since seen the issue of the *Beaver*—the *Cherwell* of LSE—which was published just before my lecture and gave the orders. It was of revolting obscenity, comparable only to the famous anti-semitic paper *der Stürmer*, published under the Nazis. I am glad that I did not see it before the event.

[1]    Lionel Robbins (1898–1984), director of the economic section of the War Cabinet secretariat 1941–5, crossbencher peer from 1959, chairman of the *Financial Times* 1961–70, chairman of the influential Robbins committee on higher education 1961–4 and of the governors of LSE 1968–74.
[2]    Following his walking holiday in Greece, T-R had written an article for the *Sunday Times*, which was published on the first anniversary of the military seizure of power (21 April 1968) under the headline 'Greece—the Colonels' coup may not have been in vain'. Arguing that 'the beginning of wisdom is to respect the reality of other countries', he reported that the Greek nation was peaceable under its military junta and that émigré dissent ('the comfortable martyrdom of Madame Vlachou or the agonised rhetoric of Melina Mercouri') should be discounted. He depicted the dismissed anti-monarchical Georgios Papandreou (Prime Minister in 1964–5) as a 'vote-buying' demagogue: 'the Communists see him as their Kerensky'. He did not admire the current Greek government, but then, he continued, there were few governments that he did admire: the Colonels 'are not fascists, but...clericals. If their intellectual standard seems low, they atone for this by an exalted, not to say tedious religiosity.'

Next afternoon I was called urgently from a committee in All Souls to speak on the telephone to Dr Adams. By this time he too had learned of the trouble. He seemed very apprehensive, and as I was preoccupied by my committee, I simply said that, being a guest, I would place myself under the orders of my chairman and do whatever he thought necessary to handle the situation. Then, I went up to London.

When I arrived at Dr Adams' office, Mummy and Xenia were already there. Mummy afterwards said that, on arrival, they had found the establishment 'windy'. I had barely arrived when a 'delegate' from the students appeared. He spoke with an American accent and presented a series of *ultimata*. The front benches were already 'occupied'. I would only be allowed to speak if I was, immediately afterwards, placed at the disposal of the students for a 'discussion' of my views on Greece. Lord Robbins behaved, as it seemed to me, with excessive compliancy. He finally agreed that if I were allowed to speak, I would be thrown to the wolves not *immediately* afterwards, but almost immediately: I might have a break of half-an-hour. Lord Robbins told us that there would be no attempt to protest at the 'occupation': the governors and guests, including Mummy and Xenia, would not enter the theatre but hear the lecture on a loud-speaker elsewhere.

I had of course agreed to whatever the Chairman should decide; but my own view was that the Chairman was craven. After all, the Governors had invited me to give the 'oration', at my own expense in labour and time—and indeed money (they didn't even offer to pay my expenses). It was their duty to protect me, not to make concessions at my expense, turning my wife and stepdaughter out of the room and forcing me to go through a second ordeal as the price of being allowed to speak. This view has hardened since.

Then I was taken to the lecture theatre. The usual ceremonial had been scrapped. No governors, no guests. The hall was packed, but the only faces I could see were the hostile faces of the demonstrators who had seized the front rows and sat everywhere, in postures of defiance, on the dais. Only Lord Robbins and Dr Adams accompanied me. We crept in by a back stair. When we arrived a loutish student walked up to Lord Robbins and presented new ultimata. Robbins replied quite skilfully and listed the compliances already made. Then he introduced me, and I began my 'oration'.

I may say that, as soon as I knew there would be trouble, I had gone through my lecture, sharpening it up. But I had the advantage over my opponents in that only I knew where the real barbs were and when they were coming; so I was able to plant them in such a manner that the enemy (who were not, I think, highly intelligent) were always too late in their protests: their slogans of dissent were uttered raggedly, sporadically, and generally too late, and were silenced by the rest of the audience. So I got through the lecture even to the end. But it was very exhausting; and I was still exhausted when I was led in again to be baited not on the lecture but on an old article on Greece which I had not even had time to re-read.

At first, it did not go too badly. But after about half-an-hour my patience, and my temper, failed. A man got up as if he owned the place: not from the audience but from, as it were, the government bench. He stood beside me and faced the audience. He was, he said, 'not a grand professor but only a humble porter at LSE'; but he owned a property in Greece, on an island, and he could give eye-witness accounts from his 'housekeeper' there. Again and again he dwelt on his Greek property and housekeeper; again and again he emphasised his humility: he was only a humble working man, only a humble trades-unionist; and as he went on and on, his voice developed a sing-song nonconformist canting unction which suddenly reminded me—hitherto I had been thinking of Uriah Heep—of my fellow-traveller in China, also so smug about his property, also so humble a trades-unionist, also dripping with cant and double-think: Ernie Roberts.[1] At that moment I heard again the familiar litany,

---

[1]   Ernest 'Ernie' Roberts (1912–94) had accompanied T-R to China in 1965, as part of a small delegation sent by the Society for Anglo-Chinese Understanding (SACU). He had started work in a coal-pit at the age of 13 and, although expelled from the Communist Party of Great Britain in 1941, never ceased to advocate class struggle. Assistant General Secretary of the Amalgamated Engineering Union 1957–77, MP for Hackney North and Stoke Newington 1979–87, and author of *Workers' Control* (1973).

'only a humble working man', and I felt that well-known sensation which has so often marked the moment of disaster: that sudden click somewhere between the eyes and the brain, that drop of an imaginary curtain which, in its fall, like a guillotine, severs reason from blind impulse, Olympian self-control from dionysiac transport. I turned on the odious porter (Xenia tells me that really he isn't a porter at all) and snapped at him, 'Cut out the cant'. Some of the audience were furious at my speaking so sharply to a humble member of the working class, who was also, because of his island-property in Greece, their prize exhibit. The porter became more sanctimonious than ever. 'Our Swedish friends…' he began. I knew that he was going to quote a committee of holier-than-thou Swedes organised by Andreas Papandreou.[1] 'Damn your Swedish friends!' I interjected. A virtuous hubbub followed, only interrupted by an invasion of other radicals, bearing huge posters, who soon found themselves fighting for possession of the hall. After an uncertain time of which I remember nothing (for the curtain having fallen, my faculties were darkened), I left the room and was given a sedate dinner with the establishment of LSE.

In retrospect, I think that the lecture at least was a success. It was a success in that I was able to deliver it at all; and it appears to have been well received. I have had a lot of letters from people at LSE who regard it as a blow struck for liberty. Lord Robbins told Mummy, after the lecture, that it was what they all wanted to say but had never dared to say.[2] But if so, I at once ask, why didn't they dare to say it? So my belief that they are a craven lot is fortified. Xenia told me that, after I had gone from the hall, Lord Robbins offered to meet the radical students at any time, in any place, at their mere will and pleasure, in a manner which was positively shameful.

---

[1]  Andreas Papandreou (1919–96) was a Harvard-educated economist: described in T-R's *Sunday Times* article as Georgios Papandreou's 'émigré son, who only returned to Greece when, his father being Prime Minister, he could start at the top' (he had been elected to the Greek parliament in 1964). He was imprisoned at the time of the Colonels' *coup d'état*, released in 1968 on condition of exile to Sweden, and was socialist Prime Minister 1981–9 and 1993–6.
[2]  Elsewhere he described the oration as 'one of the best I have ever heard'.

I must also record one other emotion. As I stood in that hall, addressing that hostile multitude, whose vocal members shouted illiterate, obscene slogans, and felt the presence behind me of my trembling chairman, Lord Robbins, I felt that that whole theatre was a great darkened barn, with a few rafters above and a sea of bird-droppings beneath, and the great dark vault of it whirring with the noise of wings: the robins coming home to roost. For it is only a few years since Lord Robbins sat complacently as chairman of the Robbins committee on University Reform, whose idiot recommendations are the origin of all our woes. Moreover, Lord Robbins himself (who has a deep personal hatred of Oxford and Cambridge, stemming from his failure to get a fellowship there) saw fit, in that report, to include a sharp attack on Oxford and Cambridge for their archaic structure which prevented them, as he complained, from making those quick surrenders to the latest fashionable nostrum which could so easily be exacted from the authoritarian vice-chancellors of provincial universities—and L.S.E. Well, we now see the results of that quick surrender, and Oxford and Cambridge may perhaps congratulate themselves on their archaic structure which, like the archaisms of the 16$^{th}$ century Netherlands or 17$^{th}$ century England, has proved useful. Perhaps—this at least is a charitable thought—Lord Robbins' cravenness is the expression of his disillusion.

I'm afraid that I feel rather strongly on this, having just heard that Orest Ranum,[1] a respectable historian at Columbia, has lost ten years' work, destroyed by virtuous radical students, and has, in consequence, had to give up a whole book.

Now I fear that I am becoming a bore. When one feels that, there is only one thing to do: to stop at once.

---

[1] On 22 May 1968 student protesters at Columbia University, New York, ransacked the filing cabinets of assistant professor Orest Ranum (b. 1933), and burnt his extensive notes for a book on early modern Europe, which he had been commissioned to write for a series edited by J. H. Plumb. Ranum transferred in 1969 to Johns Hopkins University, where he flourished as a historian of 17th-century France.

Do write, even if bored or depressed. I must confess that I never showed your depressed letter to Mummy, lest it should depress her. But I can take it!

Love from
Hugh

---

## To Valerie Pearl, 4 April 1969

Chiefswood, Melrose

My dear Valerie,

I appear, as so often, in the whitest of white sheets. I have been in America—an experience which tends to unsettle us all. While there, I arranged with the Post Office for all my mail to be re-directed into the hands of the Faculty Secretary, who had instructions to deal with it. But alas, the Post Office is not what it was. Only half my mail (as I have now discovered) was re-routed on the correct route. The other half, falling (I presume) into the hands of some creature who had previously re-directed my mail to Chiefswood, and the elasticity of whose mind had been rotted by continuous potations of office tea, was, by a reflex action, sent to Scotland; where the gardener obediently piled it, among drying onions and fresh manure, against my return. When I got back from America to Oxford, about ten days ago, I realised that something had gone amiss, from an unusual number of complaints about unanswered urgent documents which were not themselves traceable; but only today, when I arrived here, did I discover the true explanation. Among the misdirected letters was, of course, yours: hence the white sheet, which, this time, is of truly incandescent whiteness.

In New York I twice met Larry Kaplan[1]—although (maddeningly) never for more than a few brief words in a crowded room. He said that he feared you could never be persuaded to go to America. I said that I would do my best: so now I will do it.

You really ought to go. It is ghastly—and yet how can we ignore this great political force, this huge febrile society, this warning, terrifying example? The change since I was last there, four years ago, is extraordinary. The failure abroad, in Vietnam; the tension at home—in the cities, in the universities, between the races; these have unnerved Americans, and their sense of security, never very pronounced, has now collapsed. The insecurity in great cities like New York and Washington—I was only on the East Coast—is the staple of general conversation there. It was most obvious at Larry's college—City College of City University—which is on the edge of Harlem. They told me there that 45 members of the university were beaten up every *week*! We dined in Harlem, but the whole party insisted on walking the mere 50 yards from the restaurant to the car park in close formation, as through an occupied city in wartime. Columbia is no better. And once, when we were given a lift from the Opera by the Italian Consul-General, we noticed that he took the precaution of locking all the car-doors once we were aboard. Afterwards we noticed that everyone does this—in case of attack while stopped at the traffic lights. After all this we were almost disappointed to suffer nothing worse than once being stoned.

In order to have a few dollars on which to maintain a tolerable standard of life in that expensive country, I gave a few lectures. One was at Princeton, under the *aegis* not, I regret to say, of my old pupil Lawrence Stone, but of Theodore Rabb. Stone did attend my lecture, very unobtrusively, and was afterwards seen by Xandra giving a corrective, oracular commentary to a knot of his wide-eyed, docile pupils. Xandra, I may add, hated Princeton. The sexes were carefully segregated, and she had an

---

[1]   Lawrence Kaplan (b. 1934), sometime Professor of History at City College of City University of New York, and author of *Politics and Religion during the English Revolution: The Scots and the Long Parliament, 1643–1645* (1976).

entirely feminine dinner (a thing that she detests), dominated absolutely by that unchallenged queen of historical wives, Mrs Stone, who for three hours laid down the law, telling all present of the horrors of Oxford.[1] Her auditors (or auditrixes) were all either too young or, like Xandra, too cowed to differ from the ex-Oxford oracle, who gloried in her dogmatic monologue.

As a relief from such scenes, we spent some time in rural Virginia. We stayed with an English friend who is married to an American. The entire house, which was in a most romantic situation with a magnificent view of the Blue Ridge Mountains, was a Temple of the Horse. The napkins, the plates, the tiles all represented the horse—or, occasionally, the fox. The pictures were all of horses. The bric-à-brac consisted of equine trophies. There were no books—except one which was put by Xandra's bed: it was called 'The Little Red Horse'. Our hostess, needless to say, was joint-master of the local fox-hounds. The other joint-master was an orthopaedic surgeon, also English. I have moved much in hunting circles in England, but have never seen such unqualified, concentrated, fundamentalist hippolatry, such puritanical monotheism of the horse. Virginia—or at least the Blue Ridge Mountains of Virginia—seemed to me a fossil projection of upper-class Leicestershire, as Ulster is a fossil projection of lower middle-class Lowland Scotland.

But what, meanwhile, of English toadery? I have news; and I need views. Let me trade one for the other.

The great problem in Oxford is the Chichele Chair, vacated by Dick Southern, who prefers the Presidency of St John's (an odd preference). We are agreed that his successor should be a medievalist. But where can we find a medievalist who is not either painfully parochial or positively disreputable? The collapse of medieval history in England in the last generation is extraordinary. A generation ago Powicke had a man for every job. Now the whole subject is almost extinct, eaten out by that army of bloodless,

[1] Jeanne Fawtier (1920–2001), daughter of a professor at the Sorbonne, married Stone in 1943, devoted herself to his career, and collaborated in the writing of his later books.

purblind, pink-eyed, Balliol mice whom he nourished and trained. The only man who escaped that baleful influence was Bruce McFarlane;[1] but he, in a different way, had a similar effect. Instead of enlivening his pupils, he drained their life away and left them blank and sterile. Even in death, he drains them still, drawing them from the writing of their own works to the devout task of editing his own unpublished papers.[2] The result of the Balliol monopoly and the Magdalen breach of it is thus that there is not a single qualified medievalist for the Chichele chair.

There is not even a medievalist among the Oxford Electors. In fact, in an electoral board of seven, the only medievalist is the Cambridge elec-tor—appropriately enough, the last of Powicke's mice, Christopher Cheney.[3] How absurd that we should even seem to depend on him for the election of an Oxford Professor 25 years after the death of Marc Bloch![4]

Such was the position when the electors met in February. Various can-didates had of course entered, or been entered, for the race, but all of them, except mine, seemed to me impossible. Lucy Sutherland had thought of an American called Brentano[5] who—reasonably enough in these days—wanted to escape from Berkeley. But I had read Brentano's books and found them arch and trivial: elaborate archival learning, ex-pressed in an odiously affected style, and leading nowhere; so I was able to scotch him (and, even more happily, to use Cheney to do it). Cheney also showed some real genius in destroying all his own candidates (of whom there were three) before they could get started. Ronald

[1]    Bruce [K. B.] McFarlane (1903–66), Fellow of Magdalen from 1927, knew as much as any of his contemporaries about the late Middle Ages, but published only one, short book.
[2]    'Rarely can a group of scholars have devoted as much care to the *opera posthuma* of a colleague as in the continuing publication of the works of the late K. B. McFarlane,' observed Jeremy Catto in a review in the *Cambridge Historical Journal* of McFarlane's *Nobility of Later Medi-eval England* (1973), edited by J. P. Cooper and James Campbell. Other works were edited by McFarlane's devotees Gerald Harriss and Roger Highfield. All four editors were Oxford his-tory tutors.
[3]    Christopher Cheney (1906–87), Professor of Medieval History at Cambridge 1955–72.
[4]    Marc Bloch (1886–1944), co-founder of the *Annales* School of French social history. He was captured and shot by the Gestapo during the German occupation of France for his Re-sistance work.
[5]    Robert Brentano (1926–2002), a former Rhodes Scholar, who never left Berkeley.

Syme[1] (who, like me, wants a cosmopolitan scholar) floated the name of Robert Lopez,[2] who however has shown no signs of wanting to leave Yale. The All Souls party—the Warden and Mack Smith—sat pretty. So did the Vice-Chancellor.[3] When we broke up for lunch, I was satisfied that, if I played my cards well, I could get my candidate in. All depended on continuity of argument. As I chewed my lamb-chop I saw all rivals falling away in turn, and their sponsors, one by one, settling for the right man. Syme, unable to secure Lopez, would turn towards another European scholar. Mack Smith, out of conviction; Warden Sparrow, following Mack Smith, would agree; Cheney would utter a few pained squeaks, but they would be gradually extinguished as he would be firmly inserted, head-downwards like the dormouse at the Mad Hatter's tea-party, into the teapot. The V-C would slide with the majority. Only Lucy Sutherland[4] would die fighting, for particular reasons which I need not here specify, but which have no connexion with the merits of the case. With this pleasant conviction, I took a last sip of coffee and set out, with firm step, towards the Vice-Chancellor's room in the Clarendon Building.

Alas, what are the hopes of man?[5] Who can fight against the great opposeless will of God himself, who intervenes (as the Puritans constantly and, I now see, truly averred) even in our petty human elections? But I will narrate all, faithfully and in order, so that you may see how the carnal pride of man is humbled by the higher will of God, as expressed by his faithful agent, the clerical school of Powickian orthodoxy. You will also have an opportunity of reflecting on the oblique and devious manner in which the Almighty operates in pursuit of these trifling objectives.

[1]  Sir Ronald Syme (1903–89), Camden Professor of Ancient History and Fellow of Brasenose, Oxford, 1949–70, and a towering figure in 20th-century classical studies.

[2]  Roberto Sabatino-Lopez (1910–86) left Italy because of racial persecution, and had a long career (as Robert S. Lopez) as a historian of medieval European economic history at Yale. He contributed an essay on Dante to T-R's *Festschrift*.

[3]  Kenneth Turpin (1915–2005), Secretary of the Faculties at Oxford University 1947–57, Provost of Oriel 1957–80, and Vice-Chancellor 1966–9.

[4]  Dame Lucy [L. S.] Sutherland (1903–80), historian of the 18th century and Principal of Lady Margaret Hall 1945–71.

[5]  A favourite T-R question, taken from Byron, *Don Juan*, canto 1, verse 219.

Know then that when I reached the Clarendon Building, high in hope, my mind was at first fixed on immediate tactics: how I should create the opportunity for Syme to declare himself for my candidate, and thereby launch the gentle but general slide in that direction. Thus preoccupied I did not at first notice a certain confusion and stirring of persons in the vice-chancellor's ante-chamber, but pushed through to the centre of power. All this bustle outside was, I presumed, merely the ordinary, daily competition of suitors and courtiers seeking offices, benefices, perquisites, pensions, favours, immunities, etc. etc. from the throne. Only when we were seated round the table did it become clear that someone was missing. Before luncheon, we had been seven; now we were six. Further investigation revealed that the missing elector was Cheney. He had expired in the ante-room. That was the real meaning of all that bustle. And although, by the application of ardent spirits, *sal volatile* and other remedies, life had apparently been restored, memory had not. The unfortunate Cheney could not remember where or who he was, why he was where he was, or what he had been doing all morning. He had, I presume, had a slight stroke. After a doctor had been summoned, he was placed in the Vice-Chancellor's car and returned to Cambridge.

Of course, lacking an elector, we could not proceed to an election. The election is thus in suspense. It is in suspense for another month—for only in May can all the electors again be gathered together. And meanwhile, of course, the enemy is at work, sowing tares in the wheat. Lucy is not idle. And another, more sinister figure, perhaps enlisted by her, is sitting on the grassy bank to which, in his old age, he has retired, tweaking from afar the invisible strings. That distant operator is none other than the last of the apostolic succession of Balliol Regius Professors, my predecessor, Galbraith. And of course he is operating in the interests of another Balliol man, his own prize pupil, the undisputed King of all the Toads.

Half-way through the last paragraph, at 1.0 a.m. this morning, I despaired of finishing this letter, so I broke off and posted, separately, your article. I now resume the broken thread of my narrative; and since I have anyway thus broken it, let me begin again at a new point, so that all the *dramatis personae* may be manoeuvred into the right position before we come, as we will on 7 May, to Act 2 of the play.

Last summer, being in Edinburgh, I happened to call on my old friend, or at least acquaintance (for he always treats me with some disdain, as a junior officer in the great hierarchy of learning of which he so confidently adorns the summit), Denys Hay.[1] I asked him, casually, if he knew of any good medievalists for our own Chichele Chair. In the silence that followed I recognised that I might have made a tactical error; so I hastily added—'unless, of course, you are interested yourself'. Thus prompted, the Grand Toad inhaled a great puff of air and visibly swole before me. Then he said, with royal deliberation: 'Well, you know, I think that I have done my job here by now: I have put the place on its feet, and I suppose I wouldn't mind a change... Of course I won't apply; but if it were offered, I should certainly consider it'. And then he cast a glance, half-devout, half-cunning, towards the framed photograph on his desk: a photograph of his old tutor, mentor, exemplar: Galbraith.

So now you see all. In the time happily gained by the Hand of God, who obliquely struck down His inadequate agent Cheney in order to call up His reserve forces, commanded by Galbraith, the name of Hay has been put forward and, I must admit, may well provide the enemy with a powerful means of restoring the Balliol Supremacy. For think of the consequences. Lucy will clutch at this new saviour. To Syme, it will be represented that Hay is not an insular English historian: has he not pontificated on the Italian Renaissance? Cheney, now restored to health and memory, will squeak his assent. The Vice-Chancellor and the Warden of All Souls will be influenced by status: is not Professor Hay, at this moment, thanks to assiduous fraternisation with his fellow-toads, President of the Royal Historical Society? So gradually the balance will shift, and not Lucy but I will be left isolated as the voters slide gently together in order that Denys

---

[1] Denys Hay (1915–94), a war historian in the Cabinet Office 1942–5, Professor of Medieval History at the University of Edinburgh 1954–80. He specialized in the Italian Renaissance and its impact on Europe, 15th-century Italian clergy and culture, and European historiography.

Hay, like James VI, may move triumphantly, in royal progress, between avenues of obsequious, bowing and applauding toads, from Edinburgh to his new kingdom in the South.

What then am I to do? My great hope is Mack Smith. He once wrote a devastating review of Hay's worthless pomposities on the Italian Renaissance. He will be sound; and he may bring the Warden with him. But in order to mobilise the forces of light we must have a candidate who can command a majority, and who can that candidate be? I have my own, of course, but I may not prevail. There are those who regard the continent of Europe, and especially eastern Europe, in the Middle Ages, as 'peripheral': Bedfordshire, to them, is the centre of the world. Therefore I must be prepared. I too must have a reserve force to wield in the moment of battle. Ideally, of course, he must be a Christ Church man—they alone, in the general collapse of all things, can be relied upon,—but this is not essential. Indeed, there are some private disadvantages to me in promoting my Christ Church friends: it weakens the loyal vote in that college, which is also indispensable to me. It was an act of great altruism, perhaps suicidal, to procure the elevation of Blake, who commanded an army of votes in Christ Church, to the Provostship of Queen's.[1] However, first things first. *Salus Populi Suprema Lex. Fiat Justitia et ruat caelum.*[2] Etc. Etc.

Now then, I beg, come to my aid. Propose me a medievalist for the Chichele Chair. He must be good, of course; but he must also be a co-operator: we have two totally parasitic professors—Wernham and Gibbs—who refuse to sit on the Board or do anything for the government of the Faculty, thus doubling the work of the other professors; and we simply cannot carry another, even if (unlike Wernham and Gibbs) he justifies his refusal by his scholarship. At present various names are being considered. There is Barrow, who rules in Newcastle-on-Tyne and knows about Anglo-Normans; but he seems narrow in range and time, and is

---

[1]   Blake had been elected Provost of the Queen's College, Oxford, in 1968.
[2]   Famous Roman maxims: 'Let the good of the people be the supreme law' (from Cicero's *de Legibus*) and 'Let justice be done though the heavens fall'.

retreating into the unrewarding wastes of medieval Scotland.[1] There is Christopher Brooke, but he seems a lightweight: he will do for Cambridge.[2] Can you think of *anyone* who would do?[3] If so, please tell me, and soon—as soon as you can forgive me for that lamentable failure to return your excellent article on London and the Scots.[4]

yours ever

Hugh

———∞∞∞———

## To James Howard-Johnston, 28 June 1969

Chiefswood, Melrose

My dear James

Well, you have triumphed. Virtue, non-conformist virtue, has prevailed over the humane usages of society; you may glow with the inward satisfaction of the saints; the gift horse, which so unseasonably obtruded itself, has retreated back into its stable, its nose bruised, its front teeth broken by the biff which it provoked, and with its few remaining grinders is chewing the mouldy hay of disillusion; and your sister Xenia, who has

[1]   Geoffrey Barrow (b. 1924), Professor of Medieval History at the University of Newcastle 1961–74, Professor of Scottish History at St Andrews 1974–9, and Professor of Scottish History and Paleography at Edinburgh 1979–92.

[2]   The medievalist Christopher Brooke (b. 1927), author of *The Dullness of the Past* (1957), Professor of History at Westfield College, London. Brooke was elected a Fellow of the British Academy in 1970.

[3]   T-R's candidate Geoffrey Barraclough (1908–84) was appointed Chichele Professor of Modern History in 1970. He was a medievalist, who had worked in Hut 3 at Bletchley, and later as Director of the Royal Institute of International Affairs. When appointed Chichele Professor, he omitted to resign his chair at Brandeis, tried to operate as a pluralist, chafed at the ambience of his college, All Souls, and aroused the resentment of faculty colleagues who expected him to resume his medievalist interests. He abruptly left Oxford in 1972 for Brandeis, and resigned his Chichele Chair soon afterwards.

[4]   'London Puritans and Scotch Fifth Columnists', in *Studies in London History Presented to Philip Edmund Jones* (1969).

192

no such queasy scrupulosity, has become indecently rich by your preference for apostolic poverty.[1] On this subject I fear that we shall not agree.
But at least we may agree on others; and I write, partly, of course, to greet
you on your return to Washington from the Far West; partly because you
are always, or nearly always, in my thoughts; partly to tell you that I have
obeyed your orders: I have fought, as you begged me to fight, 'tooth and
nail for Barraclough'.

What a battle! It lasted, in all, four months: four months during which
one of the electors, and one of the candidates, were incapacitated by
strokes. It ended, three weeks ago, with the greatest battle of all, the battle
of Armageddon in the valley of Josaphat, at which there was much gnashing of teeth;[2] and no doubt there is more since. At one point I stated that I
had made careful enquiries of selected historical colleagues, whose judgment I trusted, and had discovered them enthusiastic for Barraclough.
Who? Who? demanded my indignant adversaries. But I did not name
you. I preserved a grave decorum, in order to emphasise and expose the
indecent denunciation of the only medievalist among us and win, if I
could, however temporarily, the decisive but floating vote of Warden
Sparrow. And in the end I prevailed. Barraclough is in; and you and I,
under God who sways the hearts of the voters, are responsible.

What, I wonder, will be the end of it? Perhaps he will be, as his opponents maintain, a disaster. Perhaps he will, as they say that he will, neglect
his duties, pick quarrels, imagine slights, and disappear on his travels
again. The Oxford medievalists—the heirs of Powicke, the continuation
of his now dessicated tradition—are furious. So are some others. Dick
Southern is speechless; Mrs Prestwich all too ready to speak; Master
Prestwich, when rendered voluble by wine at the Christ Church Gaudy,
expresses the bewilderment of the expert at such an amateur election.

[1]    Xandra had wished to settle a sizeable capital sum on both James and Xenia, but James
wrote to his mother and her solicitor refusing the gift on socialist principles.
[2]    In Joel 3 the prophecy of the gathering of heathen nations for divine judgement in
the valley of Jehoshaphat foreshadows their destruction at the Battle of Armageddon in
Revelation 16.

Isaiah Berlin goes round saying that this is my master-stroke in my campaign to ruin All Souls: for what college can survive Barraclough as a Fellow? But Trevor Aston,[1] Eric Christiansen,[2] Peter Brown are also medievalists, if not in the Powicke tradition, and they support you and me. Anyway, it was a glorious victory; and I trust that, on reporting it, as I now do, I will hear from you those welcome words, Well done, thou true and faithful servant.[3]

I am now, for two days, at Chiefswood. I have come up in order to give two lectures at Edinburgh, to Scotch schoolmasters, on Scotch history. It is my missionary zeal that has brought me: I feel that I cannot enjoy the luxury of saying what I say about Scotch education and scholarship unless I am willing to do something to improve it; and having, so surprisingly, been asked to speak to this course I must not refuse the invitation. And if I am to come for a day to Edinburgh, I want to see Chiefswood. This, of course, is a problem, now that we have no railway; and I thought that I would have to drive up and down, at which my heart shrank. But in the end all was well. By flying to Newcastle I was able to pick up Dawyck's car which he had left at Newcastle airport and can meet him on his return by train: for he has been in the south, staying with us for the Christ Church gaudy. Meanwhile I have the use of his car; have come to Chiefswood; and can go on Sunday to see my father in Northumberland, who has been ill but is now better. That is, he was taken violently ill at York races; was rushed to hospital and operated on; and we all stood by for the last exequies. But he threw off the effects of the operation, returned home ahead

---

[1]   Trevor Aston (1925–85), Fellow and History Tutor at Corpus Christi College, Oxford, 1952–85. T-R wrote (in a letter to William Thomas, 15 August 1969): 'I am devoted to him and indeed heavily dependent on him: he was an excellent chairman of the Board, has a passion for work, and is one of the few Oxford medievalists who is not imprisoned in church-historical pedantry. He also has civilised tastes and non-medieval historical interests. He seems to have enemies, or at least severe critics, who always find it convenient to emphasise the fact that he has to withdraw periodically into the Warneford [mental health hospital].' Aston was a manic depressive, whose illness caused him to take a fatal overdose in his college rooms.

[2]   Eric Christiansen (b. 1937), Fellow and Tutor in History at New College 1965–2002. T-R liked the fact that Christiansen began as a non-medievalist, with *The Origins of Military Power in Spain* (1967), before starting the work that would produce *The Northern Crusades* (1980).

[3]   Matthew 25: 21.

of time, and is now so pleased with himself for being alive that he is (I am assured) younger than ever, and has just celebrated his 85$^{th}$ birthday.

Chiefswood is wonderfully beautiful. Everything, this year, is a month late, so I see it as it normally is at the end of May. No garden flowers are out: their time is not yet; but everything is green, and the green is broken, unexpectedly, here and there, by great red and white rhododendron flowers, still in bloom, which appear through cracks of space across the sparkling water of the stream. I thought that I would take out the Allen yesterday, but when I saw the long grass full of cornflowers, I had not the heart to cut them, and deferred my action. I am enjoying being here, though alone and feeding on cold ham, kippers and spring onions. I am tired of endless committees. Why should I wear out my life sitting on them,

> et propter vitam vivendi perdere causas?[1]

So I wander in these delightful glades, and pause to read literature, not agenda or minutes, and to write to you.

We long to see you back. I hope you are enjoying the Far West, or at least the experience of it. I *hated* California, that artificial, rootless, mindless non-society. Surely, I said to myself, the Middle West is better: at least it must be real, however awful. I want to go to the Middle West; but not for long. And I suppose that what I want to savour in the Middle West is really not its character, its uniform, authentic essence, but its deviations. I would visit the Hutterites in Dakota, the Mormons in Utah. Indeed, I nearly went so far as to accept an invitation to go, with Sir Iain Moncrieffe of that Ilk,[2] to a genealogical conference in Salt Lake City in August. But no: that price, I decided, was too heavy, even for the opportunity of looking, for a short season, on that strange experiment.

Have you ever read Carl Nordhoff's book on the utopian religious communities in America?[3] I enormously enjoyed it. But perhaps my interest

---

[1] 'And for the sake of living lose what makes life worth living.' Juvenal, *Satires* 8.84.

[2] Sir Iain Moncreiffe of that Ilk (1919–85), 7th baronet, Scottish genealogist, Albany Herald at the Court of Lord Lyon, and hard-drinking clubman.

[3] Charles Nordhoff (1830–1901) wrote *America for Free Working Men!* (1865) and *Communistic Societies of the United States* (1875). Several new editions of the latter, which contained sections on Zoarites and Shakers, were published after 1960. That of 1993 had the title *American Utopias*.

in minorities does not communicate itself to you. Nor does it do me any good. The minorities themselves do not appreciate it. At present I am being attacked, in America, as an anti-semite.[1] I did not know this until Max Beloff[2] wrote a very handsome letter defending me. The trouble is that I cannot believe in the private doctrines, the exclusive virtue, or sense of virtue, of these non-conformists: I only want there to *be* non-conformists, in order that society may be fragmented and articulated and sophisticated and self-governing and responsible, and lest one good custom should corrupt the world.[3] I *hate* uniformity, which only leads to mass culture, intellectual banality and the political instability of huge mindless electorates and demagogic rulers: the world of tabloid literature and Sunday supplements, to which I would prefer even an archaic tribal society which can at least, being immune from the *media*, leave great verses to a little clan.[4] How ironic it is that America, which was the receptacle of all those minorities which we Europeans have expelled, should be the creator of that terrifying, total uniformity, conformity, banality! I sometimes think that America has preserved the shell of European diversity far more completely than we have done, while we, who have dissolved the shell, have preserved more of the substance. I mean, religious distinctions are taken very seriously in America, as they are not in Europe; but the differing social character which lies beneath those distinctions is alive with us, dead with them.

I am an uncompromising whig!

---

[1]   T-R's review of Arthur Hertzberg's *The French Enlightenment and the Jews* had appeared in the *New York Times Book Review* under the headline 'Some of my Best Friends are Philosophes'. Hertzberg, in a long riposte, compared T-R's arguments to the 'arrogant' and 'morally outrageous' case for the assimilation of Jewish culture made by Voltaire.

[2]   Max Beloff (1913–99), later Baron Beloff, became a historian of foreign policy, although his first book was a monograph on English public order and civil disturbances in the period after the Restoration. Nuffield Reader in the Comparative Study of Instititions at Oxford 1946–57; Fellow of All Souls and Gladstone Professor of Government and Public Administration, Oxford University 1957–74. T-R considered him a disastrously pugnacious ally, who only had to speak for a cause in either Oxford or the House of Lords for support for it to recede.

[3]   Tennyson, 'Morte d'Arthur'.

[4]   Keats, 'Fragment of an Ode to Maia': 'Leaving great verse unto a little clan'.

I hear the sounds of movement below. It is pleasant to lie in bed, sipping my morning tea and writing, rather discursively I fear, to you. But I must rise and cook my kipper.

Come home soon.

Love from Hugh

---

## To Frances Yates, 28 December 1969

Chiefswood, Melrose

Dear Frances

Thank you for your two letters and for the essay on Rabelais, which I have read again, with renewed pleasure. Poor Mr Bakhtin—I suppose that that discreet phrase means that he disappeared for twenty years into one of Stalin's prison-camps; which perhaps does not encourage either intellectual study or Rabelaisian laughter.[1] But I'm afraid I despair of communist scholarship: I don't believe—after my own experience of 'discussion' with communist scholars in Russia, East Germany, and Rumania—that they *can* free themselves from their intellectual strait-jacket. Like medieval schoolmen, they start from dogma, or even merely from labels, and proceed by assertion. I no longer, now, feel any desire for discussion with them. Even those who are 'heretical' seem to have been too deeply

---

[1]    Mikhail Bakhtin (1895–1975) was a Russian philosopher who also wrote literary criticism, history, sociology, anthropology, and psychology. In the *New York Review of Books* for 9 October 1969 a review by Yates with the title 'The Last Laugh' found grave defects in Bakhtin's *Rabelais and his World*, but quoted, in extenuation, a statement in the editor's introduction that in the early 1930s the author had 'tragically disappeared from the scholarly horizon' for more than two decades, and so had had no opportunity to keep abreast of modern scholarship. Bakhtin was sentenced to exile in Siberia, but after a plea of ill health was banished to Kazakhstan instead.

impregnated by the original orthodoxy to think, or at least to speak or write, freely.

And yet I fondly believe—my studies of Calvinism confirm me in this belief—that an orthodoxy *may* be intellectually stimulating *when it is in dissolution*.[1] The Dutch, the Scottish, the Swiss enlightenment all dawned when the Calvinist discipline was crumbling, and I find that some of the most stimulating writers today are those who, having been trained in Marxism, have since broken with it. In fact, just as I see the stimulating periods of Calvinism as the periods before the discipline was effectively imposed (i.e. before Beza,[2] before the French Huguenots had accepted the siege mentality of the early 17th century) and after it had begun to crumble, so I see the stimulating areas of Marxism as the areas where the discipline of communism has not yet been imposed (e.g. among the French and Italian Marxists), and where it has been repudiated.

Incidentally, in my essay on the Scottish Enlightenment,[3] I think that I emphasised too much the channels through which the solvent ideas came (i.e. the religious nonconformists and the foreigners) and didn't do full justice to those who, in the next generation (the generation of Hume), *applied* those ideas; who were largely conformists with the Established Presbyterian Church (though sceptical in their conformity), a cohesive social group of lawyer-gentry based on Edinburgh and seeking consciously, by the re-creation of a kind of Machiavellian *virtù*, to regenerate a society which, in their eyes, was sunk in barbarism and squalor. It seems to me that, after 1707, this class saw both the necessity and the possibility of a 'great leap forward' from the stagnation of the 17th century to the level of England, and that the very fact of the removal of the government to London gave them their opportunity: politics—the sterile Scottish politics of the 17th century—were now taken out of the country, and the new leaders of society could concentrate on social and economic change.

[1]   T-R makes this argument in his essay 'The Religious Origins of the Enlightenment', published in *Religion, the Reformation and Social Change*.
[2]   Theodore Beza (1519–1605), Calvinist theologian and scholar.
[3]   In *Studies in Voltaire and the Eighteenth Century* (1970); reprinted in T-R's *History and the Enlightenment*, edited by John Robertson (2010).

I also wish, now, that I had said more about James II's court (as Duke of York) in Edinburgh. James II has had such a bad press from historians that he could do with a little praise, and it seems to me that little Roman Catholic court was the centre of such economic and intellectual innovation as was to be found in Scotland in the 1680s. Incidentally, I recently discovered, at Drummond Castle,[1] a letter from Robert Boyle[2] to James, Earl of Perth,[3] from which it is clear that Boyle genuinely respected Perth (that blackest villain in whig eyes) as a patron and virtuoso of natural science. This is certainly not the usual view of him!

I liked your quotation from Sidney,[4] joining Agrippa and Erasmus. I remember that in your *Giordano Bruno* you treat Erasmus as a humanist critic of the new 'magic'. I shall be very interested to hear if you discover any further connexions, at whatever level.

Please send me—if you have copies to spare—any other articles that you write. I want to read *everything* by you.

yours ever

Hugh

⁂

*Tibor Szamuely (1925–72) was born in Moscow of Hungarian Jewish parents. He learnt English as a pupil at Beacon Hill, a progressive school in Hampshire run by Bertrand and Dora Russell: 'Dora Russell was one of the most disagreeable women Bertrand Russell ever married,' Trevor-Roper's friend Hugh Lloyd-Jones once quipped. Szamuely's father was detained during the Stalinist purges of 1937, and vanished: he himself was arrested in Moscow as an American spy in 1950, and served eighteen months' hard labour in a lumber camp.*

---

[1] The T-Rs had stayed in mid-August at Drummond Castle, Crieff, the seat of James Heathcote-Drummond-Willoughby (1907–83), 3rd and last Earl of Ancaster, and his wife 'Wissie' Astor (1909–75). The T-Rs often spent a night at Grimsthorpe, the Ancasters' house in Lincolnshire (with the north front by Vanbrugh), when travelling to Chiefswood.
[2] Robert Boyle (1627–91), natural philosopher and one of the founders of modern chemistry.
[3] James Drummond, 4th Earl of Perth (1648–1716), politician and Lord Chancellor, who introduced the thumb-screw.
[4] Sir Philip Sidney, *A Defence of Poetry*: 'Agrippa will be as merry in showing the vanity of science as Erasmus was in the commending of folly.'

*He was briefly vice-rector of the University of Budapest in 1957, and after his dismissal taught in the Kwame Nkrumah Ideological Institute in Ghana. In 1964 he settled in England, where he became Lecturer in Politics at Reading University, and a pungent critic of the Soviet system in* The Spectator *and elsewhere.*

## To Tibor Szamuely, 6 March 1970

History Faculty Library

My dear Tibor,

Thank you very much for sending me your essay, *"Left" and "Right": the False Dichotomy*. I have read it with great interest and, as always when I read your work, I have learned from it and found myself in agreement with it. I have only one general point to make. It is this.

In your essay you argue, correctly I am sure, that 'fascism' is not an ideology of the Right but rather, like communism, with which it has so much in common, an anti-liberal ideology outside and opposed to the whole political philosophy within which the traditional doctrines of Left and Right were contained. But in doing so you are, I feel, rather summary in that you draw your evidence of fascist ideas too exclusively from Hitler and thus may expose yourself to an answer which might seem to undermine your position. I can imagine a critic replying to you that there was fascism before Hitler and that, had it not been for Hitler, who imposed upon it a new and purely German character, fascism would have been seen, and rightly seen, as the totalitarianism, or semi-totalitarianism, of the Right. Even in Nazi Germany, between 1934 and 1938, fascism was actively supported by the Right—i.e. by the industrialists, the bourgeoisie, the official classes—who had brought it into power in 1933 and whose material interests it served; and if (for instance) Hitler had been killed in 1938, those classes might have made use of his revolution in order to consolidate a 'corporative state', like that of Italy or Portugal, which would then have been accepted as the classic form of fascism. Hitler's radicalism, his racialism, his social nihilism, can be seen as a Teutonic deviation which, because of German power, distorted the development of European fascism; but fascism should not be interpreted solely by reference to that deviation, for it had an independent being and philosophy as a political movement before that distortion.

Of course you can deal with this objection. You can say that you are not concerned with the (false) propaganda whereby fascist parties secured political support from the old parties of the Right any more than you are concerned with the (equally false) propaganda whereby communist parties have secured support from the old parties of the Left, whom equally they have deceived and betrayed. You are concerned with the central philosophy of both parties, which is separable from their tactical alliances. However, I think it better to spell this out in order to forestall the kind of criticism which I foresee.

The trouble is, fascism means what people want it to mean. Unlike communism, it has no agreed doctrinal base. (You will probably say that I flatter communism in saying this). I felt this difficulty, and tried to express it, when I wrote my essay for Stuart Woolf's volume.[1] I have since tried to isolate more narrowly the distinguishing and continuing content of fascism, and I find myself more in agreement with you than with anyone else: I see it as a series of tactics for the pursuit of power rather than as a particular political or social content. Seeing it thus, I recognise that the new fascism, the true heir of the fascism of the 1930s, is to be found in the 'New Left': I consider that there has been no fascism on the Right since 1938. But other people insist on seeing fascism not as the continuing political philosophy of the official and now dead fascist parties, but as the particular political form in which the philosophy was temporarily realised in the 1930s; and that was undoubtedly a form of the Right. The concept of fascism being itself so vague, even so subjective, it is impossible (I think) to disprove their thesis; so the only thing one can do is to define

[1] 'The Phenomenon of Fascism', in *European Fascism*, published in 1968 and edited by Stuart Woolf (b. 1936), a former pupil of T-R's, who has held chairs in modern history at the University of Essex, the European University Institute at Fiesole, and the University of Venice. His works include *History of Italy 1700–1860: The Social Constraints of Political Change* (1979) and *The Poor in Western Europe in the Eighteenth and Nineteenth Centuries* (1986).

one's own terms very exactly and detach and disown the meanings which one does not accept.

I don't know whether you will agree with this, but in any case it does not affect your main argument.

yours ever

Hugh

---

*Robert Blake had been a close ally of Trevor-Roper's when both were at Christ Church, though they gradually drifted apart once they were no longer members of the same college. When this letter was written Blake was working on his history of Rhodesia, which would be published in 1978.*

## To Robert Blake, 17 August 1970

Chiefswood, Melrose

My dear Robert

Will this reach you before you set off for whitest Africa? Perhaps not; but it will reach you sooner or later, and nothing in it but will keep; for it is but to thank you for your hospitable feast on Saturday. I fear that I kept you up rather late, a certain amnesia of place and time having been induced by the lavishness of your hospitality; of which the best, I think, was your own: that delicious Veuve Cliquot.

One needs a stock of champagne in these iron days of Hart[1] and Turpin.[2] The mere thought of them has obliged me to open one of my

---

[1]  Herbert [H. L. A.] Hart had chaired an Oxford University commission on relations with junior members, which had reported in 1969. He appended a section of his own composition, which analysed student revolt in penetrating terms. Hart's report was admired by T-R for its readiness to ignore fashionable doctrine and to return to first principles. Mercurius, too, was unstinting in his praise (16 May 1970): 'Truly I am almost in love with his Socratique rationality; for he asks not how far we should yield, or where resist, but proceeds always by cleer reason from generall truths.' Mercurius added, 'But some fear that he errs in presuming all men to be as rationall as he.'

[2]  T-R claimed Kenneth Turpin had not read a book for 30 years and was partly responsible for Oriel's poor showing in the league table of the performance of colleges in university final examinations, devised by Sir Arthur Norrington, President of Trinity College.

last half-bottles of Krug 1949, with which to sustain me as I pen these dismal names. I fear you are right about Hart, whom I like personally and respect intellectually: he is a highly intelligent, sophisticated, and also tough-minded man; but his views are not our views, and we, after all, hang it, are not unintelligent, or unsophisticated, or soft-minded either; so I see no reason not to presume we are right. Herbert Hart, incidentally, is the maker of Stuart Hampshire as Warden of Wadham: he told me that he had quite a struggle to convince 'them'—i.e., I suppose, the Fellows, who seem to have consulted him.[1] He also told me that 'they' are determined to go co-educational and that Stuart will support that. I think that Wadham is a dreadful college anyway, but I don't think that Stuart will make it any better.

Altogether I find myself hardening in the belief that, in Oxford, heads of houses matter. The more I see of professional university administrators surrendering to professional university agitators, and thereby betraying both the sensible dons and the sensible undergraduates, the more I put my faith in the college system and its internal hierarchy. But what if the monarchs at the pinnacle of that hierarchy let us down? With Warden Hayter in New College[2] and Master Hill in Balliol two once famous colleges slide down the drain. However, I am glad to hear—I hope it is true—that both New College and Balliol have slidden down the Norrington table too; and that may cause some people to think.

All this makes me rejoice that you are Provost of Queen's. It also makes me lament that we shall have poor old Turps for another half-generation as Provost of Oriel. Now that the corner is turned, he is visibly sinking back into cosy conformity, and I despair of building on the new foundations. He has absolutely no sense of dignity or occasion, no grasp of principle, no idea what a university is for. I fear that the river Oriel, which after its 650 year course, was about to tumble over a precipice and disappear

[1]   On 5 February 1970 the fellows of Wadham had announced the election of the philosopher (Sir) Stuart Hampshire (1914–2004) as Bowra's successor as Warden. During the war Hampshire had worked for T-R on radio intelligence.
[2]   T-R believed that Hayter was unduly influenced by his left-wing daughter.

into an abyss, has only been deflected in order to disappear in a stagnant marsh. Jeremy Catto[1] suggests that the only hope is to keep up a permanent state of crisis by bribing undergraduates to invade the Governing Body once a term; but this seems *too* radical a course.[2]

I have been reflecting on the case of Tony Trench.[3] The governors of Fettes *must* have asked why he left Eton, just as you asked me why the late Oriel chef left Oriel. They *must* (unless they are incredibly naïve) have learned the facts. Therefore I can only conclude that, with sublime Scotch confidence, they decided that *it can't happen here*. I suppose they were satisfied that, whatever may happen in the stagnant and corrupt valley of the sub-tropical Thames (that Babylonish river of iniquity), the pure, cool waters of the Firth of Forth are different, and Scotch boys are, if not unyielding, at least untempting.

The *Spectator* has gone sadly downhill since Nigel Lawson gave it up.[4] Journals, I fear, are like colleges. I wonder if Mercurius will continue to write for it: what do you think? The only compensation will be if Nigel gets into Parliament. But I see that Douglas Hurd is tipped for Marylebone,

---

[1] Jeremy Catto (b. 1939), medievalist, Rhodes Fellow, and Tutor in History at Oriel 1969–2006. His former pupil Alan Duncan, in *The Spectator* of 7 June 2006, wrote: 'He is the quintessential Oxford don—his portrait by Boyd Harte shows him in black tie and plimsolls, with his left foot shooting out of the frame. I can't detect Jeremy anywhere in his friend Alan Hollinghurst's novels, but if one were to devour C. P. Snow, *Goodbye Mr Chips* and *Porterhouse Blue*, there is a smattering of Catto in each.'

[2] In January 1970 Turpin had been provoked to take crisp and effective action to expel a group of protesting undergraduates who invaded a meeting of Oriel's governing body, but he retreated towards passivity once the crisis had subsided.

[3] Anthony Chenevix-Trench (1919–79) was a Christ Church pupil of Dundas' who gained first-class honours in classics in 1939. He spent three years as a captive of the Japanese after the fall of Singapore, and did forced labour on the Burma railway. He was coaxed back to Christ Church as a classics don by Dundas in 1951, but stayed there only a year. After various school appointments, he became headmaster of Eton in 1964, but his hard drinking, bouts of exhaustion, and zeal for caning boys led the Provost of Eton to give him notice of dismissal in March 1969. He left Eton in July 1970, but was soon afterwards appointed to succeed to the headmastership of Fettes.

[4] Nigel Lawson had resigned in May 1970 as editor of *The Spectator*, partly because of strained relations with Henry Creighton (1927–2003), chairman of the Scottish Machine Tools Corporation of Glasgow, who had bought the magazine from Ian Gilmour for £75,000 in 1967. On 16 September, after a difficult interregnum, Creighton announced Lawson's successor as editor, the bibulous *Daily Mirror* columnist George Gale (1927–90).

PLATE 1 Trevor-Roper with his pupil Alan Clark on Boxing Day 1947, before their journey to Prague. The Lagonda belonged to Clark's parents.

PLATE 2 Trevor-Roper's brother-in-law Dawyck Haig with his fiancée Adrienne Morley at Bemersyde in the Scottish borders.

PLATE 3
The Christ Church historian in
his rooms overlooking Peckwater
Quad in the mid-1950s.

PLATE 4
The Eton leaving photograph taken
in 1960 of Trevor-Roper's elder
stepson, James Howard-Johnston.

PLATE 5 Trevor-Roper outside Chiefswood, his family's Scottish home from 1959 until 1987.

PLATE 6 The Trevor-Ropers in Chiefswood's silk-lined dining-room, with James and Peter Howard-Johnston.

**PLATE 7**
Chiefswood in 1959, at the
first Christmas the Trevor-Ropers
had spent at the house.

**PLATE 8**
The Yale historian Wallace
Notestein and his wife the
educationalist Ada Comstock
visiting the London Inns
of Court in 1947.

PLATE 9 The Dacres in the Christ Church house, 8 St Aldates, where they lived from 1955 to 1980. The photograph was taken shortly before their move to Cambridge.

**PLATE 10**
The Christ Church classicist Hugh
Lloyd-Jones with a plump friend.

**PLATE 11**
Jeremy Catto, Trevor-Roper's
principal ally at Oriel.

**PLATE 12**
Alasdair Palmer, a graduate student to whom Trevor-Roper wrote regularly in the 1980s and early 1990s, outside the Cambridge house where he entertained the older man to dinner.

**PLATE 13**
Edward Chaney, a scholar whom Trevor-Roper befriended during the Peterhouse years.

**PLATE 14**
At St John's College, University of Queensland. 'I pulled a string, and behold!' (p. 329). The Dacre arms are on the lectern. The benefactor Robert Cripps looks on.

**PLATE 15**
Blair Worden, Trevor-Roper's pupil, friend, and literary executor.

and surely he will get it.[1] I like him very much—I walked across the Pelo-ponnese with him once—but he is rather too good to be true (Nigel has an engaging Ch. Ch. wickedness, while Douglas is an impeccable Eton & Trinity college, Cambridge, man), and certainly too good to be resisted by the householders of St Marylebone.

If you find the rule of a suburban white oligarchy in Africa too oppres-sive, allow me to recommend to you a book to read about *black* Africa. It is Evans-Pritchard's first book *Witchcraft, Oracles and Magic among the Azande,* first published by the Clarendon Press in 1936, still available, and one of the great works of African anthropology.[2] You will enjoy it immensely.

yours ever

Hugh

P.S. Did I tell you that a fellow of Balliol boasted to a friend of mine that Balliol is now so liberal that no undergraduate is ever sent down, or per-haps even punished, unless denounced by a cleaning-woman? So the ultimate powers of jurisdiction have been handed over by the Master & Fellows to the cleaning-women. This is just like communist countries where every intellectual dreads nothing so much as the allegation, against which there is no appeal, that he is disapproved by the working class.

---

[1]    T-R had nominated Hurd's history of the Anglo-Chinese Opium War, *The Arrow War,* together with Peter Brown's biography of Augustine, as his *Sunday Times* books of the year in 1967. Douglas Hurd (b. 1930), later Baron Hurd of Westwell, was Downing Street political sec-retary throughout Edward Heath's premiership of 1970–4. He was shortlisted but rejected by Conservative constitutency selection committees as parliamentary candidate in the Maryle-bone by-election of 1970, and the Arundel and Shoreham and Macclesfield by-elections of 1971, before being adopted for the equally safe seat of Mid-Oxfordshire, where he was elected in the general election of February 1974. He was Home Secretary 1985–9 and Foreign Secre-tary 1989–95. In later life he was a companion of T-R's at the long dining-table of the Beef-steak club.
[2]    (Sir) Edward Evans-Pritchard (1902–73), Professor of Social Anthropology in the Uni-versity of Oxford 1946–70. His acclaimed first book was first published in 1937.

*In the spring of 1972 the Trevor-Ropers spent ten days in Pakistan, as guests of the President, Zulfikar Ali Bhutto (1928–79). Bhutto, who had long been urging Trevor-Roper to visit his country, was now in a position to entertain the Trevor-Ropers as official guests. At Bhutto's first meeting with Trevor-Roper, when he was reading law at Christ Church, the older man, in his capacity as Senior Censor, had rebuked the undergraduate for not wearing a gown. Despite this difficult start the two men were soon on good terms. After leaving Oxford in 1952, Bhutto remained in contact, and often mentioned that he wished his son and daughter to study at Oxford in due course.*

*Bhutto was appointed Minister of Commerce in the martial-law Cabinet formed by President Ayub Khan in 1958, and was promoted to be Foreign Minister in 1963. Following his sacking from the Cabinet, Bhutto in 1967 formed the Pakistan People's Party, which appealed to nationalist, socialist, and Islamic ideas. His tactics in 1970–1 plunged Pakistan into civil war, war with India, defeat, and the loss of East Pakistan, which became the new state of Bangladesh. Bhutto then assumed power as President of the rump of Pakistan, and embarked on a socialist programme. When Trevor-Roper arrived in March 1972, he was impressed by the resilience of the people so soon after a calamitous upheaval.*

*The Trevor-Ropers were treated as honoured guests. They were escorted everywhere by military vehicles, with motorcycle outriders clearing citizens out of their path. Trevor-Roper was embarrassed by this privileged treatment, and pleased when an obstinate bullock refused to give way to their cavalcade. They were taken by helicopter into the Swat Valley, in the tribal area on the border of Afghanistan. Wherever they went, the President would telephone to check that they were being properly entertained. Trevor-Roper had the impression that Bhutto ran the country as a personal fiefdom.*

*The following letter, to Trevor-Roper's Oriel colleague and confidant Jeremy Catto, describes their visit.*

## To Jeremy Catto, 6 April 1972

Chiefswood, Melrose

My dear Jeremy

We have returned from Pakistan. I hope you have returned from Belfast. I telephoned you, but got no answer; but I hope this was merely because you were carousing elsewhere, not because there is some corner of an Ulster field that is for ever Oriel. Or perhaps you have disappeared again to the Balkans or North Africa or South America.

In Pakistan we had the full treatment. A splendid programme was arranged for us, and details were sent, for information and action, to all governors of provinces, commanders of armies, chiefs of police, ministers of state, muezzins, mullahs, wallahs, etc. We never travelled with less than two limousines, three armoured jeeps, a cabinet minister (to carry our bags), our own ADC, and a varying number of outriders. Special police accompanied us, at a discreet distance, in bazaars, mosques, etc. Naturally we had our own private orchestra in case we needed diversion. When we travelled along the Khyber pass, guards stood at attention on every crag. We trod red carpets, inspected guards of honour, took salutes. It happened that the British ambassador returned that day, with his wife and brother and sister-in-law, by car from Kabul. Seeing himself greeted with this ceremony, which he had not noticed on his way out, he asked the reason. He was told that the Trevor-Ropers were expected that day, and it was for them. That put him in his place. I must say that he took it quite well: he told me the story himself a few days later. The French and American Ambassadors were less well-pleased—indeed their noses were visibly disjointed—at being converted into mere background figures to emphasise our apotheosis. We spent our last day cruising in the Arabian Sea in a destroyer, *The President of Pakistan*, with the President of Pakistan. This was very agreeable. The only qualification to our pleasure hit Xandra rather than me: in the remoter parts of the country she found herself segregated among her own sex. This did not exhilarate her. While I enjoyed worldly conversation, and copious potations of whisky, with sophisticated Anglicised generals and politicians, she found herself sitting, with a glass of orangeade in her hand, among a harem of pudding-faced Moslem ladies discussing their embroidery in Pashtu. Occasionally I caught an agonized glance from the depth of the harem, but I judged it prudent to take no notice of it.

We are now back at Chiefswood, slowly and painfully re-adjusting ourselves to that more modest station to which it has pleased God to call us. Happily, having flown direct from Karachi to Edinburgh, I have been able to bring no work from Oxford, so I am enjoying a few days of complete rural indolence, as a necessary method of unwinding after such social exhilaration. On Tuesday we shall fly down & come to Oxford in order to go to the Queen's party at Windsor on Wednesday; but we shall return here on Thursday.[1]

Has anyone died while we were in Pakistan? I am always afraid of being caught napping and not being ready with a replacement at the critical time; for the Enemy sleeps not, and sows tares in our wheat. Unfortunately, it is generally the wrong people who die: the wicked flourish as a green bay tree. I suppose it is too much to hope that it has been pleased God to take the Krailer.[2]

> yours ever
>
> Hugh

---

*Sir Peter Medawar (1915–87) was a biologist who received the Nobel Prize for Medicine in 1960. He was sceptical of the value of psychoanalysis: 'It's an end product, moreover, like a dinosaur or a Zeppelin; no better theory can ever be erected on its ruins, which will remain forever one of the saddest and strangest of all landmarks in the history of twentieth-century thought.' He sent an appreciative message to Trevor-Roper after the latter's essay on Freudian history (entitled 'Re-Inventing Hitler') was published in the* Sunday Times *of 18 February 1973. In the piece, Trevor-Roper discussed Freud's psychoanalysis of Moses before considering a recently published book,* The Mind of Adolf Hitler, *by the American psychoanalyst Walter Langer. This was an updated version of a secret report which had been commissioned in 1943 by Bill Donovan, head of the US wartime Office of Strategic Services.*

---

[1]   When Xandra was divorced in 1954, Court protocol still excluded divorced women from the Royal Enclosure at Ascot and other formal Court events. Xandra, whose mother and aunts had held positions at Court, resented this general ban on divorcées, which was finally relaxed during the 1970s. Thereafter she was keen to accept royal invitations.

[2]   Alban Krailsheimer (1921–2001) won an open scholarship in French and German to Christ Church at the age of 16, and held a tutorial fellowship in French there 1957–88. His teaching of undergraduates was relentless in its pursuit of top examination results, and relied on fierce interrogatory techniques. In the 1970s he became devoted to the memory of Armand-Jean de Rancé, a Cistercian whose community, La Trappe, practised strict penitence and forbade intellectual pursuits. He was increasingly drawn into the life of this austere community, and died there.

*Trevor-Roper was withering about 'Dr Langer's confident progress from unverifiable hypothesis through arbitrary symbolism to dogmatically stated fact' and his 'clinical fairyland'.*

## To Sir Peter Medawar, 24 February 1973

History Faculty Library, Merton Street

Dear Medawar,

I shall not be able to read your book *The Hope of Progress* till after the weekend; but let me write at once to thank you for your kind letter about my article on Psycho-history. I am always delighted to find myself on the same side of the barricades as you, even though you assure me, this time, that we can't win!

And yet, can we not? Of course we shall never convert the believers; but may we not convince the waverers that the 'science' of psychoanalysis, however internally coherent and self-contained, is by that very fact, like a tautology in language, useless as a means to knowledge? The belief in witchcraft, to which I likened it, was irrefutable in its own terms; but it collapsed in the end through its irrelevance to reality.

Incidentally, your letter strengthens that comparison. The demonologists too had a perfect answer to every objection. If a 'witch' denied the charge, the denial was regarded as proof of the crime. So she too couldn't win.

Unless you forbid me, I would like (if occasion arises) to quote your second paragraph.

I treasure your article on Teilhard du Chardin,[1] and would be delighted to read anything that you write which is within my comprehension; so if you are ever distributing offprints, please include me on your list.[2]

---

[1]  Pierre Teilhard de Chardin (1881–1955), Jesuit priest and palaeontologist, who was forbidden by his religious superiors to publish his book *The Phenomenon of Man*, though it would appear posthumously.

[2]  In his review (published in *Mind*, volume 70) of Teilhard de Chardin's *The Phenomenon of Man*, Medawar declared: '*The Phenomenon of Man* stands square in the tradition of *Naturphilosophie*,

The *Sunday Times* has sent me a sheaf of furious (and prolix) letters from psychoanalysts. The most violent is from one Vincent Tilsley who, I think, gave Langer's book a long and enthusiastic puff in the *New Statesman*.[1]

yours sincerely

Hugh Trevor-Roper

———⚬⚬⚬———

*Trevor-Roper took a keen and kindly interest in a variety of graduate students over the course of nearly half a century. One of them was Jeremy Cater (b. 1940), who would later contribute a chapter on Enlightenment Edinburgh in the 1770s to his mentor's Festschrift, and would prepare Trevor-Roper's* The Invention of Scotland: Myth and History *for posthumous publication in 2008. Cater spent eighteen months teaching at Alvescot College in Oxford-shire, which combined English sixth-form education with American college education, until Trevor-Roper persuaded the Wolfson Foundation to give him a grant that enabled him to continue his research and writing. 'For four or five years,' Cater recalled, 'he inspired and spurred me on, commenting with precision and tact on what I wrote, constantly encouraging me in every way, intellectually and socially. He was supervisor, patron and friend: all to an extraordinary degree.'*

a philosophical indoor pastime of German origin which does not seem even by accident (though there is a great deal of it) to have contributed anything of permanent value to the storehouse of human thought.' He described the greater part of the book as 'nonsense, tricked out with a variety of tedious metaphysical conceits, and its author can be excused of dishon-esty only on the grounds that before deceiving others he has taken great pains to deceive himself'.

[1] Vincent Tilsley (b. 1931) came to prominence as a television serial scriptwriter with *The Makepeace Story*, a family saga set in a cotton town (1955). His adaptations of literary classics into television serials included Scott's *Kenilworth* (1957), Austen's *Emma* (1960), and Dickens's *David Copperfield* (1966). He was said to have abandoned writing for television, and became a psychotherapist, after his six-hour drama about the final days in the bunker, 'The Death of Adolf Hitler' (broadcast in 1973), was cut to under two hours' running-time. Clive James com-mented that Tilsley 'had obviously soaked himself in Hitler's table talk, perhaps to the irre-versible detriment of his own prose style' (*Observer*, 14 January 1973).

# To Jeremy Cater, 16 April 1973

Chiefswood, Melrose

My dear Jeremy

Your long letter deserves more than a verbal acknowledgment; so I now write. I was delighted by it: alike by its length, its form, its content, and by the confidence which you show in telling me so much about your work. As you know, I have complete confidence in you and am sure that you will produce an important work; but I am also anxious that it should be a striking work, something out of the ordinary, something that even the professional Scotch historians will *have* to notice because it will be read outside their little magic circle, and so they will be forced to discuss it and not bury it (as they could within that circle) with a few condescending private formulae. In order that it shall have this effect, you must elevate it, as you can (and as so few of your colleagues and competitors can), above the common run of theses. You must give it form and vitality. Form, of course, only comes from care and discipline; vitality comes from you. I know you can give this because your letters are full of vitality; and indeed your whole recent history, including your survival of Alvescot (which, incidentally, I see is moving into Oxford), is evidence of that. So I am delighted that you have now discovered the ideal form for your work also. I am quite sure that you are right. The essence of form is unity. So many writers ruin a good subject by ignoring this: their theme may have a natural unity but they do not discover it in time or present it properly. And unity entails a sense of proportion: the subordinate parts, or episodes, must be related, in their due proportion and subordination, to the central theme. If you can envisage the central episode, or problem (as you have done with the confrontation over Ferguson[1]), and will then take some

---

[1] The struggle which Cater had studied had brought into question the stature of David Hume in the Scottish Enlightenment and the principle of free thought which he represented. A party opposed to Hume tried to have his friend Adam Ferguson (1723–1816), former Professor of Philosophy at Edinburgh, replaced as travelling tutor to the young Earl of Chesterfield. The story is the backdrop to the essay contributed later by Cater to the *Festschrift* for T-R.

trouble to make this the unifying centre of your work, and then write with confidence and *brio* (which must be fed, if necessary, on champagne purchased on the credit of future royalties), I assure you that all will be well. Above all, *enjoy* writing. It is not always easy to do so. One has to get over the flat somehow. But if one is excited by a subject, or a discovery, one should be able to communicate the excitement; and after all, we write to be read. Why should we expect 'the reader' to read us unless we make some effort to interest him in our wares?

I write all this *ex animo*,[1] because I have just read a thesis, on a good subject, which defies all the sound Poloniate precepts[2] set down in that standard work which was entitled (I think) *Notes on the writing of theses in the Faculty of Modern History,*[3] but which is more popularly known (as I understand from James) as *Anonymus de These Scribendâ*. It is of enormous length, and all form is lost in a tedious accumulation of detail, presented in an illiterate, asyntactical style. Alas, I say to myself, as I struggle through chapter after chapter of apparently meaningless prosopographical *minutiae*, I preach in vain; but this, after all, is the common fate of preachers, from which I should not hope for exemption.

I forget when I last saw you. Was it before or after my visit to Amsterdam? I have been in perpetual motion since the last days of March. First I went to Holland, theoretically to attend a conference organized by the European Movement,[4] in fact to take Xandra for a few days away from the kitchen (which she hates). I don't know why I was asked, but I went. I avoided most of the conference and read manuscripts in the university library at Leiden while politicians, mainly English and American, pomped away in Amsterdam. We found a few friends there, so it was quite enjoyable. The announcement of my victory (at last) over Lord Chalfont and the BBC was published while we were there, and I am glad to say that it

---

[1]  'From the heart'.
[2]  i.e. as sententious as the advice given by Polonius to his son Laertes in *Hamlet*.
[3]  A booklet for graduate students written anonymously by T-R in 1966.
[4]  An elite campaigning group, spearheaded by Lord Harlech, Lord Gladwyn, and Roy Jenkins, and financed by business interests: its aim of British membership of the European Economic Community had been achieved on 1 January 1973.

seemed to give general pleasure—less, I think, through general love of me than through general hatred of my enemies.[1] Then we came up here. But scarcely had we settled into our rural routine when I felt it my duty to go to London to attend the annual meeting of the British Academy sections and prevent the philistines from scoring surreptitious victories in my absence. This is a battle which has to be fought every year. I *think* that we are prevailing; but the price of liberty is eternal vigilance, for while men sleep, the enemy comes and sows tares in their wheat.

Actually the great victory was won several years ago, when the medievalists were driven into a corner, in which they have since been firmly contained. I am sure you know how all historical studies in England, until quite recently, were controlled by a close oligarchy of medievalists trained at Balliol college and Manchester University. Tout and Tait were the Founding Fathers,[2] Stenton,[3] Davis[4] and Powicke the consolidators of the *régime*. By the time when Powicke sat on the throne, no historian could be appointed to any chair unless he was a medievalist trained in the right school and approved by the Elect. The Elect also invented a doctrine to preserve their own power: they maintained that 'there is no History but Medieval History': that is, that non-medieval history, since it did not

---

[1]   Alan Gwynne Jones, Lord Chalfont (b. 1919), Harold Wilson's Foreign Office minister responsible for disarmament 1964–7 and for European affairs from 1967 until June 1970, had made rash references to T-R on the live BBC2 television discussion programme *Late Night Line-Up* in August 1970. Chalfont had described T-R's contribution to a television documentary about Philby as 'gruesome'. It was 'curious', he said, that T-R should wish not to meet Philby again, 'as if there was something unclean about him', since T-R himself had been 'a spy', 'and evidently a substantially less successful one'. A letter from Chalfont to the BBC Director-General had compounded the offence by alleging that T-R had misquoted him: 'not a very good start from a professional historian!' In due course T-R's complaint against Chalfont and the BBC reached the High Court, where he was awarded damages of £2,500. He received many messages of congratulation, including a telegram from Harold Macmillan.

[2]   Thomas Tout (1855–1929), Professor of History at Manchester University 1890–1925, and James Tait (1863–1944), Professor of Ancient and Medieval History at Manchester 1902–19, were both Balliol-educated medievalists.

[3]   Sir Frank Stenton (1880–1967), Professor of Modern History at Reading University 1912–46, was an undergraduate at Keble, not Balliol. He specialized in Anglo-Saxon England and early feudalism after 1066.

[4]   Henry [H. W. C.] Davis (1874–1928), Fellow of Balliol 1902–21, Professor of Modern History at the University of Manchester 1921–5, Regius Professor of Modern History at Oxford from 1925, was a historian of England in the Norman and Angevin periods.

depend on the mystical mathematics of Councils and Cartularies, Palaeography and Diplomatic, the Wapentake and the Wardrobe, was a less exacting discipline, a second-class kind of history, in fact not history at all but trivial dilettante chit-chat whose practitioners were not even to be considered for posts of honour among true, i.e. medieval, historians. As a natural corollary of this doctrine, the medievalists acquired complete control of the historical section of the British Academy, packed it with their creatures, and kept all non-medievalists out.[1]

A few years ago, after a brisk struggle, the powers of Powicke having waxed feeble, and his numerous brood of Galbraiths, Cheneys, Jacobs etc. not being as vigilant as he, the iron rule of the oligarchy was broken, and the historical section was divided into three: Medieval, Early Modern, Modern. In consequence of this the membership of the Academy was transformed, because while the dud medievalists of course could and did continue to elect each other to their own section, they could no longer block modernists from entry through the other two doors, now suddenly opened. They are naturally very cross at this development, but they have not changed their character. Like the 15th century 'Empire' of Trebizond, they maintain their old imperial airs in the miniscule area to which they are now confined. Appropriately, my main source of information about their ceremonies and politics is that acute byzantinologist Steven Runciman who naturally, from the throne of the Caesars, looks with contempt on the petty barons and monks of the Western Middle Ages who surround and outnumber him. I dare not—as yet—tell you the details of the last battle, or his comments on them; but I will.

I came straight back here; have read two theses and the entire prose works of Milton;[2] and in a few days we go to spend Easter in the Isle of

---

[1]    In 1974 T-R secured the election of the Byzantinist (Sir) Dimitri Obolensky (1918–2001) as a Fellow of the British Academy after medievalists had declined to nominate him. According to T-R, 'the medievalists regard Byzantium as peripheral to Lincolnshire'. He went over the heads of the medievalist section and proposed Obolensky's election directly to the British Academy's Council, which vets the sections' recommendations and can make its own. Obolensky had been elected to a studentship at Christ Church in 1950, and held a personal chair in Russian and Balkan medieval history 1961–85.

[2]    This was in preparation for his lecture 'The Elitist Politics of Milton', which was published in the Times Literary Supplement, 1 June 1973.

Mull, where I suspect that the bottle will be more in evidence than the book. Then I shall return to Oxford for three days (25–28 April) before going for a week to Israel. I hope I shall see you either before I go there or after I return (if I return: I am somewhat apprehensive of Al Fatah, Kamikaze, Palestinian Liberation Force, etc., but somehow I seem committed). Meanwhile, I am launching a counter-attack against the execrable Batey[1] and am also even planning—a fond ambition of impossibility—to inject some intellectual life into Christ Church. Of course I shall fail; but no battle has been lost until it has been fought, and I shall do my best to turn even that adipose and pachydermatous flank. This last manoeuvre entails some *renversement des alliances*,[2] and I am bracing myself to behave with some nauseating sycophancy in the good cause.

But the cause in which I will stop at nothing is the higher cause of promoting the *magnum opus* of Cater. Please continue in a state of euphoria and productive industry and tell me—without distracting yourself by writing another magnificent letter (though I love receiving your letters)—how you are progressing; and do not hesitate to call upon me for any help that you think I can give.

yours ever
Hugh

───⊗⊗⊗───

*In the summer of 1973 Trevor-Roper received a letter from a stranger, Professor Rudolf Geigy, Director of the Swiss Institute for Tropical Medicine. He explained that his friend Professor Reinhard Hoeppli, who had recently died, had left documents of literary and historical value, with instructions that they should be offered to Trevor-Roper for deposit in the Bodleian. Early in August Trevor-Roper, who was visiting Switzerland in the hope of a meeting with François Genoud, the literary executor of Goebbels and Bormann, had a rendezvous at Basel airport with Geigy. He left the airport clutching the manuscript memoirs of Sir Edmund Backhouse (1873–1944), an obscure baronet and sinologist, who had made a munificent gift*

---

[1]  Keith Batey (1919–2010), the Christ Church Treasurer, wanted the T-Rs to vacate no. 8 St Aldates, where they had been tenants since 1955.
[2]  'Reversal of alliances'.

*of Chinese books and manuscripts to the Bodleian more than half a century earlier. After scandalizing his Quaker banker family by his homosexuality and prodigal expenditure at Oxford, Backhouse was in 1898 sent as a remittance man to Peking, where he lived in an increasingly reclusive style until his death. Trevor-Roper, when he scrutinized the memoirs after returning from Switzerland, found them to be of startling obscenity. He read* Backhouse's two published works, China under the Empress Dowager (1910) *and* Annals and Memoirs of the Court of Peking (1914), *and began to suspect that Backhouse had been a forger, fantasist, and confidence-trickster. Trevor-Roper was always intrigued by self-mystifying and self-aggrandizing crooks. Soon he was embarked upon researches which resulted in the publication in 1976 of* A Hidden Life: The Enigma of Sir Edmund Backhouse.

## To Jeremy Catto, 27 August 1973

Chiefswood, Melrose

My dear Jeremy

I suppose you are clearing nettles at Eydon.[1] I know of only two ways of clearing nettles at this time of year. One is sodium chlorate, which kills everything in the ground, and seeps, carrying its universal death, in all directions, and leaves the ground poisoned for six months; the other is digging them up, root by root, and all their subterranean tentacles. This is by far the best way, and very therapeutic to the mind if it is congested by such extraneous matter as Oriel college, the Provost, Wyclif,[2] Watergate,[3] etc. Of course they come again, but fewer, and then you have the pleasure of a further spell of therapy, to exorcise new *incubi* from the mind. But pause, I beg you, for a few moments among your mounds of dying weeds, to comfort me on two matters, to exorcise my two *incubi*, viz: (1) Harold

---

[1]   The Northamptonshire village where Catto has had a house since 1973.
[2]   Catto was working on John Wyclif at this time.
[3]   In July 1973, during the Watergate special committee inquiry into the burglary and attempted wire-tapping of the Democratic National Committee headquarters in the Watergate building, Washington DC, it emerged that President Richard M. Nixon had tape-recorded conversations held in his office. These proved the complicity of Nixon's White House staff, and he resigned the presidency in 1974.

Macmillan, (2) Sir E.T. Backhouse. Both have now reduced me to perplexity.

The first is relatively simple. All you have to do (since you have read all the volumes of his memoirs) is to direct me to some choice passages to which I can refer in my speech next month, which is beginning to trouble me;[1] for the great distraction of Bulgaria lies between. The second problem is greater: indeed, it weighs upon my mind.

I presume that, by now, you have read both of Sir E. Backhouse's works. What do you make of them? Sometimes when I envisage myself making the case for publication to the Curators of the Bodleian—and, in the first stance, to the Standing Committee presided over by the Dean of Christ Church—my spirit fails. No doubt I shall have the support, on different grounds, of two Curators, *viz*: Four-Letter Nell,[2] out of 'liberalism', and Hugh Lloyd-Jones, out of general outrageousness. But neither of them is on the Standing Committee, most of whom are dried-up prudes. And anyway—the crucial question: can one say that the Memoirs are genuine? Do you think that perhaps Sir E. Backhouse may have imagined it all? I am beginning to wonder. There is that diary of Chiang-Shan, which he may have forged. There is the alleged diary of the Chief Eunuch Li Lyen-Ling: is it really in Lloyd's Bank? And was Verlaine a private schoolmaster in Ascot? And if the diary of Chiang-Shan was forged, and the diary of the Chief Eunuch is not in Lloyd's Bank, and Verlaine did not teach at Ascot,

---

[1]    T-R was one among several speakers at a gathering at the Dorchester Hotel to mark the publication in September 1973 of the sixth and final volume of the political memoirs of his publisher and Oxford's Chancellor, Harold Macmillan. The current Prime Minister, Ted Heath, and his predecessor, Harold Wilson, also spoke. T-R spoke first, for ten minutes, then Heath and Wilson for five each, then Macmillan (who mentioned T-R's efforts on his behalf in the Chancellorship election). T-R remarked on Macmillan's 'historical sense', and on 'the conscious duality of his nature, wrenched, as it were, in 1914, from the quiet world of literature, which he still loves, to the necessities of life, decision, battle'. 'What I most admire him is the combination of two qualities: on one hand, courage, willingness to face and decide great issues: on the other gaiety, imperturbability, a sense of proportion, a capacity to enjoy the variety, and the comedy of human life.'
[2]    Probably Dame Helen Gardner (1908–86), Merton Professor of English Literature, who had testified as a defence witness when *Lady Chatterley's Lover* was prosecuted for obscenity in 1960. She surprised those accustomed to a certain primness in her demeanour by telling the court that the words 'fuck' and 'fucking' occurred 'not less than thirty times' in the book.

how can we believe anything? Dr Hoeppli's rickshaw man may have been repeating rumours which emanated ultimately from Backhouse himself.[1] Faced by this vortex of doubt, I look for an Archimedean point of solid fact on which to stand; but alas, I can find none. Nobody, it seems, ever knew Sir Edmund; except Dr. Hoeppli, who is now dead. By now, I almost begin to doubt Backhouse's existence; and his memoirs begin to seem a senile literary fantasy of no evidential value whatsoever. Perhaps the correct course would be to read though, in the PRO, all the diplomatic corres-pondence between London and Peking between 1898 and 1941. It is mad-dening that Hoeppli sat on the manuscript for 30 years. Had I known about it a few years ago I could have consulted Sir Hughe Knatchbull-Hugessen who was ambassador in China in the 1930s, and whom I knew;[2] but Hoep-pli has waited until all the possible critics are dead. I have written to our present ambassador in Peking, who is a Chinese scholar and may have local sources, and to the aged French bookseller in Hong Kong who (according to Harold Acton) was the only Western contact of Backhouse in Peking. I have not yet heard from either. Anyway, you have now read more of the memoirs than I have; so do tell me what you think.

I have been busy writing lectures on Burckhardt. I wonder if anyone will come to them. Magda Minio told me that the opposition to Burck-hardt, vocally expressed in the Faculty, is all imaginary.[3] She teaches Burckhardt and says that the undergraduates are not bored by him at all:

---

[1]  Backhouse had entrusted his memoirs to Reinhard Hoeppli (1893–1973), a physician specializing in parasitology who was Swiss consul-general in Peking 1942–5. Hoeppli (a portly, mischievous bachelor and gourmet, who collected jade) prepared them for publica-tion before they were handed to T-R at Basel airport.

[2]  In 1937, while British Ambassador to China, Sir Hughe ('Snatch') Knatchbull-Hugessen (1886–1971) was wounded when his car was riddled with bullets by a Japanese aircraft: he was ultimately confined to a wheelchair as a result of his injuries. He was British Ambassador to Turkey 1939–44.

[3]  Burckhardt was the set author in German in the Preliminary Examination in Modern History, for which undergraduates had to study a historical work in two foreign languages. Tim Mason (see 219 n. 2) and others wished to replace Burckhardt by a more Teutonic author. Magda Ungar (1910–87) married in 1938 Lorenzo Minio-Paluello (1907–86), who shortly after-wards left Italy because of the racial laws. Oriel's then Provost, W. D. Ross, brought them to Oxford, where Lorenzo Minio-Paluello was appointed Lecturer in Medieval Philosophy 1956, elected FBA 1957 and Professorial Fellow of Oriel 1962–75.

they are bored only by Schenk.[1] So I have squared Schenk and am going to give three lectures on 'Burckhardt as historian', *plus* one discussion, in the hope of saving the subject: for if Burckhardt goes, we shall, by Gresham's Law, have a far, far worse thing: some monstrous birth by Tim Mason[2] out of Karl Leyser.[3]

I have enjoyed writing these lectures. The trouble is, I'm afraid I take such things too seriously. I mean, I get too interested in them and what they lead me into. I have not only read or re-read almost all Burckhardt but also most of Nietzsche and much of Ranke, and so I have had no time for more urgent but less interesting subjects, and my literary creditors dun me furiously, and I do not even open any letters from them, or the Inland Revenue, or the Provost. With any luck I shall not open any from the IRA either.[4]

Did you read Rowse on Enid Starkie?[5] I enjoyed the phrase, 'her egoism was a bore'. *Quis tulerit Gracchos de seditione querentes?*[6]

yours ever

Hugh

---

[1]  Hans-Georg Schenk (1912–79), Senior Lecturer in European Economic and Social History at the University of Oxford from 1954 and Fellow of Wolfson College from 1966 until his death, gave faculty lectures on Burckhardt. He wrote *The Mind of the European Romantics* (1979).

[2]  Timothy Mason (1940–90) was a Research and then Tutorial Fellow at St Peter's College, Oxford, 1966–84. He wrote a highly adverse review of Taylor's *Origins of the Second World War* from the standpoint of a Marxist historian of the working classes in Nazi Germany. Co-founder of the History Workshop, and editor of *Past & Present*. Suffered from manic depression, fled Thatcher's Britain, and killed himself in Rome after his 50th birthday.

[3]  Karl Leyser (1920–92) was a German Jewish refugee who, like Minio-Paluello, was interned on the Isle of Man as an enemy alien in 1940. A protégé of Bruce McFarlane at Magdalen, he was a Fellow and Tutor in Medieval History there; FBA 1983; Chichele Professor of Medieval History 1984–8.

[4]  In the preceding week some ten IRA letter bombs had been delivered in London, one of which badly injured the secretary-general of the Stock Exchange. Book parcels were being double-checked at London sorting-offices, and the police had issued warnings about bank holiday weekend deliveries. On the day that this letter was written an IRA letter bomb delivered at the British Embassy in Washington blew off the left hand of Norah Murray, the military attaché's secretary.

[5]  Rowse reviewed Joanna Richardson's recently published biography of Enid Starkie (1897–1970), Fellow of Somerville from 1934 and University Reader in French Literature 1946–65, who was a conspicuous social figure and academic intriguer in the university. Hugh Lloyd-Jones had written of Rowse's review to T-R (28 August 1973), 'Everything he says about that vain, stupid, noisy old trout applies to him.'

[6]  'Who could endure the Gracchi complaining of sedition?' Juvenal, *Satires* 2.24.

*Blair Worden (b. 1945) came to know Trevor-Roper when supervised by him in the early stages of his work as a graduate student at Oxford on seventeenth-century England. In a memoir of Trevor-Roper published in* Biographical Memoirs of Fellows of the British Academy, *volume 6 (2008) he recalled that after his own move to Cambridge, at the age of 24, in 1969, 'I began to receive, to my puzzlement at the privilege, long letters from him, full of gorgeous and scandalous comedy but also of delicate intellectual guidance.' The correspondence continued after Worden's return to Oxford in 1974 as Fellow and Tutor in Modern History at St Edmund Hall and persisted through Trevor-Roper's life. Worden, who is Trevor-Roper's literary executor, prepared his book* Europe's Physician: The Various Life of Sir Theodore Mayerne *for its posthumous publication in 2006.*

*This letter was written soon after the Trevor-Ropers' return from another visit to Pakistan as guests of Zulfikar Ali Bhutto, by now Prime Minister under a new constitution.*

## To Blair Worden, 10 April 1975

Chiefswood, Melrose

My dear Blair

I wonder what makes you think there is any secrecy or secretiveness about my movements. They are as open as the migration of storks or the unvarying revolutions of the celestial orbs. We have been on a brief visit to the valley of the Indus and the mountains of the Afghan frontier and the Hindu Kush: a long-standing invitation which had been accepted last year. Admittedly, at a certain critical moment, I thought it prudent to cancel the visit: some of our colleagues are so prone to imagine devious interconnexions; but I was afterwards overpersuaded, so we went, and have had a very enjoyable time travelling with the P.M. through the Prohibited Tribal Areas. At every halt I was presented with murderous, sharp, gaily bedizened daggers, designed for use, not mere ostentation,[1] of which I now have an ample collection. They will come in very useful in the

---

[1]  In chapter 7 of his *Decline and Fall of the Roman Empire*, Gibbon writes of Gordianus the younger, who shared the Roman empire with his father: 'Twenty-two acknowledged concubines, and a library of sixty-two thousand volumes, attested the variety of his inclinations; and from the productions which he left behind him, it appears that the former as well as the latter were designed for use rather than for ostentation.'

Jungle of Academe. It was unfortunate that the P.M. had to break away owing to the assassination of King Feisal,[1] and fly to the funeral at Riyadh; but we continued our progress as planned. On our return to Rawalpindi we were able to revisit Lahore. I love Lahore: a real city, with a character of its own. And what buildings! Have you ever been

To Agra and Lahore of Great Mogul?[2]

If not, go. And besides, although worldly glory is, of course, as the earl of Clincham said to Mr Salteena (I trust you are a reader of *The Young Visiters*),[3] 'piffle before the wind', nevertheless, it is gratifying to be treated with due consideration; and in Lahore I always have been. Each time that I have been there, I have passed through those wide streets not silently or inconspicuously, not secretly or secretively as you would have me move, but preceded by outriders on motor-cycles with sirens wailing to clear the way for me—buses, bicycles and bullocks plunging briskly out of my path—and an escort of armed men following in an obedient jeep. This, I must admit, is more than I get in Oxford, or even in Melrose, where I now relax after these exhilarating oriental travels and try to compose my mind and prepare my Wiles lectures;[4] which alas will be very dull, unless the IRA can be persuaded to enliven them with their unpredictable detonations.

But alas, time whisks by, and soon—in ten days' time—I suppose that I must creep back to that dank valley of the Thames, to the impotent internecine buzzing of Oriel college, to the anarchical philistinism of Christ Church, to the cant, sanctimony and priggery of Wolfson college, and to the sustained, if modulated, bumble of the History Board. *Di meliora piis!*[5] How much I would prefer, in this quiet valley (quiet until a regional

---

[1]  King Faisal of Saudi Arabia (1906–75) was shot through the chin and ear on 25 March by his nephew, who was publicly beheaded on 18 June.
[2]  Milton, *Paradise Lost*, Book XI.
[3]  A novella written by Daisy Ashford (1881–1972) at the age of 9, but not published until 1919.
[4]  T-R's Wiles Lectures on 'The Ecumenical Movement and the Church of England 1598–1618' were delivered at Queen's University, Belfast in 1975.
[5]  'May the gods send better fortune to the righteous.' Virgil, *Georgics* 3.513.

hospital is built immediately on top of us[1] and a school for hopelessly anti-social children from Glasgow rises in front of us)

> To sit beside a running brook
> And con with inexpressive look
> An unintelligible book.[2]

But I shall look forward to seeing some of my friends who fall into none of the academic categories which I deplore: rare exceptions indeed, of whom you are one.

For really, I have to admit to myself—it is a sad and solemn admission, but we must all, one day, come to the moment of truth—I do not like dons. I suppose they were always awful, even when their awfulness was different, conformist, not non-conformist: selfish, small-minded, life-diminishing...what a parcel of envious, pretentious, purblind, complacent pedants! Do you remember what Selden said of the bishops of his time, whom he contrasted with the robust prelates of the Middle Ages: 'he gets a living, and then a greater living, and then a greater, and so he comes to govern'.[3] I often think of this remark when I hear my colleagues—and especially certain particular colleagues—sounding off: he passes an examination, and then a greater examination, and then a greater, and so he comes to lay down the law to the world. And when I read those portentous round-robins in which academics, whose only qualification is a doctorate in crystallography or social anthropology, utter their collective, not to say tabloid, wisdom on the most abstruse problems of foreign affairs, I think of that archetype of the self-important radical don, George Buchanan, who, in the words of the incomparable

---

[1]  The T-Rs had been dismayed when, in 1968, land adjoining Chiefswood had been sold as the site for a 400-bed District General Hospital. This development threatened the Arcadian isolation of Chiefswood. Although T-R belatedly organized resistance, bureaucratic momentum to build the hospital proved unstoppable.

[2]  T-R is thinking of Lewis Carroll's 'The Third Voice': 'Easier I count it to explain | The jargon of the howling main, | Or, stretched beside some sedgy brook, | To con with inexpressive look, | An unintelligible book.'

[3]  From the *Table-Talk* of John Selden (1584–1654).

Fr. Innes,[1] having never been in any employment of the state, but having spent most of his years in colleges, in the mean station of a grammarian, set up all on a sudden for a statesman, to dictate to kings the rules by which they were to govern, under pain of being pursued by their subjects, obliged to answer before their tribunal, deposed, etc[2]...But at least Buchanan knew how to write. His successors (perhaps mercifully in view of his effectiveness) are largely illiterate.

But I must control myself. Forget what I have written. When I return, the mind composed by rural tranquillity, I shall be all smiles and suavity to the whole caboodle of them. Can one go further than that? After all, the wretches all have votes, and I must remember the rules of life. Off goes his bonnet to an oyster-wench[3] (I only wish there were some oyster-wenches to unbonnet to in these iron days!) I shall be all things to all men (at least I shall try, for a time: a day or two), and as prim as the worst of them, and shall cant away like the unexpurgated Ludlow,[4] only releasing my true feelings to you, and some others, *inter pocula*, in the Eastgate, the Chequers, or the Bear.[5]

yours ever

Hugh

PS. I have been casting an eye over my collection of Afridi and Masoudi daggers. I have decided to take *four* to Oxford, leaving *two* for use against my neighbours here. I think this is the correct distribution. They are designed to slit open the belly *from behind* (the safest form of approach), and have delicately cut channels to drain off the blood. Cf Judges III 21–22.[6]

---

[1]   Fr Thomas Innes (1662–1744), an exiled Catholic priest and Jacobite who attacked the bases of Scottish national myths, and whom in *The Invention of Scotland* T-R called 'the first and greatest of Scottish antiquaries'.

[2]   A paraphrase of a passage in Innes's *A Critical Essay on the Ancient Inhabitants of the Northern Parts of Britain, or Scotland* (2 vols., 1729).

[3]   Shakespeare, *Richard II*, I.iv.30.

[4]   Worden had discovered from a manuscript in the Bodleian that the voluminous memoirs of the regicide Edmund Ludlow (1616/17–92), a standard text for the study of the Civil Wars, had been expurgated and rewritten by a late 17th-century editor, who had eliminated Ludlow's intense Puritanism.

[5]   The Eastgate, the Chequers, and the Bear are all Oxford pubs.

[6]   'And Ehud put forth his left hand, and took the dagger from his right thigh, and thrust it into his belly: And the haft also went in after the blade; and the fat closed upon the blade, so that he could not draw the dagger out of his belly; and the dirt came out.'

PPS. In Rawalpindi, a very jolly dinner was given in our honour by General Tikka Khan[1] (see the miserable Gombrich's flysheet). The PM ragged him mercilessly: 'You know, you lost me that Oxford election'.[2] But T.K. (a charming man) took it very well: 'Never mind: try again next year!'

———— ∞ ————

## To Blair Worden, 29 July 1976

Chiefswood, Melrose

My dear Blair

I am suffering from a bout of post-parturition exhaustion, and have decided, until Xandra's grand concert (Saturday) and our garden-opening (Sunday) are over, to relax, to ignore all calls of duty, and to do nothing except write private letters, on a light diet of fresh lobsters and old champagne (to be paid for by the pornographic best-seller of which I have been brought to bed). I must admit that when they held the little creature up to me, in page-proof[3]

et adhuc a matre rubentem,[4]

I was pleased with it. Whether others will be is of course another matter. It has now gone off to be nursed in the publisher's *crèche* at Bristol until it is presentable, which will be in October.

It will then be presented to you. One part of it, at least, was written for you (all books have to be written for someone), *viz*, the index. You are the

---

[1]  Tikka Khan (1915–2002) had directed the harsh military repression of separatists in East Pakistan during the Bangladesh war of 1971. After Bhutto's execution in 1979, he became a leader of Bhutto's Pakistan People's Party, and was Governor of the Punjab 1988–90.

[2]  T-R had tried to secure the award of an honorary degree for Bhutto at Oxford. He had been defeated by a campaign in which one of the most effective figures was Richard Gombrich (b. 1937), then University Lecturer in Sanksrit and Pali and Fellow of Wolfson College, afterwards Boden Professor of Sanskrit and Fellow of Balliol 1976–2004, and Director of the Oxford Centre for Buddhist Studies 2004–9.

[3]  i.e. the biography of Backhouse.

[4]  Juvenal, *Satires* 7.196: 'and still red from [its] mother's womb'.

only person (apart from Keith Thomas, who deplored it[1]) who noticed the index of *Religion, the Reformation and Social Change*; so I had you in mind when I wrote this index—or rather, when I put the frills on to Xandra's patient donkey work. (I am not sure that there is not a mixed metaphor in that sentence, but pray let it pass). I hope you will approve at least of that.

We have had no water-crisis yet, but I live in daily apprehension.[2] We depend on a private cistern, beyond a wood, a steep hill and a field of barley. We boast that our water is, in consequence, *pure*, i.e. uncontaminated by chlorine etc. On the other hand, in times of drought, agile and slender creatures—stoats, weasels, young rabbits etc.—panting for water, contrive to insinuate themselves through cracks and crannies, fall into the cistern, and quietly drown there; and their decomposing bodies give to our crystalline water a meaty tang. As walking over rough ground is painful to my shoulder, I have not been up to inspect. This is one reason for keeping to champagne.

How did you find Dunbar? I have vivid memories of it. Four whole years did I labour there: traumatic years, surrounded by Scotch boys uttering their ritual incantation of 'Bannockburn' in my ears; but at least I learnt something there, unlike my stepdaughter Xenia, who also went to a private school in Scotland and there, after four years, had acquired only two facts, *viz*: the date of the Battle of Bannockburn and the 'fact' that Scottish education is the best in the world. I may say that during my four years at Belhaven Hill, Dunbar, I was never allowed to know about the Battle of Dunbar.[3]

Incidentally, to go back to indexes, do you know the works of Samuel Butler? It was from him, long ago, that I derived the rudiments of my philosophy of indexing—that the index is a functional part of the book,

---

[1]   In his *Guardian* review Thomas described the index as 'outrageously facetious'.

[2]   A summer heatwave had begun on 22 June 1976. The ensuing drought, during which rivers ran dry, led to the appointment of a Minister for Drought, the passing of emergency drought legislation, and water-rationing in many areas.

[3]   Belhaven Hill was a preparatory school to which T-R was sent in 1924. At the Battle of Dunbar in 1650, an English army commanded by Oliver Cromwell trounced the Scots, who had held every military advantage.

which must be written by the author, not farmed out to a publisher's hack, and must be readable in itself, continuously, as an added chapter. If you don't know it already, read (after the book itself) the index of *Alps and Sanctuaries*. In fact it doesn't matter if you read the book first, because if you read the index, you will then *want* to read the book. That, surely, is one of the functions of an index. One can also, of course, put the index, in a slightly different form, first, as a table of contents. I did this in *The Last Days of Hitler*. My model there was that splendid work, Monk's *Life of Bentley*.[1]

I wonder where this will find you. Perhaps—who knows?—you are in these parts. In case you are, I enclose our house-map. As you know, Xandra hates cooking; but she has a cook till 9 August. *verb. sap. suff.*[2] There may be no water; but there are alternatives.

yours ever

Hugh

---

*Bhutto's government was deposed in July 1977 by the Pakistani military, led by General Muhammad Zia-ul-Haq, after disturbances following a general election which opponents of the Pakistan People's Party claimed had been rigged. Bhutto was charged with ordering the murder of a political opponent, Ahmed Raza Kasuri. After receiving an appeal from Bhutto's daughter, Benazir, then under house arrest, Trevor-Roper found a British barrister willing to represent her father, and pledged to underwrite the lawyer's fees. Returning from a month's visit to Pakistan, the barrister later reported that there was 'absolutely no hope of justice' for his client. Once Bhutto had been sentenced to death, Trevor-Roper appealed to the Pakistani Ambassador for clemency, urged the Leader of the Opposition, Margaret Thatcher, to make representations to the Pakistani authorities, and in an article for the*

---

[1] James Monk (1784–1856), appointed Regius Professor of Greek at Cambridge at the age of 25, afterwards Bishop of Bristol, published his *Life of Richard Bentley* in 1830. T-R relished its account of the long survival in office of the philologist and classical scholar Richard Bentley (1662–1742), Master of Trinity College, Cambridge, from 1699, in defiance of every charge of impropriety that was levelled at him by the fellows.

[2] Verbum sapienti sufficit: 'to the wise man, a word is enough'.

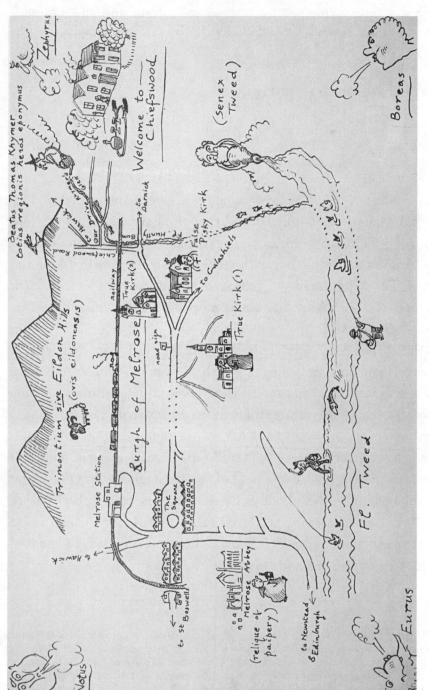

Trevor-Roper's map for visitors to Chiefswood.

New York Times (24 June 1978) predicted 'grave political consequences' if Bhutto underwent judicial assassination. 'His death could lead to the end of Pakistan and a further defeat for the West.'

## To Blair Worden, 12 April 1978

Chiefswood, Melrose

My dear Blair

Thank you *very* much for forwarding those letters. You are a friend indeed. I hope you are better. I don't like to think of you stuck in Oxford with only a virus for company, and a new term upon you. The Thames Valley is healthy only to those who are born in it: they live in it, long and slowly, like carp battening in stale ponds or primeval reptiles somnolent in the slime. We brisker fish require more bracing streams. I have *never* been well in Oxford.

Here I have been very active since we returned from Switzerland. Mainly I have been struggling on behalf of my poor friend Z. A. Bhutto. I wrote to Mrs Thatcher, who has taken some action. I also wrote to my two MPs, who conveniently represent the other two parties. David Steel has not replied,[1] but Evan Luard[2] has been helpful and reports that diplomatic representations have been made at all levels, through the British Embassy in Islamabad, to the head of the Pakistani Foreign Office (who was in London on a visit), and to General Zia personally. I also wrote to the Pakistani ambassador; and I wrote a 2500-word article which was to have appeared in *The Times* on Monday. But then, on Sunday, I had cold feet. I rang up the *Times* and stopped its publication.

---

[1]   David Steel (b. 1938), later Lord Baron Steel of Aikwood, who had succeeded Jeremy Thorpe as Leader of the Liberal Party in 1976, was MP for Roxburgh, Selkirk and Peebles.

[2]   Evan Luard (1926–91) was an expert on China who had resigned from the diplomatic service in 1956 in protest at Eden's Suez policy. Subsequently a Research Fellow at St Anthony's College, he was Labour MP for Oxford 1966–70 and 1974–9, and Parliamentary Under Secretary at the Foreign Office 1976–9.

Cold feet? No, a *crise de conscience*. On Saturday I received from the Pakistan Embassy the complete judgment in the Lahore trial. It is very long: 134 pages closely printed. I spent all Saturday reading it carefully; and the result was that I decided that I could not publish anything until I had discussed this document with the QC who, at my request, had gone out to Pakistan and reported that the trial was rigged and the verdict predetermined. And I cannot discuss it with him at present, for he is in Hong Kong.

The trouble is, on the evidence so far available, I think that Bhutto may have ordered that murder. Admittedly the evidence may have been extracted by torture. Admittedly the court may have hampered the defence and favoured the prosecution. Admittedly the prosecution case was public while the defence was heard in camera. Admittedly the trial may have been political. But having read this long document I am very uneasy. There is too much apparently concrete and converging evidence that Bhutto, if he did not positively order the murder, at least connived after the event and prevented an investigation.[1] And if this is so, certain grave consequences are entailed.

I have often asked myself at what point Hitler could and should have been stopped, and my answer has always been, after 30 June 1934—i.e. after the so-called 'Roehm Putsch', when the Chancellor of Germany, having at his disposal the police and the judiciary of the country, preferred to get rid of his political rivals by assassination. At that moment, I reply, the German establishment, which had hitherto accepted his power as legal, should have rebelled, since it had become plainly illegal, and should have removed him, necessarily, by force. But this requires us to define the force to be used. It could only be the Army. And the Army having no constitutional power to rule, there would necessarily have been, for a time, *de facto* military rule. Those who will the end will the necessary means; and so it has always seemed to me that an unconstitutional military interregnum would have been a political necessity if the rule of law were to be restored in Germany.

---

[1]    He later reverted to the view that the evidence against Bhutto was worthless. See pp. 232–3.

What is sauce for the goose is sauce for the gander. *If* Bhutto was so corrupted by power that he did in fact order the murder of Ahmad Ruza Kasuri, then, by parity of reasoning, that not only justified but required action by the legal establishment, and this in turn required the intervention of the Army and a temporary military administration. The rule of the Army may then, like that of Oliver Cromwell, have acquired a momentum, and a direction, of its own, and its promise of a rapid return to normality may have been betrayed, or at least deferred; but that is another matter. Essentially, my argument about Nazi Germany obliges me to admit that General Zia was justified—always assuming that Bhutto had used the forces of government to carry out a political murder.

On this factual question therefore—whether he did or did not order the murder—every other question depends; and until I can feel certain about it, I must fall silent. Fortunately, there is now more time than I had thought, as the appeal is not to be heard till 5 May.

I have just been attending a very melancholy function: the sale of the books in the Signet Library in Edinburgh. This is a marvellous library, built up into a great cosmopolitan collection in the late 18th and early 19th century, above all by Macvey Napier[1] and David Laing;[2] and it is marvellously housed in a magnificent building in Parliament Square. But what is learning, what is literature, what is cosmopolitanism, what are the names of Napier and Laing to the modern Writers to the Signet? Before going to view the books on Tuesday, I had lunch in the New Club,[3] the so-called 'exclusive' club which has just blackballed Ludovic Kennedy.[4] It is now dom-

---

[1]    Macvey Napier (1776–1847), solicitor and legal scholar.

[2]    David Laing (1793–1878), antiquary.

[3]    T-R had described this Edinburgh club in Princes Street to his stepson James (21 July 1966): 'The New Club has two classes of member. One is the Edinburgh W.S. [Writers to the Signet, viz. lawyers], or business-man (in so far as there is any business in Edinburgh—"that least mercantile of cities", as Lord Cockburn called it). He is a dull dog, a real Edinburgh citizen, careful, unimaginative, dried-up. The other is the rural laird who only turns up by chance when he is in Edinburgh (whereas your W.S. is there every day).'

[4]    Ludovic Kennedy (1919–2009) had been a post-war undergraduate at Christ Church after wartime service on Royal Navy destroyers. He was a BBC broadcaster of distinction, who wrote books on miscarriages of justice. There was not a blackball system at the New Club, but Kennedy's candidature there (Dawyck Haig was his seconder) was withdrawn

inated by Edinburgh WS. (An aristocratic friend told me once that his stepfather had resigned from the club because it had started admitting lawyers. Now the two chief grumbles of the Edinburgh *beau monde*, such as it is, are that lawyers have occupied the New Club and that dogs have got into the residential gardens of the New Town). As I looked round at those lean, mean, foxy faces, with their dry skin and narrow eyes, I saw in them incarnate the spirit of the new Scotland, the re-parochialisation, the return, after the Enlightenment of the 18th century, to the introversion of the 17th. Now the wretches are rubbing their hands with glee at the vast sums they are making at the sale. For the prices fetched were absurd—sometimes ten times the estimate. Real cosmopolitans were there, as buyers. I went in the hope of buying two volumes of Vanini, which went at £480, and Tho. Dempster's *de Etruria Regali* which is not being sold until tomorrow; but I shall not now bother to go tomorrow.

yours ever

Hugh

PS. 18 April. Mrs Stowell[1] has just telephoned to tell me about John Cooper's death.[2] A great blow; and how strangely similar (as reported to me) to that of his Master, McFarlane.[3]

---

after objections from Edinburgh lawyers resentful of his accounts of police misconduct and judicial prejudice in the case of Patrick Meehan, who had been wrongly convicted of murder in 1969.

[1]   Lesley Stowell was Secretary of the Oxford History Faculty.

[2]   John [J. P.] Cooper (1920–78) was a Fellow of All Souls 1948–52 and thereafter Fellow and Tutor in Modern History at Trinity College, Oxford. A scholar of passionate erudition, he contributed the appendix 'The Landed Wealth of the English Peerage under Charles I' to T-R's essay on 'The Gentry' (1953). Wallace Notestein called him 'the greatest seventeenth-scholar since C. H. Firth'. According to Raymond Carr, Cooper was the only historian T-R was frightened of.

[3]   Cooper stopped his car on the road leading from Horton-cum-Studley, the Oxfordshire village where he lived, and suffered a massive coronary. McFarlane died suddenly while walking in Buckinghamshire.

*The campaign to save Bhutto's life failed: he was hanged on 4 April 1979. Trevor-Roper became a considerate friend to his family, which was subjected to close restrictions under the military regime. In 1982, for example, he appealed to Margaret Thatcher, by then Prime Minister, to support requests to the Pakistani leader, General Zia, to allow Bhutto's wife, who had been diagnosed with cancer, to seek medical treatment abroad. Her cancer was cured by treatment in London. After Benazir Bhutto assumed the leadership of the Pakistan People's Party, she visited Trevor-Roper to seek his advice on constitutional challenges to General Zia's military rule. Following Zia's violent death in 1988, and the restoration of democratic forms, Benazir Bhutto served two periods as Prime Minister of Pakistan before her assassination in 2007.*

## To Blair Worden, 11 April 1979

Chiefswood, Melrose

My dear Blair

It was very kind of you to telephone: I greatly appreciated it. Poor Zulfikar Bhutto—I suppose that if one goes into politics in an Islamic country, one takes the occupational risks. The Turks hanged their Prime Minister (or President: I forget which), Menderes, a few years ago, with disgusting brutality.[1] The Persians are now shooting theirs.[2] But what distinguishes the murder of Bhutto is the mockery of a trial and the vindictive barbarity of that year in the death cell. The offence with which he was charged is precisely the same as that with which Jeremy Thorpe is charged.[3] I hope that even if he is found guilty, and even if, by that time, Mrs Thatcher has brought back hanging, we shall treat J.T. better.

The grim irony is that Bhutto was particularly, even absurdly, magnanimous. (That alone makes it inconceivable to me that he would have

---

[1]   Adnan Menderes (1899–1961), the first democratically elected Turkish Prime Minister 1950–60, was deposed in a military coup, charged with violating the constitution, and hanged despite appeals for clemency from world leaders.

[2]   Amir-Abbas Hoveyda (1919–79), Prime Minister of Iran 1965–77, was executed by shooting on 7 April 1979 after being tried before a 'revolutionary court'.

[3]   Jeremy Thorpe (b. 1929), Leader of the Liberal Party 1967–76, was put on trial in May 1979, a week after losing his seat as MP for North Devon, charged with attempted murder and conspiracy to murder a man who claimed to have had an affair with him. He was acquitted.

stooped, or bothered, to order the murder of a particularly obscure and impotent political adversary). Once, when dining with him, I met a fellow-guest, an enjoyable and witty old man called Dr Rashidi, who Bhutto had made head of the Pakistan Cultural Institute. When the other guests had gone, I asked Bhutto about him. He told me that Rashidi came from his own village, Larkana, in Sind, and was a client of the Bhutto family: he had known him since childhood. I said that I had found him good company. Bhutto said, yes, but he is an old rogue too. Then he told me how, when Bhutto turned against Ayub Khan, Dr Rashidi went to Ayub and offered to 'eliminate' Bhutto. I was so surprised that I checked the meaning of the word. Yes, 'eliminate, liquidate, murder'. I expressed surprise that I should find such an old rogue at Bhutto's table. He said, 'oh, he is an old man now, he can do no harm, and after all, he is a Larkana man; so I have given him this job, and he does it well'. To which I can only add that, a few months ago, Bhutto's son told me that Dr Rashidi had now changed his allegiance again and had sold himself to General Zia.

Bhutto saved a far more formidable political enemy, Sheikh Mujib, in 1971.[1] Mujib had been put in prison and condemned to death by Yahya Khan,[2] but Bhutto, on taking over, tore up the death-sentence and let him go to Bangladesh—via London, to avoid the appearance of premature recognition. The last time I stayed with him, he asked me about Richard Gombrich, who had mobilised the opposition to his honorary degree at Oxford. I told him. He then said, I hope I shall meet him. I said that I wasn't sure that they would see eye-to-eye. He said, 'but I could shake him by the hand'.

I fear we must accommodate ourselves to a different style of politics in Islamic lands now.

I am feeling rather frustrated, being immobilised and carless at Chiefswood, but I suppose I should look on the bright side of things and recognise that, if I had skidded one half-second later, I would have slid in front of the

---

[1]   Sheikh Mujib was the popular name of Sheikh Mujibur Rahman (1920–75), leader of East Pakistan, and first President of Bangladesh, who together with most of his family was murdered in a *coup d'état* by junior army officers.
[2]   General Agha Yahya Khan (1917–80), Chief of Army Staff 1966–71 and President of Pakistan 1969–71, whom Bhutto put under house arrest 1972–9.

juggernaut not into its side; and then I would not be writing this letter.[1] I am not yet ready to go, and am glad to have gained this respite. And I suppose that immobility has its advantages. I can read, and write...

What do I read? Alas, not the things that I ought to be reading. And what do I write? Alas, not the things that I ought to be writing. But why should we be constrained by duty? I was particularly incensed, this morning, to receive a formal letter from Macmillans—my own publishers—saying that they were sending me, enclosed, information about books 'which deal with your field of interest'. Who are Macmillans to define and circumscribe my interests—and to decide that I am only concerned with international relations in the 20th century? I tossed the document in the fire and went on reading Ssu Ma-ch'ien.[2]

What are you reading (and writing)? What are you making the undergraduates of St Edmund Hall read in dull Devonshire?[3] (It can't be duller than the Borders). I trust you are a subtle tempter, leading them away from Elton,[4] Plumb,[5] Stone, K. V. Thomas, Pennington,[6] *et hoc genus omne*, to the delights of Don Quixote, Jane Austen, Gogol, Dr Johnson, George Moore (I hope *you* read George Moore: I was horrified to discover, at my last meal in Oriel, that two *intelligent, young, Irish* lecturers had never even *heard* of him).[7]

I have not seen you since before I went to Rome. I tried to ring you when I got back, but the porter said you were away till Tuesday, and I was motoring

---

[1]   While driving up the M6 motorway to Chiefswood, T-R skidded in the snow on Shap Fell and collided with 'a gigantic juggernaut'. He was unhurt, but his Mercedes was wrecked.

[2]   The astrologist Ssu-ma Ch'ien (Sima Qian; 145–c.90 BC) completed a history of human-kind, which earned him the soubriquet of Grand Historian of China.

[3]   The phrase is from 'Discontents in Devonshire' by Robert Herrick (1591–1674). Worden had taken a college reading-party to Dartmoor.

[4]   (Sir) Geoffrey [G.R.] Elton (1921–94), historian of Tudor England, Fellow of Clare College, Cambridge, from 1954, Professor of English Constitutional History at Cambridge 1967–83, Regius Professor of Modern History at Cambridge 1983–8.

[5]   (Sir) J. H. ('Jack') Plumb (1911–2001), historian of Hanoverian England, Fellow of Christ's College, Cambridge, from 1946 (Master 1978–82), Professor of Modern English History 1966–74.

[6]   Donald Pennington (1919–2007), Lecturer in History at Manchester University 1946–65, co-author of *Members of the Long Parliament* (1954), which applied Namierite techniques to the 17th century. When Christopher Hill became Master of Balliol in 1965, Pennington succeeded him as History Tutor there. He and Keith Thomas co-edited a *Festschrift* for Hill.

[7]   The three volumes of George Moore's memoirs were an inspiration for the style and content of T-R's *Wartime Journals*. To Worden, T-R described Moore, Sir Thomas Browne, and C. M. Doughty as 'the trinity of my stylistic devotion'.

north (would that I had not) on the Monday. Well, Rome, like almost every-thing else this winter, was a disaster. We meant to stay a week. I thought it was hardly worth going for so short a time, but in the end we were both re-lieved when the strike of Alitalia forced us to leave a day early. Rome is both shoddier and more violent than ever. The shabbiness of this great cultural capital is unbelievable. The Piazza Navona has become a slum. Graffiti—mainly communist graffiti—cover every relic of Antiquity. There were two assassinations in broad daylight while we were there. On our first day we were taken, by an Italian friend, to the 'Protestant cemetery' (as the English call it: the 'acatholic cemetery' to the Romans) which we know well. (Xan-dra's grandfather, who died as ambassador in Rome, is buried there[1]). While we were there, our friend's locked car was smashed open, in a public place, and Xandra's bag stolen, full of all her money, papers, etc. We stayed in a grand palazzo in which we were ruled by a surly old woman who would do absolutely nothing: no service, no breakfast, not even the means of making a cup of coffee, and nowhere to get one outside. Italy has become terribly unionised, and everyone—at least in Rome—lives in terror of the lower classes: the academics who run the Accademia dei Lincei[2]—our hosts—clearly (like so many academics) dare not give orders to anyone; and I understand that they have recently been told by their staff that 'there are too many lectures', and that these lectures must be cut down for the con-venience of the porters. (Whisper this not in Gath, publish it not in Askelon,[3] lest the Clerk of the Schools[4] rejoice). However, the colloquy, when it came, was enjoyable: good lectures, good audiences. But no parties. I suppose the servants forbade that. If we hadn't had friends in Rome, it would have been very miserable. I hope that even Oxford treats its visitors a little better.

Even Oxford...I had almost forgotten the place. I wonder what is going on there. My poor college is now, politically, a shambles. They have turned

[1]  Hussey Crespigny Vivian, 3rd Baron Vivian (1834–1893), successively ambassador in Copenhagen, Brussels, and Rome.
[2]  Academy of the Lynx, an academy of science founded in 1603, and prominent in Italian intellectual life since the late 19th century.
[3]  2 Samuel 1: 20.
[4]  The officer responsible for the arrangement of the main body of lectures in the human-ities at Oxford.

down 15 (or is it 16?) candidates for the Provostship—i.e. not really 'candidates' but persons whom they have themselves invited to stand in order then to bowl them over, like successive ninepins, with malevolently and tortuously rolled balls.[1] In the stricken alley, only three skittles still stand, and, by all human prevision, none of them will be left standing next month, and no one else, seeing what has happened to his predecessors, will be willing to be set up in their stead. So unless my colleagues, in a sudden burst of panic or humility, clutch unanimously at whatever name turns up next, we shall be back where we were a year ago, only with 16 fewer potential provosts. The only message that I am sending to them from my safe retreat is that, having made such fools of themselves, they had better go the whole hog and send a delegation to Provost Turpin begging him to stay on; and I remind them of Hilaire Belloc's adjuration, to hold fast to Nurse,

For fear of finding something worse.[2]

I have been invited by the Vice-Chancellor to deliver the annual sermon on the Sin of Pride in St Mary's Church (of which Oriel is the patron) in the Michaelmas Term.[3] I shall accept, on the assumption that the patron-college will provide me with adequate matter for a cautionary tale.

yours ever

Hugh

———

[1]    Kenneth Turpin was due to retire as Provost of Oriel in 1979. Tempted by the idea of becoming, like Blake, a head of house, T-R (encouraged by Xandra) allowed his name to go forward. He claimed to be relieved when it was rejected. When all possible candidates for the Provostship had been discussed and rejected, Turpin was persuaded to stay another year. His eventual successor in 1980 was Lord Swann (1920–90), a molecular scientist who had been Principal and Vice-Chancellor of Edinburgh University before his appointment as chairman of the BBC (1973–80). When, exasperated by the minutiae of college administration, Swann resigned after nine months, T-R admitted to enjoying *Schadenfreude*.

[2]    From 'Jim' in Belloc's *Cautionary Tales for Children* (1907).

[3]    A 17th-century clergyman, William Master, endowed two annual sermons in the University Church of St Mary's, one on 'The Sin of Pride', the other on 'The Grace of Humility'. In his own sermon T-R, not persuaded that pride was always a sin or humility always a grace, asked what had led the benefactor, 'who was so careful of our spiritual health', to 'insist that this one sin should be singled out, and its supposedly opposite virtue as often extolled, from this pulpit', and to enjoin those themes on 'an unending succession of preachers, all bound together, like a continuous chain-gang moving in single file through the corridors of time'.

*Trevor-Roper was among the life peers in the first Birthday Honours list recommended by the newly elected Prime Minister, Margaret Thatcher, in June 1979. He was reluctant to be known as Lord Trevor-Roper. 'Double-barrelled titles are an invention, and a monopoly, of Wilsonian peers,*[1] *and I don't want to be in that galère,' he told Valerie Pearl. There was, he observed, already a Lord Trevor; the title Lord Roper might carry the risk of confusion with the socialist cleric Lord Soper; and under the rules of the College of Arms either peerage title would require him to change his surname to either 'Trevor' or 'Roper'. He preferred to adopt a title, Dacre, that had been held by the Roper family between 1786 and 1794, and by their collateral Trevor descendants between 1851 and 1890. When he consulted Xandra, she was at once enchanted by it. But there was an obstacle, in the form of an existing Lady Dacre. The title, which, as a Plantagenet barony created by writ in the reign of Edward II, passed through the female as well as the male line, had devolved on Rachel (1929–2012), wife of the playwright William Douglas Home. This was the peerage which had once been known as 'Dacre of the South': there was a second Dacre barony, Dacre of Gillesland, 'Dacre of the North', created in 1661 and held by the Earl of Carlisle (father of Trevor-Roper's friend George Morpeth).*

## To Blair Worden, 10 August 1979

Chiefswood, Melrose

My dear Blair

I wonder how one becomes a commoner again. It cannot be more of a business than becoming a peer. But I suppose that having begun the latter process one must complete it before beginning the counter-process of renunciation. I am having a dreadful time with the baroness (*suo jure*) Dacre. Why did I ever mention to Xandra that we once possessed that ancient, musical, romantic title? Why did I not persuade her to be content with the less romantic, but comfortable title of Lady Mold?[2]

---

[1]    Double-barrelled titles were not a Wilson coinage, as shown by the examples of Lords Cozens-Hardy (created 1914), Baden-Powell (1929), Noel-Buxton (1930), Courtauld-Thompson (1944), Pethick-Lawrence (1945), Boyd-Orr (1949), Haden-Guest (1950), Hore-Belisha (1954), Granville-West (1958), and Francis-Williams (1962).

[2]    Plas Teg, the seat of the T-Rs, is near the town of Mold in North Wales, close to the border with England. It was bought and restored by T-R's younger brother Pat.

It all began when you (bird of ill omen) were in my house: when Robert Beddard[1] rang to say that there was a message in the Lodge at Oriel to ring Lady Dacre. Scenting trouble in the wind, I did not ring her. She had already agreed that morning, and that was enough for my purposes. I went up to London next morning, registered under my new title in the House of Lords, lunched merrily at the Beefsteak Club, and then presented myself at the College of Arms to sign my application for the royal patent. When I met Garter,[2] he said, 'There has been a development. Lady Dacre has rung. She objects.'

'Impossible!' I exclaimed: 'she has already agreed over the telephone to me this morning.' This shook him, for the Baroness had prudently omitted to mention this inconvenient fact in her conversation with him. 'Anyway', I went on, 'let her object. Objection will get her nowhere. What can she *do*? I suppose she can appeal to the Earl Marshal's court, but short shrift will she get there ...' and I fingered the letter I had elicited from the Earl Marshal himself, expressing 'delight' at my proposed title. I knew that the Earl Marshal's court had met only once, in 1737: I did not see it meeting again on this issue.[3]

Garter agreed that this was unlikely, but he feared that Lady D might write letters of protest to the Prime Minister or the Queen, which would then be referred to him and interfere with his cosy sessions in El Vino. I saw his point; so after having assured myself that she had no *locus standi* in the matter and could be ignored, I agreed to what in industrial relations

---

[1]   Robert Beddard (b. 1939), historian of Stuart England and Fellow and Tutor in Modern History at Oriel 1967–2006.

[2]   Sir Colin Cole (1922–2001), Garter King of Arms 1978–92, a lumbering, ruddy-faced man whose manners and outlook resembled those of the early Hanoverian age. He spent hours sinking bottles of claret at El Vino's in Fleet Street, and until his knighthood preferred to be known as Colonel Cole by virtue of his membership of the Hon. Artillery Company. His dilatory, unbusinesslike methods so exasperated Buckingham Palace that none of the heralds was invited to the Prince of Wales's wedding in 1981.

[3]   The High Court of Chivalry, as it is properly called, had last been convened in 1954 when the Lord Mayor, aldermen, and citizens of Manchester brought a complaint against the wrongful use of the city's armorial bearings by Manchester Palace of Varieties, a theatre. The Duke of Norfolk as Earl Marshal, and Lord Chief Justice Goddard as Surrogate, presided. This was the first sitting of the Court of Chivalry since 1731 (not 1737).

is known as 'a cooling-off period'. Doubtless when she had had the position explained to her—and Garter and I agreed that we would both write emollient and reassuring letters to her—she would see sense…

Next day I returned to Oxford, found the Lady D's message in Oriel, and telephoned her. She told me that she had been suffering from mussel-poisoning when I had telephoned, and therefore could not be held responsible for anything she had said. I thought it prudent to say very little beyond advising her to wait for my, and Garter's, letters. Then I packed the car and set off for Scotland.

On arrival I found Xandra in a high state of indignation. Lady Dacre, she said, had rung up and used bullying language to her, which made her now more determined than ever to be the Lady Dacre of the North. Besides, from straws in the wind, she had sensed (correctly, I am sure) that her own bossy sister[1] would take Lady Dacre's side; so it was more than ever necessary to be firm against both of them.

I was not particularly eager for this battle, especially as I was not quite sure of the other Dacres, viz: Lord Carlisle, who, under his earldom, is Baron Dacre of Gilsland,[2] and whom, being a friend, I was particularly anxious not to offend. I had got some sort of agreement from him on the telephone; but if Lady D could recant, so could he. Of course neither he nor she has any right to block me (since the College of Arms has agreed (a) that my proposed title prejudices no one and is proper in itself, and (b) that I am a proper person to hold it), but, as you know, I am a man of peace. I do not relish the idea of driving into the House of Lords in a triumphal chariot, over the mangled and bleeding limbs of ancient hereditary peers and peeresses. On the whole, I was eager for peace on that front, and put my trust in the cooling-off period.

Unfortunately the Baroness, who perhaps is not over-employed in other matters, has not cooled off. In fact, she has used the cooling-off

---

[1] The elder of Xandra's two younger sisters, Lady Victoria Montagu-Douglas-Scott (1908–93), known to the children as 'Aunt Doria' and by T-R as the 'bossy' sister. The two elder sisters were rivals for the love of their father and both claimed to be his favourite.

[2] The barony of Dacre of Gilsland fell into abeyance in 1569, and almost certainly became extinct in 1634. Lord Carlisle's barony was properly spelt Dacre of Gillesland.

period only to hot things up. First, she mobilised her cousin, Lord Hampden,[1] who, 'as titular head of the Brand family', sent me rather a pompous letter, based on misinformation from her, urging me to desist. The Dacre title, he said, was 650 years old and very beautiful; it belonged to them, the Brand family; and no one else should breach their monopoly (he prudently avoided any mention of Dacre of Gilsland). Two days later came a letter from Lord Carlisle: a charming letter expressing delight that I was taking the title. This lifted my spirits. At least there was peace on that—the more important—front.

But the next letter that I opened soon brought me back to earth. It was from the Baroness, and was not at all charming. In fact it was very stuffy. She told me that it was bad enough that Dacre of Gilsland existed, but if I were to become Dacre of Glanton, their ancient title, of which 'we as a family [i.e. the Brands] are very proud', would become 'common'. I 'should' go choose another title. Theirs was 'over 600 years old'. She realised that 'there is little that I can do to stop you', but she would not give in willingly. She was protesting, and this was her protest, and she was writing to Garter 'to repeat my misgivings'. I have now heard from Garter. From his tortuous circumlocutions and unwillingness to quote, I infer that she has expressed her misgivings to some tune.

Oh dear, what do I do? If I had thought that the lady would make such a to-do, I would never have suggested the title. But now I have gone so far, is it possible to go back? The books are signed, the name enrolled, my ceremonial introduction fixed. The Lord Chancellor has been booked, my sponsors squared, the luncheon invitations have gone out, the robes have been arranged, my pass has been drawn up, my signature recorded. Perhaps all these arrangements, for the sake of peace, can be reversed. But dammit! I then say to myself, why should I go into reverse? And why should the Brands be so 'proud', or so jealous, of a mere title, a label, a tuft, a tassel, a coloured bead, a gewgaw, which has been bandied intermittently

---

[1]   Anthony Brand, 6th Viscount Hampden (1937–2008), stockbroker, who in 1980 published an edition of the letters exchanged between the first viscount, who was also 23rd Baron Dacre, and his wife.

from family to family for six centuries, without tradition or continuity or distinction (except for murder, litigation and extravagance) or, for the last 250 years, land? They only acquired this pretty toy, in 1829, because a Mr Brand, of whom nothing whatever is known, had married into the Trevor-Ropers (who had themselves acquired it by marrying into the Lennards). Now they behave as if they had owned it for six centuries and had a monopoly of it for ever. A fig for their stuffiness! If Lord Carlisle had objected, that would have been different: the Howards can claim some solid continuity with the medieval Dacres—lands, castles, linear descent; but the Brands, these accidental inheritors who have the insolence to be 'proud' of their accidental inheritance…

Of course the real reason is clear to me. Five or so years ago the Brands went to some trouble and expense to call the barony (for the third time) out of abeyance. Naturally they think that they have invested in a monopoly; and equally naturally, they are cross to discover that by the mere technicality of 'differentiation' (i.e. by calling myself Dacre of Glanton) I can breach their supposed monopoly. They are clearly determined to make a stink: a stink through which it will be unpleasant to advance, and from which it will be very inconvenient to retreat.

So here I am, still suspended, in my chrysalis state, in a cocoon of heraldic flummery, no longer a common caterpillar like you, not yet a noble butterfly like Lords Briggs, Bullock, Vaizey,[1] not to mention Brayley, Kagan, Plurenden, Energlyn, Grade, Weidenfeld, *et hoc omne genus*.[2] Meanwhile a

---

[1]   These three progressive-minded academics, the historians Asa Briggs (b. 1921) and Alan Bullock (1914–2004) and the economist John Vaizey (1929–84), had received life peerages on the recommendation of the Labour Prime Minister, Harold Wilson. Vaizey, however, re-signed from the Labour Party in 1978, exclaiming of its front bench in the Lords, 'Trots the lot!', and took the Conservative whip the following year. Bullock resigned from the Labour Party in 1981 to join the break-away Social Democrats.

[2]   Life peers created at Wilson's recommendation: all but Brayley and Energlyn were nominated in his notorious resignation honours list of 1976. Desmond Brayley (1917–77), who received his peerage in 1973, resigned as Under Secretary for the Army in 1974 after the De-partment of Trade opened an investigation into his Canning Town Glassworks, and was awaiting trial for conspiracy to defraud shareholders at the time of his death. Joseph Kagan (1915–95), manufacturer of the Gannex raincoat, fled to Israel with his young secretary, was extradited, and served a ten-month prison sentence for defrauding the public revenue. Rudy Sternberg (1917–81), a German refugee who made a fortune in petrochemicals and trading

dreadful habit is growing up of calling me Lord Trevor-Roper—precisely the title I wish to avoid. I am thinking of dropping the title altogether outside the House of Lords and continuing, in Oxford at least, to be *de facto* a commoner; but perhaps this is unfair and confusing to others. However, it's an ill wind... I have now got some ideas for my university sermon, next term, on 'The Sin of Pride': a sermon which I trust you will attend, for your spiritual edification.

You will understand that, what with this aristocratic *prise d'armes* in darkest Hampshire, and the flurry of opening our garden to the gaping public last Sunday (it rained all day, so not many came to gape), there has been little time for scholarship, and that little has been used up preparing a paper to give at Wolfenbüttel next month (why did I ever agree to that diversion? I already know Wolfenbüttel—have worked in the Herzog August Bibliothek there—and the other papers look desperately dull. But perhaps I can make a sortie to Bonn and pressurise in person that antiquarian bookseller who has sold a vital Mayerne MS—the key, perhaps, which will unlock a whole missing archive and force me to begin my book again *de novo*).[1] However, I am not intellectually entirely idle. Nor, I am sure, are you. I only hope that your intellectual activities are not equally distracted by concern about your contretemps with the police. Of course, if you should be disqualified from locomotion for a year by the beaks and driven to the water-wagon by penitence, your opportunities for scholarship would be enlarged; but the presentation of it might be duller.[2]

---

with the Soviet bloc in Eastern Europe, had been trustee of a confidential fund which subsidized Wilson's secretarial staff when he was Leader of the Opposition 1970–4, and was consequently created Lord Plurenden. The miner's son William Evans (1912–85), Lord Energlyn from 1968, Professor of Geology at Nottingham University 1949–78, was a bubbly expert on coal-dust diseases. Lew Grade (1906–98) was a theatrical agent, impresario, and film-producer. T-R had been fascinated by the social enterprise of the publisher George Weidenfeld (b. 1919) since the early 1950s.

[1]  Since 1972 T-R had been working on a biography of the early modern physician Sir Theodore de Mayerne, a subject that would occupy him, intermittently, for the rest of his working life. The book was incomplete at his death.

[2]  Worden was breathalysed by the police, who had mistaken his car for another, after some drinks with T-R. The test result, which Worden was awaiting when T-R wrote, found that he was fractionally below the prosecutable limit.

Remember the profound words of Samuel Butler, which got him into such trouble in Victorian England, that 'the human intellect owes its superiority over that of the lower animals in great measure to the stimulus which alcohol has given to imagination'.[1] But perhaps you had better not quote this *apologia* to the beaks, as you stand in the dock, accused of driving perfectly with .001% above the permitted level of alcohol in the blood. I still hope that by now you have received a formal note from the police that they have dropped the case. If so, I have a bottle of champagne to share with you in rejoicing....

> yours ever
>
> Hugh

---

*Nan Dunbar (1928–2005) was Fellow and Tutor in Classics at Somerville 1965–95. Her enthusiasm for Mercurius' letters had led to a spirited correspondence with Trevor-Roper in 1970. 'When I see him—as I hope I shall when I am next in Oxford—and if I should cross the High Street,' he promised her, 'I shall convey to him your kind and flattering remarks which I know will please him; for at heart he is a vain old curmudgeon and secretly relishes flattery, especially if it comes from scholars he respects, as I know that he respects you.' Trevor-Roper enjoyed corresponding with this lively, formidable woman, with her endearing chuckles and laughter, who shared his passions for classical literature, wildlife (she became an expert ornithologist in order to improve her edition of Aristophanes' The Birds), and abstruse languages (she learnt Hungarian). Nan Dunbar was a proud Scot, who retained a Glaswegian accent all her days. Trevor-Roper's essay on the Scottish Enlightenment had roused her to 'a frenzy of irritation'. Further differences ended their correspondence for a time.*

*In January 1979 Dunbar began their reconciliation by seeking Trevor-Roper's permission to set a piece of his prose for translation into Latin by candidates reading classics at Glasgow University. She described this as 'the ultimate accolade'. In his reply he addressed her as 'Nan' for the first time. He asked her to send him a copy of the paper 'so that I may purr with pleasure at the sight of it'. She duly complied with his request, and invited the Trevor-Ropers to dine with her and her husband on Burns Night—when*

---

[1]  In *Alps and Sanctuaries* (1881).

*Trevor-Roper courteously took a second portion of haggis. Later that year he dined as her guest in her college hall, and afterwards wrote conciliatingly, 'I always knew Mercurius was wrong about Somerville.' Their correspondence took on a teasing tone. On hearing that she was to preach in Glasgow Cathedral, he recommended her to consult a late-seventeenth-century work entitled* Scotch Presbyterian Eloquence Display'd. *She sent him a home-made Valentine's Day card, which she decorated with pictures of kilted Highlanders in defiant postures.*

## To Nan Dunbar, 17 April 1980

Chiefswood, Melrose

Dear Nan

Yes, I have returned unscathed from Atlanta, whose inhabitants took my lectures in good part. For the last of the series, there was a great display of tartan in the audience, and one kilt. I was told (by a lady who sat behind it) that it smelt powerfully of mothball. I was also told that, after my lecture, it is unlikely to appear again.[1]

I only discovered J. Telfer Dunbar's book[2] last term—with a slight tinge of chagrin (*pereant qui ante nos nostra dixerunt*[3]). But it is a very good book. I didn't know it was reprinted: I will look out for it. I have not read the work of the late Lord Lyon, for whom, like you, I have some contempt;[4] but on my return to Bodley, I will look at it: it may supply me with some useful detail!

I am rewriting my lecture as a series of six: two on the political myth; two on the literary myth; two on the sartorial myth. Then, I hope, I shall publish them.[5] I don't expect to convert the Scots: they are inconvertible—

---

[1]  The lecture exposed the inauthenticity of the kilt tradition.

[2]  *The History of Highland Dress* (London, 1962).

[3]  'May they perish who have expressed our bright ideas before us': Aelius Donatus, the 4th-century Roman grammarian.

[4]  Sir Thomas ('Tam') Innes of Learney (1893–1971), Lord Lyon King of Arms (an office of state in Scotland) 1945–69, compiler of *The Tartans of the Clans and Families of Scotland* (1938; revised 1964). As Lord Lyon, he regarded himself as custodian of the spirit of Caledonia: he was probably the last laird to speak unaffectedly in the Doric dialect.

[5]  He never did so, but they were published in his posthumous book *The Invention of Scotland*.

that indeed is my main thesis. Dr Johnson is right. They will cling to their myths, for the honour of Scotland, against all reason—until they are replaced by new myths.

Of course I shall not adopt a tedious moralising attitude. I am all in favour of myth, which is the soul of history. Unfortunately there is also evidence, which is its bones. So we historians suffer internal tensions.

I am so glad to hear of Mary Lascelles.[1] She sounds an *admirable* woman. I am now coming to the view that Johnson is *always* right. But I don't defend his manners to the death. All the same, even here he can sometimes be defended. I suspect that that phrase about the conversation of Scotchmen merely meant that one soon got used to their accent.[2]

Johnson was not at all anti-highland. He encouraged William Shaw to compile his Gaelic dictionary, as you doubtless know; and after all, the mere *fact* of going, at his age, to the Hebrides argues a real interest! When Boswell told Voltaire that he thought of taking Johnson there, 'he looked at me as if I had talked of going to the North Pole'. And Johnson had read Martin Martin's book.[3] (Have you? The Bodleian copy[4] has some interesting marginalia by Toland—which end up in Toland's posthumous *History of the Druids*).[5]

I'm sorry to hear that your sermon passed off 'peacefully'. No 'gangster Amazons'? No cutty-stools?[6] What is the kirk coming to? I had

---

[1]  Mary Lascelles (1900–95), Tutor in English Language and Literature, Somerville College, Oxford, 1931–60, Fellow 1932–67; Lecturer in English Literature, Oxford University, 1960–6, Reader 1966–7; editor of Johnson's *Journey to the Western Islands of Scotland*.

[2]  T-R probably had in mind the comments on accents in *Journey to the Western Islands of Scotland*: 'The conversation of the Scots grows every day less unpleasing to the English; their peculiarities wear fast away; their dialect is likely to become in half a century provincial and rustick, even to themselves. The great, the learned, the ambitious, and the vain, all cultivate the English phrase, and the English pronunciation, and in splendid companies Scotch is not much heard, except now and then from an old lady.'

[3]  Martin Martin (d. 1718), physician, natural historian, ethnographer, and collector of curiosities in the Hebrides, published his compendious *Description of the Western Islands of Scotland* in 1703.

[4]  Described in Giancarlo Carabelli, *Tolandiana* (1975), p. 14.

[5]  John Toland (1670–1722), the deist whose other works included *Christianity not Mysterious* (1695).

[6]  Within the Church of Scotland, persons convicted of a breach of the biblical commandment against adultery were made to stand on a raised platform called the cutty-stool.

hoped that you would preach for three hours, rousing the faithful, like the ayatollah Khomeini[1] or at least like Samuel Rutherford DD who, according to a friend, when in the pulpit, 'had a strange utterance, a kind of skreigh[2] that I never heard the like. Many a time I thought he would have flown out of the pulpit.' Did you not fly out of the pulpit skreighing?

I am glad to inform you that I am, next term, receiving the degree of DD.[3] I am going quite a long way to get it, but beggars can't be choosers. They offered me a D.Litt., but I said No, 'it must be a DD or nothing, *pour épater les dévots*, and to enable me to talk down to the chaplains of my various colleges.

We have spent a fortnight here, recovering from America, which was pretty awful. We suffered greatly from Bores. I'm afraid many of them claimed to be Scotch which was some advantage: it enabled me to divert them on to Xandra. The Americans—at least in the state of Georgia—give a great deal of unnecessary trouble to the Almighty too; one can't nibble a sausage on a stick without some parson invoking the blessing of the Lord on the creature, in protracted nasal tones.

I will read Walter Scott's *Letters* XI, pp. 110 foll.[4] when I am back in Bodley: I don't have it here. Do you know Scott's essay on Ossian?[5] It is marvellously fair. But he does make one grave error. He says that although Johnson is right to deny that the ancient Celt swaggered in a pair of embroidered velvet breeches, only the scepticism of prejudice could doubt his being accommodated with a tartan philibeg!

---

[1]   Ruhollah Khomeini (1902–89), Grand Ayatollah in Iran, leader of the 1979 revolution, and thereafter supreme leader of his country.

[2]   Scottish variant of 'screech'.

[3]   The degree was awarded by the University of the South in Tennessee ('Sewanee').

[4]   Dunbar had compiled a case-list of Samuel Johnson's 'gross incivility to Scottish hosts', drawn from Boswell's life, and from 'the extremely unfavourable evidence collected for Croker by that honest, scholarly and eminently fair-minded man, Walter Scott, about J's behaviour in Glasgow and at Dunvegan' (letter of 13 April 1980).

[5]   First published in the *Edinburgh Review* for 1805.

Have you ever read Pinkerton? Try *An Enquiry into the History of Scotland*.
Dip, for a start, in Chapter X, 'on the Pikish language'[1]...

yours ever

Hugh

———∞———

*Some months after being recommended for his peerage in 1979, Trevor-Roper was invited to*
*become the next Master of Peterhouse—a Cambridge college with which he had no previous*
*connections. 'It is a pleasant surprise,' he told his brother Pat. 'Peterhouse has a fine Master's*
*Lodge—said to be the best in Cambridge: an elegant Queen Anne house—as well as the best*
*cuisine and a very fine cellar.' Of course, he explained, in accepting the sudden offer, 'I was not*
*governed by such worldly considerations.' There were predictions of trouble from the outset.*
*Ian Bradley's report of the appointment in* The Times *(20 December 1979) contained an*
*ominous paragraph: 'An ex-Fellow of Peterhouse who has now moved on to considerable*
*academic eminence elsewhere warns that the new Master "will find his old-fashioned High*
*Toryism confronted with a lot of lower middle class social climbers who are trying to look like*
*High Tories". He also predicted that the somewhat High Church atmosphere of the college*
*might jar on his rationalistic and anti-clerical sensitivities.'*

*There was indeed trouble ahead. Though T-R respected, and had cordial relations with, a*
*number of the fellows, especially among the scientists, his mastership was embattled. Feeling*
*isolated in Cambridge—he once likened his move there from Oxford to becoming a colonial*
*governor—he reported his impressions of the college in letter after letter, in which he de-*
*ployed a variety of vivid metaphorical conceits.*

*After leaving Oxford, permanently as it proved, Trevor-Roper corresponded regularly*
*with his old Christ Church friend, the classicist Hugh Lloyd-Jones. In the following letter to*
*Lloyd-Jones he anticipated the challenges ahead.*

---

[1]   John Pinkerton (1758–1826) was a numismatist and collector of Scottish ballads who
wrote a vehement essay on literary forgery. His historical writings, including *An Enquiry into*
*the History of Scotland preceding the reign of Malcolm III* (1789), distressed his compatriots by their
emphasis on the congenital inferiority of the Celts, and by arguing that the Picts were descended from ancient Goths. He figures in T-R's *The Invention of Scotland*.

## To Hugh Lloyd-Jones, 27 July 1980

Chiefswood, Melrose

My dear Hugh,

I should have written to you when you were in Colorado, but I am afraid we were simply overwhelmed by the business of preparing to migrate—sorting out, thinning, selling, destroying books and papers accumulated over a generation; winding up at Oxford; preparing for Cambridge; and all correspondence (and much else) ceased until we arrived yesterday at Chiefswood, where we shall, I hope, be able to relax a little before returning to complete the move. I had over-committed myself anyway this summer—two visits to Munich, one to Monte Carlo, two to America, all between March and June—and then the election to Peterhouse came and convulsed everything. I am thankful that I had the strength of mind to refuse Colorado this year.[1] I would have enjoyed your company there, but it would really have been, as things turned out, quite impossible.

I must admit that the affairs of the U.S.A., and its position in the world, fill me with alarm. We face the most dangerous decade since 1945, and the Western world depends on the leadership of a society that is politically, in my opinion, totally bankrupt. I'm afraid I can't believe in Reagan. Ed Rozek himself—before he joined his staff—spoke very critically of him as a mere actor whose last part was to be president of the U.S. We might as well have John Gielgud as Prime Minister. In general, actors have no minds, only memories and poses, and even if Reagan has collected able advisers, they will not agree among themselves, and he must then decide. Ministries of All the Talents have never been successful. Better Mrs Thatcher commanding an obedient team of industrious nonentities than

---

[1]   T-R and Lloyd-Jones regularly lectured to a conference of teachers in Boulder, organized by Professor Edward Rozek (1918–2009), chairman of the Institute for the Study of Comparative Politics and Ideologies at the University of Colorado. Rozek, who taught a course on Communism in the Eastern bloc, became a foreign policy adviser to Ronald Reagan during the latter's presidential campaign of 1980, despite his misgivings about the candidate.

Reagan at sea among strong-minded and competitive advisers! Carter is quite hopeless; but if Carter is defeated, are we not then bound to look forward to the even more dreadful Edward Kennedy?

Owing to the pressure of impending migration I have had very little opportunity to move in the world and pick up gossip. We dined with Clarissa Avon,[1] who had a little party for Mrs Thatcher. She was more rigid than ever: power and authority have stiffened her, and small talk was not easy. When the ladies withdrew, she remained firmly with the men, and swigged brandy. But Xandra got on well with Denis T., who is exactly as portrayed in *Private Eye*.[2] I also attended—for the first time for three years (Colorado having intervened)—the Ch. Ch. Gaudy. I had to make the speech proposing the toast of the House. Having heard (from America) that the canons of Ch. Ch. were 'furious' at my DD, I could not resist the opportunity to speak on their behalf and welcome the Archbishop of Canterbury as the junior member of our select society.[3] The archbishop, by the way, made an excellent speech: at least the first half was excellent—elegant, light, witty—and if only he had stopped half-way through, it would have been brilliant; but unfortunately he suddenly remembered his cloth and it degenerated into a sermon.

I attended the AGM of the British Academy at which the attempt was made to expel Anthony Blunt.[4] I was against expulsion, considering that we are not censors of morals or politics. Blunt betrayed his friends &

---

[1]    Clarissa, Countess of Avon (b. 1920), widow of Anthony Eden and former employee of George Weidenfeld.

[2]    The Prime Minister's husband Denis Thatcher was lampooned in a long-running series of spoof letters, under the heading 'Dear Bill', written by Richard Ingrams and John Wells. The latter also played Denis Thatcher on stage and television. It was said that Thatcher began to imitate his fictional self.

[3]    At the 1980 Christ Church gaudy T-R was due to make the speech proposing the toast. On behalf of the canons, he welcomed Robert Runcie (1921–2000), recently enthroned as Archbishop of Canterbury, 'as the newest recruit to our devout fraternity'.

[4]    Following the publication of Andrew Boyle's *The Climate of Treason*, Margaret Thatcher told the House of Commons on 15 November 1979 that Sir Anthony Blunt, former Surveyor of the Queen's Pictures, had been a spy for the Soviet Union. His knighthood was annulled; he was driven to resign his honorary fellowship of Trinity College, Cambridge; he survived an attempt to revoke his emeritus professorship at London University. The British Academy's council recommended his expulsion. A counter-motion (proposed by Lord Robbins) deplored Blunt's conduct, but proposed that the Academy should not proceed further in the matter. Both these motions were on the agenda for the Academy's annual general meeting on 3 July 1980.

colleagues, but that is a matter of morality; and he betrayed his government, but since the government decided to leave him in his post, there is no call for us to be *plus royaliste que le roi*. However, I didn't need to speak. The case for expulsion was put (not very well) by T. B. Smith, the oracle of Scotch law,[1] and (very weakly) by Plumb, who is purging his own (unavowed) former membership of the communist party by showing zeal on this issue. They were both (I am told) hot for expulsion on Council. A very corrupt and dishonest speech against expulsion was made by Alan Taylor, who pointed out, as if the cases were parallel, that Sakharov had not been expelled from the Soviet Academy. (If Sakharov had been a confessed foreign spy, and not merely a critic of government policy, he would not need expulsion: he would be underground!)[2] But in the end a proposal by a lawyer—I think he is called Gower[3] and was Vice-Chancellor of Southampton University—that we move to the next item of business was carried by a 3–1 majority, so the whole case collapsed and the elaborate preparations for a secret ballot on the issue were not needed. Robert Blake, his countenance inflamed with claret and port (we had lunched together at the Beefsteak Club) rose to his feet, made a pompous declaration, and stalked out in the direction of the House of Lords, and three Fellows—Colin Roberts, Crook and a palaeographer at the BM whose name escapes me—have since resigned.[4] Yesterday there was a pompous letter in the *Daily Telegraph* from G. Huxley in Belfast denouncing the Academy for its pusillanimity.[5] It seems that your faculty takes the lead on that side. I hope you will not resign!

[1]  Sir Thomas Smith (1915–1988), general editor of *The Laws of Scotland*.
[2]  Andrei Sakharov (1921–89), Soviet nuclear physicist and dissident, had been awarded the Nobel Peace Prize in 1975.
[3]  Laurence Gower (1913–97), specialist in commercial law and Vice-Chancellor, Southampton University, 1971–9.
[4]  Colin Roberts (1909–90) of Oxford University Press; his fellow papyrologist Theodore Skeat (1907–2003), former Keeper of Manuscripts at the British Museum; and John Crook (1921–2007), expert on Roman law and Professor of Ancient History at Cambridge, resigned forthwith. Plumb, his fellow historian Norman Gash, and the Cambridge philologist William Allen issued ultimata to Dover in August that they would resign if Blunt did not relinquish his fellowship. Blunt did so on 18 August. Alan Taylor resigned the next day.
[5]  George Huxley (b. 1932), philologist and Professor of Greek at Queen's University, Belfast, 1962–83.

Kenneth Dover[1] made a very strange speech at the dinner: a miscellany of pointless learned trivialities adding up to nothing at all. I think that James is right: he has no sense of proportion, only a lucidity of irrelevant detail.

I foresee problems at Peterhouse. My impression is that the Governing Body is divided into two parties: 'the historians'—i.e. the Arts faculties, led by the historians—who believe in a cosy, introverted college community, and 'the engineers' who want to destroy the college identity and turn the place into a hall of residence for scientists. The historians, in my opinion, are far too cosy: a self-perpetuating group, whose latest abuse is the election to a teaching fellowship of an undergraduate (a crime unknown in Oxford since the election of Gordon Walker at Ch Ch).[2] The engineers are led by a renegade Peterhouse man who is very able and energetic but really detests the tradition of the place, which indeed seems to me over-ripe. The two parties are so opposed that consensus is unattainable and stalemate rules: a stalemate reinforced by the issue of co-education, which the engineers press and the historians oppose. I think it is thanks to this stalemate that I was elected: the engineers put forward a boring accountant,[3] the historians opposed them by putting forward Brian Wormald, ex-Anglican chaplain turned popish layman, now just retired.[4]

---

[1]   The classicist Sir Kenneth Dover (1920–2010) was President of the British Academy 1978–81. He was President of Corpus Christi College, Oxford 1976–86 (where James Howard-Johnston was a don).

[2]   T-R's misgivings were about the procedure of the appointment, not about the individual appointed, Harold James (b. 1956). After eight years as a Fellow of Peterhouse (1978–86), James moved to Princeton, where he is both Professor of History and Professor of International Affairs in the Woodrow Wilson School. T-R thought he had been wise to leave Peterhouse. James has published major works on German financial history, German identity, international monetary policy, globalization, and economic crises. Patrick Gordon Walker (1907–80) was appointed a History Tutor and Student at Christ Church in 1931. He was Foreign Secretary 1964–5 and Education Secretary 1967–8.

[3]   Sir Richard Stone (1913–91), economist and statistician, who would be awarded the Nobel Prize for Economics in 1984.

[4]   Brian Wormald (1912–2005), Fellow of Peterhouse 1938–79, published a study of Clarendon in 1951 (not 1941, as T-R's letter has it). In an *Independent* obituary on 8 April 2005, Nicholas Vincent described his habitual wardrobe of 'silver-buckled shoes and a monocle', and his 'loathing of pedantry, teetotalism and the creeping spread of lower-middle-class values', a sentiment which 'could be expressed in the most forthright Anglo-Saxon terms'.

Neither candidate could win the middle ground, so an outsider was brought in. Meanwhile, thanks to the same stalemate, the size of the Fellowship had dwindled: 7 years ago it was 29, now it is 23. When I suggested to Wormald that it should be increased, he said, 'that would only make it ungovernable. During the war we were down to 4: that was our golden age.' In spite of that message, I would like to increase the number—in particular, by bringing in a classical tutor. Can you find one?

The immediate issue is that of Wormald's rooms. Having retired, he has been given a college house, just round the corner, large enough for all purposes. He has of course all common room rights. It has been a rule since the war at least that retiring Fellows do not keep rooms in college—in so small a college that would be to create a geriatric institution. David Knowles was thus turned out.[1] But Wormald, having missed the Mastership, wants to live on in college and is moving heaven and earth. I have had letters from Paris, and reports from dinner-parties in the country, reporting that the college is treating him abominably, has no respect for tradition, has fallen into the hands of wicked radicals, etc. It is as if Roy, on retirement, had been allowed to stay on at 91 St Aldates but then demanded to keep his rooms in Kilcannon in perpetuity.[2] I can see that the great case of Wormald's rooms is likely to be my first and most testing battle. I am hoping it will be resolved before I take up my duties, but all the signs are that Wormald's party will procrastinate until I am in the chair in the hope of getting my support: hence the propaganda which is already being addressed to me. Wormald's special claim is based on the pretence that he is writing an important book. I will believe that when I see the book. He last published anything in 1941. It was a book on Clarendon, written in the Peterhouse style: i.e. the reader is

---

[1]    When the Benedictine monk and historian of monasticism David Knowles (1896–1974) was elected Fellow of Peterhouse in 1944, he was (with a few brief exceptions during the reign of James II) the first member of a Catholic religious order to hold a college fellowship in Oxford or Cambridge universities since the 16th century. Winston Churchill nominated him as Regius Professor of Modern History at Cambridge in 1954.
[2]    When Roy Harrod reached the retirement age for a Student of Christ Church in 1967, he vacated his rooms in the Kilcannon building.

led in circles in a verbal fog and he has no idea why he is there or where (if anywhere) he is going.

yours ever,
Hugh

---

*Trevor-Roper saw Peterhouse as overshadowed by Sir Herbert Butterfield (1900–79), who had been Master in 1955–68 and Regius Professor of Modern History 1963–8. His baleful influence, he believed, had been perpetuated by the historian Maurice Cowling (1926–2005), a Fellow of Peterhouse since 1963, and the dominant figure in a small group of bachelor dons—'leading from behind, like an old sheepdog', said Trevor-Roper—who exercised a powerful say in college affairs. Though not all of one mind, what united them, Trevor-Roper decided, was illiberalism. His relations with them soon deteriorated into open hostility.*

*Trevor-Roper had corresponded since 1950 with Noël Annan (1916–2000), whom he had first encountered late in the war. Annan later marked the folder containing his Trevor-Roper letters 'the best in all my files'. Annan had been Provost of King's College, Cambridge, 1956–66 and Provost of University College London 1966–78. Trevor-Roper liked to tease him about his progressive politics, although by comparison with some of his Peterhouse colleagues, Trevor-Roper felt that he himself was becoming dangerously radical.*

## To Noël Annan, 26 December 1980

Chiefswood, Melrose

My dear Noël

I have withdrawn from Cambridge, like some 4th century anchorite, to meditate in solitude (for I am completely alone here) on the strange turns of fortune that have landed me in that curious place. How I wish that my hermitage were nearer to you so that I could draw on your experience as head—though long ago—of a neighbouring college! Do you ever cast your mind back to your former life? Do you ever visit, even in imagination, that enclosed Fenland society? Probably not. I have not yet put my nose far outside Peterhouse;

but whenever I have done so it is to partake of gross six-course feasts among solemn academic figures wearing white-ties and scarlet robes. I think I have worn a white tie more often in the last term than in the previous ten years. There is a certain charm in finding one's self projected fifty years back in time, but it is not very stimulating intellectually. I have just been reading Maurice Cowling's new book, and am more than ever perplexed how I came to be elected head of that college.[1] How can I ever come to terms with such an institution, or speak the same language? They seem to live in the age of Newman and to want to subject history to religion—even to Anglicanism. Has *any* good historian subjugated history to *any* religion? I can't find much evidence of doctrine, or even of spiritual doubt, in Thucydides, Tacitus, Gibbon, Macaulay…I fear that Butterfield did a great deal of harm in your old university. I have never been able to understand what, at any time, he was driving at; and he seems to have imposed the obscurity of his own style on a whole generation, especially in Peterhouse.

Maurice Cowling's hero seems to be Canon Charles Smyth: a man who wrote—admittedly at too early an age—an absurd book in which he revealed that Cranmer had been a Suvermerian.[2] He never explained what Suvermerianism was, and wrote about it so grandly that no critic dared show his own ignorance by asking; until A. F. Pollard tracked it down and showed that the canon had made a particular heresy out of a latinisation

---

[1]    T-R was in the process of reviewing the first volume of Cowling's *Religion and Public Doctrine in Modern England* for *The Listener*. 'The subject is the intellectual crisis of our time,' he told Frances Yates: 'a crisis which (it appears) has been enacted, observed and faced entirely and exclusively within the walls of Peterhouse. There is a chapter on Butterfield; but Butterfield interpreted by his disciples is even less clear than Butterfield himself, and after reading it I find myself no wiser.' He later described the book as 'a series of potted intellectual biographies of a miscellany of English worthies'. It was, he judged, 'a very rum work'. 'The outer world is occasionally mentioned *en passant*,' he told Lloyd-Jones.

[2]    Canon Charles Smyth (1903–87) published *Cranmer and the Reformation under Edward VI* at the age of 23. Appointed Dean of Corpus Christi College, Cambridge, in 1937, he was passed over in 1944 for the vacant Dixie Chair of Ecclesiastical History having by his prickliness made too many enemies in his college and university. The Crown rescued him by appointing him rector of St Margaret's, Westminster, and Canon of Westminster Abbey, but he had such an unedifying squabble with Westminster School about noisy pupils disturbing his studies, and estranged so many colleagues in the abbey community, that his preferment to a deanery was impossible. He resigned early in 1956.

of the general German word *Schwärmerei.*[1] After which no one—except Maurice—took the canon seriously. I have a weak spot for him because my brother Pat was once roused from slumber in St Margaret's, Westminster, on hearing the name Trevor-Roper uttered in comminatory tones from the pulpit. He found that Canon Smyth was preaching a sermon against me. If one is going to be preached against, I am all for being preached against in a fashionable church.

One of the few items of world news that has come through to my hermitage is that you are electing a new Chancellor. Having once undertaken to challenge my own university establishment in such an election, I watch these contests with a practised eye. If you can make me eligible to vote in time, by incorporation or some such device, I will come and vote for Jones.[2] No doubt he would be quite useless and absurd; but less absurd, surely, than the official candidate.[3] I suppose she will gallop home (I choose my metaphor with care), and no doubt—if she has the same privilege as the Chancellor of Oxford of creating a batch of personally chosen doctors at her inauguration—will start a glorious reign by imitating Caligula and making her horse a doctor of divinity. (As a doctor of divinity myself, I would of course welcome such a recruit to our somewhat stodgy confraternity).

I can see how this absurd affair *developed*—i.e. how no suitable person was prepared to accept nomination against the lady—but I cannot see how it *started*. Do tell me *who* produced the official candidate (for I can't think that you did). Perhaps it was Christie, who, poor fellow, seems to have gone off his rocker: he believes that Hess is not Hess and that I must be a stooge of MI6 for thinking otherwise.[4]

[1]  'Fanatical heretics'. '*Schwärmerei*' was an insult hurled by 16th-century Lutherans at sectaries whose extremism discredited their movement.

[2]  Jack Jones (1913–2009), General Secretary of the Transport and General Workers' Union 1969–78.

[3]  Princess Anne (b. 1950), a noted horsewoman who represented Great Britain at the 1976 Olympic Games, was elected Chancellor of London University in 1980.

[4]  Ian [Ian R.] Christie (1919–98), a Namierite historian of 18th-century England, had been one of those who joined Plumb in threatening resignation from the British Academy if Blunt did not relinquish his fellowship. He held history chairs at University College London, between 1966 and 1984. Christie held the minority view that the man sentenced at Nuremberg and imprisoned at Spandau was not Hitler's deputy Rudolf Hess but an impostor. T-R contributed an essay, 'Huth: The Incorrigible Intruder', to David Stafford (ed.), *Flight from Reality: Rudolf Hess and his Mission to Scotland* (2002).

I am having a little trouble with your predecessor and am thinking of exposing him in the public prints.[1] I have drafted my exposure, but am holding my hand until I feel quite sure that he can't ruin me or any of my friends in revenge.

Do write and advise me on all these matters. Please mark the envelope *Personal*, as it may be opened by the Peterhouse college secretary. (Some highly explosive letters have unfortunately been opened by her; luckily she is sound and discreet).

Best wishes to you both.

yours ever

Hugh

*At a dinner in Oriel in October 1981 Trevor-Roper was presented with the Festschrift in his honour,* History and Imagination. *During the speeches his successor as Regius Professor, the military historian Michael Howard (b. 1922), who had been taught by him as an undergraduate, explained that the subject of his own contribution to the volume, 'Empire, Race and War in Pre-1914 Britain', had been a second choice. Originally he had written an account of the exploits of the double agent in the Second World War, 'Garbo'. Having used restricted sources, Howard had been obliged to seek clearance to publish the essay, even though Garbo's activities had already been revealed in print more than once. To his astonishment permission was refused, and he was even asked if he had used a typist not on the approved list. Howard gave a jocular description of the episode before presenting Trevor-Roper with a bound copy of it, labelled 'Confidential Annexe. Top Secret Ultra'.*

*Suddenly the Chancellor, Harold Macmillan, rose from his chair. In tremulous indignation he declared that he had never in his life heard so shocking a speech. Howard's frivolity, he continued, was characteristic of a deplorable irresponsibility in current attitudes to security matters. 'We are living', Macmillan warned the guests, 'in a period of peril*

---

[1]    Sir Cyril Philips (1912–2005), Director of the School of Oriental and African Studies 1956–77 and Vice-Chancellor of the University of London 1971–6, had obtained important correspondence by and about 'Ossian' Macpherson, which he treated as his personal property and to which he denied access to scholars. Jeremy Cater, in a footnote to his edition of Trevor-Roper's *The Invention of Scotland*, writes that in 1981 Philips 'was finally forced by mounting family, academic, and ultimately legal pressure, to disgorge what was left of the collection of Macpherson papers, which he had guarded illegitimately, jealously and incompetently for thirty-five years' (p. 251).

*comparable to that of the 1930s.' Howard, who was taken aback by the old man's vehe-*
*mence, confided to Trevor-Roper that Margaret Thatcher had told him of her regret that*
*the Ultra secret had been published. She had been got at, Howard inferred, by 'new morons'*
*in the intellgience services, who in panic after the Blunt affair were resisting disclosures of*
*any kind.*

## To Michael Howard, 5 November 1981

Peterhouse, Cambridge

My dear Michael

I am deeply indebted to you for your splendid essay on Garbo,[1] which I shall treasure as a bibliographical rarity of great value; but I am also doubly indebted, because the absurd veto of our old friends has given me *two* essays from you, and I have now read the second also.[2] It too is a marvellous work, which I have read with great pleasure and instruction. I have often been impressed by the disagreeably imperialist, racial and anti-semitic utterances of our compatriots in the late Victorian and Edwardian period, and, particularly, by the fact that such utterances were evidently quite un-self-conscious and normal. Winston Churchill, for instance, in his early letters; or the private correspondence of respectable officials in China, which became familiar to me when I was working on Sir E. Backhouse; or perhaps above all, the anti-semitic poems or allusions of Hilaire Belloc. You have put all these into a coherent context and drawn out their implications (and limits). I found your essay *most* interesting; and although, of course, I regret that *Garbo* was suppressed, I rejoice that, in consequence of that suppression (from which I, at least, have not suffered), I have been able to read a second essay by you. Many, many thanks.

---

[1]  The Catalan double agent Joan Pujol Garcia (1912–88), known by his British codename Garbo; subsequently proprietor of a books and gifts shop in Venezuela.
[2]  'Empire, Race and War in Pre-1914 Britain'.

I am still very perplexed by the extraordinary *volte face* of our Old Friends[1] over your book[2] (and that essay). Clearly they are lunatics. I consulted Dick White about the position, and he confirms that they have retreated into idiot secrecy. It looks as if the period in which reason prevailed was limited to the period when those services were dominated by the 'amateurs' of the War and that now that those amateurs have, by effluxion of time, retired, we are back in the days of the hopeless old professionals, the Menzies, Vivians and Cowgills[3] *redivivi*,[4] who are taking their vicarious revenge. I can see it all: for a whole generation the professionals have hated us, and yet also feared us because we were, in Graham Greene's phrase, of the 'untorturable class':[5] academics, public figures of one kind or another; therefore we could not be silenced or disciplined. But now our class is almost extinct, and the new heads of those Services have no personal ties with us; so they can close their empire over their docile subjects. I find this very depressing, for my opinion is that even the best of the grandees of that world—even those who were most exposed to the outer world, owing to the war—were gradually reduced to conformity with the persecution-mania of all Secret Services: how much more so those who were never ventilated!

I am thinking of republishing my little book on *The Philby Affair*, with (if you agree) an Epistle Dedicatory to you.[6] Would you allow that? I am truly *shocked* by the crabbed folly of the security services in banning your work, and would like to refer to it, if I could do so without embarrassing you. I am shocked also by our dear P.M.'s acquiescence in their folly. I sup-

---

[1]  A reference to MI6.

[2]  Authorization of the publication of Howard's *Strategic Deception in World War II* (Volume 5 of *British Intelligence in the Second World War*) had been granted, but then withdrawn, for reasons that were not made explicit. The book was not published until 1990.

[3]  Major-General Sir Stewart Menzies (1890–1968), Chief ('C') of the Secret Intelligence Service (SIS, or MI6) from 1939 until 1952; Colonel Valentine Vivian (1886–1969), Vice-Chief of SIS during the Second World War; and his deputy Felix Cowgill (1903–91), who became T-R's superior officer after the Radio Analysis Bureau was absorbed into SIS.

[4]  'Restored to life'.

[5]  The word 'torturable' is used in Greene's novel *Our Man in Havana* (1958).

[6]  T-R never republished the book in his lifetime, but a new edition is forthcoming, in a volume of his collected writings on intelligence matters, edited by E. D. R. Harrison.

pose they said to her, 'Look! see what has happened as a result of your candour about Blunt! We now have these allegations about Hollis.[1] Please keep your mouth shut in future, or the whole Service will be demoralised…' My own view is that she ought not to have been so candid about Blunt then, and ought to have been firmer against the Security Services now. But I am not, alas, her adviser.

I read, and entirely agreed with, your letter to *The Times*.[2] Do keep on in this course!

yours ever

Hugh

PS. Must I read Benjamin Kidd?[3]

—⧜—

## To Noël Annan, 17 November 1981

House of Lords

My dear Noël

You wrote me a long letter several months ago, which I am ashamed of not having answered: or rather, not ashamed (for it did not need an answer), but chagrined, because you write such good letters and I like to elicit them. Now I wonder whether I can elicit another. You are, I believe, now retired and enjoying infinite astronomical leisure; so you can, I hope, write a long letter: long and indiscreet. For I am going to ask an indiscreet question.

---

[1]  Chapman Pincher (b. 1914), in *Their Trade is Treachery* (1981), claimed that Sir Roger Hollis (1905–73), Director-General of MI5 1956–65, had probably been a Russian spy since his recruitment by MI5 in 1938. This allegation, which raised a storm of publicity, was denied by Margaret Thatcher in the House of Commons on 25 March 1981.

[2]  In an article for *The Times*, 'Case for keeping a strong conventional arms capability', responding to the proposal to deploy tactical nuclear forces in Europe, which had attracted mass protest, Howard argued that the true vulnerability of the West to Soviet attack 'still lies in the field of conventional armaments'.

[3]  The sociologist Benjamin Kidd (1858–1916), author of the bestseller *Social Evolution* (1894), which is discussed in Howard's essay in *History and Imagination*.

Two years ago, when I was suddenly whisked up into this House, you wrote me a tantalising letter. In it you remarked that, only a month before my elevation, certain of my friends had tried, very charitably, to cause the Fountain of Honour to cast a refreshing drop on me, but had been formally and decisively told that any such application on my behalf was futile: that I was *persona non grata*, indeed *ingratissima*, that my name had been erased for ever from the Book of Life, that I was cast out like an old shoe, etc. etc…I suppose my friends had suggested a K;[1] and you expressed pleasure that my enemies, having declared me unworthy of that distinction, had been obliged, only a month later, to see me elevated higher.

That is as much as you told me, and I was far too discreet (at that time) to ask you for details. But I did, by accident, learn a little more. What I learned will, if true, be known to you; but I shall spell it out before coming to the question that I want to put to you, so that you will understand my interest in the answer to that question. I was told that the idea of promoting me from my humble position among the mere Misters occurred to some of my friends who were Trustees of the B.M., at or after a meeting of the Trustees; that the business was committed to my old pupil Edward Boyle (whose memorial service I have just been attending), as the most respectable among them; and that he, presumably, having put the question, received the answer that I was beyond the Pale, totally unacceptable, a rotten orange, etc. etc.

Now let me frankly admit to you that although I have no great desire to please the Establishment, or to earn its favours, I was nevertheless surprised, even somewhat pained, to learn that I was regarded by it as such a monster of disrepute, not even to be named in the respectable company of (say) the Lord Kagan, the late Sir Eric Miller,[2] Sir Anthony Blunt, etc.

---

[1]   Knighthood.

[2]   (Sir) Eric Miller (1927–77), a property developer, received a knighthood in Wilson's resignation honours list in 1976 as a reward for helping to fund Wilson's private office. A year later he shot himself on the Jewish Day of Atonement while under separate investigations by the Department of Trade, Scotland Yard, and the City Fraud Squad. A police superintendent in the Criminal Intelligence Unit at Scotland Yard was later charged with corruptly accepting inducements from Miller to pass him secret files on the fugitive businessman Judah Binstock.

etc.; and I wondered how I had earned this disrepute. After all, though I have sometimes shown mild irreverence towards some sacred cows (without however shooting, maiming or worrying any of them), I have never been to prison, or bankrupt, or struck off the Register, or deprived of my Fellowship, or extruded from the British Academy. So how is it that my name arouses, in these influential breasts, such fierce, implacable emotions?

This question occasionally presented itself to me, but always, till now, I pushed it aside, as unanswerable, or too indiscreet to pose, and anyway no longer relevant, having been overtaken by events. But now another episode has occurred which has revived it, and indeed made it relevant, and caused me to write this letter.

Last month, some of my friends and pupils presented a *Festschrift* to me, and on that occasion there was a dinner in Oxford, and among those present was my successor Michael Howard, who had contributed an essay to the volume. After dinner, he made a little speech and presented to me a specially bound essay which, he explained, had been intended for that volume, but which the Security Services had forbidden him to publish, and for which he had therefore substituted another essay. The suppressed essay was a by-product of his work on *Deception in World War II*—a volume which he had been commissioned to write (a parallel volume to Harry Hinsley's unreadable work) and on which he had been working for three years; and it described the case-history of the Double Agent Garbo, which was of course already familiar to me from my own war-time experience, and had since been publicised in books by J. C. Masterman and Ewen Montagu.[1] There was nothing in it which was not known or knowable (if they thought it worth knowing) to any potential

---

[1]  Masterman's classified MI5 report of 1945 had been published as *The Double-Cross System* in 1972, in defiance of an official ban. Its publication in the USA, and the appearance of other unauthorized books giving garbled accounts of Allied code-breaking, prompted the authorities to sanction the revelations in F. W. Winterbotham's bestseller *The Ultra Secret* (1974). In 1977 Ewen Montagu (1901–85), who had run the wartime counter-espionage branch of the Admiralty's naval intelligence, published *Beyond Top Secret U*, which revealed how much of his work had depended on Bletchley deciphering.

enemies. The action of the Security Services in banning its publication therefore seemed to me absurd, lunatic. But Michael then told me that when he had himself remonstrated with their representative, pointing out that his article was for inclusion in an academically respectable volume in honour of a respected academic, *viz:* myself, the reaction, from negative, became violent. It was quite clear, he said, that my mere name infuriated them. He then told me that they had also banned the publication of his book on *Deception*, which they had themselves commissioned, and which had taken him three years to write—and in respect of which they (or their predecessors) had consulted me in order to be reassured about Michael's reliability, etc. He added that the Prime Minister had herself apologised to him for the suppression of his work, explaining that she now regretted that the *Ultra* secret had ever been published— although from whom she thinks it would thereby have been concealed (since the Russians knew about it from Philby nearly 40 years ago) and why its secrecy could be important now, when the whole technology of intelligence has changed, is not at all clear.[1]

From this little episode two interesting facts emerge. One is that my name is evidently a red rag to the Intelligence Services. The other is that the Intelligence Services are now controlled by complete bone-heads. Michael explains that the people now in command there are people who did not know the war and who have none of that residual tolerance and enlightenment which their predecessors derived from that experience (and from working in company with intelligent 'amateurs'); and this view is confirmed to me by Dick White, who has expressed his disgust with the new policy, and has disassociated himself from their work in consequence of the suppression of Michael's history of Deception.

---

[1]    T-R included an essay on Canaris, first published in 1950, in *The Philby Affair* (1968). He modified the original text—perhaps as the result of a talk over lunch with Dick White—to include the new revelation 'that all *Abwehr* hand-cyphers were read by the British from the beginning of 1940 and machine-cyphers...from 1942' (p. 116). This revelation—published six years before F. W. Winterbotham's book—went unnoticed at the time. See David Kahn, 'How the Allies Suppressed the Greatest Secret of World War II', *Journal of Military History*, 74 (2010) and Adam Sisman, 'The Leak that Failed', *Journal of Military History*, 75 (2011).

Now you will see, if your quick mind has not already seen (and if you are still reading this letter) why I put my question to you. What I now suspect is that the persons behind my otherwise (to me) inexplicable blacking by the Great and the Good (who in fact *were* the people who were able to black me so firmly, if also so ineffectively?) were the Security Services. I also suspect (for I can think of no other reason) that my offence in their eyes is my little book on Philby (a book, incidentally, which is required reading in the CIA!).[1] This is slightly ironical because I actually wrote that book at the positive suggestion of Dick White (who however asked not to be shown what I wrote). So my conclusion is that whereas I was, along with others, my contemporaries, trusted by the heads of the Security Services in 1968 (when I wrote that book), and indeed until 1972 (when Dick retired), and evidently later in the 1970s (when I was consulted about Michael Howard), there has been a revolution there more recently (before 1979, when—as I understand—I was 'blacked' for a K).

Moreover, it now seems that this revolution inside the Security Services—a retrogression to the mindless secrecy which characterised them before 1939 and on which I touch lightly in my book on Philby—has established itself with the political establishment too. Mrs T cannot have been enslaved by the new rulers of MI5 and MI6 in 1979, when she made me a peer, nor in 1980 when she made her statement in parliament on Anthony Blunt; but she evidently is now, since she supports them in suppressing Michael's book and utters such asininities about *Ultra*. I suspect that the Security services were cross about her statement on Blunt and then made their weight felt when the allegations were made about Hollis ('*That's* what happens when you start letting cats out of bags!'). At all events, she seems a complete convert now.

All these questions interest me because I have promised to publish a new edition of my book on Philby, with a new introduction, and I am thinking of letting myself go. I feel sure that one of the reasons why the Security Services hate me (and Michael is quite positive that they do) is that I have somehow escaped their power. I am no longer, in Graham Greene's phrase, 'torturable'. They can stop Michael from publishing

---

[1]  Richard Helms (1913–2002), Director of Central Intelligence 1966–73, enjoined 'all his senior officers' to read T-R's 'splendid essay on Philby'.

because he has entered into a contract with them; but I am free and, in spite of them, too well established to be frightened by them. So why not use this freedom? But of course I want to be sure of my facts.

So my positive request to you is this. Since the 'blacking' of me in 1979 *seems* to fit into the general picture which I have reconstructed, I would like to know more about it. Can you tell me anything about the background or the source of the objections? I would be very grateful if you could.

yours ever
Hugh

———⌖———

*Trevor-Roper was as intrigued by Kenneth de Courcy (1909–99), the self-styled Duc de Grantmesnil, as he was by Edmund Backhouse. De Courcy had launched himself as a roving foreign policy consultant to uninfluential Conservative politicians during the 1930s. From 1938 until 1976 he compiled and circulated a fierce anti-Communist newsletter with many subscribers in the American Midwest. After his sentence in 1963 to seven years' imprisonment for fraud, forgery, and perjury, he shared a cell in Wormwood Scrubs with the spy George Blake. Always susceptible to titled company, his genealogical self-aggrandizement intensified after his release from prison. Trevor-Roper's pleasure in de Courcy's absurdities, and patience with his pretensions, were however not without limits.*

## To Jeremy Catto, 21 August 1982

Chiefswood, Melrose

Dear Jeremy,
Where are you spending August? At home, I hope. It is folly to go abroad (see below). If you are at Eydon, please keep a very close watch on Squire Ford (and more especially Lady Ford).[1] Has anyone bought the house? But my interest is not in the new owners.

---

[1]  The courtier Sir Edward Ford (1910–2006), who suggested the phrase *annus horribilis* to the Queen to describe the events of 1992, was married to Virginia Brand (1918–95), a cousin of Lady Dacre and Lord Hampden. The Fords lived at her Palladian house, Eydon Hall in Northamptonshire, from 1963 until 1982. Catto was a neighbour.

I think I told you that Sir E.F. tackled me at a dinner party in London and said that they were selling the Dacre portraits: would I be interested?[1] I said 'yes' in a somewhat non-committal way. Lady F also told me this, at the same party, in a somewhat more distant way. Well, I have now had a letter from Sir E.F., written on behalf of Lady F (who is the owner of the house and the pictures)—why, I asked myself, couldn't she write herself?—and enclosing a list of the Dacre portraits, some to be sold, some to be kept: in other words, allegedly, a complete list. However, I note that the Trevor-Roper portraits (the only ones in which I might be interested) have been omitted from the list. And yet I have seen them myself in the house. What is the meaning of this? We can only assume that Lady Ford, being unable (so far) to kill me, as she told you that she would gladly do, is seeking to re-write history by eliminating the Trevor-Ropers from the history of the Dacre title—rather as Stalin eliminated Trotzky from the history of the Russian Revolution. Ominous precedent! Perhaps, like Stalin, she is determined to destroy her enemy too, and is only biding her time till she has found a hatchet-man prepared to insert himself into my household…

We have been back at Chiefswood for a week; but it will take far more than a week for me to recover from the psychological shock of the previous fortnight. I will tell you all.

I *hate* going abroad in August: too hot, too many tourists, and all one's foreign friends have anyway fled from their homes. But this year I was weak enough to yield to Xandra's desire to accept what she thought (I never did) a tempting invitation. We were invited to spend a fortnight as the guests of a friend who had taken a ducal villa in Tuscany. Apart from my dislike to travel at that time, I had my suspicions of our host, and as I enjoy quietly working at Chiefswood in the summer, I uttered grave reservations. But Xandra said that it would be, for her, a welcome escape from the kitchen-sink, and to this powerful argument I surrendered.

---

[1]   Lady Ford had inherited several ancestral portraits of the Dacre family from her father Lord Brand. T-R did not succeed in buying them.

We were told that there was a swimming-pool, that there would be a house-party of eight, and that the ducal owner had guaranteed every comfort. So I reconciled myself to the prospect, thinking that I would take plenty of books, reserve to myself a cool, well-lit corner of the library, square the butler to ensure a constant supply of refreshing liquid, and only move when I heard the dressing-bell for a convivial and elegant dinner.

At this point, perhaps I should name our host in order to clarify my reservations. He was none other than the father of your former pupil Joseph (I think) de Courcy: now I suppose Lord Joseph, since his father, *mero motu*,[1] has created himself a duke in order to exorcise a psychological trauma due to his lack of a title of nobility; and if one is going to ennoble one's self, I suppose one might as well go the whole hog. At any rate he is now duc de Grantmesnil, and takes his ducal status very seriously. He has ducal emblems embroidered on his shirts and slippers; his title is printed in his cheque-books and on his labels and engraved on his writing-paper; and his road-atlas (for he motored us out), and no doubt his other books (if he has any), are inscribed, in his own hand, with the words 'Property of His Grace the Duke of Grantmesnil'. I noticed that in France, when referring to himself, he would contrive to use the third person, so as to drop the phrase, which seemed very musical to his ears, 'Monsieur le duc'— just as Walter Annenberg, when ambassador to the court of St James, contrived, by the same device, to make repeated use of the phrase 'his Excellency'.[2] However, I also noted that when we were staying, *en route*, with a real French marquis, he became Mr de Courcy. The marquis, I observed, was a keen and learned genealogist, whom perhaps it would have been difficult to deceive.

But I am running ahead too fast. We are still only in March, when I rashly allowed Xandra to accept the invitation. Then came the war for the

---

[1]  'Of his own accord'.
[2]  Richard Cawston's BBC television film *Royal Family* (1969) contained footage of Walter Annenberg (1908–2002), the publishing tycoon who had been appointed by President Richard Nixon as U.S. Ambassador to the Court of St James's, presenting his credentials to the Queen with excruciating orotundity.

Falkland Islands. I saw a ray of hope. Mrs T (it seems) wanted me to conduct the enquiry into the preliminaries to that war, and that task, I
thought, though otherwise unenviable, would at least get me out of the
Italian holiday. But alas, I was vetoed (as I understand) by Mr Foot,[1] and
there was no escape. Indeed, the Falklands war had the very opposite result: for while we were doomed to go, the rest of the house-party made it
an excuse to run out—one couple because their sons were due back from
the Falklands in August, another because they had a furious row with our
and their prospective host on the subject of the Falkland Islands: indeed,
it seems, the war in the South Atlantic was child's play compared with the
battle which raged over the dinner-table, with verbal bombardments
shattering the calm of the dining-room and exocets[2] sinking the port de-
canters with all contents. So my hope that the conversation of our host
would be diluted and dispersed by the company was confounded, and we
were doomed to be with him for a fortnight, alone.

When we arrived at the ducal villa, we found that this too was very different from our expectation. Instead of a luxurious Renaissance *chateau*,
with terraced gardens, elegant statuary, quiet ilex-groves, a swimming-
pool fed with crystallised water from the mouth of a baroque animal
holding the ducal coat-of-arms, and polite Italian servants periodically
wheeling in the drink-trolley, we found a dark and poky farm-house in a
field, with no conveniences of any kind, and a perpetual lack of water.
The swimming-pool was a communal pool a mile away, in a field of nettles, surrounded by a barbed-wire fence. There were no servants, and the
nearest shops were in a hideous *borgo* about five miles away over execrable
roads. In this squalid bothie we were doomed (since we had a fixed-day
return air-ticket) to spend a fortnight, listening to endless monologues by
the *soi-disant* duke on his imaginary pedigree, his own social grandeur,
his importance in the councils of the great and the Secret Service, his butlers, footmen, valets, stewards, secretaries, etc. Xandra said it was like a

---

[1]   In the event, Lord Franks was appointed to conduct the inquiry.
[2]   Exocets (from the French word for a flying-fish) were French-made missiles lethally
used by the Argentine navy against British ships in the Falklands conflict.

Chekhov play. I thought it was a cross between *Nightmare Abbey* and *Cold Comfort Farm*.

We made various plans of escape. We tried to take refuge with Harold Acton;[1] but he had just had Princess Margaret to stay, after which all his servants, exhausted by the strain, had claimed an immediate holiday. We tried the Hotel Universo in Lucca; but it was full. So we had to sit it out and find some relief by seeking to lead our host on to the subjects which he seemed most anxious to avoid and so to reconstruct, behind the tedious fantasies of his phony autobiography, some few solid facts of his real history. For he is, I soon realised, a Backhouse; and indeed I have now enough matter for another book on another hidden life; but I am determined not to write it.

We flew back from Pisa a week ago, our suitcases groaning with clothes for all social occasions, never used. Xandra says that she has a callus on her bottom from the hardness of the kitchen chairs (the kitchen was the only living room). We only once escaped from the (pseudo-) ducal monologues: that was when we found the British Ambassador to Prague in a house nearby.[2] He was a Cambridge man, and was much exercised by the problem of the authorship of the letters of Mercurius Oxoniensis, which he seemed to know by heart. He asked me if the problem had ever been solved, so I told him the truth: that it had aroused a great deal of speculation, and many wild suggestions, but that it remained one of the insoluble mysteries of literature.

yours ever
Hugh

———— ∞∞ ————

[1]    Sir Harold Acton (1904–94), aesthete and historian, lived in princely style in an imposing villa, La Pietra, north of Florence. His offer to bequeath La Pietra to Christ Church was declined.
[2]    John Rich (1928–95), Ambassador to Czechoslovakia 1980–5 and to Switzerland 1985–8.

*In 1974 Trevor-Roper had been appointed as one of the four 'National Directors' of Times Newspapers Limited charged with upholding the editorial independence and probity of* The Times. *In 1981, when Rupert Murdoch's News International bought control of Times Newspapers, Trevor-Roper was one of the 'Independent Directors', as the National Directors were renamed, responsible for 'protecting editorial freedom from interference by the proprietor'.*

*Two years later, in March 1983, Trevor-Roper was asked by* The Times *to assess the authenticity of documents, supposedly Hitler's diaries, for which the German magazine* Stern *was offering syndication rights for sale under terms of strict secrecy. Murdoch was keen to secure the rights if the diaries could be authenticated. Trevor-Roper flew to Zurich on 7 April, and was allowed a few hours to scrutinize them in a back room of a bank and to question* Stern *executives, who gave him assurances that later proved to be worthless. Afterwards he submitted to pressure from the editor of* The Times *and gave a tentative authentication, on the basis of which Murdoch bought the English-language rights. The following letter was written after Trevor-Roper had given his opinion that the Hitler diaries were genuine, but before their discovery was announced to the world's press at a press conference in Hamburg on 25 April (attended by him). It shows his mind ranging far from the subject of the diaries.*

## To Blair Worden, 14 April 1983

Chiefswood, Melrose Alas, till 17 April only

My dear Blair,

When you were at private school, did you ever (as I did) read Conan Doyle's *The Lost World*?[1] Probably not; your generation probably read science-fiction at that age. *The Lost World* was about a plateau in South America which was so inaccessible and isolated behind natural barriers that its fauna had not had to compete in the struggle for existence, and had thus been exempt from the process of evolution. Consequently it was stuck in the Mesozoic age. Dinosaurs swished their long tails as they roamed through the prehistoric vegetation, and pterodactyls flapped their

---

[1]  First published in 1912; its hero, Professor Challenger, reappears in its sequel, *The Poison Belt* (1913).

leathery wings as they descended on their carrion or prey. This 'world that we have lost', as Laslett[1] would call it, was found again, and boldly penetrated, by a learned and adventurous *professor* from the outer world— I think he was called Professor Challenger—who had various uncomfortable adventures in it. In the end, as far as I remember, he beat a hasty and hazardous retreat, pursued to the frontier-precipice by romping megatheria and snorting brontosaurs.

Well, I am that professor and Peterhouse is that Lost World: an unreformed, unevolved, unreconstructed island, or preservative bottle, left over from the past.[2] And no doubt my escape, in the end,—if I escape— will be similar. Already I seem to hear the whirr of those leathern wings, and to feel the scaly horror of those swingeing tails. And yet, is it not flattering Peterhouse to describe it as a plateau? Is it not rather a dank, sunken cavity in which the surviving animals are not huge, roaming dinosaurs and air-borne pterodactyls but immobile molluscs and torpid gastropods? I believe that in fact Conan Doyle's biology was at fault: that animals which survive in insulation dwindle in bulk and vitality, becoming—like the Carthaginian elephant—miserable shrunken relics of their former selves...

However (though I shall return to this topic) let me not complain. For four weeks I have not looked on that place, nor even thought about it much. I have been sitting at Chiefswood reading the philosophical works of Cicero, Squire Waterton's *Wanderings in South America*,[3] and the Travels in Tartary and Tibet of the abbé Huc.[4] I will not press Cicero upon you—I have

---

[1]    Peter Laslett (1915–2001), who had worked at Bletchley decoding Japanese naval intelligence, discovered John Locke's library in a damp Highlands shooting lodge and instigated Paul Mellon's gift of it to the Bodleian. A Fellow of Trinity College, Cambridge, from 1953, and co-founder in 1962 of the Cambridge Group for the History of Population and Social Structure, he urged social historians to focus on demography and on the history of the family. *The World We Have Lost: England before the Industrial Age*, which exemplified this approach, appeared in 1965.

[2]    The reluctance to hold open elections to fellowships seemed to T-R to typify the 'unreformed' condition of the college.

[3]    Charles Waterton (1782–1865), naturalist, traveller, owner of plantations in Demerara, created the first English bird sanctuary on his Yorkshire estate in 1826.

[4]    Evariste Huc (1813–60) wrote with graphic, racy charm of his visit to Lhasa in 1846.

special reasons for reading him—but so do you know Waterton, and Huc? I first discovered Waterton as a boy,[1] from reading an article in the *TLS*, which I used to purchase weekly at the bookstall of the now obsolete railway station at Alnwick.[2] The article was re-printed recently. He has been a hero of mine ever since; and last month, breaking our northward journey at Nostell Priory, the house of my dear if distant cousin Lord St Oswald,[3] I made a pilgrimage to the squire's house, Walton Hall; which, alas, is now tamed and trimmed as a country club for the inhabitants of Wakefield.

As for the abbé Huc, he is a new discovery. I have his work; and yet I had never read it until I had to write a hack article in order to pay the plumber's bill. Do you know the book? No, or you would surely have sung its praises to me. He dates from the 1840s. He was a Lazarist priest who, after creeping incognito across China, was then nestling in Mongolia, where, with a colleague, he conceived a heroic plan. Since the worldly and sophisticated Jesuits had failed to convert the worldly and sophisticated Chinese, and had merely caused Christian missionaries to be excluded from the Celestial Empire on pain of death, these two evangelists decided to go to Tibet, to convert the holy city of Lhasa, and, through it, the whole Buddhist world of central Asia. So they set out on a terrible journey, in mid-winter, across the Pamirs. They reached Lhasa, set up their chapel, and began their work; but then they were squeezed out by Chinese pressure, and had to make another terrifying journey back through China. Fr Huc's account is marvellous: beautifully written, with an agreeable mixture of simplicity and quiet irony. Unlike the *mondain* philosophers of the previous century, he did not like the Chinese at all: thought them worldly,

---

[1]   He was 18.

[2]   A leading article, 'The Squire', in the *Times Literary Supplement* of 29 December 1932 (unsigned, but written by Richard Aldington), begins: 'Like many other human beings, Charles Waterton of Walton Hall suffered from the world's calumny and misrepresentation. After the publication of his "Wanderings in South America" he was accused of a "strong propensity to dress facts in the garb of fiction". Even though he had ridden regularly to hounds with Lord Darlington, his account of riding a live alligator was received with derision; and his description of the three-toed sloth, proved afterwards to be accurate, met a storm of contempt and contradiction...Time, he said, would prove he was right; and in most cases it did.'

[3]   Rowland ('Rowley') Winn, 4th Baron St Oswald (1916–84), a former war correspondent.

cowardly and corrupt. He liked the nomads of the steppes, even the brigands who haunted the caravan with which they crossed those terrible mountains. Just as the Jesuits saw Confucianism as compatible with Catholicism (give and take a few details, such as the crucifixion), so these missionaries saw Tibetan Buddhism as a mirror-image of popery: Tibet = the Papal States, the Dalai Lama = the Pope, the Grand Lamas = the cardinals, etc. But they did not draw any unorthodox conclusions.

Apart from these purely intellectual journeys to South America and Central Asia, I have, since I saw you, had a real outing to the Caribbean. I went—having been invited to give some elementary lectures to some rich Canadians, as they cruised in a four-masted schooner among those tropical islands—with three ulterior motives. First, it was an opportunity to give Xandra a holiday at the end (as I thought) of the winter. Secondly, I thought that I might discover, and exploit, some Canadian millionaires. Thirdly, I must confess I was quite happy to show my lack of interest in Peterhouse by going off—without revealing my destination—for ten days in full term. The schooner was very luxurious: it had belonged to Miss Post, the heiress of all the Post Toasties in the World, and, after her, to the dictator of Ste. Domingo, Rafael Trujillo.[1] The Canadians were *very* boring (I would rather have been Trujillo's guest). And I did not, I must admit, think much of those tropical islands: miserable run-down places populated by white drop-outs and black slugs. At St Eustathius, the Dutch island, which was once the great slave emporium of the Western world, I was proudly shown the island's public library: a room full of trashy paperbacks—the only titles that suggested anything to me were *The Works of Sigmund Freud* and *1,000* (or was it *10,000*?) *Homosexuals*. I have acquired one Canadian friend—the only person on the boat whom we found interesting, and who promises well for my fund-raising purposes; and now I feel that I need never go back to the Caribbean.

---

[1]    *Hussar II* was the largest private yacht in the world when it was built in 1931 for Marjorie Merriweather Post (1887–1973), the breakfast cereal heiress who acquired Birds Eye Frozen Foods for her conglomerate General Foods. In 1955 Miss Post swapped her yacht for a second-hand Vickers Viscount aircraft. Its new owner, Rafael Trujillo (1891–1961), renamed it *Angelita*. After his assassination, it changed ownership several times, and was renamed *Sea Cloud* in 1978.

Meanwhile do not think that I have forgotten those essays.[1] They are being sedulously polished, arranged, re-arranged, deranged, etc. Nor have I forgotten my friends. Though I have not written many letters to them (or anyone else) I think of them *constantly*, seeking to earn their approval, or at least to avoid the open signs of their disapproval.

How is your life? How are your studies? St Edmund Hall, as we all know, is a well-ordered college, sustained by the tribute of that Winery in New York and the unavowable subsidies of President Marcos of the Philippine Islands.[2] Everything there, I am sure, runs on oiled wheels. You have, I trust, ample leisure for literature, scholarship, society and observation. You are in touch (oh happy state!) with intellectual life: with Catto and Cobb,[3] and such great names as these. Toss to me, I beg, in my Fenland prison-house, some crumbs from your feast of the Muses. Have you written on Marvell?[4] Have you read Keith Thomas on cats and dogs?[5] And the Regius Professor on the Bomb?[6]

Give me also, if you will, your views on a subject which has much exercised me of late. The Peterhouse historians have for some time been

[1]  Worden had persuaded T-R to gather, in a series of volumes, essays which had appeared individually in miscellaneous and often obscure publications.

[2]  In 1966, in an effort to raise funds, penurious St Edmund Hall began exporting its own branded blends of brandy, whisky, gin, Madeira, port, and mead to a New York outlet, Sherry-Lehmann. The scheme was the brainchild of Reginald ('Reggie') Alton (1919–2003), Fellow and Tutor in English at St Edmund Hall 1953–87. Alton and Sam Aaron of Sherry-Lehmann were co-authors of *A Few Words from Oxford about the Pleasures of the Bottle* (1966). After a St Edmund Hall undergraduate, Ferdinand ('Bongbong') Marcos (b. 1957), son of the President of the Philippines, failed some of his PPE examinations, a Foreign Office man visited the college to say, very politely, that although it was a matter for the college, the British government would be pleased if he were kept on, as he was.

[3]  Richard Cobb (1917–96), Fellow and Tutor in Modern History, Balliol College, Oxford, 1962–72; Reader in French Revolutionary History, Oxford University 1969–72; Professor of Modern History 1973–84. A few days before the meeting of the electors to the Chair of Modern History, a tipsy Cobb fell downstairs at a sedate function at the British Academy. T-R ensured that no whisper of the incident reached the electors. His frequent letters to Cobb were destroyed shortly after Cobb's death.

[4]  Worden published an essay on Andrew Marvell's 'Horatian Ode' in the *Historical Journal* for 1984.

[5]  *Man and the Natural World: Changing Attitudes in England, 1500–1800* (London, 1983).

[6]  Howard, whose essays on *The Causes of War* had been published in February 1983, had argued in 'Ultimate Test of Nuclear Deterrent', *The Times*, 8 February 1983, that the NATO decision of 1953 to base the defence of Western Europe upon nuclear deterrence had been taken on grounds of cost. This argument aroused a public controversy involving Max Beloff and others.

telling the world that the Peterhouse school of history has a special, indeed unique, character, and that this character raises it far above the ordinary vulgar historians of our or any time. Maurice Cowling, in his book ('the book of a *voyeur*', as John Elliott described it) and in the *Sunday Times*,[1] Roger Scruton (ex-Fellow of Peterhouse) in the *Times*,[2] Peregrine Worsthorne (ex-undergraduate of Peterhouse) in the *Sunday Telegraph* and the *Spectator*,[3] have all banged this drum and blown this trumpet, so that I am beginning to believe that there really is, and must be, such a school. But what is it? What are its distinguishing views?

When I, timidly, ask such questions in Peterhouse, the answer (like all answers from that quarter) is oracular but opaque. However, I begin to detect, through the fog, some faint lineaments of a definition. For instance, I learn that the Peterhouse historians are all *philosophic* historians, and *tory* historians (they regard me as a 'Whig'—an Anglican Whig, says Cowling; an infidel Scottish Whig, says Worsthorne). I also learn that their founding fathers are the philosopher Michael Oakeshott[4] (why is he not honoured by the Crown, cries Worsthorne; 'nothing less than an O.M. will do') and the historian Butterfield. Now I have to admit that I have not read much of either of these *gurus*—only enough to convince

---

[1]  Maurice Cowling, 'Place for Women?', *Sunday Times*, 6 March 1983, regretted the imminent admission of women to Peterhouse. 'Those who have thwarted them have been moved not by dislike of women but by dislike of fashion', he wrote. 'In this respect the college has done its duty [and] stood out against nonsense.' He added, 'Peterhouse has a distinctive tone which is at once learned and imaginative, serious and satirical, hard-nosed, hard-minded and hard-working.'

[2]  Roger Scruton (b. 1944) had been a Research Fellow at Peterhouse 1969–71. In an article deploring the college's decision to admit women undergraduates ('Stay with the men, Peterhouse', *The Times*, 22 March 1983) he described 'the spirit of Peterhouse' as 'an acute, and poetic, scrupulousness', and explained that 'if the Peterhouse style seems scornful...this merely reflects...an impatience with fraud'. Scruton praised its 'moral and intellectual' power. He was editor of the conservative *Salisbury Review* (1982–2000) and Professor of Aesthetics at Birkbeck College, London, 1985–92.

[3]  (Sir) Peregrine Worsthorne (b. 1923), then associate editor of the *Sunday Telegraph*. Like T-R he was a member of the Beefsteak. In the *Sunday Telegraph* of 27 February 1983 Worsthorne had maintained that T-R was unsympathetic to the Peterhouse historians because 'he detests all religions in general and Christianity in particular'. Under pressure from T-R, Worsthorne publicly retracted those words four days before this letter was written.

[4]  Michael Oakeshott (1901–90), Professor of Political Science at the LSE 1948–96, whose *On History* appeared in the year this letter was written.

myself that they are not worth reading. In this I may well be wrong. But I am prejudiced against Butterfield by seeing his legacy in Peterhouse—and also the historical *mafia* which, by his patronage, he created there and elsewhere, largely in Ireland (an academic colony of Peterhouse). To Peterhouse he gave the genius of Cowling; to Dublin that of Desmond Williams.[1] Another member of the *mafia* is Brian Wormald. Cowling has some pupils whom he tries to force on us, but none of them have written anything to indicate their character, except a young man called David Wootton whom Cowling sent to me as a research student in Oxford and then tried to force on Peterhouse as a Fellow; but the Papists stood firm against him, being a Marxist (Cowling has declared, in his book, his own opinion that Marxism is 'right but unimportant').[2]

Now what is the common denominator of this 'school'? They—or rather those of them who can utter—seem to me to have *some* common qualities. First, they are all ideologues in search of a dogma. Butterfield was a Methodist tub-preacher. Cowling is a resentful inner *émigré* from Anglicanism. Wormald is a convert to popery. Secondly, their writing is always opaque and circular and seldom finished—which hardly matters since it has no direction. Butterfield rambles round his Methodist tub. Wormald (as Noël Annan put it) 'wrote half a book, backwards'. Cowling is writing an open-ended part-work of which vol. 1 the only one in print—leads nowhere. Williams flounders hopelessly in an alcoholic

[1]  Desmond Williams (1921–87) became a research student at Peterhouse under Butterfield in 1944, and by Butterfield's influence was appointed Professor of Modern History at University College, Dublin, in 1949 (a post he held until 1983).

[2]  David Wootton (b. 1952), now a professor at the University of York, is an authority on cultural and intellectual history across the period 1500–1800. Having begun a doctoral thesis under T-R's supervision at Oxford, he abandoned it after the two had found themselves intellectually at odds. Instead he published his findings as a book, *Paolo Sarpi: Between Renaissance and Enlightenment* (1983). In 1976, when Wootton was a Junior Research Fellow of Peterhouse, Cowling put his name forward for a teaching appointment there. Cowling himself stated that the resistance to Wootton was prompted not by religious allegiance, or by the Marxism to which Wootton at that time subscribed, but by the expectation that he would vote for the admission of women as undergraduates. When, many years later, T-R and Wootton were reintroduced as they boarded a bus to bring members of a conference back from an expedition, the mention of the word 'Peterhouse' instantly gave their relations a much happier turn. A gleeful exchange of memories between the two occupied the long journey home, and thereafter they got on very well.

Irish bog. Finally, all these Peterhouse historians praise each other in ex-aggerated language. They do so in such terms, and with such conviction, that the scientific Fellows of Peterhouse, and the undergraduates (two in-nocent, credulous classes) really believe—or did believe, as one scientist said to me 'until you came'—that 'the Peterhouse school of history' is an intellectual power-house which has transformed the subject and laid the philosophic base for a revolution in political thought. As this 'school', through their friends in the media, have captured columns in the news-papers and programmes on the radio and television, they are now im-posing their claims on the world.

Now the question I ask myself is, do I misjudge them in regarding the whole lot of them as a gaggle of muddle-headed muffaroos bumbling and fumbling blindly after each other in broken circles? The words of Oliver Cromwell haunt me: 'in the bowels of Christ I beseech you, consider that you may be mistaken'.[1] I suppose that the only way to determine this question is to sit down with a damp towel round my forehead and read the works of Oakeshott, Butterfield, etc. But No! That I *will* not do! Life is too short. So I turn to you as the most trusted of my advisers. Have you read this stuff? Can you discover the spinal cord that animates and dir-ects the corpus of their work, and that of their disciples? Please enlighten me so that I can avoid doing an injustice to my colleagues.

In a review of a book on the English historians of the French Revolu-tion, published in 1968, Richard Cobb remarked that those of these histor-ians who lived in Cambridge not only 'never bothered to cross the Channel' but 'were clearly too fixed in their ways, too embedded in their comfort-able colleges, even frequently to make the journey to London'. Among these 'rather idle men', he singles out, as 'the arch-sloth', one Smyth who spent sixty years in Cambridge ('no wonder he was an important figure there'),[2] and remarks that the author of the book under review 'writes that

---

[1]  Cromwell's letter to the general assembly of the Church of Scotland (3 August 1650) included the words, 'I beseech you, in the bowels of Christ, think it possible you may be mistaken'.

[2]  A review of Hedva Ben-Israel, *English Historians of the French Revolution*, *Times Literary Sup-plement*, 28 November 1968.

he [Smyth] had great influence on his pupils, while admitting, rather rue-fully, that his work was little known outside Peterhouse'.[1] Is Smyth, per-haps, the Founder of the Peterhouse School?

yours ever,

Hugh

On the morning of Saturday 23 April, the very morning that Trevor-Roper's article announ-cing the discovery of the Hitler diaries was published in The Times, he spoke by telephone to the editor, Charles Douglas-Home (1937–85), and told him that he could no longer stand by the judgement he had made. Though the Sunday Times was due to start serializing the diaries the next day and planned a banner headline headed 'World Exclusive', Trevor-Roper's volte-face was not transmitted to its editor Frank Giles, who had been Trevor-Roper's friend for over thirty years, or to anyone else on the newspaper, until Giles telephoned him at 7.00 o'clock on Saturday evening. Trevor-Roper's admission that he had changed his mind caused consternation at the Sunday Times offices, where the presses had already started to roll. Rupert Murdoch's response, when contacted by telephone in New York, was 'Fuck Dacre. Publish'.

That Monday, Trevor-Roper attended a press conference in Hamburg at which Stern announced its discovery to the world's press. The event, which became chaotic, was excruci-ating for him. When, after the press conference, the documents were swiftly proven to be forgeries, he was humiliated and his reputation damaged. The standing of the Sunday Times as an investigative newspaper was also diminished by these events. In contrast, Trevor-Roper's enemies at Peterhouse were exultant.

[1] Richard Cobb, *Tour de France* (1976).

## To Frank Giles, 10 July 1983

The Master's Lodge, Peterhouse

My dear Frank

At Steven Runciman's birthday party I got a formidable drubbing from Kitty[1] for not having apologised to you personally over the unfortunate affair of the 'Hitler diaries'. I was in rather a weak state at that party. I have had a prolonged and disagreeable crisis in this college which reached its climax at a long college meeting on Monday. Immediately after that I had to fly to Hamburg to give evidence to the tribunal investigating the part played by *Stern* in that same affair of the diaries. I returned from Hamburg on Wednesday afternoon so exhausted by events, and so enervated by the heat, that I tried to get out of that party; but Xandra was determined to go. So I felt in no state to argue or resist, or, after that, to discuss so inappropriate a matter with you: I decided to reserve it for a letter.

I have genuinely forgotten some of the details and order of events in the hectic period 22–25 April; but let me begin, without *ambages*[2] or qualifications of any kind, by expressing to you (since my public apology was evidently insufficient)[3] my great regret that, through an initial error of mine, which I have admitted, you were, most improperly (as I believe), put in an embarrassing and indeed impossible position. I think you were treated very badly, and you certainly deserve an apology from those who put you in that position. I *thought* that I had sufficiently apologised to you, but if not, let me do so now. I apologise very sincerely, *ex animo*. That said, let me explain the reasons which have governed my action or inaction hitherto. I was asked to look at those diaries by The Times, not the Sunday Times; I reported to The Times; and on the basis of my first report (which

---

[1] Lady Katharine ('Kitty') Sackville (1926–2010), daughter of the 9th Earl de la Warr, had married Frank Giles in 1946.
[2] 'Equivocation'.
[3] T-R's apologia appeared under the headline 'Hitler: A Catalogue of Errors' in *The Times*, 14 May 1983.

I had never expected to have to give by telephone within a few hours of seeing the stuff) the management of *The Times* took over and thereafter forced the pace. At the request of *The Times* I wrote (under great pressure) my first article. In none of the history was the *Sunday Times* involved. What I understood is that Rupert Murdoch, having acquired the rights from *Stern* on—I think—21 April, imposed (if that is not to strong a word) the stuff suddenly on the *Sunday Times*, which had no opportunity of examining, considering or criticising it. If this is true (for I speak from hearsay), then it is my opinion that you were badly treated, though not by me, and were owed an apology, though not directly by me.

In fact I believe that I too was badly treated, both by *Stern*, which misled me with false evidence of fact (which I could not doubt unless I was to accuse them of bad faith) and, to some extent, by *The Times*, which did not allow me the conditions which I had at first been promised to check the material (i.e. a typed transcript of the German text on which I was to make a written report). However, I have refused to make any complaint or excuse on these grounds, for I recognise that I should have been firm and have refused to commit myself in the circumstances which actually obtained. So, when I first doubted the authenticity of the material, I decided to take the whole blame on myself—and I must admit that the *Times* and the *Sunday Times* were very happy to place it there. I apologised in writing to Rupert Murdoch (who wrote very civilly in reply, accepting part of the responsibility), and in print to the editors of the *Times* and the *Sunday Times*.

Kitty suggested that I owed you an apology for not having made it possible for you to stop publication of the articles on 24 April. I was quite unaware of this situation. Perhaps my memory is at fault. My recollection is that, after my return from Hamburg on 20 April, the pace was suddenly quickened by *Stern*'s action in bringing the publication date forward. This obliged me to write my long article for the *Times* under great pressure. My doubts then began and by the morning of 23 April I had to face the fact that the documents might be forged. But this entailed such large consequences— grossly unprofessional standards, even bad faith, by *Stern*—that I could not, at that stage, call them more than doubts. I telephoned Charlie Douglas-Home early on Saturday morning and told him the position. I *understood* that my doubts would be passed on to you. Charlie's attitude was that so long as there was any chance that the diaries were genuine, we should keep to our course: I should go to Hamburg next day (Sunday) for the Press Conference on Monday, and handle the matter as best I could. In fact, by the time of the conference in Hamburg, I had grilled Heidemann[1] (on Sunday night) and my doubts had been confirmed; so I spoke more explicitly than I would have done in London. If I had thought that I could have stopped—or postponed—the publication in the *Sunday Times* on the Saturday, I would certainly have done so; but matters were out of my hands.

All this is *vieux jeu*[2] now. It was a horrible experience for me: I was savaged by almost the whole press—the *Observer* went on for five weeks—and was powerless to answer because I did not wish to say anything that might make the position worse for the *Times* or the *Sunday Times*. It was a horrible experience for you too—and less deservedly, for I at least must admit to an error, which you need not. If my understanding of events is correct, the *Sunday Times* alone comes out of the affair quite blameless.

There are still many problems to be solved, and *Stern* is going through an agonising reappraisal which I have seen at close quarters. There are also some general conclusions which I dare not express even in this letter which I prudently send to your private address.

yours ever

Hugh

---

*Zeev Sternhell (b. 1935) was Léon Blum Professor of Political Science at the Hebrew University of Jerusalem, working in its Centre of European Studies, and Fellow of the Israel Academy of Sciences and Humanities. In his book* Ni droite ni gauche *(translated into English as* Neither Right nor Left) *he argued that the ideological origins of fascism were French: the populist reaction of Boulangisme in the 1880s; Georges Sorel's syndicalism; and Proudhonism.*

[1]  Gerd Heidemann (b. 1931), the *Stern* journalist who claimed to have found the diaries.
[2]  'Old hat'.

*Trevor-Roper was a supporter of Sternhell when he was sued for defamation in 1983 by the political economist Bertrand de Jouvenel.*

## To Zeev Sternhell, 1 August 1983

The Master's Lodge, Peterhouse

Dear Professor Sternhell

I am a bad correspondent at the best of times and especially, I am afraid, when people are so kind as to send me their books. Of course, sometimes one can answer that one 'looks forward to reading the book'. But your work so interests me that I want to read and digest it first, and acknowledge it intelligently. You may well have forgotten by now that you sent me a copy of your book *Ni droite ni gauche*. Well, I shall not forget it. I find myself very preoccupied at present, trying to combine some historical work with the problems of ruling a strange college in a strange university: so I get far too little time to read outside my immediate preoccupations; and your book is a profound work, not to be read hastily. But now that I have read and digested it, let me write, however belatedly, to tell you how much I have enjoyed reading it, and have learned from it, and how much I respect your writings, which I have found the most illuminating work that I have read on a fascinating and important subject. I really cannot sufficiently express my admiration for it.

You take issue with me on one important point. In my essay on 'the Phenomenon of Fascism' I argued that fascism, as we came to know it in action, differed from country to country, and differed so widely that the term was unsafe as a generalisation (I have not my essay at hand, but I think that is a fair summary). You have certainly shown, as no one else, to my knowledge, not even Nolte,[1] has done, how the social content and philosophy of fascism was built up in France. However, looking at fascism as a form of

---

[1]  Ernst Nolte (b. 1923), Professor of Modern History at the Freie Universität Berlin 1973–91, was a philosophical historian who in *Der Faschismus in seiner Epoche* (1963; translated into English as *The Three Faces of Fascism*, 1965) made a comparative study of German Nazism, Italian Fascism, and the counter-revolutionaries of Action Française. He identified fascism as a reaction against modernity.

government and a philosophy of government, as realised in power, I still feel that the term ceases to be useful. Perhaps this is because I am arguing on a more superficial level. I think of the vulgar application of the term to the governments of Hitler, Mussolini and Franco. It seems to me that an essential, perhaps the essential, element in national socialism—the element which, historically, came to distinguish it from international socialism—is anti-semitism. And yet anti-semitism was absent from Mussolini's Italy and Franco's Spain: it was the Germans who brought it into Italy when they occupied it after Mussolini's fall. This seems to me more than a mere local variation. Indeed, it seems so fundamental a difference that whatever unity the national socialist philosophy may have had in opposition seems to me to have been broken by the compromises, and *Realpolitik*, of power.

However that may be, your work on the history of national socialism in opposition and on the way to power seems to me of the greatest importance. A movement that has been captured by power (rather than has captured it) and been ridden to disaster by it, is historically discredited and all its early prophets, contributors, deviationists, heretics, fellow-travellers, are customarily thrown into the same dust-bin. You have shown what the movement was before it was captured, and done so, if I may say so, in a really historical way (I was particularly fascinated by your account of Henry de Man[1]). I hope that your book is as widely studied as it deserves to be: it is a great work.

Over a year ago—in May 1982—I gave a lecture in Düsseldorf of which I am taking the liberty of sending you a copy. If you read it, please read it in English, not in German! I wrote this lecture after I had read your book *La Droite Révolutionnaire* but before I had received *Ni droite ni gauche*. You will see that I am, as I hope that many others will now be, indebted to you.

yours sincerely
Hugh Trevor-Roper

---

[1]  Henri de Man (1885–1953), Belgian socialist leader who welcomed the Nazi occupation of Belgium in 1940.

## To Blair Worden, 28 December 1984

Chiefswood, Melrose

My dear Blair

I have before me two letters of yours, which I have not answered: one of 11 Sept, the other of 9 Oct. I feel guilty about this; but then I have been remiss in so many other matters too in the last few months—ever since I went into hospital in March, which slowed me up and I seem never to have caught up again. And then that seventh centenary![1] Those endless functions and junketings! And when I protested against them—against the lack of any intellectual content to celebrate our real purpose over those seven centuries—that only entailed more work, and absorbed more energy, from *us*.[2] I can still hear the sullen growl (or was it a snarl?) of Cowling, from the far end of the table in the obscurantist gloom of the Combination Room (where our Governing Body meets), 'If you want *that* sort of thing, do it yourself!' And indeed, if anything has to be done in Peterhouse, the motive force has to come from us. However, I organised the lecture and Xandra organised her concert, both of which were afterwards allowed to have been a great success, and I hope that Peterhouse is beginning to be associated with something other than rich food, deep potations and bad manners (as a colleague explained when I spoke of Cowling's rudeness to guests, 'Maurice doesn't *believe* in being polite to guests'!). Our wedding anniversary also took some organisation, but we enjoyed that, and I was very touched that you should come from Oxford. Now I am at Chiefswood and am reading books and writing letters and not thinking (much) of Peterhouse. How pleasant to be writing to you!

Owing partly to all these preoccupations I did not make my customary visits to Oxford during last term; but I hope to come next term (although I propose to escape to America for part of it), and I hope I shall see you.

---

[1] The year 1984 marked the 700th anniversary of Peterhouse's foundation.
[2] i.e. the Dacres.

Meanwhile, let me repeat what I said on the telephone, *viz*: that I thought your two essays, on Marvell's Horatian Ode and on Cromwell's toleration,[1] splendid: the former so subtle, so penetrating, and so well written; the latter so agreeably heretical; and both so scholarly and persuasive. I was delighted by them. Many thanks for sending them. Please send me anything you write.

I will of course see anything you publish in *Past and Present* (if I keep up my subscription); but how irritating to be censored by Christopher Hill![2] I'm afraid I now feel about him as I do about Stone (although I *like* Christopher, which makes a difference): I simply do not read anything he writes because nothing that he writes can be trusted: he has no scholarly method. The turning-point for me was *The Intellectual Origins*; the last straw (if I may mix my metaphors) *Milton*.[3] I suppose that both he and Stone are the victims of their respect (if Stone can respect anyone) for Tawney, who had exactly the same fault. Neale once said to me that it was useless to discuss evidence with Tawney: he simply didn't know what it was.

I am delighted to hear that you have started a Further Subject on 'Literature and Politics in Early Modern England'. This will strike a blow, incidentally, against certain trends in the Eng. Lit. World. I don't know about Oxford, but I understand that in Cambridge the ruling doctrine is internalist—i.e. that literature should be separated entirely from its context and considered without any reference to it. Eng. Lit. dons are anyway often so silly that you can only do good among them, though you will have to read some very boring literature as well as Sidney and Bacon, Clarendon, Marvell and Milton. Presumably you are now immersed in Lyly, Gabriel Harvey, and Sylvester's du Bartas.[4]

---

[1]  In *Studies in Church History* (1984).

[2]  Worden had submitted an article to *Past and Present* on 'Providence and Politics in Cromwellian England', which was published in that journal in 1985. Members of the editorial board, of whom Hill was one, act as referees. Worden was loath to adopt Hill's suggested changes, though these hardly amounted to his being 'censored'.

[3]  Hill's *Intellectual Origins of the English Revolution* (1965) hinted at links between the spirit of scientific enquiry and social or political radicalism; *Milton and the English Revolution* (1977) discussed the influence of radical ideas on the poet.

[4]  T-R names Elizabethan writers who command the interest of specialists but not of a wider readership: John Lyly (1554?–1606), Gabriel Harvey (1550?–1630), and Josuah Sylvester (1563–1618), the last the translator of an epic biblical poem by the Frenchman Guillaume du Bartas.

Did you read Geoffrey Elton's first Butterfield Memorial Lecture, delivered at Belfast and published in the *Historical Journal?*[1] Alternate showers of soft soap and hatchet blows. I particularly relished the remark that Butterfield's aura (rather a fuzzy aura, I would say) caused Peterhouse to be regarded as a historical college 'long after it had ceased to be one'.

You went for four days to Madrid. I wonder why. Spain is so fascinating and Madrid, except for the Prado, to me, so dull. But perhaps you went to visit the Prado. I hope you took Ford![2]

You say some very kind things about *The Last Days of Hitler* which greatly encourage me. Many thanks! Since you say them, I will admit to you what I have never been so immodest as to admit to anyone hitherto, *viz:* that when I wrote it I *intended* it to be a classic. If you think it is, I have my reward. My reasons for thinking that I *could* write a classic on that subject were two. First, I realised that I had an extraordinary, perhaps a unique opportunity, for here was a dramatic episode in contemporary history that was not only self-contained but also, as far as I could see, evidentially limited. I mean that, unlike nearly all such episodes, the complete truth about it was in the grasp of a contemporary writer. All the action took place within a hermetically sealed area; there were no secret documents buried in the archives; if I could examine the personal witnesses, and could find such documents as they had written or were carrying, and such messages as they contrived to send out, there was a chance, at least in theory, that I could write an account of it that would not be superseded. This was a great incentive to collect all the evidence and, of course, to interpret it aright. Secondly, I believed that in this instance I, and only I, *could* interpret it aright. This was a very vain belief, but it had a basis which I still think, equally vainly no doubt, was sound. I was, I think, one of the very few people in England who had taken the trouble to read *Mein Kampf* in German (for only a fraction of it had been available in England till the war, and then people were too busy or too prejudiced to read it).

---

[1]   'Herbert Butterfield and the Study of History' (1984).
[2]   The connoisseur Richard Ford (1796–1858) published his remarkable pioneering *Hand-Book for Travellers in Spain* (1845).

It was a general, perhaps the universal, belief in England in 1945 that Hitler was a mere adventurer, a gangster solely intent on power, a Pied Piper who bewitched a gullible people, or, alternatively, a pawn manipulated by powerful interests. I read *Mein Kampf* in the autumn of 1938 as a result of reading an article by R. C. K. Ensor,[1] which greatly impressed me, on Munich. Ensor there wrote that 'to have read *Mein Kampf* in German is the beginning of wisdom in international affairs'. Having been to Nazi Germany, and having read *Mein Kampf*, I had a different view of Hitler, and in writing about him, and believing that I had a chance (owing to accidental circumstances) of writing for posterity, I was determined *not* to write in the current mood but to see the whole episode, and the persons involved, though they were contemporary, in a long-term historical context. It pleases me to think that I may have succeeded.

There was also another factor. I wrote that book *for* someone. The person was dead when I wrote it; but I had him always in my eye. He was Logan Pearsall Smith, whom I knew very well during the war, and who revived in me the desire (almost extinguished in my philistine years) to write elegant prose. He died in March 1946, just as I was beginning to write the book; but his spirit guided my pen.

You see what an exhibition of vanity your much valued compliments have provoked!

yours ever

Hugh

PS. 31 Dec. I see in today's paper that Geoffrey Barraclough has died, whom, by a bold *coup*, I once made Chichele Professor: not an ideal election, as it turned out, but at least he was a more colourful professor (and a more stimulating historian) than his predecessors and successors. Will there be a memorial service for him in All Souls? I suspect that there will not. Nor in St John's college Cambridge neither.[2] Perhaps an austere,

---

[1]   The article appeared in *The Spectator* a week after Chamberlain's return from Munich. Sir Robert Ensor (1877–1958) had been a journalist before becoming Senior Research Fellow at Corpus Christi College, Oxford.

[2]   Barraclough had been a Fellow of St John's 1936–45.

secular function in Brandeis. I see him as one of the migratory, truculent humanist scholars of the 16th century, fleeing from university to university, leaving a bad name everywhere, but better than all his more sedentary critics. I hope that someone will strike a blow for him in Oxford: perhaps his old schoolfellow and fellow collegian at Oriel, Alan Taylor.[1]

---

*On 29 January 1985 the dons of Oxford University decided by a majority of more than two to one not to award an honorary degree to the Prime Minister, Margaret Thatcher, who had read chemistry at Somerville. It was an unprecedented slight to withhold an honorary degree from an Oxford graduate who had become Prime Minister. Some hailed the university for displaying its independence of power politics, or its resentment of government policies towards academia. Others condemned the vote as uncivil and imprudent. The controversy resembled that ten years earlier surrounding the proposed honorary degree for Zulfikar Ali Bhutto. Both cases exposed the difficulty of awarding honorary degrees to politicians.*

## To Hugh Lloyd-Jones, 2 March 1985

The Master's Lodge, Peterhouse

My dear Hugh,

I think I owe you two letters. I must apologise for my silence. My term has been somewhat disordered. I was not well during that frightful cold period, and when I at last recovered, we went off to America, where I had committed myself to give three lectures in New York and two in Chicago, and also to speak at a colloquy organised by Ed Rozek in Colorado Springs; all of which was exacting, but it was a relief to escape from this introverted village.

At Chicago we had a very grim lunch with members of the History Faculty. There was McNeill, who is more sedate and humourless than ever

---

[1]  Both Barraclough and Taylor had been schoolboys at Bootham in York and Oriel undergraduates; Taylor was two years Barraclough's senior.

and gave us a series of lectures on Ceylon, Troy, China, etc;[1] and there was a dreadful man who never uttered a word but merely yawned grossly throughout the meal. We did not enjoy the experience; but the Committee of Social Thought (which had invited me) is much better: we liked Saul Bellow and his Rumanian wife,[2] and Shils[3] and Momigliano[4] are both members of it.

Syme's meanness is squalid, and painful to witness in so distinguished a man. I have heard some dreadful instances of it. He stayed with us when he received an honorary degree at Cambridge last summer. He wanted us to drive him to the station, which we couldn't do, as the car was being repaired: it was fascinating, but pitiful, to watch him avoiding the question of taking a taxi, at the cost of £1.25. (He asked me if I could not scrounge a lift for him from the Lord Chief Justice[5] who was staying at Trinity).

The affair of the PM's degree is scandalous and was, in my opinion, also very badly managed by Council. As soon as I saw the flysheets, I asked the Vice-chancellor[6] who had written the Council fly-sheet, which I thought feeble, illiterate and unreadable: it read like the small print on the back of an insurance policy. To my astonishment, he said that he didn't know: it was 'someone in the office.' In such a matter Council's view should have been put tersely and forcibly by the V-c himself. I then urged Robert[7] to

[1]   William H. McNeill (b. 1917), who held a history chair at Chicago, was author of such Toynbee-esque volumes as *The Rise of the West: A History of the Human Community* (1963) and *The Human Condition: An Ecological and Historical View* (1980).

[2]   The novelist Saul Bellow (1915–2005) was married (1974–85) to the mathematician Alexandra Ionescu Tulcea (b. 1935).

[3]   Edward Shils (1910–95), sociologist, was a specialist in the works of Max Weber, on whom T-R had contemplated writing in the 1950s. Shils held joint appointments at Chicago and other universities, was a Fellow of Peterhouse 1970–8 and an Honorary Fellow of the college from 1979. At Chicago, he attracted leading European scholars to teach at the university, including Arnaldo Momigliano and Raymond Aron.

[4]   Arnaldo Momigliano (1908–87), historian specializing in historiography, had been dismissed on racial grounds (he was Jewish) in 1938 from his post as Professor of Roman History in the University of Turin, though he was reinstated as a supernumerary professor in 1945. Momigliano moved to England, and became a professor at University College London 1951–75. T-R arranged his election as a Visiting Fellow of Peterhouse.

[5]   Geoffrey Lane (1918–2005), Lord Lane, Lord Chief Justice 1980–92.

[6]   Sir Geoffrey Warnock (1923–2005), philosopher, Principal of Hertford College 1971–88; Vice-chancellor 1981–5.

[7]   Blake.

use the constitutional device whereby two members of Congregation, by standing up and objecting, can postpone the whole affair (as was done in the Bhutto business). Time could thus have been gained during which the opposition could have been divided and had second thoughts—as many of them must be having now, if they think of the consequences to the university. But Robert said no, it was better to go through with the vote as scheduled. I thought, and still think, that he was wrong.

What is so mortifying is the sheer bad manners of it, as if the government, in seeking to close uneconomic academic pits[1] (snake-pits too) was actuated not by a view—whether right or wrong—of necessity but by malevolence, to be opposed by counter-malevolence. But dons, in general, I fear *are* boors. I had thought that this was true only of Cambridge dons; but alas, it is general.

Not only boors but also so silly, and so self-important: they believe that they are an intellectual *élite* whereas in fact they are, for the most part, an insulated and protected species of lemming. Most of the names on the flysheet, as far as they meant anything to me (who, for instance, are Cronk of Pembroke coll. and Dronk of Linacre?[2]), were predictable; but I was distressed to see that of Peter Oppenheimer[3] on it: I had thought better of him.

I think nothing of Foucault,[4] and even less of Daniel Bell.[5] The former seems to me a typical 20th century French *guru* (like Sartre and Levi-Strauss). Why is it that the French, who used to be so rational and clear, have become so frothy and opaque? When did it all begin? 1870, I suppose, with the German conquest; and then Bergson.[6] As for Bell, whose real name is, I think, much longer, I made up my mind about him at a

---

[1]   In March 1984 the National Union of Mineworkers had called a strike to resist the closure of 20 'uneconomic' pits.

[2]   Nicholas Cronk (b. 1954) is Director of the Voltaire Foundation in Oxford, Professor of French Literature, and Lecturer in the History of the Book; Ursula Dronke (1920–2012) was Vigfússon Reader in Old Norse at the University of Oxford 1976–88.

[3]   Peter Oppenheimer (b. 1938), economist, Student of Christ Church 1967–2008.

[4]   Michel Foucault (1926–84), Professor of the History of Systems of Thought at the Collège de France since 1970.

[5]   Daniel Bell, né Bolotsky (1919–2011), a Harvard sociologist who raised a stir with *The End of Ideology* (1960), *The Coming of Post-Industrial Society* (1973), etc.

[6]   Henri Bergson (1859–1941), Professor of Philosophy at the Collège de France from 1900, Nobel laureate for literature 1927.

conference in Venice a few years ago.[1] He pomped away on 'futurology' and gave himself great airs. Because of his intellectual grandeur, he insisted on travelling first-class in the aeroplane from Venice to Milan, and sat there alone while all the rest of us had a gay party in the tourist part of the machine. I have a full (illustrated) private record of that conference: most of the illustrations are of D. Bell, in various animal forms.

About Lord Stockton, reluctantly I agree with you: σκοπέειν δὲ χρὴ παντὸς τὴν τελεύτην, κῆ ἀποβήσεται.[2] I recall the judgment of an Anglican divine of the 1670s, who looked back at the pre-Revolutionary period: 'Archbishop Abbot's *Yield, and they will be satisfied at last* was a great miscarriage; Archbishop Laud's *Resolve, for there is no end of yielding* was great policy.'[3] But Laud's great policy led to revolution. Perhaps it need not have done, had things been managed better. I see Mrs T. as Laud.

All this is very topical to me as I lectured on the subject—the 17th century part of it—in Chicago. I expanded into two lectures the single lecture on 'The New Right in the English Universities 1660–1646' which I gave (rather maliciously, I must admit) in the new theatre of Peterhouse in our seventh centenary year.

---

[1]   T-R had described Bell at the Venice conference in a letter to his stepson (4 April 1971): 'Futurology, I now see, consists of making random guesses about the future and calling them scientific in order to draw large funds from gullible Foundations. In order to call them scientific, it is necessary to dress them up in pompous, polysyllabic jargon and utter them in oracular, dogmatic style. The futurologist himself is like the *New Yorker*'s caricature of an administration egg-head. His head is really like an egg, only inverted, with the small end at the top. A thin circle of black hair conveniently marks the place at which you strike with the egg-spoon. He has a black toothbrush moustache and large, heavy, black-rimmed spectacles. He never stops to think, or inhale, before speaking, having an instant supply of pompous jargon to turn on in response to any question or criticism.'

[2]   'One must look to every matter's end, how it will turn out.' Herodotus 1.32. In a letter of 24 February 1985, to which this was a reply, Lloyd-Jones had commented on Harold Macmillan, Oxford University's Chancellor, who had been created Earl of Stockton a year earlier: 'Every time Lord Stockton speaks, he confirms my opinion about him. When he let the finance ministers go in 1958, he began what Wilson, Heath and Callaghan carried on. He is a charming and cultivated man, but he lives in the world of the thirties and has no real courage, at least not for dealing with what happens now.'

[3]   From *State Worthies, or The Statesmen and Favourites of England since the Reformation* (1670) by the royalist clergyman David Lloyd (1635–92). T-R explored this theme in his essay 'Laudianism and Political Power', published in *Catholics, Anglicans and Puritans*.

But perhaps it is Wilson and Callaghan rather than Stockton who are the parallel to Abbot.

Thank you for sending me that article on Braudel.[1] I have to admit that I can't *entirely* disagree. I think *La Méditerranée* a great book, although there are large areas of it that don't bear rigorous examination. It is full of ideas, has a majestic sweep, and much of it is well documented. It is also well written. But since then Braudel seems to me to have gone off disastrously: airy-fairy generalisations decorated, but not necessarily supported, by a parade of somewhat arbitrary statistics, and the whole covered over with a film of rhetoric. The *Annales*, which he took over from Lucien Fèbvre,[2] have gone sadly downhill, and his disciples, who edit it, are miserable termites (There is a very funny description of them in a review by Richard Cobb of a book by Furet, who is one of them, and another, in *TLS*, reprinted in one of his volumes: I think, *Tour de France*[3]). I gave up taking the *Annales* about ten years ago. I must admit that Braudel himself told me that he too now found them unreadable.

One great fault of Braudel and his disciples is their total ignorance of the Anglo-Saxon and German worlds. Whenever Braudel generalises about England, he shows himself an out-dated ignorant dilettante: about as sophisticated as Arthur Bryant, but less well read.[4] The contrast between his real historical knowledge, both literary and archival, of Spain, France, Italy, Belgium, and his abysmal ignorance of England, Scandinavia, Holland, Germany, is astonishing; but it is common to many French historians: I suppose the religious division is impassable—although

---

[1]  Lloyd-Jones had sent T-R, with a letter of 24 February 1985, an article by David Gess, 'The Pride and Prejudice of Fernand Braudel', *New Criterion*, April 1983. Gess argued that Braudel should have learned to think and write as T-R did in his 'famous' essay 'Religion, the Reformation and Social Change'.

[2]  Lucien Fèbvre (1878–1956) and Marc Bloch (1886–1944) had in 1929 founded the influential journal *Annales d'histoire économique et sociale*.

[3]  François Furet (1927–97), anti-Marxist historian of French revolution and president of École des Hautes Etudes en Sciences Sociales 1977–85. In the *Times Literary Supplement* of 8 September 1966 Cobb had reviewed Francois Furet and Denis Richet, 'La Révolution française'. He described them as possessing 'the faculty to restate obscurely and in a French almost Sartrean in its muddiness, what previous...historians have stated clearly'.

[4]  Sir Arthur Bryant (1899–1985), prolific High Tory author of patriotic histories.

Lucien Fèbvre himself was a Germanist and wrote a book on Luther (but knew nothing of England). On the whole, I think that English historians understand France better than French historians understand post-Reformation England. The exception is Élie Halévy; but he, of course, was a Jew.[1]

I am not quite sure in what sense I am 'diametrically opposed' to Braudel!

> yours ever
> Hugh

---

*In March 1985 Trevor-Roper attended a dinner party at 10 Downing Street, organized by the historian Hugh Thomas[2] and his wife Vanessa, for the Prime Minister to meet writers and scholars. Afterwards Trevor-Roper wrote to tell Blake that he had been 'shaken' by some of the things Mrs Thatcher had said. 'She has no friends, listens to no-one, and never relaxes.' The following letter was written afterwards to another of the guests, Noël Annan.*

## To Noël Annan, 10 April 1985

The Master's Lodge, Peterhouse

My dear Noël,

How delightful to wake up every morning and feel glad to be alive! And to regard your period as head of a Cambridge college as the happiest time of your life! How I envy you your happy temperament! I suppose it comes from being a man of the *Left*: a dangerous Marxist radical in the eyes of our colleague Lord Beloff; at least heir to the Enlightenment, optimist,

---

[1]  Halévy emphasized the moral and social effects of evangelical religion in his *Histoire du peuple anglais au XIXe siècle*.

[2]  Hugh Thomas (b. 1931), Baron Thomas of Swynnerton, historian and chairman of the Centre for Policy Studies, 1979–91, which aided Margaret Thatcher. His wife, Vanessa (née Jebb; b. 1931), was a graduate of St Hugh's College, Oxford, who in 1956 had replaced Antonia Pakenham in George Weidenfeld's office, where she remained until 1960.

forward-looking, a believer in the doctrine of Progress and the National Goodness and Perfectibility of Man, attainable by Nationalisation, Trades Union power, and abolition of the House of Lords. Perhaps I should change my party and come and sit on your Benches, if not for the greater good of the country, at least for my own mental comfort. As your fellow-radical Stuart Hampshire once said, 'to be a socialist is a small price to pay for a good conscience'.

But seriously, do you think that our dear P.M. has gone bananas? I was rather shaken by some of the things she said at that curious dinner-party—her impatience of obstruction by the organs of society: committees of enquiry, parliamentary procedure, courts of law, and, no doubt now, the House of Lords. Her toryism seems to be rather that of Charles I than of Edmund Burke. And I was horrified to hear and see her on television, telling her hosts in Malaysia that she had 'seen off' the miners, and that Trades Unions were children which needed to be spanked by Nanny for their own good. I should have thought that the nursery-governess image was one which she ought particularly to avoid! But I suppose it comes naturally, irresistibly, to her.

What do you think lay behind that party? Did someone say, we must improve your public image, especially in universities and places where they brain-wash the young! Get some *dons* and *writers* to dinner? But what an odd collection! Who, for instance, can have recommended Theodore Zeldin?[1] And the idea that Tony Powell and V. S. Naipaul and Iris Murdoch would be her literary paladins is very comic. As for the Lord Quinton, *no* one could have done more harm to her cause than he did by his ridiculous flippant speech in Congregation at Oxford on the day of the vote...[2]

My dear Noel, you Stoics[3] (I am sure) hang together. Could you not persuade that noble lord to go into a retreat in Buckinghamshire for a time: to hide his light (and his voice, and his face) under a bushel (whatever that

---

[1] Theodore Zeldin (b. 1933), historian of modern France, read history at Christ Church, where he was taught by T-R.

[2] Anthony Quinton, Baron Quinton (1925–2010), philosopher, Fellow of New College, Oxford, 1955–78, and President of Trinity College, Oxford, 1978–87.

[3] Old boys of Stowe School.

is in this context)? No doubt it is a very comforting thing to be a peer and a head of a house, etc., but I confess that, when I look at Mrs T's other academic peers (Quinton, Beloff and now the Lord Butterworth),[1] I do not feel the same complacency.

I hope you are enjoying the knockabout turn of the Right Reverend Prelates on the matter of the Resurrection.[2] Why can't they behave like the sensible 18th century bishops 'whose sound understanding', as Gibbon wrote, 'is perhaps seldom engaged with that abstruse mystery'?

On which orthodox note I end and sign myself,

yours ever

Hugh

⸺◦◦◦⸺

*On an early evening train from London to Cambridge, Trevor-Roper began talking to a young man whom he saw reading a work of philosophy. This was Alasdair Palmer (b. 1959), a Cambridge graduate student working on a philosophy Ph.D. under the supervision of Bernard Williams, Provost of King's. Palmer had gained a first in history at Corpus Christi College, Cambridge, before switching to philosophy. Finding that Palmer was free that evening, Trevor-Roper invited him for a simple supper at the Master's Lodge; and it was only then, as the train approached Cambridge, that the younger man realized with whom he had been talking freely. Intrigued by his character and invitation, Palmer agreed. Trevor-Roper returned to the Lodge by taxi, while Palmer bicycled there. At the Lodge, Trevor-Roper warmly welcomed him, uncorked a bottle of delicious white wine and made a passable cheese omelette. At the end of the evening, after they had consumed a second bottle of wine, Palmer swerved home on his bicycle, feeling uplifted by the evening's conversation, in which Trevor-Roper had surpassed himself in well-turned anecdotes. Palmer's subsequent note of thanks initiated a long*

---

[1]  John Butterworth (1918–2003), Fellow and Tutor in Law at New College 1946–63, founding Vice-Chancellor of the University of Warwick 1965–85. The peerage that he received on Thatcher's recommendation was his reward for having withstood attacks on him by E. P. Thompson and student radicals when he raised donations for a business school in the early 1970s, and for inviting Thatcher to open the university's privately funded Science Park in 1984 (which provoked further disturbances).

[2]  On 7 April David Jenkins, Bishop of Durham, in his first episcopal Easter Day sermon, cast doubt on the reality of the resurrection, which, he said, is 'neither to be pinned down, nor wholly proved. It is to be lived by faith in the God who raised Jesus from the dead.' Sermons by other bishops dissented from him.

*correspondence. This young man's enthusiasm and energy inspired Trevor-Roper to write some of his most enjoyable letters.*

## To Alasdair Palmer, 15 July 1986

The Master's Lodge, Peterhouse

Dear Alasdair

Thank you for putting me right about the reason why Keynes, Russell & co. fell for the ideas of Moore.[1] How remiss of me not to have thought of this obvious explanation! It may not apply to Russell, but I see that it is a reason which clearly operated in some directions (and co-operated in others), and I ought not to have excluded it from my calculations. Sheer carelessness by me.

In about 1950, when I was a Student (*anglicè*[2] a Fellow) of Christ Church, there was a disreputable old don called Dundas who had been at Eton, in the same election as Keynes, who no doubt taught him a trick or two in the boskage. One day he announced portentously that he was having an important guest to stay, one Swithinbank, 'a friend of Keynes'.[3] When Swithinbank came—the first of several visits—we junior Students were surprised

---

[1]  George Edward [G. E.] Moore (1873–1958), Professor of Mental Philosophy and Logic at Cambridge and Fellow of Trinity 1925–39, and a founder of the analytic tradition in philosophy; author of *Principia Ethica* (1903), which had a powerful impact on Keynes and his fellow Apostles. In the letter to which this was a reply, Palmer had written: 'Moore's extraordinary impact must have had something to do with the fact that half his followers were in love with him; but it was also that he seemed to give a rational ground for everything that Bloomsbury desperately wanted to believe.' Moore's *Principia Ethica*, added Palmer, 'was experienced as so liberating by Keynes, Russell and others because it enabled them to disguise their own preferences as the dignified and elevated results of insight into the objective realm of…truth. They wanted their rejection of the previous generation's values—the stern Victorian emphasis on public service and political activity—to have a suitably intellectual wrapping. Moore gave it to them, and enabled them to turn away from the boring and impersonal tasks of imperial administration for which they had been raised, and instead to concentrate on those two most un-Victorian values, intimate friendship and purely aesthetic experience. No wonder they worshipped him!'

[2]  'In English terms'.

[3]  Bernard Swithinbank (1884–1968), Eton and Balliol, had been a male beauty before joining the Burmese civil service in 1909.

and disappointed: we found him a dry stick of morose manners and no conversation at all. At that time, of course, we derived our view of Keynes from our colleague Roy Harrod, his disciple and biographer. Later, when Holroyd's Life of Lytton Strachey let the cat out of the bag,[1] we realised that we had been looking for the wrong qualities in 'a friend of Keynes'.

You make another point, which I expected you to make and should perhaps have forestalled; but I was afraid of being too prolix—viz: that Wittgenstein's disciples were at Oxford. My answer to this (though of course, in offering sociological models, one must never be too dogmatic or absolute in their illustration) is that Freddie Ayer,[2] who brought the doctrine to Oxford (Gilbert Ryle,[3] who was his tutor, was, in this respect, his pupil), gave it a very different, Oxonian look. Language, Truth and Logic, which is now celebrating its 50th anniversary, has a light-hearted touch which distinguishes it from Cantabrigian earnestness. Freddie himself regards it with indulgence, as a juvenile jeu d'esprit. Miss Anscombe,[4] who took those austere doctrines seriously, gathered her hair-skirt around her and migrated to sit (upside-down no doubt) on a smaller pillar in the mini-Nitria[5] of Cambridge.

You remark, truly enough, that Leavis was not universally accepted in Cambridge.[6] My picture of Cambridge as a guru-oriented society does

---

[1]   The two volumes of Lytton Strachey by (Sir) Michael Holroyd (b. 1935) were published in 1967–8.

[2]   (Sir) A. J. ('Freddie') Ayer (1910–89) was a Philosophy Lecturer at Christ Church until 1939. T-R saw him regularly in the late 1930s, and read with excitement Language, Truth and Logic on its publication in 1936. Ayer was Wykeham Professor of Logic and Fellow of New College, 1959–78.

[3]   Gilbert Ryle (1900–76), Student and Tutor in Philosophy at Christ Church 1925–45 and Waynflete Professor of Metaphysical Philosophy at Oxford 1945–68, served under T-R in the Radio Analysis Bureau, together with Charles Stuart and the philosopher Stuart Hampshire. Ryle was an inspiring influence on the young T-R, and his boon companion, as described in Wartime Journals.

[4]   Elizabeth Anscombe (1919–2001) was Fellow of Somerville College, Oxford, 1946–70, and thereafter Professor of Philosophy and Fellow of New Hall, Cambridge, 1970–86. She spent eight years studying with Wittgenstein, who became her tenant and named her as his executor. During her first undergraduate year she had converted to Roman Catholicism, and for the remainder of her life engaged in causes inspired by her passionately held religious belief.

[5]   An abandoned site of early monastic activity.

[6]   Frank Raymond [F. R.] Leavis (1895–1978), Director of Studies in English at Downing College, Cambridge, from 1932, was not asked to join the English Faculty Board until 1954 and was not awarded even a readership until the age of 64.

not entail a monarchy of one guru universally accepted, or even an oli-garchy similarly accepted. What I see is a plurality, as in the original desert, of several pillars, some high, some low, with groups of varying size around their base. Newton's pillar was very high; but even he did not command universal loyalty, and if his views on the Trinity had got out, there would no doubt have been a schism among the faithful and, per-haps, a secession to the pillar of Dr Waterland or some other more orthodox prophet.[1] My point is that—at least in my time—there were *no* gurus in Oxford: the whole social structure seemed to me more open. Some persons were perhaps more respected, and listened to, than others, but if there was such respect there was also a certain amount of ridicule, of which I did not find much in Cambridge.

So far, I flatter myself, I have repelled, or at least evaded, your replies. But now you produce that formidable gladiator William of Ockham, a pedantic glint in his eye, drawn razor in hand. At this point I take cover until I have thought out an answer. On the face of it, I allow that you have a point; but I am inclined to think that Ockham was too long ago to count: that the peculiar character of the two institutions had not yet, in his time, become established. It was the Reformation (I say desperately) that established it.

'The two great national seats of learning', says Macaulay, 'had even then [i.e. in the reign of Queen Elizabeth] acquired the characters which they still retain.'[2] So far, so good, and the implication is that it was then that they acquired these characters. Of course my submission to the judgment of Macaulay doesn't go on to the next sentence: 'In intellectual activity, and in readiness to admit improvements, the superiority was then, as it has ever since been, on the side of Cambridge.' That seems to me going a little too far.

The ups and downs of institutions fascinate me. In Oxford, in 1600, Christ Church and St John's were the only centres of anti-puritanism in a

---

[1]  Daniel Waterland (1683–1740) was, as Master of Magdalene College, the leading moderate Whig in early Hanoverian Cambridge, and a defender of Anglican theological orthodoxy.

[2]  From Macaulay's essay on Francis Bacon, first published in the *Edinburgh Review* in 1837.

puritan university. Laud converted the university to high Anglicanism in seven years, and it retained that character for centuries. But within the university the character of particular colleges remained remarkably stable: in the 19<sup>th</sup> century Mark Pattison wrote that Christ Church and St John's were the two colleges 'most corroded with the canker of ecclesiasticism'.

In Cambridge the character of Peterhouse—the only college I know— seems always to have been total reaction. In the 1630s it was more Laudian than Laud. By the 1930s it seems to have been Methodist— Butterfield (a *guru* of cloudy reaction) preached from tubs all over the Fens; but Methodism was by then a form of abject reaction. Whether de-votion to a guru, and the corresponding inverse relationship, is 'a feature of some character types' rather than socially conditioned by (say) col-leges in the Fens is a debatable question and depends, I suppose, on the answer to the precedent question, whether character-types themselves are socially conditioned. I believe that they often are; but I am prepared to leave so difficult (if not insoluble) a question in suspense. Meanwhile, I am glad that you have changed the title of your thesis to something that I can understand. The previous title makes me wonder who your first supervisor can have been!

yours ever

Hugh

⎯⎯∽∾∽⎯⎯

*Another of Trevor-Roper's younger friends was Edward Chaney (b. 1951), who lived in Flor-ence from 1978 until 1985 and had a doctorate from the Warburg Institute in London. He was the Shuffrey Research Fellow in Architectural History at Lincoln College, Oxford, 1985–90, and later historian to the London region of English Heritage and Professor of Fine and Decorative Arts, and Chair of the History of Collecting Research Centre, at Southampton Solent University. Just as Trevor-Roper was supplanted at a late stage as Pearsall Smith's testamentary heir, so Chaney was Harold Acton's literary executor until Acton made late changes in his will. At the suggestion of the publisher and naval historian Richard Ollard, Chaney sent a copy of his first book* The Grand Tour and the Great Rebellion (1985) *to*

*Trevor-Roper, whose biography of Laud he had used. In the covering letter he declared that Trevor-Roper was one of the book's ideal readers. Trevor-Roper invited Chaney to meet him at Peterhouse. After Trevor-Roper's return to Oxfordshire, the two men often went walking together.*

## To Edward Chaney, 6 August 1986

Chiefswood, Melrose

Dear Mr Chaney

I was delighted by your letter: delighted, charmed, flattered (perhaps all these represent the same response), but also touched. Especially since I suspect there is a little intellectual gulf between us. I do not put myself into any category, but I see myself periodically described (among other less flattering adjectives) as a *whig*; and I suppose that may be as accurate as any such labels are. You, I deduce, with the same general reservation, are a *papist*:[1] so that in the 17th century, at least, and indeed at any time up to that of Lord Acton,[2] we would be irreconcilable—although now, perhaps, drawn closer together by the emergence of more radical believers such as Christopher Hill. In any case, I am delighted to find myself on the same side as the writer of so learned and fascinating a book and such a charming letter.

I write now from my home in Scotland. Always when I come here— the journey a recurrent trauma—I leave something important behind. This time we had to turn back from Peterborough because we suddenly realised that we had left all the silver on the dining-room table. Only on unpacking here did I discover that I had left some vital papers behind, which include your letter (though not, happily, your book); so I write

[1]  Chaney describes himself as 'a Catholic-supporting atheist'.

[2]  John Dalberg-Acton, 1st Baron Acton (1834–1902), historian and moralist, was a leader of the liberal Catholics from the 1860s, and conspicuous for his European rather than insular outlook. In 1869 he and Lord Edward Howard were the first Catholics to be promoted to the peerage since the 1680s. As a historian he had the fatal inhibition that he would not begin to write until he had read all the sources.

without having it in front of me and may not take up all the points you raised. However, I remember some of them.

First, Ussher.[1] I would still (unless corrected) describe him as of a Protestant family. I think I am right in saying that his uncle Richard Stanyhurst[2] was originally a Protestant, but converted to Catholicism by Edmund Campion. Ussher's mother followed later; but I *think* the whole family started as Protestants. There was not much love lost between Ussher and Uncle Richard, at least after Ussher published his book *de Christianarum Ecclesiarum…perpetua successione*.[3] Ussher had civil relations with Catholic scholars, but he was, I think, pretty paranoid about popery. You mention someone—was it Richelieu?—expressing interest in Ussher's works. I am interested in that. May I ask for a repeat?

You asked me about Berenson. I knew him very well and used to stay regularly at I Tatti. It was a wonderful house to stay in: a marvellous library, interesting company and good conversation. He had a house in Vallombrosa, to which he went in the summer when his servants went on holiday, and I used to go there too. I look back with the greatest pleasure to my time at I Tatti—with such pleasure that I am reluctant to visit the place now (although I did stay there once after his death, with Myron Gilmore, who, as Director, preserved some of the *douceur de vivre* of the house).[4]

Thank you for the information about the correspondence of Cassiano dal Pozzo.[5] I will pursue that. I do not believe that Mayerne ever went to Italy, after his return from the Grand Tour with the Duc de Rohan in

[1]    James Ussher (1581–1656), Archbishop of Armagh and Primate of All Ireland from 1625. He is the subject of an essay by T-R in *Catholics, Anglicans and Puritans*, in which T-R acknowledges that 'the family's Protestantism was not very firm and there had been relapses'.

[2]    Richard Stanyhurst (1547–1618), Irish alchemist, historian, poet, and chaplain to Archduke Albert of Austria. Chaney had pointed out that he became a priest and that two of his sons became Jesuits.

[3]    Ussher's staunchly Protestant *Gravissimae quaestionis, de Christianarum Ecclesiarum…continua successione & statu* appeared in 1613.

[4]    Myron Gilmore (1910–78), sometime Gurney Professor of History and Political Science at Harvard, was Director of Harvard's Center for Renaissance Studies at Villa I Tatti 1964–73. Chaney had been a Fellow at the Center 1984–5.

[5]    Cassiano dal Pozzo (1588–1657), connoisseur, antiquarian, patron of Poussin, and an alchemist.

1600,[1] or had any Italian friends; so Petersson's[2] remark surprised me. I suspect that you are right and that he is merely mentioned in the correspondence of others.

I spoke to Noel Malcolm.[3] He said that he had not received a copy of your book, but that he would try to get a review copy. I hope he will review it. I hope that I will too; but I am frightened of promising more than I can do at present.

Poor old Christopher Hill—I understand that, after a lifetime of trying to keep ahead of the latest radical undergraduate fashion, he has now sunk exhausted by the wayside and is regarded by undergraduate historians as *vieux jeu*. In the 1930s he was (in a discreet, semi-sophisticated way) a Stalinist—not all that discreet and only very superficially sophisticated: he published a book, *Lenin and the Russian Revolution*, in which Trotsky is not mentioned.[4] In about 1951–2 I remember the visit to Oxford of Academician E. A. Kosminsky, who, by a scholarly dissection of the Pipe Roll of 1292 (I think) established the entire class structure of medieval England as a Marxist paradigm.[5] When there was a reception for the History Faculty to meet the great man (at Balliol of course), he was flanked by Christopher and Max Rothmann (do I recall the name aright?[6] A bone-headed Stalinist bigot) to protect him from any profane contacts. In 1956, in the Khrushchev era, Christopher moved to keep up with the anti-Stalinist young and

[1]  Henri (1579–1638), Duc de Rohan, soldier, Huguenot leader and writer, was the friend, patient, and patron of Mayerne.

[2]  Robert Torsten Petersson (1918–2011), whose books included *Sir Kenelm Digby* (1956).

[3]  Noel Malcolm (b. 1956), Fellow of Gonville & Caius College, Cambridge, 1981–8 and of All Souls since 2002; Hobbes scholar, political columnist, historian, and campaigner for justice in Bosnia. He gave Chaney's later book *The Evolution of the Grand Tour* (1998) a favourable review in the *Sunday Telegraph*.

[4]  In fact the book mentions him a number of times, albeit in a hostile spirit.

[5]  Evgeniĭ Alekseevich Kosminsky (1886–1959) studied the Hundred Rolls of 1279–80 and was co-author of *Studies in the Agrarian History of England in the Thirteenth Century* (1955).

[6]  As T-R explained in a later letter, he meant Andrew Rothstein (1898–1994), a Balliol graduate, who had been a founder member of the Communist Party of Great Britain in 1920 and remained a party member until his death. He was press officer to the Soviet mission in Britain 1920–45, and Lecturer at the School of Slavonic and East European Studies 1946–50 (when, as he claimed, he was 'purged'); author of numerous propagandist works, including studies of Soviet foreign policy; critic of Communist revisionism in the 1980s.

quarrelled with Rothmann, who denounced him as a *wankender Intelle-ktueller*[1] (I only saw the record of the C.P. meeting in German). Then, in 1962, he jumped on the sociology bandwagon (see *Intellectual Origins of the Puritan Revolution* 175–6). In 1968, when Marcuse overtook Marx, he made a further great leap forward: he dyed his hair black, advertised that he was still young by feats of physical agility, and found historical progress the property no longer of austere, disciplined puritans but of antinomian Ranters. The climax of this phase seems to me to be his *Milton*: a monument of perverse industry, in which the Muggletonian Milton (like a radical Balliol undergraduate in the King's Arms) haunts taverns, swapping radical thoughts with plebeian revolutionaries who take tobacco 'as a means of heightening consciousness, akin to drug-taking in our own society'.

Beyond this point it is difficult to see where one can go, and the poor old thing now seems to have given up. I met him a few weeks ago at a posh luncheon at the Dorchester to celebrate the 75th birthday of Veronica Wedgwood (whom he had tried to blackball for the British Academy; but this *inter nos*, as Aubrey would say). He has ceased to dye his hair. No doubt he lives very comfortably on the royalties of his Marxist books, still required reading in the Open University.

However, I have always found him very genial, and he has a sense of humour, and I can't help liking the old wretch. Recently we found ourselves in unexpected alliance across a wider gulf than separates you from me: against the Cambridge neo-tories. So you can see how useful a central whig position can be! Not that I am entirely against the new toryism. My whiggism is very relative. I regard crude whiggism as being the logical forerunner of crude Marxism: the idea that 'progress' is the possession of a particular political party.

I hope you will call on me if you come to Cambridge. I shall return there at the beginning of next term, 5th October—perhaps before.

yours sincerely

Hugh Dacre

---

[1] 'Wobbly intellectual'.

PS. (*sotto voce*) May I, very tentatively, as the self-constituted guardian of the purity of our language, *beg* you not to use that dreadful word (if it can qualify as such) 'tutee' (pp. 133, 420, &—I fear—elsewhere).

---

*In a letter of 15 August 1986, Palmer commented on a passage in Trevor-Roper's valedictory lecture as Regius Professor, 'History and Imagination', delivered in May 1980. Trevor-Roper had asserted the importance of individuals in history, and had dwelt on the significance of Franco's refusal to allow Hitler to attack Gibraltar, which he saw as crucial to the outcome of the war. 'If General Franco, at Hendaye on 23 October 1940, had effectively substituted one syllable for another—if instead of No he had said Yes—our world would have been quite different: the present, the future, and the past would all have been changed. But once they had been changed, no one would have dwelt on that little episode. The German victory would then have been ascribed not to such trivial causes but to historical necessity.'*

*'Decisions made by individuals are the stuff of history,' Palmer wrote, 'and if they had been made differently, history would be different, as you stress. But I agree with Marx at least when he said that "men make their own history, but they do not make it in their own heads"... No individual is an "unmoved mover": not even Franco when he said "No" instead of "Si" was that. And though we do not know, and perhaps could not know, what the causes of the decision in that particular case were, we do know that it is not going to be totally mysterious that he chose to say one thing rather than the other. There were causes—his character, his upbringing, his psychology, his history, his society—perhaps even his neurophysiology—and they together determined what he did. The arbitrary and the accidental do indeed play a vital role in history, but something is arbitrary only in relation to some principle or law.'*

## To Alasdair Palmer, 29 August 1986

Chiefswood, Melrose

Dear Alasdair,

What, you ask, do I think of the great problem of Free Will and Necessity? What a large question! The philosophical angels in *Paradise Lost*, you will recall, debated these questions.[1]

> And found no end, in wandering mazes lost.

If they could not answer, how can I? And yet I am so flattered by your question (perhaps it was merely a rhetorical question—but I brush aside that probability), that I shall try to answer it.

I do not think that we disagree. Of course there is no absolute freedom of choice. Society is glutinous and so is philosophy—mental patterns outside of which we theoretically can but in practice, at a given time, cannot think. And yet there are occasions when the mental habit is broken, the social restraints do not operate or are overcome, and choice, freely made, transforms (ultimately, when a generation is worn out) both society and thought.

I can think of many moments in history when such decisions, freely made, have effected great changes which otherwise would not have occurred; and not only decisions but accidents, which need not have happened. Let me offer a few examples.

Think of the vast consequences of the Hellenisation of the East. But was it bound to happen? If Alexander had not existed, can we say that that extraordinary history would have occurred?

Or of the christianisation of the Roman Empire. Let us allow that *one* of the new oriental religions—of Isis or of Mithras or of Christ—would have been adopted, but which one? Diocletian would have chosen one; Constantine chose another. No doubt whichever was chosen would have

---

[1]   Milton, *Paradise Lost* II.557–61: 'Others apart sat on a hill retir'd, | In thoughts more elevate, and reason'd high, | Of providence, foreknowledge, will and fate, | fixt fate, free will, foreknowledge absolute, | And found no end, in wandring mazes lost.'

absorbed many of the same elements; but there would still have been a great difference.

If Hitler had won the war of 1939, no one can deny that Europe, and the world, would look very different today. And (as I said in my lecture) there were many occasions when he might have done so. If Churchill had been killed by the taxi which knocked him down in New York a few years earlier, would there have been the leadership necessary to avoid rational surrender in Britain in 1940? If the Germans had forestalled us with the Atom-bomb? If we had not had *Ultra*? My remark about Franco was (predictably) challenged, when I made it, by Mr Southworth: an elderly Marxist who lives in bourgeois comfort in a castle in France and allows no one to differ from him on the subject of the Spanish Civil War.[1] But I stand by it. There were of course pressures on Franco which inclined him to say No; but there were also pressures which inclined him to say Yes. In particular, there was the power of the Germans, already at the frontier, and the prospect of sharing the spoils. Serrano Súñer, his Foreign Minister,[2] wished to say Yes. Hitler had his plans—'Operation Felix'—prepared. Franco *was* prepared to say yes on conditions. It was touch and go, a gamble. If Franco's personal temperament had been different—if like Hitler he had been a gambler—he might well have said, Yes; and if he had done so he would, I believe, have backed a winner as well as changed the face of the world.

When I published my lecture I got many silly letters from people saying that such and such an accident or free choice would have transformed the world thus or thus. I call them silly because they ignored the social and mental prisons in which we live. I get impatient with people who say,

---

[1]   Herbert Southworth (1908–99) was born in poverty in an Oklahoma township, and self-educated in the Carnegie public library in Abilene, Texas. He worked for the republican Spanish Information Bureau in New York in the mid-1930s, and for the US Office of Psychological Warfare in Algeria and Morocco 1943– 5; then bought US Army surplus radio equipment to found Radio Tangier, which made him a small fortune before it was nationalized in 1960. He lost money in a company that failed to popularize potato crisps in France, before settling in Château de Roche, Concrémiers, south of Tours, where he wrote pugnacious, anti-Franco works of contemporary Spanish history.

[2]   Ramón Serrano Súñer (1901–2003) was also Franco's brother-in-law.

for instance, that in 1945 we should have gone on to occupy all Germany and organise for war, if necessary, against Russia as the next enemy. Such a decision was inconceivable at the time. It took a mental revolution before we could think in such terms. I equally get impatient with people who ascribe *particular* long-term consequences to such free decisions or accidents (as Arnold Toynbee[1] ascribed the whole social history of modern Italy to the impact of Hannibal). I believe that the freedom of the will operates only within very narrow limits and can achieve particular results only for a short time (for we cannot limit the freedom of will, or the objective forces which limit or direct that freedom, of our successors); but I believe that *general* changes of potentially vast importance can sometimes—perhaps even often—be ascribed to human choice or accident.

Who are we to say that if (say) Caesar, or Richelieu, or Lenin, had not existed, some other unknown person would have fulfilled his historic function?

History is not a science (if it were, how dull it would be!), but it is limited by science: limited but not totally controlled; and the same applies to us.

*Dixi!*[2]

I am glad that your thesis is not boring you. I hesitate to advise, because I believe that everyone who writes has his own method; so I will only say that I always find new ideas coming, and old ideas being modified, as I write. I believe that there are people so well-organised that they think out everything in advance and then write it down. This is no doubt an enviable gift, but I lack it; and in fact I *enjoy* the sense of re-thinking with the pen (though it is expensive of time and ink).

I am sorry that you suffer from 'black clouds'—though of course, as you say, we all do—and glad to learn that I may do something to disperse them. I wish I could do more. I feel very much for those who, in these iron days, are under the sort of pressure that you are. But you have intellectual vitality which you must not allow to be stifled (or, if I may

---

[1]  The 12 volumes of *A Study of History* by Arnold Toynbee (1889–1975) had been ridiculed by T-R in *Encounter* in 1957.
[2]  'I have spoken'.

dare to say so, dissipated in dilettantism), and if I can help you I shall be happy to do so. Don't be too perfectionist. A thesis is not your last word, but what you can show for three years of research. Do not let yourself be oppressed by it.

And then, *you have survived Cambridge*! I respect you for that! You must have great spiritual resources to have done so, generated perhaps at Marlborough,[1] perhaps in Highgate Cemetery,[2] perhaps elsewhere: it is not for me to speculate. Man is a mystery. Psychology is not a science either—and psychoanalysis *is* an imposture.

One of the shocks which I experienced on my arrival in Cambridge was when I was approached by a colleague—a university reader—and invited to join 'the Peterhouse Book Club'. The members, as I afterwards learned (for of course I didn't join) vote to buy such and such a book, and then it is handed round from Fellow to Fellow to read—I thought of the *Graiae*, those three old women of Greek mythology who had but one eye and one tooth between them and handed it round for successive use. Last term I discovered that the latest book that they had bought for such circulation was Sarah Keays' book on the process which led to her illegitimate child.[3] Such is the intellectual life of the oldest college in Cambridge. It is like a Women's Institute at Ely.

But I see that I am losing that ἀταραξία,[4] or *sang froid anglais*, which is recommended by the Epicurean philosophers. Let me forget about Peterhouse. Let me interpose the thought of Northumberland, that delightful county. I nipped over into it yesterday, to refresh my spirits: went to the little Norman church of Old Bewick, where my parents are buried, an

---

[1]   Palmer had been at school at Marlborough College.

[2]   Palmer had been brought up in a house backing on to Highgate Cemetery. In his childhood, during which attempts were made to bomb Karl Marx's tomb there, he explored the cemetery, which was semi-derelict, overgrown, and spooky: votaries of black magic sometimes exhumed buried bodies or broke open coffins in mausoleums, so that visitors were liable to be confronted by corpses.

[3]   Sara Keays (b. 1947) published *A Question of Judgement* (1985), her memoir of her years as personal secretary and lover of the Conservative politician Cecil Parkinson. Her revelation that she was pregnant with his child forced his resignation from the Thatcher Cabinet in 1983.

[4]   'Freedom from passion; calmness'.

isolated church in a crease of the moors, surrounded by a little wood and a stream, an enchanting spot, and then over those pastoral uplands to my native village of Glanton: for I please myself with the thought that, like Antaeus,[1] I recover vigour by touching my native earth. There I received a message from the present owner of the house in which I was born, who wants to change its name to 'Dacre House'. That, I must admit, tickled my vanity enormously. Of course I said Yes!

My dear Alasdair, do not die intellectually at the age of 35! It takes a conscious effort not to do so! This, I fear, has become an obsession with me. I think of that grim Druid cirque of black-gowned creatures, silent by candle-light, while the decanter circulates, like some primitive eucharist, squeezed from acid, if not poisonous berries (but it does not poison them, they are immunised by addiction)…But of course you will not: I apologise for even suggesting the possibility.

yours ever

Hugh

---

## To Alasdair Palmer, 4 October 1986

The Master's Lodge, Peterhouse

Dear Alasdair,

Of course you are right. A scholar, even for the sake of his scholarship, as well as for that of his life, *must* have other interests. Scholarship which is confined to one rut becomes antiquarianism: it needs a context, and the possibility of comparison, and the invigorating infusion of reality, and life. But then, of course, there is the opposite danger of dilettantism, the

---

[1]  In Greek mythology, Antaeus was a giant who compelled all passing strangers to wrestle with him, and proved invincible because each time that he was thrown down in combat, he gathered new strength from touching his native earth.

occupational hazard of the journalist. I think that one needs to be a disciplined specialist in one area in order to have a corrective standard outside that area—and meanwhile to have interests outside that area in order to preserve one's balance and keep intellectually alive.

You see how I keep harping on intellectual vitality! It is the evidence of its decay around me that obsesses me and makes me such a bore on the subject.

I am indeed interested in 'the might-have-beens of history'—but very cautiously. I believe that history must be read forwards as well as backwards: one must see, or rather try to see, the actualities of any historical situation, before the options were closed by the event: otherwise one takes the reality, the life, and perhaps the lessons out of the past. But one must recognise also the limits of freedom of choice and the possibility of accident, which can interfere with the alternatives too. It is here that discipline is required—the corrective standard which I have mentioned.

I seem to be fated to take up subjects which involve me with lunatics; which has made me very cautious. Hitler, witches, the authorship of Shakespeare's plays, are all subjects which attract undisciplined minds, and having exposed myself (though tentatively) on all these subjects, and thereby drawn upon myself much unwelcome, not to say lunatic correspondence, I am very conscious of the dangers. The might-have-beens of history are another such subject: a treacherous green quagmire into which incautious and inexperienced travellers are easily tempted and are almost certain to sink.

How much more agreeable to sit at ease in 'a villa in the Tuscan hills between Arezzo and Siena'! Visions of Cicero's Tusculan Disputations,[1] of Machiavelli at San Casciano[2] (wearing his best clothes in order to read the great writers of Antiquity), of Galileo at Fiesole, spring to the

---

[1]   Philosophical writings composed at Cicero's villa at Tusculum, close to the present-day Frascati.

[2]   Machiavelli's country home at Sant'Andrea in Percussina, south of Florence, where he spent his days managing his properties, his evenings in the tavern, and at night withdrew to his study and wrote *The Prince*.

mind! Of course there are villas and villas, and I have had disappoint-
ments recently with villas which have turned out to be not Phaeacian
country-houses with exquisite gardens and archaic *douceur de vivre* but
seedy farm-houses surrounded by pigs and hens. But some of my happiest days have been spent in a Tuscan villa with a great library and intelligent people and delicious meals and a constant flow of stimulating
conversation;[1] which is perhaps why I find collegiate life in the Fens,
and the dull and deep potations[2] and unedifying talk of my collegiate
colleagues so depressing by comparison. I have no doubt you are right:
that there are lively and intellectual circles tucked away in the recesses
of Cambridge; but alas, I have not found them. No doubt there were
some sophisticated Sarmatian clubs and convivia in Tomi in the time
of Ovid,[3] but he seems not to have discovered them either. Perhaps that
is our fault (mine and Ovid's, I mean): we should have sought them
out...

Was Oxford so different? you ask. Well, perhaps not—although there I
had a world of research students and a few of my colleagues were lively
and had lively friends; and a few is enough. And Christ Church, when I
was there, was full of life. It was, of course, just before and just after the
war, a very political college in a very political time—in 1938–9 four of the
Students (Fellows to you) were standing for Parliament against each other,
passions ran high, and half the rest were canvassing for or against them.[4]

---

[1]   T-R refers to Kenneth de Courcy's holiday rental and to Berenson's I Tatti.
[2]   Gibbon in his autobiography described the fellows of Magdalen College, Oxford: 'Their
conversation stagnated in a round of college business, Tory politics, personal anecdotes, and
private scandal: their dull and deep potations excused the brisk intemperance of youth.'
[3]   Tomi was the city on the Black Sea to which Ovid was banished by the Emperor Augus-
tus. Ovid describes the region as Sarmatian and complains of the barbarous conduct of the
Sarmatians.
[4]   In the by-election for the Oxford University seat in 1937, Lindemann ('the Prof') stood
as an Independent Conservative and Sir Farquhar Buzzard as the official Conservative candidate. In the Oxford City by-election of 1938, Quintin Hogg, a former scholar of Christ
Church and a Fellow of All Souls, was the successful Conservative candidate, whereas the
Labour candidate, Patrick Gordon Walker, a Student of Christ Church, reluctantly stood
down in favour of a Popular Front candidate, A. D. Lindsay, Master of Balliol, and was replaced as Labour candidate at the 1945 general election by another Christ Church man,
Frank Pakenham.

In that cathedral foundation there were also internal battles—'Students' v. canons, free-thinkers v. clergy; but the battles were fought by agile gladiators with polished rapiers, not by lumbering peasants with rustic cudgels.

Do I perhaps romanticise the past? I cannot exclude that possibility. In general I fear that you are right when you say that colleges are 'no longer conducive to the generation of a society of scholars' ('No longer'? Were they ever? Read the correspondence of the poet Gray, or Mark Pattison's memoirs!) Certainly I have now come to believe this. I believe it so much that I am now genuinely reluctant to recruit lively young scholars as permanent teaching Fellows of this college, as I had once hoped to do, because I feel that to do so would be to destroy them. I will bring them in very gladly as Research Fellows, but if they are made permanent will they not either be dreadfully frustrated or, if they are not strong enough to resist, corrupted by the spirit of the place? And yet, I say to myself, scholars must live, and be enabled to live; the college system works for undergraduates; it has other merits too, as was shown in those dreadful years 1968+: it stabilised Oxford and Cambridge when the universities of America and Europe were convulsed and half-ruined. It is better to reform than to destroy. Unfortunately, they are self-governing corporations, and, as such, are *almost* irreformable.

You describe the atmosphere of combination rooms, 'torpid, heavy, oppressed by a sense of failure'. How well I recognise that atmosphere. It is a terrible commentary on that phenomenon which has come to obsess me: the death of the spirit which threatens every man unless he is conscious of the danger and has a real purpose which can keep it alive and enable it to thrust its way through the choking weeds and thorns to the air and to the sun.

I enjoy reading your letters so much that I am perfectly happy to leap-frog over the erasures and decipher the palimpsests. But I enjoy your company too and hope to have it: I am selfishly glad that you are, after all, still here. Perhaps, before winter descends on these gloomy fens, I can persuade you to come for a walk again. Autumn is a delightful time, if there are woods and streams to be touched by them.

yours ever

Hugh

———∞∞∞———

*James Stourton (b. 1956) was one of the younger friends whom Trevor-Roper met at the Beefsteak Club. Stourton joined Sotheby's in 1979 and was its UK chairman 2006–12. He is the author of four books on the history of collecting and patronage. For a while he ran his own private press.*

## To James Stourton, 5 October 1986

The Master's Lodge, Peterhouse

Dear James

I am glad to hear such a tribute to the Post Office! And I hope you enjoyed Greece and Turkey.

I'm afraid I have a weakness for frauds like the Sobieski Stuarts:[1] at least if they are *fantaisistes* who live their own fantasies, as they did. We need a touch of fantasy to irradiate this dull world of orderly, respectable virtues. My hero (if I can so describe him) Sir Edmund Backhouse, bart., was another such; and did not your hero, Sir Iain Moncrieffe of that ilk, also have such a streak?[2] A certain amiable *snobisme* is, it seems, a necessary ingredient

---

[1]    In his essay 'The Invention of Tradition: The Highland Tradition of Scotland', published in 1983, and later in *The Invention of Scotland*, T-R discussed the imposters John Sobieski Stolberg Stuart, *soi-disant* Count d'Albanie, and Charles Edward Stuart. These were the brothers John Carter Allen (1795?–1872) and Charles Manning Allen (1799?–1880), who pretended to be legitimate grandsons of the Young Chevalier, Charles Edward Stuart. In 1842 they published *Vestiarium Scoticum, or The Garde-Robe of Scotland*, asserting the antiquity of the use of clan tartans on the basis of a fifteenth-century manuscript, which Walter Scott dismissed as fraudulent. Their monumental *The Costume of the Clans* (1844) pictured medieval, Catholic, Celtic Scotland as a jewel of sophisticated European civilization.

[2]    Stourton's private press had recently issued a volume of essays edited by John Jolliffe, *Sir Iain Moncreiffe of that Ilk*. T-R's phrase 'your hero' was a tease, as he knew that Stourton had found Moncreiffe difficult.

in the character: one escapes from the humdrum world into faery castles, invests oneself with glittering titles, conjures with imaginary wealth. One such person whom I know is convinced that he is a duke.[1] 'Dukes *here*', he once said to me contemptuously in Italy, 'are two a penny'. I always humour him and write to him under his ducal title, which he takes very seriously.

Scott himself, I believe, had something of this character—which indeed is what made his greatness. At Abbotsford he realised, and lived in, a fantasy world, imagining himself an ancient Scottish magnate, romanticising loyalties which, in Scottish history, were imaginary rather than real—to the Duke of Buccleuch, his 'chief', to a Hanoverian king tartanised for the occasion—dispensing open-handed hospitality, scattering in the end unreal wealth. And yet, like most of these people, he combined these fantasies with practical, rational behaviour in other areas of life: sensible in historical judgment, honourable in personal relations, efficient in his work as sheriff, punctual in completing his books. It is the contrast, or tension, between his Augustan and his romantic character which makes him so attractive to me.

I believe—I may have said this before: if so, forgive me—that Scott wrote six great novels, all published between 1814 and 1819: *Waverley, Guy Mannering, The Antiquary, Old Mortality, Rob Roy, Heart of Midlothian*; then came *Ivanhoe* and a long list of second-rate best-sellers, redeemed only by *Redgauntlet*. Best of all, in my opinion, is *Old Mortality*. Then, towards the end of his life, he wrote that marvellous *Journal*, a most moving work, from which the reality and the charm of his character emerge. Do you know it? They emerge also from Lockhart's *Life* which I think a wonderfully good biography, to be read in its entirety, not in the potted version. Perhaps the best bits in it are by Scott himself—'the Ashesteil fragment'[2] of his autobiography and the journals of his Lighthouse Tour.

I thought Paddy Leigh Fermor's essay on Iain splendid. It brought out the romantic fantasy in his character and conversation, happily

---

[1]  Kenneth de Courcy.
[2]  The autobiographical account composed when Scott resided at Ashestiel, on the Tweed near Melrose.

abbreviated! I was amused by your experience of authors who objected to being deprived of letters after their names. They must have been Cambridge men. One of the many differences that I notice between our two ancient universities is that Cambridge men (who as a rule take themselves so much more seriously—you don't, which is one reason why I so like you!) insist on their little doctorates. In Oxford it is regarded as a solecism, even a vulgarity, for anyone except a DD, DLitt, D.Mus., or DCL to call himself 'Dr Smith'. The D.Phil may, by now, be a professional necessity, but one is quiet about it (although even here, alas, there is a hint of change, brought in by self-important Cambridge immigrants).[1] In Cambridge they are all 'Dr' and I have to be very careful always to use the title if I want their votes in my college meetings.

I fear that our Scottish life is coming to an end. Xandra, who made me live in her native country, now wants to leave it. I, who would have preferred my native Northumberland, would be happy to stay. We have a charming house, with woods and a stream, which are so necessary to me—like Virgil I can say *flumina amem silvasque inglorius*[2]—and if our neighbours are dull, I have books, which are not. But Xandra says that she has now no friends there and it is too cold in winter: 'it is all very well for you: you will gad up to London at the expense of the House of Lords. I shall be stuck here alone!' And next June we have to leave our fine Queen Anne house in Cambridge. So a great migration to some London suburb lies before us. It is very distracting; and since there are horrible economic implications, we ask ourselves what we can sell. If we should meet, perhaps at the Beefsteak on Wednesday, when I hope to come to London, or, if not, on a postcard, perhaps you could tell me whom at Sotheby's I could consult about pictures—I have two 17th century paintings (Roelant de Savery and Valerio Castello[3]) which, reluctantly, I would flog, but only if they would make a material contribution towards this dreadful change in our way of life.

---

[1]  The 'change' at Oxford had progressed further than T-R knew.
[2]  Virgil, *Georgics* 2.486. 'May I love the waters and the woods, even if without fame?'.
[3]  Roelant Savery (1576–1639) was Dutch; Valerio Castello (1624–59) worked in Genoa.

I have not yet braved the Beefsteak in its temporary lodgings,[1] but I am determined to do so; and I hope that I shall find you there one day soon.

yours ever

Hugh

———⊗⊗⊗———

## To Alasdair Palmer, 23 October 1986

The Master's Lodge, Peterhouse

Dear Alasdair

Yes, I am better, though it took a long time, and I must still be careful.[2] It mortified me to see those beautiful autumn days and not to be able to go out and enjoy them. But your handwriting on an envelope always cheers me.

I sense that you need to be cheered too, so I am glad that Bernard Williams[3] is so encouraging. I sympathise with people in your state, especially when, as now, I have just read 133 applications for 2, or at most 3, research fellowships. With my mind's eye I see them all, 133 slaves in a Roman quarry, or mine, or treadmill, of whom only half-a-dozen, in the end, will be emancipated—if it is emancipation and not a more comfortable but more deadly slavery that they are seeking...Let us not ask too many questions about that. Dons, and supervisors, are very critical—it is their occupational disease—and sometimes very negative and do not, in the poverty of their spirit, appreciate the agony of those who are still going through the process which has given them their petty doctorates.

---

[1]   Because of building work, the Beefsteak had vacated its club premises at 9 Irving Street, which joins Leicester Square to Charing Cross Road. During the closure, Beefsteak members decamped to the Travellers in Pall Mall.

[2]   He was recovering from a prostate operation.

[3]   (Sir) Bernard Williams (1929–2003), Provost of King's College, Cambridge, 1979–88, had recently published his major works *Moral Luck* (1982) and *Ethics and the Limits of Philosophy* (1985).

How can I boost your morale? Only, I fear, in a somewhat egotistical way—since I cannot comment on your work, only on your letters—by saying, truthfully, that I find in you, and in them, qualities which I admire: a warmth, a vitality, an intelligence, a love of literature; and that I value your friendship and hope to keep it; and that if your philosophy does not exclude or suppress these amiable qualities I shall willingly be converted to it.

You write about Evelyn Waugh. My relations with him were curious. I contrived never to meet him, which required some ingenuity, for we had many common friends and fashionable hostesses sometimes sought to trap me into a confrontation. But I was determined to avoid him because I genuinely admired his writing but knew that he would be offensive and did not want to be involved in disagreeable scenes. He picked a quarrel with me in 1947—wrote me, out of the blue, a very nasty letter, attacked me in the *Tablet*, and then in other papers. I hit back occasionally, and he then became, as it seemed to me, somewhat paranoid. I heard many stories of his wild, and often intoxicated denunciations, and since his death his published (and unpublished) letters have given further evidence of his hatred of me. He evidently regarded me as a particularly poisonous serpent who had slid into the garden of Brideshead and was corrupting its innocent Catholic inhabitants; which perhaps, to a certain extent, I was— or, as I would prefer to say, was provoked into being. In the end I tried to make peace with him, but my civil letter received only a curt formal acknowledgement.

Now that the dust has settled, what do I think of him? I think he was a writer of genius, and I forgive him a great deal because of his genuine love of our language. His wild fantasy and black humour are aspects of his genius as well as of his warped character. He was, I believe, utterly cold-hearted: all his emotions were concentrated (apart from his writing) upon his social snobisme and his Catholicism, which was a variant of it, or rather, perhaps, the ideological force behind it. He was a true reactionary—not just a troglodyte like the Peterhouse *mafia* but a committed, believing, uncompromising, intellectually consistent reactionary like (say) de Maistre.[1] I wonder if he had any friends. He kept up a regular correspondence with Nancy Mitford,[2] much of which has been published, but she (whom I knew well) was equally, behind a witty, entertaining *persona*, a cold-hearted selfish person, chiefly interested in malicious private gossip. After his death a volume of essays about him was published—I can't remember the editor, some 'Mayfair Jezebel', I think (to use Logan Pearsall Smith's phrase).[3] Most of the essays were thin and worthless, but there was one which was splendid. It was by the late Lord Birkenhead who had found himself living, during the war, in German-occupied Yugoslavia, with Tito's partisans, in the company of Waugh and Randolph Churchill. The essay was wonderfully funny and wonderfully good-tempered. I wrote to Birkenhead about it and received a letter which I treasure. I enclose a copy of it; but please destroy it when read: I don't want even a whiff of it to reach the one person mentioned in it who is still alive (and dangerous)![4]

Evelyn Waugh's original offensive letter was provoked by an admittedly injudicious remark by me about Jesuits in *The Last Days of Hitler*,[5] and I assumed at the time that this was my initial offence. However, since his

[1]    Joseph de Maistre (1755–1821), the chief French theorist of the counter-revolution, emphasized the necessity of suffering and war, and insisted on the role of the public executioner in the preservation of social stability.

[2]    Nancy Mitford (1904–73), novelist and biographer.

[3]    David Pryce-Jones, *Evelyn Waugh and his World* (1973).

[4]    In a letter of 29 October 1973, Birkenhead had written: 'After my three months with E. Waugh at really close quarters, I came to the conclusion that he was an odious, indeed a psychopathic character. It must always be anxious work incarcerated in a pig-sty in an enemy-occupied Balkan country, but to be so in the company of two such Freudian characters is authentically gruesome. It must be seldom that you can find simultaneously a couple so totally divorced from all human kinship, both born without the bowels of compassion…The other essays are mostly contemptible—all stressing the charm and innate loyalty of E. Waugh, who had not the slightest comprehension of either. I should have dealt far more hardly with him…had I not wished to avoid, perhaps cravenly, the insane malice of his repulsive son', Auberon Waugh. In a letter to Anthony Thwaite (3 September 1976), declining to review a biography of Waugh for *Encounter*, T-R explained that he was 'frightened of incurring the insane malice' of Auberon Waugh: 'I have other things to do than to contend with irrelevant vendettas!' Later, however, T-R and Auberon were on good terms, not least because of T-R's admiration for him as a wine correspondent.

[5]    He mistakenly wrote that Joseph Goebbels had been 'the prize-pupil of a Jesuit seminary', who 'retained to the end the distinctive character of his education: he could always prove what he wanted'.

death, I have seen letters from him which attacked me well before that publication, so I no longer know the original cause of his hostility. The general background to it was certainly ideological. During the war, and throughout the 1950s, a group of very articulate, socially reactionary Roman Catholics—all, or nearly all, converts—pushed themselves forward and evidently thought that they could be the ideologues of the post-war generation. They established themselves, by patronage and infiltration, in certain institutions (the British Council, the Foreign Office) and they wanted to establish themselves in the universities. They behaved in a very aggressive, boastful manner: their public line was that there was no alternative to them: there *is* no culture except Catholic culture, there *are* no English novelists except Catholic novelists, there *is* no political thought or system, in the discredit of Nazism, fascism, communism, except that of the neo-Catholic. Frank Pakenham, now Lord Longford, used to 'teach' his pupils that modern thought is dominated by 'the three Ms: Marx, Mannheim[1] and Maritain;[2] and the greatest of these is Maritain'. Frank, of course, was not one of them, having become a socialist; but as a fellow-convert of Father D'Arcy[3] he was an ally in religious zeal, and his mind was sufficiently muddled, not to say chaotic, to entertain any jumble of inconsistent ideas. Graham Greene was similarly one of them ideologically, though different in political orientation. Their spiritual centre was the Jesuit Church of Farm Street in Mayfair. In his controversies with me, Waugh used to write to the Jesuits there for ammunition (I have seen one of his letters seeking such ammunition and have a copy of it).

All these people regarded me as a dreadful enemy—I sometimes think (but this is vanity) as public enemy no. 1. The reason was that I was thought to be influential in Oxford, and particularly in Christ Church—precisely the places which they were most eager to conquer. 'You are not going to send your son to be taught by that *dreadful* man?' Evelyn Waugh exclaimed

---

[1] Karl Mannheim (1893–1947), founder of the sociology of knowledge, author of *Ideologie und Utopie* (1929), who fled from Nazi Germany to the London School of Economics in 1933.

[2] Jacques Maritain (1882–1973), France's leading 20th-century Catholic philosopher.

[3] Martin D'Arcy (1888–1976), Jesuit priest and Master of Campion Hall 1933–45.

to a Belgian friend of mine; and then, turning to the company, 'Does this poor foreigner know what he is doing?' And on another occasion he would say, rather unrealistically, that the prime objective of himself and his friends was to have me removed from Oxford. Graham Greene once walked out of a restaurant in Abingdon simply because he saw me there. In my old age I regret having aroused such feelings in such distinguished literary men.

Time and events have made that phase of history, or biography, seem very remote, and the internal contradictions of what then seemed a solid party have disintegrated it. Waugh sank into abject, total, eccentric reaction. Greene found himself supporting Castro (I remember a letter from him, published in the *Times*, protesting that Castro was *not* a communist but a romantic radical Catholic, like himself) and Philby (whom he praised—after his defection and exposure—as the modern equivalent of the Elizabethan Jesuit martyrs like Edmund Campion, the hero of Evelyn Waugh[1]). The Papacy of John XXIII was a body-blow to them—although I suppose that Greene has found some ingenious way of compromise with Latin American 'liberation theology'. Frank Longford, of course, has long been insulated from reality by unlimited vanity and unqualified love of publicity. But Waugh remains a cult-hero to a little band who live in an imaginary mini-Brideshead.

I would love to come and dine on 30 Oct. and meet your friends. You know my problem: I *have* to go out occasionally in the evenings— Governing Body nights, guest nights, House of Lords—and Xandra doesn't like being left alone too often; but I will try to ration myself next week so that I can come on Thursday. It will be a great pleasure to see you again.

yours ever

Hugh

---

[1] Greene wrote a sympathetic introduction to Philby's memoir *My Silent War* (1968), in which he compared Philby's subterfuge on behalf of Soviet Russia to the activities of the persecuted Catholics in Elizabethan England who plotted for the victory of Spain. Greene suggested that Philby served Stalinism in the spirit that 'many a kindly Catholic must have endured the long bad days of the Inquisition with this hope...that one day there would be a John XXIII'.

## To Alasdair Palmer, 2 November 1986

The Master's Lodge, Peterhouse

Dear Alasdair,

You are a very good host. You took a lot of trouble and gave us an excellent dinner. I only wish you had not been *quite* so good, and so had not had to spend so much time in your kitchen! But it was nice to see you when you emerged. Many thanks.

I think that I carelessly left my raincoat in your house. May I collect it in some way convenient to you?

Would you care to dine with me on Tuesday or Wednesday? I shall telephone you, for time is short; and who knows? Perhaps you have been hooked by Granada Television and have already left these drab Fens for Manchester. I rather hope not. I mean, I absolutely hope not, but I have to qualify the absolutism because I naturally want you to find agreeable and profitable employment.[1] But I must admit that I am now very prejudiced against the media, and I have always especially disliked Granada: they were such *thugs* when they came to our house in Oxford! They even *smoked* in our drawing-room.

I dislike Tebbit,[2] whom I meet occasionally in London. I think he is a thug too. But I fear that he may have *something* of a case against the BBC. There is now (as in the media generally) a destructive, irresponsible, *mesquin*[3] ethos in it. But you will not, I am sure, be corrupted by such an ethos, there or anywhere.

I am sorry about your 'domestic storm', whatever its nature may be. I hope that you have not been hurt by it. You seemed, or contrived, to be very cheerful on Thursday, and I hope that you have recovered. We all, at

---

[1]   Palmer had a successful career as a journalist, especially as Public Policy Editor for the *Sunday Telegraph* 1998–2013. He is now a speech-writer for the Home Secretary, Theresa May.
[2]   Norman Tebbit (b. 1931), Baron Tebbit, a member of the Thatcher Cabinet 1981–7, whose election to the Beefsteak was resisted by many of its members including T-R.
[3]   'Mean, petty-minded'.

times, have doubts. Again and again I think of those lines by Housman (whom, like Waugh, I admire at one level and dislike intensely at another)

> When the bell justles in the tower
> The hollow night amid,
> Then on my tongue the taste is sour
> Of all I ever did.[1]

But nothing will persuade me that you have not behaved perfectly!

I agree with you about Catholic converts. I can't take 'em; and I fear that I showed it in respect of E Waugh. I also dislike 90% of Christians and Christianity. But I will not join you as 'a solid atheist'. I am fascinated by religion as a sociological phenomenon. I enjoy observing the foibles— the harmless foibles—of its various adepts. I recognise that it has done *some* practical good. And then, think of its contribution to art and music and poetry! How mean, how insolent, is the claim that we can dispense altogether with it; how jejune a philosophy which leaves no mystery be-hind it! But of course, when people smugly claim to solve that mystery with theological explanations, I shut off.

I like to think that there are mysteries beyond the reach of human reason—totally beyond it, so that all theological explanations are neces-sarily wrong. I would happily be a Greek pagan in the youth and freshness of the world. But then I say to myself, why did that happy system prove in-adequate? Was it not, perhaps, like so much of Greek civilisation, the care-free cult of an *élite*? Did not a slight shift in secular happiness make it seem insubstantial and useless? And then, when the hitherto stable foundations of society seemed to tremble, men turned to oriental religions of salva-tion, the response to a *sens tragique de la vie*.[2] Who are we, I ask myself, sit-ting in academic insulation, with security of tenure and three meals a day, to despise the consolatory fantasies of suffering humanity, especially

---

[1]   A. E. Housman, *A Shropshire Lad*. The first line should read, 'When the bells justle in the tower'.
[2]   'The tragic sense of life'.

when those fantasies have produced heroic poetry, towering cathedrals, real saints, great conquests and memorable crimes, while we can only pick holes in each others' theses. No, I find 'solid atheism' too mean and cold a system with which to challenge the wonderful organisation of the world.

As for Christianity, I accept it as the established religion of my country, which, by being established, is an inoculation against worse diseases: for an established Church only demands conformity while a sect expects belief. I consider it most unfortunate, and indeed indecent, that bishops have now begun to argue about beliefs. They should leave that to Dissenters. It is like modernising the liturgy, whose whole value—psychologically—depends on its beautiful unintelligibility. What a fool the Bishop of Durham is to bother about the Resurrection! He should behave like those sensible 18th century bishops 'whose sound understanding' (as Gibbon wrote) 'is perhaps seldom engaged with that abstruse mystery'.

You see that I have given some attention to these matters, and you will, I hope, sympathise with me when I feel pained that Dean Norman[1] has never invited me (though a DD) to preach in my college chapel.

The Habsburgs were splendid patrons—more splendid than I wrote in that little book;[2] for I had no space to include the Emperor Maximilian at the beginning of my period (I have remedied that in a later essay)[3] or Philip IV at the end. As for the Medici, do not forget that they include not only Cosimo and Lorenzo but Leo X and Clement VII and the later Grand Dukes of Tuscany... But I must correct myself: I must not forget that I am writing to the latest choreographer of Tuscany.

No, don't type your letters. As you see, I reject the impersonality of the machine; and your hand, though sometimes stumbling, is always legible.

yours ever

Hugh

---

[1]   There was antipathy between T-R and Edward Norman (b. 1938), Dean of Peterhouse 1971–88.
[2]   *Princes and Artists* (1976).
[3]   'The Emperor Maximilian I, as Patron of the Arts', in *Renaissance Essays* (1985).

# To Alasdair Palmer, 23 November 1986

The Master's Lodge, Peterhouse

Dear Alasdair

I am so glad that you found dinner in Peterhouse enjoyable. I am always rather apprehensive in bringing guests to that unpredictable table: some of them have had remarkable experiences. Sometimes I think it best to provide a protective bodyguard of janissaries. But I felt that you, who have toughened your spirit among exhumed corpses, spooks, were-wolves and hooting night-owls in Highgate cemetery, could cope.

In any case, I greatly enjoyed your company; as I always do. Your conversation and correspondence cheer me in my village life.

I am more indulgent than you to our dear Prime Minister. I deplore some of her chosen helpers: Tebbit, Archer,[1] Currie.[2] I deplore the philistinism of the government. I agree that she has broken the consensus, and that consensus must be restored (which the Tebbits and the Curries will never do). But the consensus that she broke was an illusion, under cover of which our institutions were being destroyed. No other politician had the courage to face the fact and confront the destroyers. It was, I believe, a necessary confrontation.

You write of religion. You tell me that you were once 'a committed Christian'. This delights me, because it enables me to ask a question: a question which I cannot decently put to a professed Christian but may, I suppose, risk putting to an ex-Christian. Did you, at that time, really believe, or believe that you believed, those quaint, superannuated doctrines of Incarnation, Resurrection, Ascension, etc., which, in the Creed, we solemnly say that we believe, and which, if words have any meaning, are

---

[1]  Jeffrey Archer (b. 1940), later Baron Archer of Weston-super-Mare, had resigned as deputy chairman of the Conservative Party in October 1986 after the *News of the World* reported that he had, through an intermediary, paid £2,000 to a prostitute.

[2]  Edwina Currie (b. 1946) had been appointed as junior Health Minister in September 1986 amidst a storm of interviews and photo opportunities. 'Yes, I am pushy,' she told *The Guardian* (14 September) for an article headlined 'How Edwina Promoted Herself'.

indeed essential beliefs; for, as the Apostle says, with unusual clarity, 'if Christ rose not from the dead, then is all our faith vain'.[1]

Do 'committed Christians' really 'believe' such stuff? Merely to pose such a question makes me somewhat dizzy; for if the answer is Yes, I must resign myself to thinking that I am in a madhouse, or the Floating Island of Laputa; but if it is No, then what is the meaning of being 'a committed Christian'? This is a problem—a semantic, an epistemological, perhaps an anthropological problem—which exercises my poor, well-meaning brain, and exercises it more severely than ever now I have survived into a more serious-minded generation and migrated from the sunlit uplands of Oxford into these dismal Dissenting Fens. Now, and here, I have come to realise that there are people, even in what Gibbon would call 'the full light and freedom of the 20ᵗʰ century', who apparently take this stuff not (as is surely permissible) as an agreeable allegory, or harmless poetic myth, into whose historically consecrated shell successive generations have poured a permanent philosophic or moral content, but *literally*. I have even heard tell of 'born-again Christians': grown persons who, having previously been rational creatures, have suddenly and deliberately—horrible thought!—chosen to take up this bizarre mental apparatus. Ex-President Carter,[2] I believe, is one of them, and I have a dark suspicion that there are one or two in the university of Cambridge.

All this is extremely worrying to me as I sit, now and then, in the chapel of Peterhouse, placing myself, by versatile imaginative effort, as the various parts of the service succeed one another, among the fanatical bedouin of ancient Judaea, the hooligan clergy of Byzantium or the Roman Maghreb, the scholarly Anglican bishops of the 17ᵗʰ and the

---

[1]   A loose rendering of 1 Corinthians 15: 13–14: 'if there be no resurrection of the dead, then is Christ not risen: And if Christ be not risen, then is our preaching vain, and your faith is also vain.'

[2]   'Jimmy' Carter (b. 1924) had declared in 1976 that he was a born-again Christian. He was the first born-again Christian to be President of the United States (1977–81). At the presidential election of 1980 the three chief candidates (Carter, Reagan, and John B. Anderson) all stated that they were born-again Christians.

snivelling Methodist hymnologists of the 19<sup>th</sup> century. I hope you will be able to put me at ease on this subject.

Do you know E E Evans-Pritchard's great work, *Witchcraft Oracles and Magic among the Azande?* It is a marvellous and fascinating book. I have found it most illuminating when faced by such problem; especially since I came to Peterhouse. But the intellectual world of the pagan Azande (they live in the southern Sudan) has a consistency and a coherence which has disappeared from the etiolated and anaemic Christianity of today.

I am glad that you are now better disposed towards the Medici. In my brief list of *some* members of that family whom you had evidently over-looked, I inadvertently omitted Catherine de Médicis, the builder of those exquisite châteaux and the creator of those splendid masques and pageants of the Valois court, and Marie de Medicis, who commissioned Rubens to decorate her new Luxembourg Palace. Surely Lipsius was not wrong who called them *stirps quasi fataliter nata ad instauranda vel fovenda studia*.[1]

> yours ever
> Hugh

PS If you should answer my question (as I hope you will), it will not be enough to say that you committed yourself only to the current moralities of Christianity, taking the doctrines on trust; because the current moralities are not exclusively Christian and entail no such commitment. What is exclusively Christian can entail no such commitment. What is exclusively Christian, the authentic and only valid badge of Christianity as distinct from other religions, or its own later incrustations, is the doctrine that those who, in his time on earth, gave up all and followed him would, after death, in the *near* future, be bodily resurrected and sit with him in a local heaven, judging the similarly resurrected twelve tribes of Israel. If

---

[1] 'A family as it were destined at birth to renew and foster the arts'. This quotation from Justus Lipsius (1547–1606), epistle VIII *ad Germanos et Gallos*, is probably taken from Edward Gibbon's *Memoirs*.

you merely adhered to, or conformed with, the religion of your country, I would not of course press you; but since you *committed* yourself, you presumably read the small print of Holy Writ before taking this serious step.

It is a pity that our religion is based on such gibberish. Judaism and Islam are so much more sensible. If only Roman paganism, which was good enough for Cicero (provided that he didn't have to believe it—he was a sound 18th century deist), could have held out for two or three centuries longer, perhaps—as Burckhardt thought—we should have been won for Islam instead. Of course, we would have been heretical within Islam (though the Scots no doubt would have been Wahabi bigots of orthodoxy): perhaps Shi'a Moslems, so that we would now be ruled by a hierarchy of ayatollahs—which you perhaps would prefer to Mrs Thatcher. On which happy speculation I shall end this letter and switch my mind, perforce, to the dreary task of countering, with strong metaphorical insecticide, the constant furtive depredations of our college death-watch beetle, M. Cowling.

H

—⁂—

*In 1960 Trevor-Roper had engineered the election of Harold Macmillan as Chancellor of Oxford University, by persuading the then Prime Minister to become a candidate and by acting as his campaign manager. The death of Macmillan in December 1986 created a vacancy for a new chancellor. Trevor-Roper was encouraged by the medievalist Peter Godman, a Fellow of Pembroke, to consider standing, but failed to recognize that the stain of the Hitler diaries made his election impossible, even if he would otherwise have been a strong candidate, which was doubtful. His illusions were reinforced by Xandra, which proved awkward when James was expected to agree that his stepfather should stand. Trevor-Roper assumed that Robert Blake, his oldest friend among the university's senior figures, would not consider standing, because Edward Heath, who had made him a peer, was known to be poised to enter the contest; so he was surprised when Blake announced his candidature. Trevor-Roper consulted Charles Stuart, who pleaded with him to 'keep out of the battle in dignified silence', warning that 'the Philistines' were 'numerous and hostile—don't let them have the pleasure of doing you down'. This was sound but perhaps unwelcome advice. 'I shall not compete with Robert,' Trevor-Roper replied; 'our natural constituencies overlap and I would not wish to drain away any votes: so I have asked my supporters to proceed no further.' He informed Blake of his decision, and wished him well.*

*Heath's Balliol contemporary and political opponent Roy Jenkins also entered the contest. Trevor-Roper did not vote in the ensuing election because he was in Australia. The Conservative vote was split evenly between Blake and Heath, allowing Jenkins to triumph with less than 40 per cent of the vote. Blake came second, with 32 per cent. Heath was third with 29 per cent.*

## To Blair Worden, 12 April 1987

Chiefswood, Melrose

My dear Blair

It seems a long time since I communicated with you, and much has happened since then. You have elected a new Chancellor. I have been to the Antipodes—and was thereby spared a difficult choice in that election. I wonder how you will find your new Visitor.[1] He will enjoy your feasts, if you give him plenty of claret (only the *best* claret, please); and on such convivial occasions you will find him very good company. I see him quite often, as we belong to the same monthly dining club in London, and I always enjoy sitting next to him. Whether his presence will lend tone and dignity on ceremonial occasions, time will tell.

My old friend the Lord Blake seems to have been behaving very oddly. Nobody loves a bad loser, but he seems not to have digested that truth. I had always credited him with the mind of a politician, not a bureaucrat. Bureaucrats cannot bear to be defeated, and in order to avoid that ultimate indignity, they tend to dig themselves into fixed positions which they then defend regardless of cost or changing circumstances; and if, in the end, they are overpowered, they sulk and meditate revenge. Politicians normally adopt a more genial attitude, recognising that we all get defeated now and then, and cheerfully take the rough with the smooth. But dear Robert seems now to be seething with resentment at not having

---

[1]   The Chancellor of Oxford University is *ex officio* Visitor of St Edmund Hall.

been supported by the Tory Party, whom he never consulted before standing (reasonably enough, since he then presented himself as a non-political 'academic candidate'), and who surely has as much right to lobby for their chosen candidate as Christ Church and Queen's had for theirs. This attitude seems to me very irrational.

Ted Heath is also very cross, but at least his public behaviour has been more dignified. He tells me that his personal relations with Robert are now 'very disagreeable', so there has evidently been recrimination. He considers that Robert, whom he made a peer, ought not to have stood against him and split the vote by claiming tory support. Robert maintains smugly that it was Heath who challenged him, since he announced his candidature first. But this is sophistry: he knew perfectly well that Heath was going to stand and deliberately jumped in first. Compared with all this, the famous election of 1960 was a very genial, good-tempered affair: a jolly Eatanswill[1] election reeking deliciously of that unreformed 'Old Corruption' so dear to our new tory revisionist historians.

I enjoyed my visit to Australia—unexpectedly, for I went reluctantly. As so often, I yielded to cajolery and flattery and then found myself committed beyond recall. I really couldn't afford the time, at this crisis in our affairs (see below) and I shrank from that long and tedious journey, which, if I had to make it, I would gladly have broken in Bombay or Singapore, or Bangkok or Bali, but could not, having promised Xandra to be back in a fortnight. I spent most of that time in Brisbane—a dull provincial city, far too hot—but I made a brief sortie to Sydney and Melbourne, which I liked.

The only begetter of this enterprise was John Morgan, who was chaplain of Oriel when I was there.[2] He is a truly admirable person who almost reconciles me to Christianity. I tried to have him made a Fellow of Oriel (as chaplain he was kept below the salt) but my efforts were defeated (how

---

[1]   *The Pickwick Papers*.
[2]   John Morgan (b. 1941), Chaplain of Oriel 1969–76 and of the University of Melbourne 1979–82; Warden of St John's College, University of Queensland, 1982–2013; Canon of St John's Cathedral, Brisbane, Hon. Professor Univ. of Queensland, sometime President of Australian Association for Professional and Applied Ethics.

I *hate* these smug sub-dons!). So Morgan returned to his native Australia to be head of a college of Brisbane university, and last year, when he had study leave, I had him made a Fellow Commoner of Peterhouse, where he was a great success; and no doubt it was for this reason that he invited me to Brisbane, and flattered me into accepting his invitation.

The ostensible purpose of the visit was to open a new graduate centre at John Morgan's college; which I did. I pulled a string, and behold! a curtain parted, revealing a brass plaque elegantly (and no doubt expensively) inscribed with my coat-of-arms and stating that I had opened the as yet non-existent building; after which the plaque disappeared into some secure place, lest it be vandalised by yahoos from the Outback, until the building has been run up to flaunt it. I also earned my fare by preaching a sermon, holding seminars, delivering lectures, talking to rich reactionary business-men in Sydney, and dining with virtuous and loyal Cambridge men in Melbourne, in a club which, according to John Adamson,[1] who looked after me there, 'made the Athenaeum seem like a Parisian go-go club'. Wherever I went, I found among my audience—among the Sydney business-men and among the Melbourne lecture-audience—my old friend, colleague and fellow Oxford wine-taster, Max Hartwell.[2] He had also been in my audience last year when I lectured in Chicago. I don't know how to interpret this: do you think he is shadowing me?

But a fig for lectures and seminars, universities and clubs, plutocrats and dons! The great triumph of my visit was not among them. It was my encounter, at last, face to face, in the flesh, with a creature of which I have been enamoured—a romantic, remote, platonic and, I had supposed,

[1]    John Adamson (b. 1959) took a first in classics and history at the University of Melbourne. Early in 1986, after completing his doctoral dissertation at Christ's College, Cambridge, a committee chaired by T-R had elected him to a research fellowship at Peterhouse. He deferred the research fellowship for family reasons, and was a Visiting Fellow at the University of Melbourne for the northern academic year of 1986–7. He has remained at Peterhouse since 1987. His *The Noble Revolt: The Overthrow of Charles I* was published in 2007.
[2]    Max Hartwell (1921–2009), born in the northern tablelands of New South Wales; historian of the Industrial Revolution; collector of fine vintages; an irreverent teacher and provocative controversialist. He was Reader in Recent Economic and Social History at Oxford, and Professorial Fellow of Nuffield College 1956–77.

hopeless passion—ever since I was at my private school in Dunbar. I refer, of course, to that amiable eccentric of the mammalian world, the duck-billed platypus, whom I saw (sufficient compensation for that long and arduous journey) in the Zelman Cowen Platypusary at the Melbourne Zoo;[1] at which I also saw many other animal reminders (especially the wombat) of my Cambridge Combination Room: creatures which, by long insulation in a protective enclave, have developed characteristics so distinct and specialised that they no longer seem to belong to the same species...But enough of this: let me return to my main narrative.

Having seen much of John Adamson at Melbourne, I have come to like him. I found him a very civilised and agreeable host and companion, who took a great deal of trouble for me, for which I could imagine no interested motive. Perhaps he is more at ease in Melbourne than in Cambridge (or Oxford). I am sorry that I shall not be at Peterhouse when he is there.[2]

We are going through a traumatic period. I cease to be Master of Peterhouse on 19 June (by statute, my office ends on the last day of term: no interval for the upheaval of emigration). So we have the problem of a hurried removal to Didcot.[3] Unfortunately, at the very same time, we must clear out of Chiefswood too. We had hoped to postpone that second move till the first was over, but my hand has been forced by our gardener who, last January, suddenly declared himself ill and renounced all work. Since we *must* have someone here while the house is empty, and since we *must* have the grounds and garden looking respectable while we are trying to sell the place, I have had to bribe him to stay, on full pay, while

---

[1]    Sir Zelman Cowen (1919–2011) was Governor-General of Australia 1977–82 and Provost of Oriel 1982–90.

[2]    Adamson comments (4 February 2013): 'It was the first occasion on which I had spent any extended time alone in Hugh's company, and he was on excellent form throughout the visit: relaxed, cheerful, and clearly relishing the respectful, nay reverential, treatment he received from the Melbourne "establishment", from the Governor down. I don't know how I appeared to him; but *he* was certainly more at ease in Melbourne than I was ever to see him in Cambridge.'

[3]    The Dacres felt they had been hurried into leaving the Master's Lodge at Peterhouse by T-R's successor as Master, Henry Chadwick, and his wife. They had to fit their possessions from both Chiefswood and Cambridge into the Old Rectory at Didcot, which they had bought for £180,000 in early 1987.

myself doing all the work, and finding contract labour to do it when we are not here. You can imagine that not much historical work is being done: my days are divided between packing up, selecting books to get rid of, and shovelling manure; to which will soon be added correcting proofs of *Essays*, vol 2. Next term, trying to rule the factions of Peterhouse and cope with two empty houses 350 miles apart, will not be easy. But I hope I shall see you: perhaps also your friend, to whom I am indebted, von Maltzahn.[1]

yours ever

Hugh

PS. I have just received a curious piece of intelligence from a former pupil, now a journalist, who recently secured an interview with Maurice Cowling. Cowling told him that he was making 'a collection' of my letters to other persons. I don't really believe this—I trust those of my friends to whom I write freely, and the claim seems merely a reflection of the malicious and *mesquin* mind of Cowling, who loves to see himself, and to make others see him, as the great operator who knows all the secrets and has his hand on all the levers of village life. As he himself has said, 'Not a sparrow can fall to the ground in Peterhouse but I know it':[2] fit boast for an alpha mind!

---

[1]    Nicholas von Maltzahn (b. 1959), then a part-time tutor at Lincoln College, Oxford, Professor of English at the University of Ottawa since 1998, wrote his Oxford doctoral thesis on Milton, and commented on the typescript of the essay by T-R on Milton which appears in *Catholics, Anglicans and Puritans*.

[2]    Matthew 10: 29: 'Are not two Sparrows sold for a farthing? And one of them shall not fall on the ground without your Father.'

## To Edward Chaney, 5–11 May 1988

House of Lords

Dear Edward

Many thanks for M. Strachan on Sir T. Roe:[1] I see that I have some solid reading ahead of me; and for your letter, with all that delicious flattery glistening through the transparent pretence of censorship. Do I identify with Burckhardt? I never ask myself such questions. But I *don't* identify with Macaulay, whom I admire for his robust political sense but find ultimately unattractive: he is so insensitive, so complacent in his upstart, patrician whiggism: how his rhetoric glows when he thinks of Chatsworth, Woburn or Bowood! Do you know that passage about the Highlands of Scotland in the 17th century—their primitive, anarchic social system, so different from today when a gentleman can travel speedily and comfortably in a first-class railway carriage from his London club to his Highland grouse-moor? There is something insufferable (to me) about *his* identification with that imaginary gentleman, whom all Creation, it seems, aided by whig midwives, has been groaning and travailing to produce. Macaulay seems to me, for all his brilliance, to date far more than (say) Gibbon. Reading Gibbon, one feels that one is listening to a contemporary; with Macaulay, one is listening to a very successful, self-satisfied Victorian.

Burckhardt does refer to Gibbon, whose work of course he knew, but distantly: they were *very* different and I suspect that B wished to show his independence. Gibbon was a straightforward deist, Burckhardt a deeply religious spirit who had discarded Christianity. Gibbon set out to answer

---

[1] Michael Strachan (1919–2000) had been a Borders neighbour and fellow member of the New Club in Edinburgh. He was chairman of steamer shipping lines and a pioneer of oceanic container transport, as well as Director of the Bank of Scotland 1973–90 and chairman of the trustees of the National Library of Scotland 1974–90. Among other works on travellers and seamen of the early modern period, he published in 1989 a biography of Sir Thomas Roe (1581–1644), ambassador to the Great Moghul in India. Chaney had sent the typescript to T-R in the hope that he might help find someone to publish it.

a great philosophical question—why do Empires rise and fall?—by the method of Montesquieu. Burkhardt sought to analyse a great cultural crisis—one world-culture replacing another—in the spirit of Goethe. I think their difference is shown most clearly in their treatment of the early Christian ascetics. Gibbon despised them for contracting out, for their lack of *virtù* in the crisis of civilisation. Burckhardt respected them for disengaging themselves from a corrupted world and beginning again. I don't think Burckhardt ever expressed his opinion of Gibbon's work; but I think it can be deduced.

If I am Burckhardt and you are Nietzsche, I would warn you that Burckhardt was a somewhat timorous elderly gentleman who was rather frightened of the formidable young Nietzsche (though he learned a lot from him).

You should have gone to Magdalen: an invitation to it is a very rare experience.[1] I dined there only twice in fifty years. The first time was before the war, when I was a candidate for the fellowship to which they (rightly) elected A J P Taylor: not a very relaxed occasion. The second time was on the occasion of some Gibbon anniversary, when 'the monks of Magdalen'[2] tried to reclaim him. I regard that college as the Oxford Tibet: an inaccessible group of lamaseries, closed to the outer world. Oriel is rather a dull place, but quite hospitable: they don't deliberately *insult* guests.

You ask if you can pass on the Ten Commandments.[3] Of course! It has suddenly occurred to me that I am probably the only surviving member of the Society for Pure English. This was a society which was founded in 1913 by Robert Bridges and expired, with the birth of the (then) much trumpeted 'age of the Common Man', in 1946. It published numerous tracts with such titles as, 'On Hyphens and Shall and Will', 'The Split Infinitive', 'The Fate of French É in English', 'The Plural of Nouns ending

---

[1]   Chaney had been invited to dine there by the historian John Stoye (b. 1917), Fellow of Magdalen College, whose books include *English Travellers Abroad* (revised edition 1989), a work admired by both Chaney and T-R.

[2]   As Gibbon called the fellows.

[3]   The Ten Commandments (reproduced below, pp. 336–7) were a set of rules for the writing of prose which T-R had composed for the guidance of graduate students. They derived from comments that he had made on a draft of his stepson's thesis in 1971.

in —th', etc., on all which subjects I am now prepared to hold forth to a firmly captive audience in any saloon-bar. So I am naturally very glad to have found a missionary who will spread my much simplified evangel…

11 May 1988

I began this letter six days ago, but never then finished it: there was a division bell, and then, seeing the Earl Russell[1] (who sits on the Liberal benches) rising to speak (yet again) in the Committee on the Reform of Education Bill, I decided that it was time to leave for Paddington. Then, next day, I went to Cambridge, for a Feast at Peterhouse; after which I collapsed with gastric 'flu, from which I am just emerging to resume the pen.

I find that, in the House of Lords, we have some jolly moments. On Tuesday last there was a very agreeable episode. The Bishop of London[2]—one of the few sensible bishops (I think of Gibbon's description of Adhemar bishop of Puy: 'a respectable prelate, alike qualified for this world and the next')—was moving an amendment requiring religious teaching in schools, when up stood the Lord Sefton. This is not the 7th Earl of Sefton, High Constable of Lancaster Castle: he, alas, is now dead, to the impoverishment of White's, Bucks' and the Jockey Club,[3] and a new peerage of that title—Sefton of Garston—has been created for the former Labour leader of Liverpool City Council.[4] This new Lord Sefton is a roaring atheist, and he now made a long speech, denouncing all

[1]    Conrad Russell, 5th Earl Russell (1937–2004), specialized in 17th-century English history; held chairs at Yale (1979–84), University College London (1984–90), and King's College London (1990–2002); and in the 1980s bestrode the Tudor–Stuart history seminar at the Institute of Historical Research. A party spokesman in the House of Lords, he was described by his colleague John Morrill as 'the Micawber of the Liberal Democrat Party'. A few months before this letter a jaundiced review by Russell of *Catholics, Anglicans and Puritans* had been published in *The Spectator*.

[2]    Graham Leonard (1921–2010), Bishop of London 1981–91, and brother-in-law of the sometime Provost of Oriel, Lord Swann, moved his amendment on the Education Reform Bill on 3 May 1988.

[3]    The earldom became extinct because Hugh Molyneux, 7th Earl of Sefton (1898–1972), chairman of the Stewards of the Jockey Club, had determined that he should not have children after seeing his sister become insane in their nursery.

[4]    William Sefton, Baron Sefton of Garston (1915–2001), trained as a plumber and worked for years in a tannery. He was a tub-thumping self-styled Marxist who served as Labour leader of Liverpool City Council 1964–73 and of Merseyside County Council 1974–7.

religion and quoting Tom Paine's *Age of Reason*. Undeterred by various traditional signs of dissent, he then turned on the Bishop and demanded peremptorily whether the Rt. Revd. Prelate believed in the Virgin Birth (cries of 'Oh!'). But the Bishop, at this critical juncture, did not lose his *sang froid*: he replied that this question was hardly appropriate to the Committee stage of the Bill (thus implying that it would, of course, be perfectly in order at Report Stage or at Third Reading). Further prosecution of the interesting subject was then promptly stopped by the Baroness Seear,[1] who launched what the ex-Lord Chancellor called 'the *ultimum decretum*': i.e. she moved 'that the noble Lord be no longer heard'—an extreme device, very seldom used, and then only, in my experience, against Lord Hatch of Lusby,[2] the Bore of Bores, who also has the misfortune to be equally unpopular on all sides of the Chamber. The motion was immediately carried without a division (unprecedented even in the case of Lord Hatch); and so the House returned to the quiet drone of Christian conformity. Do you have jolly episodes like this in the Lincoln College Governing Body meetings?

I did not enjoy the Peterhouse Feast. I do not really enjoy these institutional beanos anyway, and at Cambridge they are rather gross. But at Peterhouse I have to show the flag, for a time at least. I do it to show appreciation of my supporters, who made me an Honorary Fellow, and also, I must admit, to hear, with my inner ear, that delicious music, the gnashing of the teeth of those who tried to block the election. My (limited) pleasure was not enhanced when I met, on arriving for pre-prandial champagne, an unexpected guest, the Earl Russell. It seems that I cannot avoid him.

yours ever

Hugh

---

[1]  Nancy Seear, Baroness Seear (1913–97), former Reader in Personnel Management at the London School of Economics and Liberal Leader in the House of Lords 1984–8.

[2]  John Hatch, Baron Hatch of Lusby (1917–92), former Director of the Extra-Mural Department at the University of Sierra Leone and of the Institute of Human Relations at Zambia University, was a general irritant.

P.S. I should be delighted to have a 'long walk and talk'—in Wytham Woods or on the Berkshire Downs—provided you are not *too* Zarathustran.

⊶⊷

## THE TEN COMMANDMENTS

1. Thou shalt know thine own argument and cleave fast to it, and shall not digress nor deviate from it without the knowledge and consent of the reader, whom at all times thou shalt lead at a pace which he can follow and by a route which is made clear to him as he goeth.

2. Thou shalt respect the autonomy of the paragraph, as commended by the authority and example of the prophet Edward Gibbon; for it is the essential unit in the chain of argument. Therefore thou shall keep it pure and self-contained, each paragraph having within it a single central point to which all other observations in it shall be exactly subordinated by the proper use of the particles and inflexions given to us for this purpose.

3. Thou shalt aim always at clarity of exposition, to which all other literary aims shall be subordinated, remembering the words of the prophet commandant Black, 'clarté prime, longueur secondaire.'[1] To this end thou shalt strive that no sentence be syntactically capable of any unintended meaning, and that no reader be obliged to read any sentence twice to be sure of its true meaning. To this end also thou shalt not fear to repeat thyself, if clarity require it, nor to state facts which thou thinkest as well known to others as to thyself; for it is better to remind the learned than to leave the unlearned in perplexity.

4. Thou shalt keep the structure of thy sentences clear, preferring short sentences to long and simple structures to complex, lest the reader lose his way in a labyrinth of subordinate clauses; and, in particular, thou shalt not enclose one relative clause in another, for this both betrays crudity of expression and is a fertile source of ambiguity.

---

[1] Perhaps the *nom de guerre* of Gustave Bertrand (1896–1976), a French military intelligence officer who made vital contributions to the decryption of German Enigma ciphers.

5. Thou shalt preserve the unities of time and place, as commended by the High Priest Nicolas Boileau,[1] placing thyself, in imagination, in one time and one place, and distinguishing all others to which thou mayest refer by a proper use of tenses and other forms of speech devised for this purpose; for unless we exploit the distinction between past and pluperfect tenses, and between imperfect and future conditional, we cannot attain perfect limpidity of style and argument.

6. Thou shalt not despise the subjunctive mood, a useful, subtle and graceful mood, blessed by Erasmus and venerated by George Moore, though cursed and anathematized by the Holy Inquisition, *Pravda*, and the late Lord Beaverbrook.

7. Thou shalt always proceed in an orderly fashion, according to the rules of right reason: as, from the general to the particular when a generality is to be illustrated, but from the particular to the general when a generality is to be proved.

8. Thou shalt see what thou writest; and therefore thou shalt not mix thy metaphors. For a mixed metaphor is proof that the image therein contained has not been seen with the inner eye, and therefore such a metaphor is not a true metaphor, created by the active eye of imagination, but stale jargon idly drawn up from the stagnant sump of commonplace.

9. Thou shalt also hear what thy writest, with thine inner ear, so that no outer ear may be offended by jarring syllables or unmelodious rhythm; remembering herein with piety, though not striving to imitate, the rotundities of Sir Thomas Browne and the *clausulae* of Cicero.

10. Thou shalt carefully expunge from thy writing all consciously written purple passages, lest they rise up to shame ye in thine old age.

---

[1]  Nicolas Boileau-Despréaux (1636–1711), satirist, critic, and poet, who self-mockingly called himself '*régent du Parnasse*'.

## To Alasdair Palmer, 29 May 1988

The Old Rectory, Didcot

Dear Alasdair,

I am always delighted and cheered by your letters, which, I'm afraid, I have done little lately to deserve. I have had rather a depressing time—a fire in the house (luckily we got it under control before it had taken over and destroyed the work of a year), illness (including House of Lords salmonella: the result of my dutiful attendance during the debate on the Education Bill[1]), and, on top of all this, continued difficulties with the Peterhouse mafia. But let us not think about them. Let us (as Logan Pearsall Smith wrote) 'interpose the thought of Kilimanjaro, that highest mountain of Africa', rising from 'grassy slopes and the green Arcadian realms of negro kings' through 'dim elephant-haunted forests' to its white crown of eternal snow.[2]

There are of course alternatives to Kilimanjaro as refreshing screens between ourselves and sordid reality. I hope you have a supply of them for everyday use. You will need them if you have much to do with David Steel (a man whom I have reason not to like,[3] though I must sympathise with him in the long futility of his public career), David Owen[4] (whom I do not know directly) or even Enoch Powell (whom I know and, to a certain extent, respect, respect but cannot like—who can? he is not human).

---

[1]    The Education Reform Bill, which instituted a national curriculum and abolished the Inner London Education Authority, was debated in the Lords for several weeks from 18 April. Major amendments were tabled, with speeches from Noël Annan, Max Beloff, Robert Blake, and sundry vice-chancellors and professors (but not T-R).

[2]    'As I sat inside that crowded bus, so sad, so incredible and sordid seemed the fat face of the woman opposite me, that I interposed the thought of Kilimanjaro, that highest peak of Africa, between us; the grassy slopes and green Arcadian realms of Negro kings from which its dark cone rises; the immense, dim, elephant-haunted forests which clothe its flanks, and above, the white crown of snow, freezing in eternal isolation over the palm trees and deserts of the African Equator' (*Trivia*).

[3]    As the local MP, David Steel had supported the scheme to build the hospital that blighted Chiefswood, and had failed to reply to T-R's letter about Bhutto's trial.

[4]    David Owen (b. 1938), later Lord Owen, Foreign Secretary 1977–9 and Leader of the Social Democratic Party 1983–92.

In general I am not fond of politicians: however enjoyable they may be at first, they are soon corrupted by their environment and the necessity of acquiring a public *persona*: only whig grandees like Harold Macmillan or Alec Home[1] seem able to withstand that subtle pressure—Macmillan because he was, among other things, a lover of literature; Home because he never really took politics seriously. As for Enoch Powell, I have never been able to regard him as human since he published his concordance to Herodotus,[2] in which he solemnly records, with chapter and verse, every occasion on which that robust and genial historian uses the word 'and'. I once made this point at a dinner party in Los Angeles, and no one would believe it; but luckily our host, the Byzantinist Milton Anastos,[3] had a copy of that portentous work—the only copy, I am prepared to wager, in California—and I was able to demonstrate it. There is something impressive about Powell's austere, inflexible virtue: it is like the lifeless frozen core of Kilimanjaro; but I prefer the grassy slopes, the sylvan elephants and the negro kings.

I am sure you are not being corrupted by your life in the media, because I am sure that you are aware of the danger and can see (and see through) the necessary triviality, even vulgarity, which it entails, from a stable point outside it. If I see signs of incipient corruption, I will tell you; and then, if I am right, you will be cross with me; but no doubt I shall be wrong and you will not.

You mention Tebbit. I have only met him once and disliked him strongly. I think of him and Edwina Currie as the typical Thatcherites Mark II—i.e. after the last election which gave Mrs T such power, and perhaps also such *folie de grandeur*. Before that election, Francis Pym said to

---

[1]  Alexander Douglas-Home (1903–95), Lord Home of the Hirsel, Prime Minister 1963–4 and Foreign Secretary 1960–3 and 1970–4.

[2]  Enoch Powell (1912–98) published *A Lexicon to Herodotus* in 1938.

[3]  Milton V. Anastos (1909–97) studied patristics, theology, and Byzantine intellectual history at Harvard Divinity School, and was a Fellow at the Dumbarton Oaks Center for Byzantine Studies 1941–64. He had a wartime Washington post in charge of the 'Greek desk' in the Office of Strategic Services. In 1964 he became Professor of Byzantine Greek at the University of California, Los Angeles. His ironic humour, erudition, and lofty character appealed to T-R.

me, 'if she wins this time, *none* of our friends will be in the Cabinet';[1] and effectively he was right. Tebbit's remarks about the Prince of Wales did not surprise me at all.[2] Or rather, their substance did not surprise me, though I would have thought that even he would have been more cautious in the expression of it. I do not regard Mrs T as a Tory at all, in any historical sense: she is rather the heir of Joseph Chamberlain:[3] a radical who found himself a place in the tory party through opposition to a common enemy: in his case, whig grandees; in hers, lackadaisical Butskellism, the common denominator of Macmillan, Wilson, Callaghan. Macmillan was, after all, also a whig grandee, and Harold Wilson was a great admirer of Macmillan. Mrs T is, very definitely, not.

A new menace has recently been brought into our public and academic life by the untimely death of the late Earl Russell, the eldest son of Bertrand Russell. He only once entered the House of Lords, I think, and then made a speech in favour of the I.R.A., which was not well received.[4] However, his death is much lamented there because his successor, his

---

[1]   Francis Pym (1922–2008), later Baron Pym, survived Thatcher's purge of the 'wets' in her Cabinet in 1981; but his paternalist notions seemed obsolete to her, and she peremptorily dismissed him as Foreign Secretary after the 1983 general election.

[2]   In an interview broadcast on 11 April 1988 in a BBC television programme entitled 'Charles: Prince of Conscience', Tebbit said that the Prince was becoming 'dangerous' in his campaigning for such 'socialist' causes as inner city revival, jobs creation, architectural standards, and environmental protection. 'The Prince of Wales feels extra sympathy towards those who have not got a job, because in a way he has not got a job,' said Tebbit. 'He is 40 and yet he's not been able to take responsibility for anything. I think that is really his problem.'

[3]   Joseph Chamberlain (1836–1914), the Birmingham MP and Leader of the Liberal Unionists.

[4]   John Russell, 4th Earl Russell (1921–87), attended the Lords intermittently, and indeed died on a train to Cornwall after attending the chamber. His suggestion in the Lords (30 July 1985) that the Thatcher government should recognize that the IRA had 'a legitimate role' in any negotiated Irish settlement was roundly condemned, although in fact Sinn Féin would play a crucial part in the Good Friday Agreement of 1998. His speech in a debate on the victims of crime (18 July 1978) recommended such crime prevention techniques as universal nude bathing, giving bags of Hatton Garden diamonds to potential criminals, and polygamy for women: he accused the police of molesting young people, forcing them to work in brothels, and 'raping them in gaol...part of a plot which is designed to destroy the human race by making it subserve dead spirits instead of live ones'. In a debate on the Public Order Bill (13 June 1986) he declared, 'We should free the prisoners, and learn to have fun...If you do not look after other people, you have chosen suicide yourself.'

half-brother Conrad Russell is not only constant in the Chamber but almost permanently on his feet. He has also taken to writing pompous letters to the Press (see today's *Sunday Times*).[1] He also hopes to succeed to the Regius Chair of History at Oxford, for which he hoped to qualify by giving the Ford Lectures last term. (I attended the first lecture, which was *very* bad—pedantic, niggling and vulgar). He has been publicly tipped for this chair by the new Oxford oracle, Jonathan Clark[2]—ex-Peterhouse, now at All Souls—in tandem with Edward Norman, also ex-Peterhouse, now, or shortly, going to be chaplain to a training-school for primary school-teachers at Canterbury.[3] For this reason I am not as distressed as I should be by the decision to freeze the Regius Chair—and indeed, no less shocking, the Regius Chair of Greek too, although that, since the field is presumably limited to those who know Greek, is less likely to be at the mercy of politics.

At first sight, Conrad Russell might seem an unlikely candidate because he is opposed to the govt: was a Labour candidate for Parliament once and now sits, in the Lords, on the Liberal benches. But there is an alliance between Left and Right-wing historical revisionists, both attacking whig history. This was brought out very clearly in the House of Lords, last year, when there was a debate on the celebration of the Glorious Revolution of 1688, and the Roman Catholic tory Lord Mowbray[4] was joined, in condemning that revolution, by the former Labour minister Ted Short, now more musically re-named Lord Glenamara. It was also brought out in a recent radio or T/V programme (which I didn't hear or see myself) when an innocent producer, expecting a lively controversy, brought together

[1] Russell's *Sunday Times* letter was 'in defence of academic freedom', by which he meant guaranteed tenure of university posts—the subject of a recent vote in the House of Lords.

[2] Jonathan [J. C. D.] Clark (b. 1951), Research Fellow at Peterhouse 1977–81 and at All Souls 1986–95, was appointed to a chair in British history at the University of Kansas in 1995.

[3] Edward [E. R.] Norman was Dean of Chapel 1988–95 at Christ Church College, Canterbury, which had been founded in 1962 to train teachers (not primary school teachers, as T-R states) for church schools and diversified into health studies during the late 1980s.

[4] Charles Stourton, 26th Baron Mowbray, 27th Baron Segrave, and 23rd Baron Stourton (1923–2006), noted that the Glorious Revolution had deprived his ancestors of their right to sit in the House of Lords until the Catholic Emancipation Act of 1829. He was a keen historian, who promoted the National Heritage Act of 1980, and father of T-R's friend James Stourton.

Jonathan Clark—see above—and Tony Benn, and found them joined in perfect anti-whig harmony.

A further reason for welcoming the otherwise shocking decision to freeze those Regius Chairs is provided by the personality of the present Patronage Secretary, whose duty it is to collect evidence and advise the PM. This office used to be held by sensible men who dined in the right Oxford and Cambridge colleges and consulted the right people. But the present holder of it, a man called Robin Catford,[1] does not fall into this category at all. He graduated at St Andrews in agriculture and until 1982, when he became adviser on academic chairs to Mrs T, he led a blameless life as an agronomical bureaucrat, mainly in black Africa. Worse still, I read in today's *Sunday Times* that he is a religious enthusiast and, as church-warden of his parish in Sussex, is dictatorially reconstructing his parish church in order to accommodate corybantic dancing round the altar,[2] which is to be uncanonically shifted for the purpose, thus turning our staid and decorous Anglican ritual into something like the ancient bacchanalian orgies on Mount Cithaeron[3] or the antics of whirling dervishes in Northern Iraq.[4] I think it will be difficult for the Earl Russell to catch up with these practices in the next two years (the period, we learn, for which the chair of History is to be frozen), but perhaps Edward Norman, in the seclusion of Christ Church, Canterbury, will be able to adjust himself, and thus qualify himself for it.

What a strange county Sussex is! Coming from the innocent north of England, and only visiting there, I have always seen it as a comfortable green county, prosperous, sensible, serene; but now I discover, it is full of

---

[1]  (Sir) Robin Catford (1923–2008), Appointments Secretary at Downing Street and ecclesiastical secretary to the Lord Chancellor 1982–93.

[2]  Corybants were priests of the Phrygian goddess Cybele whose rites were celebrated with music and ecstatic dances.

[3]  In Greek mythology Mount Cithaeron was a centre of Dionysian rites.

[4]  The evangelical Catford, as churchwarden emeritus of All Saints', Lindfield, led proposals to alter the church's interior to facilitate mime shows, clapping, and dancing in the aisles. One of Catford's opponents told the *Sunday Times*, 'Those people in favour of the plan were saying God had spoken to them and that if anybody spoke against it, the devil was in them.'

ancient, esoteric superstition. A few years ago a nest of Muggletonians was discovered there, which caused great excitement among our modern radical historians (see Christopher Hill, Barry Reay and Wm Lamont, *The World of the Muggletonians*) who unearthed a whole Muggletonian archive, since sold at Sotheby's. Then, a few years later, a legal prosecution revealed that, close to the noble mansion of Sheffield Place, where Gibbon corrected the proofs of the last volumes of *The Decline and Fall*, the country was honeycombed with diabolism, and that my kinsman Lord Hampden, at Glynde, had paid £35,000, no less, to an alleged prisoner of the Devil, so that he could buy a new Rolls-Royce and thus so impress Satan by his enhanced social status that the Fiend would relinquish his hold and set him free.[1] And now we learn that the Patronage Secretary to the Prime Minister, who appoints the Regius Professors of the two Kingdoms, and lives under the shadow of the patrician house of the Earl of Stockton, is a whirling dervish! No doubt (if I may vary my metaphors) this is but the thin end of the wedge, the tip of the iceberg, and further research will uncover new evidence. I expect to hear that those placid villages are secretly dominated by covens of witches and that the air above them, every night, is dark with self-propelled broom-sticks, carrying old ladies in tall hats, intent on bewitching their neighbours' pigs.

But indeed it now seems that No. 10 Downing Street itself is deeply infected. After all, there is also John Selwyn Gummer, son of Canon Selwyn Gummer, and himself a Selwyn man[2] (like Dr Norman)—all this emphasis on Selwyn presages no good—who preaches and prays at us and writes books with titles like *To Church With Enthusiasm* (Enthusiasm! what horrible vulgarity!); and now the P.M. herself has taken to preaching sermons (written for her, I understand, by Mr Catford) to the General

---

[1]  In 1986 Lord Hampden gave £39,000 to a fraudster who had undertaken to use the money to break a Satanists' ring but instead bought a Rolls-Royce.

[2]  John Selwyn Gummer (b. 1939), later Baron Deben, who had graduated from Selwyn College, Cambridge, in 1961, was a Conservative MP and minister. A member of the General Synod of the Church of England 1979–92, he converted to Catholicism in 1993. He was a contributor to the essays in *To Church with Enthusiasm* (1969) and author of *Christianity and Conservatism* (1990).

Assembly in Edinburgh.[1] Perhaps we are in for a religious revival, with born-again Christians dominating (as in the Bible-belt of America) prime time on television.

We are going to Colorado on 19 June, for three weeks. I go with reluctance, solely in order to keep the wolf from the door. It will be very dull. Will you be in London before that date? Anyway, if you have time, write to me: in my present state I need to be cheered up. And if you have read any good books (do you have time to read *any* books?), please tell me. I want to take something to read, or re-read, in Colorado. Something substantial, but portable, and written in exquisite prose. Not *Don Quixote*, that incomparable, inexhaustible book—the only book, Dr Johnson said, that we wish were longer:[2] I have re-read it too recently. Doughty's *Arabia Deserta* and George Moore's *Hail and Farewell*, two marvellous works of antipodean difference of style, are alas too bulky to carry. Perhaps I shall re-read Boswell's *Johnson*, or *The Golden Bough* (the original version, before it was swollen to intolerable length), or *The Brothers Karamazov*. Or perhaps even something *new*: is there any great work of literature or perfectly written work of scholarship that you will recommend?

yours ever

Hugh

---

## To Edward Chaney, 26 June 1988

College Inn Conference Center, 1729 Athens Street, Boulder

Dear Edward

Sitting in Boulder, Colorado, condemned to eat waffles for 'brunch', my imagination transports me to Vallombrosa, where you sit in the

---

[1]   Catford provided much of the content of her address, which was delivered on 21 May 1988.

[2]   According to Mrs Piozzi, Johnson once asked, 'Was there ever yet anything written by mere man that was wished longer by its readers, excepting *Don Quixote, Robinson Crusoe*, and *The Pilgrim's Progress*?'

overarching, embowering shade of those great beech-groves[1], sipping the wine of Orvieto and discussing, with a scholarly *élite*, the delights of literature. I brought with me your unfinished paper, which I have read and re-read, and greatly enjoyed.[2] On Milton's visit to Vallombrosa you speak to the converted. I save myself a lot of trouble on controversial questions by a simple formula: I ask, on whom lies the burden of proof? Did Milton visit Galileo? Possibly, and possibly not; but since he says that he did, that must be allowed to be evidence; the burden of proof is on those who deny it, and till they produce better evidence than that of the grotesque and paranoid Swede Liljegren, the balance of evidence is in favour of the visit.[3] Did he visit Vallombrosa? He never claimed to have done so; there is no contemporary evidence that he did; so the burden of proof is on those who maintain that he did. Till they produce it, the balance is against them and I shall happily—after reading your learned paper (what a lot you have read!) even more happily—regard the visit as a fantasy.

Your examination of Milton's Catholic contacts is fascinating and I was delighted by it, and frustrated by its incompleteness, and the missing footnotes. What a mysterious person Milton is! Why do you think he made that sudden attack in *Lycidas*?[4] Remove it, and (with your evidence) he appears almost as a papist. But it can't be removed. He must have suffered from a sudden attack of the spleen just as he was writing that poem.

---

[1]   An allusion to *Paradise Lost* I.301–4 where Satan's legions 'lay entranced | Thick as autumnal leaves that strew the brooks | In Vallombrosa, where the Etrurian shades | High over-arched embower'. The vividness of this description has led scholars to suppose that Milton visited Vallombrosa.

[2]   This paper became chapter 12, 'Milton's Visit to Vallombrosa: A Literary Tradition', in Chaney's book *The Evolution of the Grand Tour: Anglo-Italian Cultural Relations since the Renaissance* (1998). At the time of this letter Chaney was attending an international Milton conference held in Vallombrosa: he gave a paper which caused indignation among American Miltonists by denying Milton's visit to Vallombrosa and emphasizing his Catholic connections.

[3]   Sten Bodvar Liljegren (1885–1984), author of *Studies in Milton* (1918), was Professor of English Philology at the University of Greifswald 1926–39, and later at the University of Uppsala.

[4]   Milton in lines 113–31 of *Lycidas* (1637) assails the condition of the Church in the reign of Charles I: 'The hungry Sheep look up, and are not fed, | But swoln with wind, and the rank mist they draw, | Rot inwardly, and foul contagion spread: | Besides what the grim Woolf with privy paw | Daily devours apace.' T-R returns to this and other themes discussed here in his essay on 'Milton in Politics', published in *Catholics, Anglicans and Puritans*.

Perhaps the image of Dr Chappell[1] floated before his imagination, or he remembered Christ's College and some rankling impertinence by a mere serving man there. Anyway, we must admit that his retrospective cover-up has been very effective. I long to read your paper in full.

Why did Milton so detest France and the French? Did he detest them before going to Paris? Perhaps the French *literati* didn't pay enough attention to him. Long ago, after mobilising the Master of the Rolls,[2] I discovered the Scudamore Mss, which had been locked up in consequence of a Chancery case in 1830 (I think). See *Archbishop Laud*, 1940 (appendix). I had no time to read all the papers in that dust-covered chest, and I have often wondered if Lord Scudamore made any reference to Milton when he turned up in Paris with a letter from Sir H. Wotton. The Mss are now available to anyone at the PRO.

To return to Milton. You say that his morality, in his grand-touring days, was 'flexible enough'. I wonder what you mean. Even allowing for his retrospective self-idealisation, I had thought that the balance of evidence was in favour of his austere morality. But perhaps, like Dr Chappell, you know some dark secret. Heinsius, I think, explicitly denied the report that Milton had 'sold his buttocks to the Italians'.[3] But I suppose it depends on the degree of 'loose-living' that you ascribe to Codner/Salvaggi.[4]

I like to imagine the conversation at Fr. Fitzherbert's hospitable table.[5] How unfortunate that no Boswell recorded it. Perhaps we should write an imaginary account of it, in the name of Henry Holden, or Patrick Cary, or

---

[1]    William Chappell (1582–1649), whom John Aubrey claimed had whipped Milton when he was the youth's tutor at Christ's College, Cambridge; Provost of Trinity College, Dublin, 1634–40, and Bishop of Cork from 1638.

[2]    Wilfrid, 1st Baron Greene (1883–1952), Master of the Rolls 1937–49.

[3]    In a letter of 1653 Nikolaas Heinsius (1620–81), Dutch bibliophile, philologist, classicist, and traveller, refuted this allegation levelled by Milton's literary adversary Claude de Saumaise (Salmasius).

[4]    Chaney argued that the Benedictine David Codner, *alias* Selvaggio, was the 'Selvaggi' who wrote a complimentary couplet to Milton, which Milton included in the collection of his own poems in 1645.

[5]    Father Thomas Fitzherbert (1552–1640), the Jesuit rector of the English college in Rome 1618–39, entertained Milton, Holden, Cary, and Fortescue at a dinner in the college in 1638, as described in Chaney's book and cited in *Catholics, Anglicans and Puritans*.

Sir N. Fortescue,[1] and slip it into some appropriate archive, in order to dis-concert the Miltonists and keep up the trade in D.Phils. But we had better not mention, as you do, the port: an anachronism that may well get you into trouble with the enraged and vengeful Dr Krapp/Adams[2]—whom, I must admit, I regard as hardly worth the honour of your kindly (to me) footnote. How absurd to say that Milton the politician is not worth powder and shot when Krapp/Adams' fellow Stalinist Christopher Hill has recently published a large book insisting that the poet was a polit-ician to his finger-tips. (I have learned from an American friend who shared lodgings with him as a graduate student that K/A was one of Sta-lin's 'useful idiots' and tried to recruit him for the cause). All the same, many thanks for the dewdrop in that note. I don't know *quite* what you mean by 'Johnsonian', but as I regard Johnson as the greatest of English prose-writers, I naturally purr with pleasure.

We are not *greatly* enjoying our visit to Boulder. It is a dull place which makes Didcot seem exciting. Xandra, who made me come here so that she would not have to cook (she *hates* cooking!) is finding that advantage somewhat offset by the necessity to be up for breakfast at 7.0 a.m. I am dutifully lecturing to people whose political views would please you—*far* to the right of Dr Scruton but whose intellectual level is discouragingly low. But needs must when the Devil drives. Could you not fix up a little job for me in (say) Lecce or Naples or Florence? Then I would scrap Boulder. We had a dreadful journey out: our plane had to return *twice* to London through mechanical failure: dreadful noises and the shadow of the plane against a cloud showed its innards hanging out. In the end we had to spend the night at Heathrow and come out on another plane next day. I understand from our American hosts that American air-lines have all been taken over by predatory entrepreneurs who are cutting costs by

---

[1]   Henry Holden (1596–1662) was a Catholic priest and theologian; Patrick Cary (c.1624–57), brother of Lord Falkland, was a Catholic exile and poet; the Catholic royalist Sir Nicholas Fortescue (c.1605–44) was mortally wounded at the battle of Marston Moor.

[2]   Robert M. Adams, né Krapp (1915–96), American editor, anthologist, and translator of Voltaire, Stendhal, and Machiavelli; author of *Ikon: John Milton and the Modern Critics* (1955).

keeping them in service till they disintegrate in mid-air. If we survive such hazards, we shall be back on 10 July and I hope we shall meet. (I shall probably now *bring* this letter with me and post it at Didcot: it has now been hanging about as I desperately mug up or write down my lectures).

yours ever<br>Hugh

———⊶⊷———

## To Alasdair Palmer, 14 August 1988

The Old Rectory, Didcot

Dear Alasdair

I am glad to hear that you are married and hope that you will be very happy. Marriage, says my oracle, Dr Johnson, has many trials, but celibacy has few pleasures; and the few pleasures indulged by the celibate Fellows of Peterhouse do not encourage me to wish that any friend of mine should be condemned to share them. So I send you—belatedly as always—my congratulations and best wishes.

Of course, as a sound Anglican and a Doctor of Divinity, I deplore your resort to the Registry Office. Unless there are undisclosed and overpowering other reasons, I have to assume, what I understand you to intend me to assume, that you took this curious step for *theological* reasons, because you had *doubts* (or perhaps even more than doubts) about the identity and nature of your Creator. What an absurd scruple! You are the first person I have heard of, since cardinal Newman, to take any vital step in life on such grounds. Surely the whole point of having an Established Church is that we pay our clergy to believe doctrines which we cannot believe ourselves (and indeed why should we? It was they, not we, who invented them), just as we pay the electrician to mend a fault in the wiring which, if we meddled with it ourselves, might well give us a fatal shock. On this convenient basis we then call on the Church to provide a dignified ceremony on special occasions, useful *rites de passage*, and a loose, elastic, metaphysical envelope within which we can insert our view of morality and our ideas (if any) about the economy of the universe.

I have never set foot in a Registry Office, so I don't know what it was like, but I have attended an atheist funeral, and a pretty grim experience it was. It was the funeral of Theodore Besterman, an earnest atheist if ever there was one (he always wrote God with a lower-case g and made this correction in the writings of his contributors to *Voltaire Studies* etc.)[1] I was his executor, so I had to go. We stood silently round the coffin in the crematorium. No clergyman, no music, no articulate sound. Then suddenly the floor gaped and hey presto! the coffin sank out of sight. Whereupon we trooped silently away. I hope that my DD will at least save my corpse from such an undignified disposal: like waste going down the sink.

I am very sorry to hear of your *two* burglaries. It is a horrible experience to come back and find all one's possessions scattered higgledy-piggledy by profane hands, and not even to know what has been taken. We were burgled at Peterhouse once, while we were in Scotland, and had to motor down to deal with the consequences. I hope you did not lose anything of great value to you.

You tell me of some of your experiences with the media. Let me tell you some of mine.

---

[1]  T-R was intrigued by Theodore Besterman (1904–76), whom he thought 'a mystery man', as well as 'a great scholar and patron of scholarship'. Besterman had been born in Poland (the son of a diamond dealer), but by 1925 was chairman of the British Federation of Youth Movements. Between 1927 and 1935 he was the investigating officer to the Society for Psychical Research; his criticism of a book on an Italian medium caused Arthur Conan Doyle's resignation from the Society. The first edition of his great *World Bibliography of Bibliographies* was published in 1939. Besterman was an undiplomatic departmental head at post-war UNESCO. In the 1950s he began collecting, translating, and publishing Voltaire's writings, including much unpublished correspondence. He leased Voltaire's house in Geneva, where he founded the Institut et Musée Voltaire, and published 107 volumes of Voltaire's letters. T-R contributed to his journal *Studies on Voltaire and the Eighteenth Century*. After dining with Besterman at the Paris Ritz in 1963, he reported to his stepson: 'I found him a sort of English guardee officer, both in looks and voice and manner…and then, with an effort, I had to remind myself that he is really a wonderful scholar, far superior to me.' T-R continued, 'I suspect he is illegitimate and half-caste; nobody seems to know the source of his great wealth. He reminds me, both by his ostentation and by his reticences, of Lord Cherwell.' Besterman bequeathed his books and manuscripts to Oxford University.

Recently I was conned into taking part in a programme produced by N.B.C.[1] I didn't want to do it at all but was pushed into it by the Oxford University Press which has just re-printed *Hitler's Table Talk*, with a preface which I wrote for it when first published 35 years ago. (As I had sold the copyright in my preface outright to George Weidenfeld, the original publisher, I had no financial interest in it and was really rather cross at being pushed into this stunt to advertise the book for the Press, which had not even given me the chance to revise my preface in the light of intervening evidence; but as it was the Oxford Press I yielded). Well, I went up to London—the programme was at *midnight*—prepared for rational discussion of the subject. But what did I find? It was a 'phone-in' programme. The man in charge of it was a moron: he referred—in the programme— to Hitler's early days in Vienna 'in the 1920s'. The programme was regularly interrupted by vulgar interludes, and the questions which were put to me (as one might imagine from the sort of people who would listen to that sort of programme) were mindless and lowering—mainly about Hitler's sex-life. And the Oxford University Press had obtained this programme, and coerced me to take part in it, in order to advertise a serious work! It is experiences like this—of which I have had several (mainly with independent television companies)—which make me despair of the media and look back with regret to that self-important old Scotch megalomaniac Lord Reith.[2]

I felt the same when Rupert Murdoch took me round the printing works at Wapping.[3] All that technology was wonderful, all that energy so admirable, and then, in the last room, I saw the finished product of this

---

[1]  The National Broadcasting Company (USA).

[2]  John Reith, 1st Baron Reith (1889–1971), Director-General of the BBC 1926–38, whose diaries Charles Stuart had edited for publication. T-R wrote to Stuart (20 September 1975): 'I believe that he read engineering. Surely this is a perfect example...of the happy combination of the sanctimony of the Manse with the mechanical rigidity of the engineer.'

[3]  Printing of *The Times, Sunday Times, Sun*, and *News of the World* was transferred in 1985–6 to News International's new premises at Wapping, where new electronic systems enabling journalists to input their copy directly were installed. The labour-intensive, hot-metal linotype printing processes were rendered obsolete: so, too, were the Fleet Street printers, with their exploitative, disruptive shop stewards (called 'Fathers of Chapel').

miraculous process pouring out: infinite copies of *The Sun*. And it is for this, I reflected, for this systematic cretinisation of our people, that whole rain-forests are being consumed, the world of irreplaceable Nature—of exquisite birds and exotic butterflies—turned to pulp...

I hope that the programmes that you are producing are of a different kind and that your natural virtue—for in spite of everything I still believe in natural virtue—and your expensive education will save you from sliding into satisfied subservience to that degrading system!

I am less surprised than you are by the insistence of that grand French official on speaking French with you. The French are cultural imperialists and deeply resent the eclipse of their language, the language of civilisation, by the inferior English tongue. So it is a matter of policy for French officials to make no concessions. When I was in Israel some years ago I was told how the French historian Robert Mandrou came to give a lecture in Jerusalem.[1] In Israel the educated classes all know English but no one knows French. Mandrou can speak English perfectly well. But he refused to lecture in English: *'un français'*, he said portentously, *'en mission culturelle à l'étranger, ne parle jamais que le français'*.[2] So the lecture had to be delayed while interpreters were found, and then itself held up while sentence after sentence was translated, rather than sacrifice that important principle.

I would love to see you, but this is a bad time for me to come to London—House of Lords in recess, clubs closed, general suspense of life; and Xandra doesn't like being left alone. In a week's time we are going to Bayreuth. I have never been there and am not, in general, a lover of Wagner. But every five years I make the effort, recognising that, like Carlyle and Victor Hugo and others, though a monster, he was also a man of genius; and art and learning should not be judged by the personality of the author, nor (what with Wagner is particularly relevant) by the practical

---

[1]   Robert Mandrou (1921–84), one of the *Annales* School, co-author with Georges Dubuy of *Histoire de la civilisation française* (1958) and author of a study of medieval superstition, *Magistrats et sorciers en France en XVII siècles* (1968).

[2]   'A Frenchman, on a cultural mission abroad, speaks nothing but French.'

consequences later drawn from them, or fathered on him. Also we went to *Parzifal* in London recently and I actually enjoyed it. Whether I shall enjoy the whole *Ring*, in what seems a poor production, and on what I am assured are very hard seats, I am uncertain, indeed doubtful. We shall be back in September. Will you still be coming to London then? Have you a telephone number in Stockport? If I go to London it is often at rather short notice, and the post is so slow.

Does your life as an expert on every topical subject leave you leisure to read any books? Michael Bloch has just sent me his book *The Secret File of the Duke of Windsor*.[1] It is a fascinating but horrible story. I now see that there is a good deal to be said for a Republic. I fear that in my old age I am becoming very radical. After Peterhouse I doubt the value of the college system, and after Bloch of the monarchical system; but I must overcome these doubts. Indeed, by going to Oxford occasionally, I am gradually prevailing over the former, and no doubt attention to the Presidential Election in America will gradually cure me of the latter.

Although I do little to deserve them, I enjoy your letters greatly. I hope I shall receive more of them and hear more of your experiences in that horrible world (you see how *deeply* prejudiced I am on the subject; but I have suffered much from the media). And I hope that, when I come back from Bayreuth, we can meet in London.

yours ever
Hugh

———∞———

[1]   Michael Bloch (b. 1953), barrister, employed by Maître Suzanne Blum, lawyer of the Duke and Duchess of Windsor, to write books advocating their views on the Abdication and its sequel. *The Secret File of the Duke of Windsor*, describing the ex-king's bitter relations with the court, had been published in July. T-R had praised Bloch's *Operation Willi* (1984) in a *Sunday Times* review, and contributed a preface to Bloch's biography of Ribbentrop (1992).

# To Noël Annan, 20 October 1988

House of Lords

My dear Noël

You flatter me too much, but I love it (as who does not?) and lap it up. Many thanks for that offering—butter in a lordly dish (and the *best* butter, too)! But what have you seen in the *FAZ*?[1] The context into which you casually throw this fragment of omniscience suggests that it was something on 1688; and it is indeed true that I have written something on that subject for that paper. But has it appeared? Or are you referring to the *Werkbesichtigung* which *has* appeared (on 14 Sept)?[2] If my article on 1688 has been published, you will have noticed, I am sure, that I have referred, in suitably arcane language, to J. C. D. Clark. My general policy is never to *name* him if I can avoid doing so, for to name is to advertise (as Alan Taylor once put it, 'All publicity is good publicity'—adding, *exempli gratia*, 'I would rather be mentioned as A. J. P. Taylor the notorious sexual pervert than not be mentioned at all').

Please let me know when you appear in the *Independent*, which I only see when I am in London or Oxford: here in Didcot (which is not a very literary town) my reading is limited.

Though I am forced to admire your world-wide intelligence system, I am slightly chagrined to find that it extends to the *F.A.Z.*, for I have agreed to write another piece for them—one which I had hoped thereby would escape your eagle eye; for you will not approve of it.[3] But I now see that that hope is vain. Clearly, if I am to hide from you, I must find a more

---

[1]  T-R is referring to his articles for *Frankfurter Allgemeine Zeitung*. His article on 1688, 'Umstrittenes Erbe, Kontroversen um Englands Revolution', was published there on 2 November 1988.

[2]  In *Frankfurter Allgemeine Zeitung*, 14 September 1988: 'Trevor-Roper über Trevor-Roper: Werksbesichtigung XI, Hitlers letzte Tage: Rückblick auf Recherchen der ersten Stunde'; reprinted in Henning Ritter (ed.), *Werksbesichtigung Geisteswissenschaften* (1990).

[3]  Probably the piece comparing Oxford to Cambridge, to the former's advantage, which was published in *Frankfurter Allgemeine Zeitung* on 25 March 1989.

esoteric vehicle for my questionable writings. I did once write for an Icelandic paper—a very arcane paper, published not in cosmopolitan Reykjavik but in provincial Akureyri, on the Arctic sea. Unfortunately that vent is now closed. The editor (with whom I used to go fishing for salmon on two noble rivers in that country) suffered from the common infirmity of Scandinavia (cf. Strindberg, Ibsen, Kierkegaard, *et. al.*), *viz:* manic depression, berserk rages, Viking bravado, and seasonal lunacy, and flung himself through the plate-glass window of a high-rise hotel in Stockholm. So whither shall I now turn to escape your panoptic eye? Do you read Hungarian?

I am glad to learn that my BBC programme, *Desert Island Discs*, gets some favourable comment in your cultured circles.[1] The only comment in Didcot came from my dentist. 'I heard you on the radio', he said, when he had rendered my mouth totally incapable of reply: 'I didn't think much of your choice of records'. Some time later, when he allowed me to rinse, I ventured to say, 'what records would *you* have chosen?' 'Oh, I don't know', he replied; and then, after deep thought, 'perhaps a few nursery rhymes for the children'. I also had a fan letter from a lady in Blackburn, *Auslanddeutsche*[2] by origin, who expressed a great desire for an exchange of views on Germany. Not waiting for my agreement to this proposal, she gave me the benefit of her own views, which were, that Hitler was a very good thing; that we—the British—made a great mistake in stopping him; that his policy was 'wholesome and healthy'; that 'above all he was a great *German* leader'; and that all Germans approved of him except 'the upper classes and people with connexions (JEWS!!) [sic]'—and some others who didn't count because they were in concentration camps. Xandra, who, like you and Isaiah, had appeared on the more Olympian programme

---

[1]   The programme was broadcast on 21 August 1988. The favourite work of music allowed him as a castaway was Maurice Ravel's 'Pavane pour une infante défunte'. His other choices were Mozart's Piano Concerto no. 27 in B flat major and his 'Traurigkeit' from *Die Entführung aus dem Serail*; 'Ombra mai fu' from Handel's *Xerxes*; J. S. Bach's 'Sheep may safely graze' (from Cantata no., 208); Wagner's *Siegfried Idyll*; Bartók's Concerto for Orchestra; and Beethoven's 'Pastoral' Symphony. He chose the collected works of Virgil as the book he would take to his desert island. His luxury was paper, pen, and ink.

[2]   Ethnic German.

as 'Woman of Action',[1] told me that 'Desert Island Discs' was 'a down-market version' of that programme, although she charitably, if condescendingly, added that perhaps they were trying to improve it by bringing me in. Any euphoria induced by this somewhat qualified commendation was soon corrected: my successor, I discovered, was one 'Dame Edna Everidge', who, I understand, is a male clown who appears in drag for the diversion of the vulgar.[2]

You mention Chris Andrew.[3] I think highly of him. Indeed, as you may recall (for you were there) I gave him a puff in the House of Lords:[4] a puff which was later taken up and cited, in the same chamber, by the Lord Jenkins of Putney.[5] So he has received lordly bouquets from right and left. But alas, what is the value of such tributes? You were there, and were heard (sensible as always), when that ass Frank Longford paid a similar (though less rational) tribute to J. C. D. Clark![6]

Incidentally I was not there on the last day of the last session when you discussed the proposed amendment of section 2 of the Official Secrets

[1] When the first letter of invitation reached Xandra, stating that as she was a woman the programme would be called 'Woman of Action', the T-Rs assumed that it was a spoof, and she did not reply.

[2] The catchphrase of the Australian Dame Edna Everage—*alter ego* of Barry Humphries (b. 1934)—was 'Hello Possums!' T-R did not know that Humphries is a discriminating bibliophile.

[3] Christopher Andrew (b. 1941), Fellow of Corpus Christi College, Cambridge, from 1967, Professor of Modern and Contemporary History at Cambridge 1993–2008, official historian of MI5, and a specialist in the history of intelligence.

[4] T-R had made one of his few House of Lords speeches in the debate (17 December 1986) on the accountability of the Security Services. He praised Andrew's *Secret Service: The Making of the British Intelligence Community* (1985) and the journal *Intelligence and National Security* (which Andrew co-edited) for their historical value and for providing 'psychological therapy for bringing the intelligence community out of the closed mentality from which the recent traumas have grown'.

[5] Hugh Jenkins, Baron Jenkins of Putney (1908–2004), campaigner for nuclear disarmament, Labour politician, and Minister for the Arts 1974–6. He had initiated the Lords debate on Secret Service accountability after the Thatcher government's failed attempt to suppress Peter Wright's paranoid memoir *Spycatcher*.

[6] During a discussion of the exhibition to mark the tercentenary of the Revolution of 1688 in the Banqueting House at Whitehall, Longford extolled 'an admirable article in the *Sunday Times* yesterday written by a brilliant academic, Mr Clark, in which the claims made on behalf of the so-called Glorious Revolution are revealed as a total nonsense'. T-R's opinion of Clark was influenced by Clark's 'revisionist' assaults on whiggish accounts of English history, especially of the 18th century.

Act. I wish I had been. But I read the debate in Hansard. Your reply to Lord Hatch of Lusby was *splendid!*[1]

I enjoyed Bayreuth (and also Coburg, which we visited). What a *monster* Wagner was! And yet how can one withhold a grudging tribute to the old egotist who persuaded King Ludwig and others to pay for the erection of a *huge* opera-house (holding 9000 persons) & designed by himself, for the sole and exclusive purpose of performing his own works in perpetuity— and has been proved right 100 years after his death? The production was *dreadful* (Bernard Levin was quite right on that[2]). I am glad to say that the East German producer[3] was booed, louder and ever louder, whenever he appeared. In the end he prudently did not appear at all. Even so, some of the music is wonderful.

I hope to see you very soon.

yours ever

Hugh

———— ✗ ————

*After he left Cambridge, Trevor-Roper corresponded with Max Perutz (1914–2002), who had been an Honorary Fellow of Peterhouse since 1962. Perutz was Director of the Medical Research Council Unit for Molecular Biology from 1947 to 1962 and Chairman of the Medical Research Council Laboratory of Molecular Biology from 1962 to 1979. By the time of his death the laboratory counted 13 Nobel prizewinners among its former staff, including Fred Sanger who had won twice. Perutz was himself awarded a Nobel Prize in 1962, and was*

[1]  On 29 July 1988, in a debate on reform of the Official Secrets Act, Annan complained of Hatch, 'month in and month out for two years he went banging on about the "Belgrano", attempting to cover the Prime Minister with slime', and added, 'in a military engagement the lives of our mariners and soldiers are far more important than his own degree of self-righteousness'.

[2]  Bernard Levin, 'Wagner, Twaddle and Mustard', *The Times*, 3 September 1988, complained of 'galumphingly obvious sexual symbolism in Harry Kupfer's production', although he liked the use of lasers, gantries, and catwalks. He was less impressed by gods traipsing around with transparent, empty suitcases, Siegfried and Brünnhilde living in a coal cellar, and the Norns spinning their rope among a forest of television aerials planted outside a multi-storey car park.

[3]  Harry Kupfer (b. 1935): 'a wretchedly limited man', but 'ingenious', according to Levin's account.

*nominated as a Companion of Honour in 1975 and to the Order of Merit in 1988. Like his colleague Aaron Klug, Perutz was an erudite man with a wide range of cultural, historical, and political interests. As an active book reviewer, Perutz brought to bear his enviable general knowledge, his thorough investigative habits, and his defence of science from its detractors. Many of his book reviews were reprinted in two collections, Is Science Necessary? (1989) and I Wish I'd Made You Angry Earlier (1998).*

*Neil Plevy, the Development Director at Peterhouse, brought Perutz and Trevor-Roper together in a tape-recorded discussion to compare their experiences of life. Perutz was four months younger than Trevor-Roper and died a year before him. He had been born into an assimilated Jewish family in Vienna and had come to Cambridge to carry out research work in the mid-1930s. During the war he had suffered the indignity of being interned as an enemy alien, before he was brought back to Cambridge, where he continued his research in the Cavendish Laboratory. Modest, polite, and generous, Perutz was the quintessential laboratory scientist, who remained an active experimentalist almost until the end of his life.*

## To Max Perutz, 7 January 1989

The Old Rectory, Didcot

Dear Max

Many thanks for sending me *I Cani di Gerusalemme*.[1] I have read it, and enjoyed it; but I have to admit—since you ask for my opinion—that, in the end, I found it disappointing. It starts with a happy idea, but then makes so little of it. Perhaps the fault is mine: I have missed some profound allegorical significance, or some deep philosophical content.

The parallel (as far as the machinery goes) with *Don Quixote* is dangerously close: dangerously because, being so close, it challenges comparison. Don Quixote is an eccentric *hidalgo*; he goes out with a simple peasant from his village as his attendant, and with his horse Rocinante; he leaves, in his village, his niece and the curate, who together deplore his follies. Nicomede is an eccentric baron; he goes out with a simple peasant from his castle as his attendant, and with his mule; he leaves, in his castle,

---

[1]    A novel by the Italian film director Fabio Carpi (b. 1925).

his sister and the priest, who together deplore his follies. The parallel is very exact. And both books, in different ways, are satirical 'romances of chivalry'—though the Italian book is on a different scale and in reverse: Nicomede is a mini-Quixote through the looking-glass. However, having challenged comparison, how does Nicomede compare with Quixote? The fascination of *Don Quixote*, to me, is at several levels. There is the rich context, the real Spain of the 16th century in which these absurd adventures take place. There are the marvellous conversations between Don Quixote and Sancho—the grave, magniloquent fantasies of the one, the stolid proverbs of the other; the emergence of character; the alternation of tragedy and farce. Even Rocinante has a character; and of course there are other characters too. But how jejune, in comparison, is the furniture of Nicomede: a shed, a tree, an occasional bird; how thin and banal the conversations; and where is the touch of fantasy apart from the initial idea, which could have been taken from Albert Speer's *Spandauer Tage-bücher*[1]– not a very imaginative source? When I began the book I liked the idea and thought that there was going to be some philosophy in it—like the philosophical subtlety of Lewis Carroll; but if there was, I didn't find it. Have I been very obtuse?

*Basta scambiare le parole con le cose, il reale con l'immaginario*,[2] says the summary on the cover; but apart from the original idea, there is not much imagination. The port of Taranto, the walls of Nicaea, the 360 towers of Antioch...but they are walls and towers of rather thin paper, I say to myself, and then I think of Don Quixote's splendid account of the two armies which he sees about to do battle in the mountains, and which are really two flocks of trans-humant sheep (Part I chapter xviii). Every time that I read that chapter, I laugh aloud at it: at the wild, grandiloquent fancies and the instant rationalisations which make all those fancies coherent within an imaginary world-picture created by those 'romances of chivalry'; and I am reminded of that wonderful book by Edward Evans-Pritchard, *Witchcraft*

---

[1]    German edition 1975; published in English as *Spandau: The Secret Diaries* (1976).
[2]    'It's enough to swap words with objects, the real with the imaginary.'

*among the Azande* which shows the same coherent rationalisation within a different imaginary world, reminding us that we too are prisoners of our world-picture and that our reasoning operates within it and cannot, by itself, break through it, or out of it.

Looking through your earlier letters, I feel ashamed at my lack of response. I go through periods when I find it very difficult to write.[1] Let me now try to answer some of the questions which you, perhaps, have now forgotten that you asked.

In one of your letters you ask how it was that British Intelligence, in 1945, was able to track down wanted persons so easily. I evolved my own method, which was really very simple. I asked myself what I would have done if the Germans had occupied Britain in 1940 and I had been thought worth hunting. I decided that I would have gone to my home in Northumberland and lain low there, because there I could lie low and could, thanks to friends, survive without a ration card. So when the boot was on the other leg, I assumed that Germans would do the same. Therefore, when I decided that I wanted to find any particular person, I always made enquiries about his home or village. (At the same time I circulated his name to all Allied Prisoner-of-War camps: the British and Americans kept records and answered promptly; the French and Russians *never* answered). If necessary I went there myself. The local burgomasters were required to register all inhabitants. So if the wanted person was living under his own name, it was easy. Johannmeyer, about whom you asked, was living under his own name. I had more trouble with those who were living under false names; but in the end I generally found them. Defeated Nazi Germany was full of rancour and enmities and I could generally find someone who had a score to pay off!

You told me about Kendrew and his interest in the pictures at Peterhouse.[2] It was clear to me, when I went through the files—unfortunately too near the end of my mastership—that he had taken a lot of trouble, but

---

[1]  Perhaps because of his near-blindness; perhaps because of low spirits.
[2]  Sir John Kendrew (1917–97), molecular biologist, Fellow of Peterhouse 1947–75 and President of St John's College, Oxford, 1981–7.

that when he left, an era of neglect set in. However I think things are better now, Philip Pattenden[1] having taken over the enquiry and Richard Skaer[2] put in charge of the pictures. Before I left, we discovered some fragments of stained glass lying under a bedstead in the cellar of the William Stone Building. Skaer discovered them when acting as college auditor and informed me. I went and saw them with Pattenden, and we decided that they were the remains of a window of the chapel, smashed by the Puritans in 1644.[3] We decided that the window represented Christ washing the feet of St Peter; and from this we deduced that the original windows (replaced with plain glass in 1644 and then with the present German windows in the 19th century) had represented—naturally enough—scenes from the life of St Peter. Since I left, Pattenden has had the window (now agreed to be by van Linge, who also worked in Oxford and made the windows in Christ Church) restored and set up in the Lubbock Room in the Library Building.[4] Have you seen it? It has been very well done, but Pattenden told me, when I went to see it, that none of the Fellows had made any comment on it. I have urged him to have it photographed and an account printed in the *Peterhouse Record*.[5] Perhaps the old members will be more appreciative.

You asked me about Simon Schama's book.[6] I have not read it. I can't read Schama. I admit to prejudice. I tried to read his previous book[7] on the Netherlands in the 18th century, but soon foundered in it. I don't like *displays* of erudition!

[1]  Philip Pattenden (b. 1950), Classics Fellow of Peterhouse since 1976.
[2]  Richard Skaer (b. 1936), Fellow of Peterhouse and Tutor in Biology 1961–2004.
[3]  The parliamentary commission to demolish monuments of superstition in Cambridge, led by William Dowsing, got to work in Peterhouse in December 1643.
[4]  During the 1630s the Dutchman Abraham van Linge (fl. 1625–41) painted beautiful windows in Christ Church which were smashed by the Puritans. Some of his work survives there.
[5]  An article by David Watkin in the *Peterhouse Annual Record* for 1998–9 mentions the stained glass, though without identifying the subject as the washing of Peter's feet.
[6]  Simon Schama (b. 1945), who then held a Harvard history chair. Perutz had mentioned in a letter dated 11 November 1988 that his daughter had been reading and enjoying Schama's *The Embarrassment of Riches: An Interpretation of Dutch Culture in the Golden Age* (1987), and had asked him if he knew Schama.
[7]  *Patriots and Liberators: Revolution in the Netherlands 1780–1813* (1977).

You also asked about Bacon: should you read the *Novum Organon*? Well, yes, if you have time; but Bacon wrote such beautiful English (and repeated his ideas in so many forms) that I would recommend rather *The Advancement of Learning*, being the embryo from which the rest of his philosophical works grew, and *The New Atlantis*, which is his last work, published posthumously, and is his testamentary utopia, the embryo of the Royal Society.

We miss Cambridge—Xandra especially, who had many friends there and was very active in the musical world. She is going back for a weekend at the end of January to go to the opera, of which she is Patron. I shall be coming up to talk to the undergraduates at Caius on 6 Feb and shall probably take lunch in Peterhouse. I hope I may see you. Meanwhile, if Dutton or Barrie & Jenkins write to me, I shall do all I can to help your book, which I am sure needs no puff from me.[1]

All good wishes for 1989.

> yours ever
> Hugh

———❧———

*In a letter to Perutz of 7 December 1989, written a month after the breaching of the Berlin Wall, Trevor-Roper described the changes taking place in Europe as 'the most exciting and moving in a generation'. He wrote to Perutz again a fortnight later.*

---

[1] *Is Science Necessary? Essays on Science and Society* (1989). T-R picked it as one of his 'Books of the Year' in *The Telegraph*. Reviewing the book in *The Spectator*, T-R commented of Perutz: 'He makes the most difficult subjects intelligible and writes with the warmth, humanity, and broad culture which has always characterized the great men of science.'

## To Max Perutz, 23 December 1989

The Old Rectory, Didcot

Dear Max

How very kind of you to send me that record of Bach's cello suites. I have played them all and been greatly cheered by them. It was a charming thought, and I am very grateful. We have both had the epidemic 'flu pretty badly and still have not shaken off all the after-effects of it. I hope you will avoid it: it is very disagreeable. I was very sorry that it prevented me from going to Cambridge and seeing you there.

Henry Chadwick[1] has written to me that you have accepted the college's invitation to give the Dacre lecture on 14 March, and I have reserved that date so I can come and hear it. I have heard you lecture, and know that it will be good.[2]

Inspired by my little puff in the *Telegraph* and the *Spectator*, my stepson (who is a Byzantinist) is now reading *Is Science Necessary?* I am sure he will profit by it.

I have just written my last piece for the *Independent Magazine*, to appear on 30 Dec.[3] I have written it on the Revolutions of 1848, making the comparison with those of 1989. There is one consequence of the revolutions of 1848 upon which I have *not* dwelt but which lurks uneasily in the back

---

[1]   Henry Chadwick (1920–2008), Fellow and Chaplain of Queens' College, Cambridge, 1946–58, Regius Professor of Divinity at Oxford, and Canon of Christ Church 1959–69, was a scholar of massive erudition. He was Dean of Christ Church 1969–79 and would succeed T-R as Master of Peterhouse 1987–93, thus becoming the first person in four centuries to have headed a college at both universities. T-R considered him too malleable to be a head of house.

[2]   The subject of the lecture was 'Life with living molecules: an account of some of the crucial discoveries that led to the "biological revolution" of the present day.'

[3]   During 1989 T-R contributed 11 columns entitled 'Home Thoughts' to the Saturday magazine supplement of *The Independent*: 'The Legacy of Spycatcher' (27 May); 'The Myth of a Chinese Utopia' (3 June); 'On Salman Rushdie' (10 June); 'On German Reunification' (17 June); 'On Bad Language at Oxford' (24 June); 'German Facts and Fantasies' (25 November); 'On Christian Reunion' (2 December); 'The Peterhouse Effect' (9 December); 'Hitler's British Hit List' (16 December); 'History's Bloody Legacies' (23 December); and 'Europe's New Order' (30 December).

of my mind. In 1848 the Germans demanded, at first, *Einheit und Freiheit*.[1] Gradually they developed this into *Einheit, Freiheit und Macht*.[2] Sir Lewis Namier, who really understood Central and Eastern Europe—he was brought up as a Catholicised Polish-Jewish landlord in (Austrian) Galicia—pointed (in 1944) to the proto-nazi aspects of 1848 in Germany. I have remarked that 1848 was described—in 1916, by Friedrich Naumann[3] I think—as *Napoleonismus ohne Napoleon*.[4] 1989 *might* develop into *Hitlerismus ohne Hitler*.

At present we cling to the television screen to watch the dramatic but also horrible events in Romania: a country which I know quite well and in which I have friends. The overthrow of Ceausescu, if only it can be completed without further bloodshed, fitly crowns this extraordinary year.[5] But I don't suppose that it exercises the minds of the Peterhouse historians: things mortal move them not at all.[6] They live in their comfortable little mouse-holes squeaking quietly to themselves about the shocking advance of liberal theology in the 19th century. I am reminded of a passage in Mark Pattison's *Memoirs* in which he describes his emancipation from the similar preoccupations of Oxford Common Rooms in the 1840s: how, after 1845, all conversation centred on the conversions of Newman & co; but then came, 'in 1848, the universal outburst of revolution in every part of the Continent. It seemed incredible, in the presence of such an upheaval, that we had been spending years in debating any

---

[1] 'Unity and freedom'.

[2] 'Unity, freedom, and power'.

[3] Friedrich Naumann (1860–1919), a liberal imperialist member of the Reichstag who was first president of the German Democratic Party.

[4] Bonapartism without Bonaparte.

[5] On 21 December the henchmen of Nicolae Ceaușescu (President of Romania since 1965) dragooned his subjects into attending a mass rally in support of him. To his visible astonishment a riot against him erupted. On 22 December his army deserted him, and he was deposed, although bloody street fighting continued in Bucharest. He and his hated wife Elena were captured on 23 December (the day that this letter was written) and were executed by firing-squad on Christmas Day.

[6] In a letter to T-R of 25 November 1989, Perutz had described his elation at what was happening in Prague, but 'when I tried to convey my joy to some of the Fellows of Peterhouse I found that they could not have been less moved if last night's momentous events had taken place in Polynesia'.

matter so flimsy as whether England was in a state of schism or no'. *Plus ça change...*

All my Israeli friends express horror at the actions of their government against the Arabs;[1] but I suppose that, as so often, it depends what company one keeps. It seems to me that Israel is *driven*, by 'reason of state', to behave in the Middle East, politically, as Prussia behaved in Europe. I was last in Israel soon after the war of (?) 1968[2]—when Sinai, the Gaza strip and the West Bank were secured. I was taken to all the conquered areas and was deeply shocked by the aggressive chauvinism of the Israeli officials whom I met: they boasted, uninhibitedly, about their brutal methods of keeping the Arab population in awe. I recalled my experiences in Nazi Germany in 1935, after which I did not revisit Germany until 1945; and I have not wanted to revisit Israel since. I was also very struck by the defiant militarism of the national day celebrations in Jerusalem: a country the size of Wales advertising its armed strength in tanks, armoured cars, war-planes sufficient for a great power: a great *militarist* power.

You ask me about Arnold Goodman.[3] I know him well. He is a marvellous person, very public spirited, invariably kind and helpful. He has bad health and always looks ill, but he is always ready to help. I don't know what his views on Israel are: I have never discussed the subject with him. I suspect that, as an assimilated English Jew, he is anti-Zionist, but I don't know; and anyway one can only be anti-Zionist for oneself, not for others who could not be assimilated. We are dining with him on 28 Dec,

---

[1]  During 1989 the right-wing Likud party in Israel's coalition government had asserted its primacy in policies towards the Arabs. West Bank schools were closed by military order for many months, Jewish settlement of the West Bank continued, and two years after the start of the Palestinian uprising, over 600 Arabs had been killed by Israeli forces, and at least 150 more by Arab vigilantes who suspected them of collaboration with Israelis. Israel's government and public opinion settled into a pattern of violent attrition.

[2]  T-R probably means the Six Day War of June 1967.

[3]  Arnold Goodman, Baron Goodman (1913–95), was a solicitor whose firm specialized in media and libel law. He was Harold Wilson's indispensable adviser and abetter during his years of power, and an Establishment fixer of high influence until Thatcher came to power in 1979. He was chairman of the Arts Council 1965–72 and Master of University College, Oxford, 1976–86.

so if you wish me to explore any matter with him I will look for an opportunity.

I envy you your mobility, your visits to Germany and Austria: I wish I could visit Eastern Europe now.

All good wishes for 1990. When are you coming to Oxford?

yours ever

Hugh

---

## To Alasdair Palmer, 24 December 1989

The Old Rectory, Didcot

Dear Alasdair

You entertained me nobly at Duke's Hotel[1] and I should have written to thank you; but two days later, I was struck down by the epidemic 'flu, which in due course I gave to Xandra; we both had it badly, and are only now recovering from the after-effects. This has slowed everything up, and I am only now catching up with correspondence. But my memory of that day is still vivid: I greatly enjoyed seeing you again, and hope you will let me know when you are back in London and meanwhile write to me: I greatly enjoy your letters.

The debate, of which you heard the beginning, turned out to be quite interesting, though I didn't hear it all: there were 45 speakers and it went on till 11.30 p.m.[2] I would not previously have believed that an unintelligible point of theology could occupy so much legislative time. The essential question—for although some speakers tried to extend it to genetic manipulation in general, it was clear that this was not really an issue—was

---

[1]  Duke's Hotel in St James's Place serves expensive but good teas and cocktails.
[2]  The Human Fertilization and Embryology Bill was debated in the House of Lords on 14 December. The Duke of Norfolk and his fellow Catholic peers feared that it would liberalize existing abortion laws.

simply whether embryos in the first 14 days after conception have an identity (or soul) or not. The Archbishop of York,[1] who has a degree in natural science, thinks not. The Duke of Norfolk,[2] who of course is briefed on these delicate matters by the cardinal,[3] thinks yes. So (of course) did all the other RC peers who spoke: Perth,[4] Longford, Ryder,[5] Sidmouth,[6] and two naval officers who, for all I know, may be RCs too.[7] So did Lord Robertson of Oakridge,[8] son and grandson of generals: he is a low-church Protestant fundamentalist who believes that Jesus was conceived by the Holy Ghost. The cat was let out of the bag (as usual) by Lord Longford, who stated that he had been urged to speak by the Duke of Norfolk. I have no doubt that the other RCs had received the ducal whip too. The mystery man, to me, was Lord Kennet, alias Wayland Kennet, whom I had regarded as a man of sense, but who joined the RCs and the admirals and the generals. Perhaps he is RC too: I must investigate.[9]

One of the things that fascinates me in the House of Lords is that, whatever the subject of debate, and however abstruse and arcane the point

[1] John Habgood (b. 1927), Archbishop of York 1983–95, thereafter Lord Habgood.
[2] Miles Fitzalan-Howard, 17th Duke of Norfolk (1915–2002), had taken a third in history at Christ Church in 1937. Retired as Director of Service Intelligence at Ministry of Defence, with rank of major-general, 1967; became a merchant banker, specializing in Eurobonds and Eurodollars; England's leading Catholic layman.
[3] Cardinal Basil Hume (1923–99), Archbishop of Westminster since 1976.
[4] John Drummond, 17th Earl of Perth (1907–2002), an efficient, emollient Minister of State for Colonial Affairs 1957–62 during the thorny period after the Suez crisis; bibliophile, connoisseur, and devout Catholic.
[5] 'Don' Ryder, Lord Ryder of Eaton Hastings (1916–2003), a former financial journalist who was an industrial adviser to the Wilson government in the 1970s.
[6] John Addington, 7th Viscount Sidmouth (1914–2005), had lived with Ronald Knox in the Catholic chaplaincy while reading Greats at Brasenose. He attended Catholic mass every day, and said the rosary with his wife every evening. His Lords speeches were usually confined to the subjects of horticulture or railways. He had pioneered the supply of cut flowers to England from his Kenya nursery during the 1960s, and had 26 acres at Slough where he grew carnations and cucumbers under glass. As a former operating superintendent of the Kenya–Uganda railway, he was the only member of the Lords who was a qualified signal-box operator.
[7] He probably means John Godley, 3rd Baron Kilbracken (1920–2006), and Thomas Shaw, 3rd Baron Craigmyle (1923–98), a Catholic, who was concerned to ensure that 'a claimant who came into the world by modern hi-tech adultery, euphemistically called AID [artificial insemination by donor], would be refused a seat in the House of Lords'.
[8] William Robertson, 2nd Baron Robertson of Oakridge (1930–2009).
[9] Wayland Young, 2nd Baron Kennet (1923–2009), writer and politician. He was not a Catholic.

raised, there always seems to be, in the Chamber, the acknowledged expert on the subject. In the course of this debate, Lord Longford, as usual, wandered off the subject and dwelt on the moral problem of cannibalism, as when an airplane crashed in the Andes and the survivors of the crash managed to survive till they were rescued by eating those who had been killed in the crash. Whereupon it appeared that there was in the Chamber, in the person of Lord Shackleton (the son of the explorer and himself an Arctic and Antarctic explorer),[1] a peer who had actually been in the same situation: i.e. had been in a party which had had to decide whether they should survive by cannibalism, although in fact they were rescued before getting down to the meal. This suggests to me that our method of recruitment is better than that of the House of Commons: our net, cast more at random, brings in a wider variety of fishes. I doubt if there is a cannibal in the House of Commons.

On the other hand, when I consider how in fact we are recruited, I have to admit that the method is, to say the least, somewhat whimsical. A few weeks ago, I was in the Chamber when a new recruit took the oath.[2] He was a spry old gentleman of 84 who, after sixty years of legal and genealogical research, had proved to the satisfaction of the College of Arms that he was the only surviving direct descendant of any of the three aunts and co-heiresses of the late Lord Grey of Codnor, who died in 1496. So hey presto! He suddenly became a hereditary legislator, and incidentally jumped the queue of precedence, ahead of everyone, going back to 1299. I wonder if such things can happen after we have been rationalised in 1992.[3]

You are probably in America now, grilling the executives of Pan Am.[4] I look forward to hearing the results. You will have no time, I fear, under

---

[1]   Edward Shackleton, Baron Shackleton (1911–94), a former Labour cabinet minister.
[2]   Charles Cornwall-Legh, 5th Baron Grey of Codnor (1903–96), former chairman of Cheshire Police Authority.
[3]   The Labour Party was pledged to establish an elected upper chamber if it won the next general election (due in or before 1992).
[4]   Palmer was researching an ITV drama documentary (broadcast 26 November 1990) entitled 'Why Lockerbie?' about the destruction of Pan Am flight 103 by a Libyan bomb while flying above Dumfriesshire on 21 December 1988. The film depicted Pan Am's security failures, public relations cover-ups, and slackness.

these and the other ordinary pressures of life, to fill the surprising gaps in your reading of our literature—Dryden, the most robust of our poets, Halifax,[1] the most Attic of our observers of public life: between them, the types of our Augustan age. But to cling to literature is, I have found, a great resource in times of pressure. That is why I venerate the memory of Logan Pearsall Smith, who fed me with literature, and led me to new discoveries in it, in the dreariest and most depressing period of the war. But perhaps public affairs, with the crumbling of the corrupt despotisms of eastern Europe, are more exhilarating now, and the elevation and excitement of your daily life raises you above that spiritual need. Macaulay has a splendid passage on the redemptive quality of world literature—I wish I could find the reference: written, I suppose, when he was in India and was overwhelmed by his sister's death and the daily battle with those predatory and philistine Scotch colonists.[2] I found the same refuge when I was at Peterhouse.

One of the results of the Gorbachovian thaw in Russia is that the (then) young man who was our guide in Leningrad thirty years ago has now dared to write to us. He has offered to arrange another visit. Perhaps we shall go. But where I would really like to be now is Romania: a country which I know and where my friends have been *incommunicado* for seven years or more. I find it rejuvenating to witness, even from a distance, this *dégringolade*,[3] this *écroulement*,[4] of those rotten regimes; but always I think of 1789, the enthusiasm which it generated, the terrible *peripeteia*[5] which

---

[1]  George Savile, 1st Marquess of Halifax (1633–95), whose *Works* had been published in three volumes by Oxford University Press in 1989.

[2]  T R may have been thinking of the passage at the start of Macaulay's essay on Bacon (written in India) which expresses an educated man's gratitude 'towards the great minds of former ages' and continues: 'They have filled his mind with noble and graceful images. They have stood by him in all vicissitudes, comforters in sorrow, nurses in sickness, companions in solitude.'

[3]  'Rapid collapse'.

[4]  'Crumbling'.

[5]  'Sudden reversal'.

had to be played out before the end. On which sobering note I end. If you ever find that lost letter, please send it to me: even if it seems out of date to you, it will add to the pleasure of

yours ever

Hugh

———⚬⚭⚭⚬———

*The fall of the Soviet empire produced an impetus towards the reunification of Germany after forty years of division between east and west. In the letter that follows Trevor-Roper recounted his experiences as one of a group of academics invited to Chequers on 24 March 1990 to discuss with the Prime Minister, Margaret Thatcher, problems that might be posed by a reunited Germany.*

## To Max Perutz, 15 August 1990

The Old Rectory, Didcot

Dear Max

Many thanks for your article on Peter Medawar. I only met him once, but I had a great admiration for him, as a very distinguished scientist who (like you) could write for laymen (like me), and had wide humane interests and a clear English style! I thought he was splendid on that old humbug Teilhard de Chardin.

You ask me about the Prime Minister's now famous 'seminar'. What happened was this.

I was invited to lunch at Chequers on 24 March in order to discuss with the PM and others the problems created by a re-united Germany. I was not told who else had been invited. Before the meeting, I was sent a document—a sort of 'discussion paper'—which made certain generalisations about the German character, in the form of questions. I thought them rather naïve.

369

I feel reasonably sure that they represented the PM's views: they were not unlike those which re-surfaced later as those of Nicholas Ridley.[1]

When I arrived at Chequers I met the other participants. Apart from the PM, her private secretary Charles Powell,[2] and Douglas Hurd,[3] they were George Urban, Timothy Garton Ash, Norman Stone, Gordon Craig and Fritz Stern.[4] After lunch we had a long discussion—it did not end till 6.30—in the course of which it became clear that all the invited participants basically agreed that the presuppositions of the questionnaire—which was not explicitly mentioned—were wrong. The PM did not speak much: she acted as a chairman, and a very good chairman too.

No document was shown to us afterwards, but it was noted that the PM, in her public utterances, was much less anti-German, and this—which culminated in her speech at Houston—was commonly seen as a result of our meeting (the fact—though not the content—of which had somehow got into the Press: it was published, with the names, in the *Sunday Telegraph*).

Then, on 15 July, the *Independent on Sunday* published, *verbatim* and *in toto*, the summary of our discussion which had been drawn up for the PM by Charles Powell. It took all of us by surprise. There was much telephoning that morning. Some wanted us to make a joint statement. Of course the Press and the television companies telephoned me, but I kept them at bay, and persuaded the English participants that we should neither appear on

---

[1]  Nicholas Ridley (1929–93), afterwards Lord Ridley of Liddesdale, resigned on 14 July 1990 as Secretary of State for Trade and Industry after publication in *The Spectator* of an interview during which he denounced European economic and monetary union as 'a German racket designed to take over the whole of Europe'.

[2]  Charles Powell (b. 1941), later Lord Powell of Bayswater, Private Secretary and Adviser on Foreign Affairs and Defence to the Prime Minister 1984–91.

[3]  Douglas Hurd had been Foreign Secretary since 1989.

[4]  George Urban (1921–97), Hungarian-born Director of the conservative 'think tank', the Centre for Policy Studies, who later published *Diplomacy and Disillusion at the Court of Margaret Thatcher: An Insider's View* (1996); Timothy Garton Ash (b. 1955), foreign editor of *The Spectator* 1984–90 and commentator on the Communist regimes of central and Eastern Europe; Norman Stone (b. 1941), Professor of Modern History at Oxford 1984–97, with special knowledge of Eastern Europe; Gordon Craig (1913–2005) and Fritz Stern (b. 1926), two pre-eminent American academic historians of modern Germany.

television nor write articles. My view was that our meeting had been confidential and remained confidential even if there had been an unauthorised leak. However, almost immediately after agreeing explicitly that he would *not* do so, Norman Stone appeared, that same day, *both* on BBC *and* on ITV television *and* wrote an article in the *Times*, which was published on the following day. I was rather annoyed about this, but not really surprised.[1]

Our objection to Charles Powell's summary was not that it misrepresented our views but that it put the main emphasis on the views put forward in the preliminary questionnaire as if we had advanced these views, whereas in fact we had not even mentioned them. They had been set out in Powell's questionnaire or discussion document but had in fact been tacitly ignored and implicitly rejected. But in his summary Powell brought them back and made them, retrospectively, the centre-piece of the discussion. So it looked as if we had taken them more seriously than we did, and had indeed ourselves advanced them.

After it had blown over, I wrote an article in the *Sunday Telegraph*[2] expressing the views which I had in fact expressed at the meeting—and indeed a little earlier in a speech in the House of Lords. (I didn't intend to make a connexion with the seminar, but of course the *Telegraph* made it). I enclose a copy of my article.

The question which remains is, who leaked the document? It seems that the *Independent* got it from Germany; and certainly the first details to be printed were published in the *Rheinischer Merkur*. Charles Powell says that the only copy of the document to be sent to Germany was sent to our ambassador there, Christopher Mallaby;[3] so it *looks* as if there is a mole in his embassy.

---

[1] Shortly after the Chequers meeting, Norman Stone was contacted by Gina Thomas of *Frankfurter Allgemeine Zeitung*, who knew about the meeting and Charles Powell's record of it. Stone wrote in a personal communication of 26 March 2013 that 'I thought the first thing was just to say it hadn't been at all sinister—and to say so publicly (I had my own German friends who might otherwise have been taken aback). Anything else would have been just horse-bolting stable-door stuff. Hugh T-R no doubt inured to discretion obviously thinks I was wrong, but anything I did was after it had all become public knowledge'.

[2] 'How Nations Can Change their Spots', *Sunday Telegraph*, 29 July 1990.

[3] Sir Christopher Mallaby (b. 1936), ambassador at Bonn 1988–92 and at Paris 1993–6.

As a final judgment, Tim Garton Ash wrote to me recently that 'it seems to me that, in spite of all that we have said and written in different ways, it is now firmly established as historical fact that we participated, at Chequers, in March 1990, in an anti-German cabal'.

Since you are so kind as to send me your articles in the NY Review,[1] I am sending you one of mine: the result of our recent visit to Budapest.[2]

On 24 August we are going to Mexico. It has been uncertain for some time, since Xandra had an operation and then had to go back to a second hospital—with a virus (I think) contracted in the first. She is still rather lame. But the doctor says that she can go, and she is eager to go, so we are going: for a conference on—Eastern Europe!

yours ever
Hugh

—∞∞∞—

## To Edward Chaney, 20 April 1991

The Old Rectory, Didcot (Hitler's birthday)

Dear Edward,

'How delightful the Chaneys are!' So writes Kitty Farrell, which makes us feel, complacently, that our lunch-party was successful.[3] And now many thanks for your letter. I am most grateful for your comments on my

---

[1] Perutz had been a regular reviewer for the New York Review of Books since 1985.

[2] 'Reunion in Budapest', an article on the exhibition of Bibliotheca Corviniana, New York Review of Books, 19 July 1990.

[3] Charles Farrell (b. 1919), who had matriculated at Christ Church in 1937, and his wife Katharine (b. 1922) were old friends of the Dacres. Xandra wrote to the Chaneys afterwards to explain that 'the father of Kitty Farrell was the Marquis of Anglesey and her mother was the sister of Diana Cooper. Her parents were wonderful people, both handsome, artistic and good company. She is the twin sister of the present Marquis who is a military historian.' In a postscript, she added, 'Kitty's ancestor lost his leg at Waterloo and the Prince Regent went looking for it. This is the kind of history I know!'

(unfinished) piece for the *Festschrift*.[1] Thanks to you, I have got Harley on Pigments from the London Library. They haven't got the American feminist's work on Artemisia Gentileschi's unfortunate experiences in England (is it a book or an article, and what is its title?); but perhaps I can afford to omit that not altogether necessary detail.[2] I shall also omit Inigo Jones and the snails, reserving that *bonne bouche* for my book, whose substance I don't want to leak too copiously in this premonitory article.[3] And can you tell me where the detail about the mercury-damage to the Mantua pictures is recorded?[4]

*Festschrift* essays are a problem. One writes for the dedicatee, but one must assume that the laity (some of them, at least, however few) will read what one writes. So I can't bring myself to refer to Vasari's *Lives of the Most Excellent Painters*…etc. any more than I could refer to Cervantes' *The Ingenious Hidalgo Don Quixote de la Mancha*. My public must be content with the customary abbreviated translation! But I am frightened of those damned art-historians, *genus irritabile* if ever there was one, with their blow-pipes and arrows steeped in wourali[5] poison.

I know nothing about the alleged TV play about the Hitler diaries except what reaches me through casual gossip; from which I understand that it is based on a book by one Robert Harris, which I haven't

---

[1]  Sir Oliver Millar (1923–2007), Surveyor of the Queen's Pictures 1972–89, was presented with a *Festschrift* (edited by David Howarth) entitled *Art and Patronage in the Caroline Courts* (1993). T-R's contribution discussed 'Mayerne and his Manuscript'.

[2]  The Italian baroque painter Artemisia Gentileschi (1593–*c.*1656) is the subject of a feminist biography by Mary Garard (1991). T-R is referring to facetious comments by Chaney on Gentileschi's sexual affair, at the age of 17, with her tutor Agostino Tassi. Her father, who was Tassi's former artistic partner, prosecuted him for rape. Chaney's reading of the trial documents, as published by Garard, suggested that the case would not have been brought if Tassi had agreed to marry the girl. T-R misunderstood Chaney as having said the rape occurred in England rather than Italy.

[3]  This is a reference to Mayerne's recipe for Jones's melancholy, which was 'a diet of cold snails for breakfast'. At the time Chaney was contemplating the biography of Jones eventually published in his two-volume edition of *Inigo Jones's 'Roman Sketchbook'* (2006). In fact T-R did not use this *bonne bouche* in his book on Mayerne.

[4]  While being shipped from Italy to London, pictures bought for Charles I were damaged by mercury, which was being carried in the hold of the same ship. As Chaney explained in his reply, this event was documented by Alessandro Luzio in *La Galleria dei Gonzaga venduta all'Inghilterra* (1913).

[5]  Waterton's word for curare.

read.[1] I don't suppose that I shall see the film. I consider that I am the only person who knows the whole discreditable story, but there is no point in arguing with the media, which I despise, and I assume that they will have taken care to protect themselves against libel actions, so that there is no point in my watching the programme in the hope of netting a cool half-million (less legal fees of an equal amount).[2]

One day (perhaps) I shall spill the beans—but are they worth spilling? So far I have (very decently, I think) forborne to name any of those who were really responsible; for which my only reward has been that they all, with one accord, made me their scapegoat; whom the media were then delighted to butcher. So you see why I have some contempt for them and am not very interested in their further developments of the theme!

John Pope-Hennessy[3] is giving a lecture (the Neurath lecture, in honour of the *émigré* Austrian founder of Thames & Hudson[4]) next week, on the art of art-history, or some such title. I don't think I shall go: I don't really regard him as a historian, and I don't like that arrogant Bluntish *hauteur*. To be fair to him, he hated Blunt; but that was perhaps merely part of the general jungle-war of his profession.

I hope to see you again before long—I hope you will not be sucked out of our world by the business of commuting to London and that you will not suspend work on Inigo Jones![5]

yours ever

Hugh

---

[1]    A five-part ITV drama-documentary, based on the book *Selling Hitler: The Story of the Hitler Diaries* (1986) by the novelist, political columnist, and broadcaster Robert Harris (b. 1957). T-R was played by Alan Bennett, who had been a pupil of K. B. McFarlane's.

[2]    Toby Low, 1st Baron Aldington (1914–2000), had in 1989 been awarded £1.5 million, plus £500,000 costs, in the libel action which he brought against Count Nikolai Tolstoy about the repatriation of Cossacks to Stalin's Russia.

[3]    (Sir) John Pope-Hennessy (1913–94), art historian and Director of the Victoria and Albert Museum 1967–73, and of the British Museum 1974–6. T-R had first met Pope-Hennessy when they were fellow guests and protégés of Pearsall Smith in wartime Chelsea.

[4]    i.e. Walter Neurath (1903–67). T-R gave the second of the lectures, published as *The Plunder of the Arts in the Seventeenth Century* (1970).

[5]    Chaney had just become historian to the London region of English Heritage, a post which required him to commute to London from Oxford.

*Trevor-Roper met Adam Sisman (b. 1954) in 1977, when the latter was a junior editor at Oxford University Press. They were in occasional contact over the next decade, when Sisman was pursuing a career in publishing. After the death of A. J. P. Taylor in 1990, Sisman began work on his biography. This brought him into more regular contact with Trevor-Roper, who offered him generous and unselfish help. Trevor-Roper talked about his relations with Taylor, lent Sisman copies of his letters from Taylor, and in due course commented on drafts of certain passages of the biography. 'Of course I think that you have presented a one-sided account of the great controversy over* The Origins of the Second World War,' *he wrote, 'but then I would, wouldn't I?' When the book was published in 1994, Trevor-Roper reviewed it generously in the* Sunday Telegraph.

## To Adam Sisman, 21 June 1991

The Old Rectory, Didcot

Dear Adam

Thank you for a postcard which I see is dated 3 June. How quickly this dismal, cold summer month has gone! We have just returned from Scotland, to which we had to go for some exhausting ceremonies celebrating the 70th birthday of the British Legion, which was founded by my father-in-law; so much time was spent in high military circles. I am now back at Didcot and shall be fairly free from the beginning of July (I have to go to Berlin for a couple of days first).

You ask what I think of AJPT's *Letters to Eva*.[1] I have read them and written a review of them for the *Daily Telegraph*. I think the review will appear on Tuesday. I would have liked more space than I was allowed. What struck me most was (1) Alan's *trauma* over his first two marriages, which obviously (unless he was over-dramatising it) deeply affected him and damaged his self-confidence; (2) his egotism, which dominates his letters; (3) his *passion* for publicity—of which of course I was aware, though not of its full extent. I was amused by his resentment at not having the OM,

---

[1] The publishers had recently circulated review copies of *Letters to Eva: 1969–83*, edited by the Hungarian historian Eva Haraszti (1923–2005), who married Taylor in 1976. The letters are notable for their self-doubt, anxiety, and pangs of bitterness.

combined, very typically, with a repudiation of it (and the veiled attack on Isaiah Berlin ('the socialite Sir I. B.' as he once described him in print) who, in some ways, was his *bête noire*, as one who received, unfairly, the *official* recognition which was, equally unfairly, denied to himself). Similarly, Alan wonders whether Blunt will resign from the British Academy and adds 'It would give me an excuse for resigning from it too'. In other words, Alan wants an excuse to make a gesture against the Academy *before* he knows whether, or in what circumstances, Blunt may resign, just as he wants the OM in order then to show contempt for it. It seems to me the same syndrome as in his most outrageous act—one which many people at Oxford would never forgive—his creation of an unreal grievance (being 'deprived' of his university lectureship) in order to kick the (in this case) university establishment.[1]

So altogether, although I enjoyed reading the book (but will the great public, to whom the *dramatis personae* are unknown?), I felt, at the end, that Alan was lowered by it. He writes as if public applause was necessary to his self-esteem, the real measure of his worth; which I found depressing. Thus, when some anonymous journalist describes him as one of the 'Brains of Britain' (and he then quickly, by elimination, gives himself the first, and only just, place among them) he seems really to think that this is proof of his quality. This surely shows great lack of self-confidence. I suppose that his self-confidence was undermined by his mother ('She was a bitch') and wives nos. 1 & 2, and restored, to some extent, by the apparently uncritical hero-worship of Eva. I note that his autobiography (which I have not read, because everyone said it was so sour and querulous) was written for Eva.

I thought that Alan's relations with his sons came out as very attractive.

---

[1]   Special lectureships, which excused the holder from some teaching responsibilities, were awarded to scholars of distinction for a finite term. Taylor's special lectureship was due to lapse in 1963, after ten years; but in 1962 he contacted journalists with the tale that he had been 'sacked'. His orchestration of the ensuing outcry was resented in the Oxford History Faculty.

Eva remains a mystery to me. I suspect that, as a historian, she was no great shakes and that her work on the Anglo-German naval agreement—which Alan tries, but with very visible effort, to praise—is not an important contribution to history. I have not read her book on life with Alan.[1] I presume that you have. I have seen it described as 'one of the oddest books of this age'. Is that a fair judgment? What do *you* think of these letters?

yours ever

Hugh

PS. Re-reading this letter, I ask, have I been too severe, too negative? One of Alan's charms is the way that modesty, self-deflation, keeps reasserting itself. But I cannot help noticing (what I experienced to my cost) that in the end it is the vanity which prevails—he really thinks that he *ought* to be OM and that the organs of the establishment are absurd, pompous, arbitrary, etc. not merely in general, so that their awards can be treated with indifference, even hilarity, but because they do not recognise his particular claims. His remark about Ronald Syme, as a 'mediocrity' who had written a book on *The Roman Revolution* thirty years ago (as if he had written nothing since) seemed to me monstrously unjust: Syme is a better historian than Alan. But who of us would wish to be judged by our private letters, in which one is licensed to be frivolous and irresponsible? (I wonder if he knew that Eva would publish his).

Incidentally, in my article on Alan in the *Telegraph* two rather important qualifying words were omitted. I wrote, 'he should be judged, as all writers should be judged, not by the perishable froth, of which no doubt he generated too much, but by his *best* work'. The printed version omitted the word 'best', making the sentence meaningless.

H

---

[1]    Eva Haraszti Taylor, *Life with Alan: The Diary of A. J. P. Taylor's Wife, Eva, from 1978 to 1985* (1987).

## To Blair Worden, 14 July 1991

Ye Olde Rectory, Didcot

My dear Blair,

It was very kind of you to give up so much time and to take so much trouble for that grave comedy on Thursday.[1] I felt ashamed at having imposed the task on you; but whom else could I have trusted? And you did it so well. Many thanks: I am most grateful, and I will try to show my gratitude by cooking up something on Grotius.[2] I fear that it will be something of a *rechauffé*: I have, after all, already dished him up, or part of him, in *Catholics, Anglicans and Puritans*.[3]

My life, all last week, was centred on my poor orphan hedgehogs. At first I thought, since they were mobile and since the gardener assured me that one of them had gobbled up a proferred worm, that they could fend for themselves. A zoological Fellow of Oriel assured me that they could. But gradually I came to doubt this. None of them would sip the milk which I set out for them, and they turned their noses away from the most succulent of worms. Soon their gait became uncertain and the pallor of death tinged their cheeks. In despair I constantly telephoned Animal Rescue and the RSPCA, only to hear dry metallic voices referring to each other. By this morning three of the four had died and been buried, and I was merely waiting for the fourth to die. But then—oh happy moment!—I managed to persuade it, perhaps through mere physical weakness, to open its mouth; whereupon I force-fed it with milk through a surgical syringe; after which it revived. And then—a second happy chance!—the RSPCA actually responded on the telephone with what seemed to me a live voice. 'Are you a human being or a machine?' I asked; and the lady

---

[1] Worden had interviewed T-R on film about his historical philosophy at the Institute of Historical Research, which recorded a series of such interviews with historians.

[2] For a conference of the Anglo-Dutch Historical Society arranged by Worden at St Edmund Hall. The lecture, entitled 'Hugo Grotius and England', is printed in *From Counter-Reformation to Glorious Revolution*.

[3] Grotius figures in three of the five essays in that book.

admitted her humanity. So a conversation ensued. She told me of an in-firmary for ailing hedgehogs near Princes Risborough. So I carried off the last survivor and it is now installed there in a private ward and will, I am confidently assured, quickly recover: all it needs is a hot-water bottle and warm milk. Perhaps Horlicks will be best. My pleasure is tinged with melancholy by the thought that, if only I had heard that human voice earlier, all four might have been saved.

I love hedgehogs and cannot quite forgive Sir T. Mayerne for recommending dried intestines of hedgehog *au vin blanc* as a sovereign quickener of reluctant urine (*urinam potenter ciet*). What was wrong, I ask, with the powdered bees (also *au vin blanc*) which worked so well on archbishop Ussher?

As I always take any comment by you very seriously, I have been considering the grave question of the alleged abbreviation of my sentences.[1] Perhaps you are right: but let me point out that as there is no general rule or tendency that may not, on special occasions, be deliberately flouted; so, if you should look at *Hermit of Peking* pp. 184–5 (Penguin edition), you will find one sentence of such serpentine length and sinuosity as has no parallel since the time of the late Lord Clarendon.[2] This, I admit, was deliberate.

As your life is convulsed and distracted by college chores, so mine is by incessant attendance at the hospital—generally I go by train, Xandra needing the car, and it being impossible to park it there; which is very

---

[1]  In a review of *Catholics, Anglicans and Puritans* in the *London Review of Books*, Worden had suggested that T-R's sentences were becoming shorter.

[2]  'The unnamed Chinese "authorities", the provincial governors, the rifles and machine-guns so exactly described and dated, the flotilla of ships, and the whole dramatic history of their journey from Hankow to Canton, which had kept cypher clerks busy in Peking and London, caused legation officials to be sent to Shanghai and Hong Kong and commanding generals to be initiated into profound secrets; which had sent the British Minister Plenipotentiary to wait on the President of China, ruffled the diplomatic waters in Tokyo and Petrograd, fetched two million pounds from London to Peking, and nearly brought a Japanese battle-cruiser into the South China Sea; which had agitated pens in the Foreign Office and the War Office, exercised the Army Council and Lord Kitchener himself, drawn in the personal intervention of the Foreign Minister and the Colonial Secretary, been reported to the Cabinet, the Prime Minister, and the King; all this, it now seemed, was an insubstantial pageant, the baseless fabric of a dream, now suddenly dissolved, leaving not a rack behind.'

tiring. But I have sent in my latest volume of essays, which have been a millstone round my neck.[1] I am not pleased with it, only glad to be rid of the burden which I had weakly accepted. Now I hope to be undistracted (except by Grotius) until I have to think of the lecture which I am to give in Spain in April. But I hope to be often distracted by your company before then.

yours ever

Hugh

---

*James Shiel (1921–2010) was an Irish-born scholar of classics and the early history of the Christian Church, and a friend of the classical scholar E. R. Dodds. From 1954 he was Lecturer in Classics at University College Dublin; in 1963 he moved to Sussex University, first as Lecturer in the History of Classical and Medieval Thought in the School of European Studies, and then Reader in the History of Hellenic Thought, until his retirement in 1980.*

## To James Shiel, 21 January 1992

The Old Rectory, Didcot

Dear Mr Shiel

I have owed you a letter for a long time. You wrote on 19 September. Since then, I have been to America—rather an unfortunate visit, as my wife was ill there most of the time—and have been very preoccupied ever since. I am glad to say that she is fully recovered now and I have caught up with the accumulated arrears; so I have begun to write letters again.

In your postscript you flatter me by describing me as a successor of Symmachus.[2] This comparison—not of myself personally but of this

---

[1]  *From Counter-Reformation to Glorious Revolution* (1992).

[2]  Quintus Aurelius Symmachus (*c.*345–402) was an orator and man of letters, who sought to preserve Rome's traditional religions at a time when the aristocracy was converting to Christianity. He led an unsuccessful delegation of protest against the Emperor Gratian, after the latter ordered the Altar of Victory removed from the Senate's principal meeting place in the *curia*.

institution[1]—clings to my mind. Though only some of us have great *latifundia*,[2] and some of us (not many) have a love of antique culture, and no doubt some of us would wish to restore the Altar of Victory, I fear that the closest parallel lies in the fact that we are regularly over-ruled by the combination of the Emperor and the People and the new demotic ideology.

As for poor old Toynbee and his protégé, disciple and biographer McNeill[3] (who has tried so hard and so faithfully to praise him and has only succeeded in letting some very unattractive cats out of the bag), I believe that 'universal history' is an impossibility in their terms—or in those of Hegel, Ranke, Spengler and the Marxists. The lessons of history, in my opinion, must be allowed to emerge out of history: they are complex and tentative and conditional: the idea of a 'science of history', as proclaimed by the positivists of the late 19ᵗʰ and early 20ᵗʰ century, is, to me, a chimera. There are rules *in* history, but not *of* history. And so my favourite historians are Gibbon (who never forces the pace) and Jacob Burckhardt, whose historical understanding was so sensitive that he alone, of all the 19ᵗʰ century historians, succeeded in prophesying, cautiously but in fact accurately, the most important developments of the 20ᵗʰ. καὶ περὶ μὲν τούτου, as Heradotus says, τοσοῦτο εἰρήσθω.[4]

I often reflect on the teaching of the classics as I experienced it before the war. I was very well taught, at Charterhouse, by Frank Fletcher, then headmaster, and A. L. Irvine, a Wykehamist.[5] I am *very* grateful to them. But in retrospect I feel that, at that time, it was taken for granted that the classics were an education in themselves, the literature transplanted from its own soil into ours, and turned, too often, into a mere game—turning bus tickets into Greek iambics, or at least conjuring with conjectural and unscientific 'emendations'. There was a very silly fellow at Cambridge

---

[1]  The letter was written on House of Lords writing-paper.
[2]  'A great landed estate'.
[3]  William H. McNeill, with whom T-R had lunched in Chicago five years earlier. His biography of Toynbee had been published in 1989.
[4]  'And that's enough of that.' Herodotus 6.55, to which T-R brings an echo of 1.92.
[5]  (Sir) Frank Fletcher (1870–1954), headmaster of Charterhouse 1911–35, and Andrew Irvine (1881–1967), who taught at Charterhouse 1914–46.

called A. Y. Campbell, who filled the *Classical Review* (or *Quarterly*) with his proposed improvements of Sophocles, etc.[1] He had no literary sensitivity whatever. That sort of thing still goes on in Cambridge, but in Oxford, I am glad to say, it has been overtaken. I think that E. R. Dodds deserves much of the credit. I well remember the rage in the classical establishment when he was appointed and the outrageous things that were said about him, especially by Maurice Bowra, a disappointed candidate. If *he* had been elected, the change would not, I think, have been for the better.

At Cambridge, it seems to me, the influence of Housman, which still persists there, was disastrous. His arrogance cowed other scholars into flight or silence, while his textualism, excluding all considerations of content, ideas, literary character, and everything that is included in *Altertumswissenschaft*,[2] effectively removed classical literature from the laity who had once drawn inspiration from it. Frances Yates once told me that she could not forgive Housman for having *terrorised* all historians of ideas from reading Manilius, who was a great influence on Renaissance thought; but Housman, by his contemptuous and brutal textual purity (or pedantry) effectually discouraged anyone who was not himself a textual pedant from reading or trying to understand him. In his editions of Juvenal and Manilius, both of which I possess, there is not the slightest concession to the reader who wishes to see past the text to the ideas. And yet the textual purity, of which he so boasted, has—I understand—been invalidated since: for his 'emendations' have been undermined by the evidence of the papyri.

I would like classical studies to be restored to their position as a humanist education, but also the ancient world to be studied in its own right, in its own context. I do not think that this has yet happened in Cambridge,

---

[1]  Archibald Campbell (1885–1958) was a lecturer until 1922 at Cambridge, where he returned to live after his retirement in 1950 as Professor of Greek at the University of Liverpool.

[2]  *Altertumswissenschaft* ('the science of antiquity') was the late 18th-century intellectual programme which introduced an interdisciplinary, unifying approach to the separate disciplines of the study of the ancient world, and invented the seminar as its institutional meeting-ground.

where the pseuds (i.e. the psychologists, deconstructivists, etc) divide the field with the bus-ticket gang!

But I fear I am becoming a bore; and anyway this is the end of the page.

yours sincerely

Hugh Dacre

---

## To Alasdair Palmer, undated (February 1992)

The Old Rectory, Didcot

Dear Alasdair

My turn to apologise; which I do, *ex animo*. Your last letter, which I have just re-read, and re-enjoyed, is dated 5 August. You were then expecting to go to the Middle East. (Did you go?) So I did not hurry to write. Then, in November, I made a grave mistake. I accepted an invitation to America. I didn't want to go, but somehow allowed myself to get committed—partly because Xandra, to my astonishment, said that she would *like* to go. I was astonished, because she already knew the place, the University of the South in Tennessee, and therefore knew, as I did, that it was not intellectually or socially scintillating. However, she said, 'it will be a change'. So we went. It was disastrous, because she was ill, and in pain, all the time there, and doctors, though very expensive, were of no help, merely differing from each other. This made the whole stay—three weeks—very harrowing. Then we had a very uncomfortable return journey, and the English doctors took over and continued the argument for another three weeks. All that is now over and she is restored to health, but it has been a miserable winter.

Apart from that, what have I done? Very little. I had another—briefer and more splendid—outing last month. I was suddenly invited to a colloquy in the Vatican and found myself in animated *tête-à-tête* with the

Pope.[1] There was a clicking of cameras, and next day the *Osservatore Romano* sent me colour photographs of our conversation. I am thinking of making one of them into a Christmas card to send to certain of my friends[2]—to the papists, who will be outraged for one reason, and to the infidels, who will be equally outraged for another. How sad that Evelyn Waugh and Freddie Ayer[3] are both out of reach! I would have loved to send such a card to *both* of them!

I envy you your visit to Russia. I have not been there since 1965. I long to revisit Eastern Europe after these extraordinary changes. But I cannot now either take Xandra (it would be too much for her) or leave her behind alone. However, perhaps in August…for then she is due to go, with a small aristocratic party of descendants of heroes of Waterloo, on a suitably *de luxe* tour of the battlefields of Flanders. So perhaps I shall then slip away to (at least) Romania: the country, in those parts, that I know best.

I was interested by what you wrote about Gordievsky.[4] I watched him on television and was fascinated by him. Robert Armstrong has promised to arrange a dinner for me to meet him, but seems to have forgotten.[5] I will remind him. But at the back of my mind I have the same reservations which you express. Having been in the world of secret intelligence and known personally not only Blunt, Philby, Burgess but also some of their German opposite numbers, I am deeply sceptical about the whole business and those, however virtuous or sincere, who are involved in it. Intellectually, and as psychological cases, they may be fascinating, but how can they be trusted, either intellectually, as sound (by either side, or by historians), or personally: for they must necessarily have betrayed not only their employers but their friends? Also, most of them—if they are any good and not mere venal spies (who are then totally

---

[1]  According to a memorandum which T-R left among his papers, Pope John Paul II (1920–2005) questioned him about recent events at Peterhouse.

[2]  He did circulate a Christmas card bearing the photograph in 1992. Palmer received one: see p. 387.

[3]  Ayer was an atheist.

[4]  Oleg Gordievsky (b. 1938), a former KGB colonel who was an MI6 double agent 1974–85.

[5]  Robert Armstrong, Baron Armstrong of Ilminster (b. 1927), Cabinet Secretary 1979–87.

unreliable)—are, or soon become, paranoid, dotty, *fantaisistes*, and, as such, positively dangerous.

I once wrote a little book on Philby. In it I ventured the opinion, which I formed during the war and still firmly hold, that better intelligence is to be obtained from intelligent people studying public evidence than from less intelligent people studying secret evidence. This remark elicited a letter from George Kennan who declared his support for it.[1] I was very pleased by that support. I am not in favour of 'Freedom of Information'. I do not want Granada Television poking its nose into all the *arcana imperii*.[2] But I have always regarded the CIA and SIS as more dangerous to us than the KGB.

However, I see that I am treading on dangerous ground. I have to re-mind myself to whom I am writing. I'm afraid I have come to hate the media more and more. Of course there are exceptions—personal ex-ceptions. I have a great respect for some individuals, among whom I wish to include you. But the ever increasing size of the papers, and the ever sharper competition of the television companies, has led to such vulgarity, and such invasion of privacy, and so, indirectly, to such deg-radation of public standards, that I am in danger of becoming an in-ternal *émigré*, like the anchorites of the Desert or the Stoics of the later Roman Empire (or the Neo-stoics of the 17th century). But I hope that, if I end, like St Simeon Stylites[3] (on whom read—or re-read—Gibbon), sitting on a high stone pillar on the Berkshire Downs or the Lambourn gallops, you will keep me in touch, somehow, with the less disagreeable aspects of reality.

I am also in danger of ceasing altogether to write letters. I have had some disquieting experiences recently. First, in Chicago, a young scholar told me casually that he had spent the day reading my letters to Wallace

---

[1]  George Kennan (1904–2005), US Ambassador to Soviet Russia 1952–3 and to Yugoslavia 1961–3; professor at Princeton 1956–74 and author of authoritative works on Soviet foreign policy and American diplomacy.

[2]  'Secrets of state'.

[3]  St Simeon Stylites (c.390–459), a Christian ascetic saint who lived 37 years on a small platform on top of a stone pillar.

Notestein—a distinguished historian, of Yale, who was a close friend of mine and to whom I wrote very uninhibited letters. I trembled on hearing this and asked how it had happened. He told me that Notestein had bequeathed his papers to Yale University; that they were all now in the Bynum Library there,[1] and that xerox copies of my letters had a wide circulation throughout the academic freemasonry of that great continent. This was a great shock to me; but worse was to come. For yesterday, in the House of Lords, Noel Annan gave me a copy of a document which had been sent to him (because he was mentioned in it) by a third party. It turned out to be a transcript of a letter from me to a historian—a Peterhouse man, incidentally—who is now dead. It concerned the election to a chair of history at Cambridge (to which I was an elector) in 1963, and I wrote unguardedly and confidentially (there was such a thing as confidentiality in those days) about all the candidates: genial but somewhat critical portraits of (among others) Elton and Plumb. It now appears that this letter, or a copy of it, was passed, at some time, to Herbert Butterfield, then Master of Peterhouse, and is now among his papers in the Cambridge University Library.[2] I have no doubt that Noel's informant (a Peterhouse man) who found it there, and had no scruple in sending it (in breach of copyright), without my knowledge, to him, will also distribute it to others: perhaps to Maurice Cowling, who, *of course*, seeing a chance of making trouble, will pass it on to Elton and Plumb...So what remedy is there for the future except a Trappist silence? I am more and more in love with that pillar in the Desert; from which however I would hope to make

---

[1]   In fact the Beinecke Library.
[2]   In a letter to Desmond Williams (dated 29 May 1963), which Williams copied to Butterfield for his information if not delectation, T-R weighed Elton and Plumb before plumping for Taylor. 'Elton would be an unpopular choice. I am told that he has become an arrogant bore (I can believe that too), a stiff opponent of reform, and in general the bane of the Faculty. I don't myself much like what he writes, or the style in which he writes it, but there is no denying his energy and ability.' As to Plumb, 'well, I couldn't vote *very* enthusiastically for him. There is something small about his character, something vulgar about his *arrivisme*, something trivial about his attitude to history. I do know him pretty well, so it would be embarrassing if I had to say this (and have it reported back by Rowse, who would probably vote for Plumb as a fellow-devotee of the great god Mammon): I do hope I will not!'

occasional furtive descents in order to see my friends, of whom I hope that you, in spite of my long silence, are still one.

I hope also to hear about your visit to the Middle East (if you went).

yours ever

Hugh

———— ∞ ————

## To Alasdair Palmer, 17 December 1992

The Old Rectory, Didcot

Dear Alasdair

What a pleasant surprise to receive a letter from you! Your last letter to me was dated 19 Feb 1992, and it was my firm belief that I wrote back to you, at some length; and in this conviction (or, as you will perhaps say, illusion) I sat back and hoped, for some months, to hear a squeak from you. But as time passed, but no squeak came, I said to myself, Well, he is very busy constructing anti-establishment television programmes for Granada in Beirut, or Nicaragua, or Peru: I must not expect him to write…and as I don't like to 'cram-throat' my friends, whether with books or with letters, I forbore to intrude on those public-spirited activities. 'But I shall send him a Christmas card', I thought, 'just to show that he is not forgotten'. As indeed I now do, and it is here enclosed, and will show you, incidentally, what grand and holy company I now keep. I am not sending this particular card to everyone: in the wrong hands it might be misinterpreted; but I feel reasonably safe in sending it to you.

In your present letter you tell me of your adventures, in the course of your duty of public enlightenment, in Lebanon and in Oregon. Clearly it is better to fall into the hands of Hezbollah terrorists than into those of the American police. My stepson had a somewhat similar experience in America some years ago, when he was a research student at Dumbarton Oaks and was driving an American friend's car to the West. He charitably

387

assumed that, the car being thought too posh for his years, he was sus-pected of having stolen it; but I think that it was merely normal behaviour by the police in that great country. It is a great mistake to arm policemen: it affects their psychology, encouraging aggression, etc. I hope we shall never arm ours.

I hope all has gone well with the *accouchement*, and that you are now the proud father of a bouncing child. I'm afraid I have no great love of small children. They all look alike—i.e. like prawns, only noisier—and can be very tiresome in the house. Careful culture over a long time is ne-cessary to make them tolerable (this of course applies to humanity in general). No doubt the population must be kept up—but not too much. Please do not positively increase it. I regard over-population as the great-est menace to our planet—far greater than global warming, or the grand eschatological *finale* promised by the doctors of the Church. I fear that Hitler's Final Solution and Mr Karadjic's Ethnic Cleansing[1] will seem mere child's play compared with what you may expect in the next cen-tury, when the 'dash for growth' has been achieved and 1000 million Chinese and at least as many Muslims, having grown accustomed to pri-vately-owned motor-cars, washing-machines, refrigerators, transistors, mobile telephones, etc (and exterminated the entire animal world except pets and vermin *en passant*), feel the need for *Lebensraum* and a call from God to achieve it.

Do you read the works of Henry Fielding? Even if you do, I bet you have not read, or seen acted (as I have) his poetic drama *Tom Thumb the Great*. In it there is a memorable scene, the marriage of Tom Thumb, in which the parson blesses the happy couple and urges them to be fruitful and multiply:

> As when a Cheshire cheese a maggot breeds,
> Another and another still succeeds;

---

[1]  The Bosnian Serb psychiatrist and politician Radovan Karadžić (b. 1945) was indicted in 1995 by the International Criminal Tribunal for crimes against humanity in the former Yugoslavia as well as violations of the laws of war.

By thousands and ten thousands they increase
Till one continuous maggot fills the rotten cheese.[1]

(That last fine Alexandrine, you must admit, is worthy of Dryden). I sometimes see our planet as a cheese—not a Cheshire but a round Dutch
cheese, flattened slightly at the poles—rotating in the void, but almost
eaten out by maggots—human maggots, of course—and clearly destined
for disintegration. I do not see how the process can be reversed, or even
controlled, short of some cataclysm. The increase has been exponential
throughout history. In the 17th century it was generally believed that the
population of the Western world had declined since Antiquity (although
only at the expense of a Dark Age of a thousand years). However, David
Hume, with his famous essay on the Populousness of Ancient Nations,
destroyed that comfortable illusion. So you see the danger with which
you are threatening the world by procreation of infants. However, I allow
*one*, or even two for company and mutual cancellation; and since my own
father was the youngest of fourteen, and Xandra's father the youngest of
thirteen, I hesitate to press my doctrine (or any doctrine) to extreme conclusions, as your hero Derek Humphry seems to have done—although I
am not sure what his doctrine was.[2] You say that he favoured euthanasia,
but you give the impression that his victims did not necessarily assent to
the process. Perhaps he believed that death (for others) was an absolute
good. No doubt your programme will clarify this point.

The events in Yugoslavia are indeed horrible. They were equally horrible during the War—the Croatian *Ustaša*, blessed (because RC) by Pope
Pius XII of infamous memory, were just as bad as the Bosnian Serbs today,
but no one noticed it at the time, and though amply documented, it has
never, I think, been published. How ironical that the Croats provoked the
first world war through their efforts to escape from the Austro-Hungarian

---

[1]    Slightly misquoted, like much else drawn from T-R's deep memory of poetry and verse.
[2]    Derek Humphry (b. 1930) was a former *Sunday Times* journalist who became a leader in
the American right-to-die movement after helping his cancer-stricken wife to kill herself in
1974. His handbook to committing suicide, *Final Exit*, became a bestseller in the 1990s. He was
principal founder of the Hemlock Society USA.

Empire and be united with their brethren the Serbs! Now they would probably welcome federation with Austria (a variant of the 'trialism'[1] for advocating which the Archduke Franz Ferdinand was assassinated)—under the presidency of Otto von Habsburg...[2]

But as far as intervention[3] is concerned, I am a minimalist. We cannot sort out the world. The Americans would like to lord it safely (and briefly) in the skies, in order to advertise their virtue, while we mop up bloodily on the ground. I would prefer to supply arms to the Bosnians and hold the ring until the time is ripe for diplomacy. What else can we do which would not make the situation worse? Surely the danger of being sucked into a Balkan Vietnam is great? I blame the Germans, for prematurely recognising the independence of Croatia, and thus starting the *dégringolade*—and ourselves for weakly following their lead. With the experience of Ulster, we should have known better.

I fear I am becoming didactic, not to say dogmatic. Time to shut up. Thank you for persevering in correspondence in spite of your (in my opinion) erroneous belief that it was my turn to write and that I had dropped you, which I certainly had not. I would love to see you again.

yours ever

Hugh

---

*Geoffrey Wheatcroft (b. 1945) was a scholar in modern history at New College, Oxford. As an undergraduate he was taken by his near-contemporary James Howard-Johnston to a party at 8 St Aldates, where he met James's mother and stepfather. Thereafter he occasionally encountered Trevor-Roper while he pursued a career first in publishing, and from 1975*

[1]   Supporters of 'trialism' urged that the dual monarchy of Austria and Hungary should be reconstituted into a triple monarchy in which the Serbs held equal political status.
[2]   Archduke Otto von Habsburg (1912–2011) was Crown Prince of Austria-Hungary 1916–22, and thereafter Pretender to his father's thrones and Duke of Lorraine. A champion of European unity, he represented Bavaria in the European parliament 1979–2004, and in the summer of 1989 instigated the 'Pan-European Picnic' which accelerated the collapse of the Soviet bloc in Eastern Europe.
[3]   In the Bosnian civil war.

*onwards in journalism. As literary editor of* The Spectator, *1977–81, he commissioned a number of reviews from Trevor-Roper. At the time of this letter he was working as a freelance journalist, and preparing a piece on Taylor which would appear in* The Guardian *under the heading 'Love Life of a Telly-Don' three weeks afterwards.*

## To Geoffrey Wheatcroft, 12 January 1994

Old Rectory, Didcot

Dear Geoffrey

You ask me, in wide general terms, for my opinion of Alan Taylor. How can I answer so open-ended a question? The subject is so large—and so difficult. I too have read Adam Sisman's book, which I think very good, but it leaves Alan as difficult to understand as ever. My feeling is that, between its sympathy and its admissions—warm sympathy and dreadful admissions—it will confirm whatever preconception the reader may hold before reading it.

One thing that I have learned from Sisman's book is Alan's grotesque vanity, which I had not fully realised before. In general, and outwardly, he seemed good-humoured, genially irreverent, fully aware of *la comédie humaine*. I realised that, although he regarded history as a chapter of accidents, he somehow, inconsequently, assumed that such accidents ought not to happen in his career: the rules of world history ceased to apply when they touched him. He *ought* to have been made Regius Professor and it was not an accident, or an error, but a crime that he was not. His treatment of Namier was, in my opinion, shocking.[1] Namier told me that, when asked by the Prime Minister, he had given his opinion of Alan and of me separately, without preference. This is what I normally do on such occasions. It is not for us, but for the PM to decide: we are merely asked for information. But Alan obviously considered that Namier had a *duty* to impose him on the PM. This seems to me extraordinary egotism. Alan

---

[1]  Namier had been Taylor's mentor in Manchester in the 1930s, and was fond of him; but after the Regius Chair eluded Taylor in 1957 he refused to speak to Namier again.

was an impulsive person, capable of great generosity and also of great meanness, and the meanness always seems to have sprung from this kind of egotism. His behaviour towards Nicko Henderson, described by Sisman, is another instance of it.[1]

In this Alan reminds me of Rowse. Rowse also regarded every accident in his career—failure to be elected at Christ Church, failure to be elected Warden of All Souls—as an injustice and a crime, to be remembered and resented; and Rowse also, like Alan, would afterwards say, 'Of course I never wanted the thing anyway'.

Another fact which emerges from Sisman's book is the real enmity which Alan aroused. I had not previously realised how deep it ran. I always took his *boutades*[2] and gestures lightly, but I now realise that they were not always so lightly based. Sometimes at least they were the expressions of Rowsian egotism, and those who had to live with him more closely than I—the Fellows of Magdalen, for instance, and his first two wives (though they seem to have been pretty difficult themselves)—were well aware of this.

I do not think that Alan had much respect for the truth—in spite of his vehement insistence that he had. It was often said, at the time, that he wrote things that he knew were untrue. He always denied this very emphatically. But I can give instances which I think are unanswerable: falsifications which cannot be explained innocently. It was this that really shocked me in his book on *The Origins of the Second World War*. At Oxford he forfeited all sympathy by his ostentatiously publicised pretence that he had been victimised by the expiry of his university lectureship. He lied a great deal over that episode—and indeed over its sequel, his election as a Research Fellow at Magdalen.

---

[1]   Sir Nicholas ('Nicko') Henderson (1919–2009), British Ambassador to the United States 1979–82. At a dinner party co-hosted by Henderson, to mark the publication of Taylor's autobiography in 1983, Taylor overheard Henderson murmur to Michael Foot, 'I don't think the truth is what he's particularly concerned with.' Taylor reacted pettishly to this irreverence: 'There are many things in your life and career I particularly dislike,' he snapped, before leaving the party early. He never spoke to Henderson again.
[2]   'Quips, sallies'.

As a historian, I found Alan always stimulating. He was a natural heretic who never accepted any orthodoxy unexamined, so his opinions were always worth considering (and elegantly expressed). I have heard it said that he did not allow that there were great men in history. He denied this and pointed out instances—Bismarck, Churchill, Bright etc. I think he was right there, and that it is salutary to look behind the reputation of the great. Whether he admired *human* greatness or intellectual greatness I am not sure. My suspicion is that he was psychologically and philosophically ill equipped to do so. His toadying to Beaverbrook nauseated me. At the time it seemed merely comic, but in cold print it is horrible—especially since, after Beaverbrook's death, Alan admitted that he was not worthy of his adulation (See *Letters to Eva*).[1]

To take your specific points *seriatim*: I agree with you that, in academic life, he suffered from a succession of grievances, most if not all of which were unjustified. I think he was totally unintrospective and so never asked himself how he had incurred the damage. With your impression of him in politics I don't agree. You suggest that he was 'an entirely cynical and unillusioned power-worshipper'. This seems to me very wrong. Alan was really a professional 'anti'. He prided himself upon being unillusioned and to that extent could be seen as cynical, but I don't think that he was really cynical. He believed passionately in CND on humane and rational grounds, but (as always) fell out with the organisation. He was really, I think, unpolitical, an individualist who could never work in any party, an intellectual and to some extent an idealist; but his idealism was eroded by his intellectual acumen, his impatience of humbug. This is what I liked about him. At different times he expressed wildly incompatible opinions, but perhaps not seriously. He liked to shock (though he would deny this), and being so unintrospective and self-centred, did not realise when he was going too far for his own good. I suppose he parodied

---

[1] 'I seem to have been enslaved to that old man for ever,' Taylor complained to Eva Haraszti in 1970. By the time his biography of Beaverbrook was ready for publication, he had begun to question whether it had been worth the effort. 'I did it because I loved him, but that memory fades too. Now I often remember the times when I found him exasperating and wonder why I ever wasted my time in his company.'

himself, saw himself as a free spirit, and could not see why people were shocked by his cult of Beaverbrook and Mosley. Like the Antinomians of the 16<sup>th</sup> & 17<sup>th</sup> centuries, he believed that to the Pure all things are pure and that a free spirit like himself remains free from any corruption: another form of egotism.

Boswell, describing his social triumph in bringing together Johnson and Wilkes,[1] says that he always practised the intellectual chymistry which consists of distinguishing the good from the bad in the same person. On this basis I liked Alan, enjoying his liveliness of mind, geniality, acumen, wit and style, and treating his exhibitionism, shocking judgments and occasionally outrageous behaviour as mere necessary ingredients in the mixture. On balance, even after reading Sisman and seeing on what a foundation of egotism they rested, I still think he was a good thing. He was the enemy of all pomposity, orthodoxy, humbug, and the people who disliked him most were people whom I disliked—Poole,[2] McFarlane, *et al*—though I cannot say that his friends were always my friends. The Press, that odious instrument which we both use, tried to present Alan and me as permanent enemies. On the contrary, we were always friends, although I sometimes found it difficult to advocate his cause in the university, or endorse his actions; and he wrote an extraordinarily generous tribute to me in, I think, 1980, which, alas, I never acknowledged because I never saw it until it was shown to me (by Adam Sisman) after his death.[3]

---

[1] On 15 May 1776. 'Two men more different could perhaps not be selected out of all mankind,' Boswell boasted.

[2] Austin [A. L.] Poole (1889–1963), medieval historian, Fellow of St John's College, Oxford, from 1913, and President 1947–57. Poole's criticisms of Taylor were published in Sisman's book. Unlike Taylor, Poole was slow to publish; but like Taylor, he contributed a volume to the Oxford History of England (entitled *From Domesday Book to Magna Carta*).

[3] In a review, published in the *London Review of Books* in October 1981, of the *Festschrift* for T-R, Taylor wrote: 'When I read one of Trevor-Roper's essays tears of envy stand in my eyes. It is not only that his essays are models of English prose. Each has a clear theme which is gradually brought into shape. At the end, we feel there is at least one inevitable characteristic in history: the conclusion of the argument to which Hugh Trevor-Roper has been leading us from the beginning. The quality that binds together the essays in this festschrift is not a shared outlook in history, still less an interest in a single period. It is devotion to the writing of history as clear forceful exposition which delights the reader, while also instructing him.'

Well, I have written five pages; but have I answered your questions?

You are right to suppose that I was not responsible for the headline of that article.[1] I winced when I saw it. Since Charles Moore[2] is a literate man (did he not, as editor of the *Spectator*, run a regular column exposing the solecisms of *The Times*?), I have been thinking of sending him a draft circular to be sent to all his staff on the *Sunday Telegraph*, telling them, in simple language, when to use 'I' or 'me', 'he' or 'him', 'who' or 'whom' (a very common solecism in print now is in the form of 'whom he considered would make the best person...'). I shall rely on your support in such a crusade.

yours ever

Hugh

PS. I don't think I ever heard, or read, Alan expressing any philosophical, intellectual or speculative idea. I believe he was totally uninterested in ideas, and a bad judge of them. He was only concerned with the politics which they were used to justify. So he would puff Tom Paine but dismiss Burke as 'a corrupt whig hack'.

Since I have made a parallel with Rowse, perhaps I can press it further. Both Alan and Rowse seem to me to have suffered from a rather childish resentment against others who, by the mere accidents of life, have gained more public recognition (of some kind) than themselves. Rowse habitually describes such people as 'second-rate' or 'third-rate' (Sparrow, when elected Warden of All Souls against Rowse, was 'a second-rate man elected by the third-rate'). Alan, reflecting that he was not among the holders of the OM, described them all as 'mediocrities' far less distinguished than himself (though they included—apart from *very* distinguished scientists—Ronald Syme, a better historian than himself). Both of them particularly resented the high reputation of Isaiah Berlin. Rowse

---

[1]  T-R's piece 'A. J. P. Taylor and Me' had appeared in the *Sunday Telegraph* on 16 September 1990, shortly after Taylor's death. Wheatcroft sent him a postcard asking 'Whatever happened to the nominative?'

[2]  Charles Moore (b. 1956), editor of *The Spectator* 1984–90 and of the *Sunday Telegraph* 1992–5.

runs him down in his latest book.[1] Alan described him, in print, as 'the socialite Sir Isaiah Berlin', who had been 'knighted for his conversation', and, in one of his letters, as having been given the OM 'for his talk'. Now it may be that Berlin has been over-praised, over-decorated: he is a cult-figure of the international *haute juiverie*. But even if so, what of it? I find it very odd that these accidents should be resented as if it was contrary to Nature, Justice and History that accidents should happen.

What rum creatures dons are!

H

---

## To Noël Annan, 28 September 1994

The Old Rectory, Didcot

My dear Noël

You flatter me too much. Not that I reject flattery: I love it—provided always that it comes from the right people. From you it is delicious; but still excessive. I will try to keep a cool head, avoid *hubris*, etc.

I absolutely agree with you about Philby and the Philby industry. These writers have no conception of the structure, the hierarchy, the division of labour and of responsibility, within which Philby and all of us worked. Philby could occasionally suppress a document. He could leak a document. This might, on occasion, have an indirect effect on policy. If he had been a *German* spy, it could have been disastrous. But even then he could not have organised an assassination or blocked a treaty. But these people want to find single causes for great events and find him a useful *deus ex machina* to resolve all difficulties.

---

[1] 'He could have written three or four substantial books for us on Russian thinkers,' Rowse wrote of Berlin in *All Souls in my Time* (1993): 'He never did, he devoted himself to essays, skimming the European cream; his little book on Marx was only half a book.'

You ask a specific question. Why did Dick White leave Philby on the strength in Beirut?[1] I once asked him this question. His reply was that he was dismayed to find that Philby was back on the strength, but, on re-flexion, decided that it was safest to leave him there because if he were brought back to London it would be impossible to convict him or to pre-vent him from seeing his old colleagues in SIS and picking up old threads; and he hoped, by keeping him in Beirut, and sending Elliott out to con-front him, to get valuable information from him in return for immunity.[2] I agree with you that Elliott was a poop—a typical member of the old-boy network on which SIS relied—but Dick thought that he was close enough to Philby to get him to confess, which was the first necessity; which he did. Unfortunately the intended second stage didn't follow.

You ask about Cave Brown.[3] He is a monster: gross, loud, aggressive, vulgar. I can't read his prolix, prosy block-busters. He wanted to talk to me when he was writing his book *Bodyguard of Lies*. I asked Dick White whether I should see him. He advised against. But in the end Cave Brown simply barged into my office unannounced. I was very reserved, and he regards me as an enemy. He accumulates material but is very unreliable in his use of it, laying on his social prejudices and circumstantial colour quite irresponsibly, pretending to have met and known people whom, at most, he has only trapped into a telephone conversation. I am told that his only contact with Menzies was one telephone call in the course of which Menzies only uttered one word, *viz*: 'No'. But in his book he appears as a welcome guest at Menzies' country house—the evening shadows lengthening as his host uncorked another bottle of Krug, etc. He is also—or was—a dipsomaniac. The late Fred Winterbotham[4] had some horror stories of him: how he rang up from Winterbotham's club in London

---

[1]  After *The Observer*, with Foreign Office encouragement, appointed Philby in 1956 as the newspaper's Middle East correspondent based in Beirut, Philby resumed work for MI6.

[2]  Nicholas Elliott (1916–94) of MI5 and MI6, head of Beirut station 1960–2, was sent back to Beirut to interview Philby.

[3]  Anthony Cave Brown (1929–2006), journalist and author.

[4]  Frederick [F. W.] Winterbotham (1897–1990), RAF officer who supervised the distribu-tion of Ultra intelligence during the Second World War.

demanding that Winterbotham order the Club to give him accommodation and credit there; how one Sunday the Winterbothams (who lived near Torquay) returned home from church and found Cave Brown sitting in their house, having climbed in through a window and already polished off a bottle of their whisky... I advise you not to let him near St John's Wood Road,[1] or to bring him into the House of Lords.

I trust you will not leave this letter to the Library of King's College—at least not till he and/or I are safely coffined.[2]

Do you think that *anything* can be believed that comes out of the KGB archives, or (*a fortiori*) the well-lubricated lips of old KGB hacks? I am inclined to believe that it is *all* either fantasy or disinformation.

I doubt if I shall read Cave Brown's book.[3] I hate these huge, turgid volumes of which American readers are thought by publishers to be so fond. I am spending the little leisure I have re-reading Tacitus: 'the philosophical historian', as Gibbon calls him, 'who will be read by the last generations of mankind'.[4] I don't think that could be said of Cave Brown.

The dinner for Max Perutz was a very jolly affair. Those present were essentially Peterhouse and Molecular Biologists. I sat next to a *very* distinguished and very unworldly molecular biologist—I have momentarily forgotten his name: Nobel Prize winner, OM, etc., and very pleasant, but seemed totally unaware of the world outside the Molecular Biology lab: the ultimate Cambridge mind.[5]

Yes, I too deplore the lack of eccentrics in our House, and regret the loss even of Lord Hatch of Lusby. Those boring heavyweights from the House of Commons take up too much time. They seem to forget that they now have no constituents to impress by the record of their oratory. Our hope of diversion must come from the hereditary peers—one good

---

[1]   Where Annan lived.

[2]   He did.

[3]   *Treason in the Blood: H. St John Philby, Kim Philby and the Spy Case of the Century* (1994).

[4]   From chapter 12 of the *The Decline and Fall*: 'the philosophic historian, whose writings will instruct the last generations of mankind'.

[5]   This was a dinner for Perutz's 80th birthday on 21 September 1994. The 'unworldly' molecular biologist was probably Frederick Sanger (b. 1918), who had been Perutz's colleague in the Medical Research Council's Laboratory of Molecular Biology in Cambridge 1961–83.

reason for keeping them, at least if we see the Upper House as one of the decorative rather than the functional organs of the constitution. Do you think that Michael Onslow is qualifying to succeed Lord Hatch as the essential irritant in the system?[1]

In answer to your P.S., I think I shall leave my papers to the bonfire—a bonfire of vanities. *Non male vixit qui vivus moriensque fefellit.*[2] David Cannadine's biography of Trevelyan (a good book) depressed me in one respect.[3] Trevelyan took such care to discourage and prevent biographers, and yet all in vain. But he was a public figure. I am not, and hope to be safe. Leaving papers to university libraries is very unsafe—as you must know, since you kindly (or was it maliciously?) presented me with a copy of a very indiscreet letter of my own dug up by some excavator in the CUL. I am told that my letters to Wallace Notestein, now (alas) in the Bynum Library at Yale, circulate in microfilm or Xerox all over the broad continent of America. I have almost ceased to write letters in consequence. Now I shall be very careful what I write to you.

yours ever

Hugh

---

*In the early 1990s Xandra suffered a series of small strokes, and began to succumb to Alzheimer's disease. The first sign for Trevor-Roper was when, during supper at Didcot, she suddenly asked him, 'Do you know my husband Hugh?' He was obliged to take charge of everyday chores as her mind slipped away. 'I have been having a very difficult time,' he told his friend Patrick Reilly in 1995. 'I have to be permanently here in case of mishap, which is a great restraint of liberty. I also have to be*

---

[1]    Michael Onslow, 7th Earl of Onslow (1938–2011), was a voluble (and self-styled disloyal Conservative) peer with strong views on many subjects: he opposed capital punishment, police racism, and racial discrimination; he upheld asylum seekers and human rights legislation. Ebullient and gossipy, with flamboyant clothes, booming voice, and a taste for mischief, he irritated the drones in the Lords. He also upset T-R's friends at the Beefsteak by proposing Norman Tebbit for membership.

[2]    'He has not lived badly who from birth to death has passed unnoticed.' Horace, *Epistles* 1.17.

[3]    (Sir) David Cannadine (b. 1950), who has held chairs in history at the universities of Cambridge, Columbia, and London, published *G. M. Trevelyan* in 1992.

*cook, housekeeper, chauffeur, shopper, etc etc.' Trevor-Roper's failing eyesight made it impossible for him to continue driving, and increasingly difficult for him to write as well as to read. He cared for Xandra tenderly and ungrudgingly, though his attentions to her left him little time for intellectual activity. Her son James tried to exercise her failing memory by talking to her about the past. He asked her when Hugh had come into her life. She could not remember. He tried a different question: had Hugh been in her life while she had been at Cambridge? 'Yes,' she said, after much thought, 'but that was another Hugh.'*

*His devotion to Xandra, and his distress at her deterioration, came as a surprise to his stepchildren. It seemed to James that his stepfather had changed beyond recognition. This became even plainer when James and Xenia organized a conference with three professionals to settle their mother's future care. When it was clear that she must enter a nursing home, their stepfather, usually so cool and in command of himself, burst into tears. Both James and Xenia were amazed; this was a side of Trevor-Roper previously unfamiliar to them.*

*When he visited Xandra in the home, she received him politely, though it was evident that she had no idea who he was. She died in August 1997, at the age of 90.*

## To Hugh Lloyd-Jones, 6 November 1997

The Old Rectory, Didcot

My dear Hugh

It was kind of you to write on Xandra's death. As I think you know, she had been failing for a long time—2½ years. I looked after her at home till it became impossible; then we found an excellent nursing home, near enough for me to visit her regularly, where she was very well cared for, and quite happy—though not an enviable kind of happiness. I miss her terribly and find life rather empty without her, especially as I now suffer from serious glaucoma and can only read with great difficulty. But I have some very helpful ex-pupils and friends, who are a great help, so I have no right to complain of the ordinary incidents of human life.

I hope that you are well and that Mary is not only unharmed by the Amazonian armies of Negrophilia and Political Correctitude but is turning the tide.[1] When are you coming to Oxford? I hope I shall see you before long.

Public affairs here are in a pretty sorry state. Oh for an hour of the Iron Lady—although admittedly she went mad at the end. We had a great orgy of mass-hysteria on the occasion of the funeral of 'the People's Princess'.[2] Oleg Gordievsky, the ex-KGB man, compared it to the scenes in Moscow on the death of Stalin. I recalled rather those in America on the death of Rudolf Valentino.[3] But I retain a touching, if also dwindling, faith in the ultimate common sense of the British People, and hope it will soon have passed—or turned into a ritual burning, on the anniversary of the Death, of effigies of the Fayed family, those chosen instruments of Fate. Our dear Prime Minister's reading of the New Testament lesson at the Funeral Service (in all references to the Death, capital letters are obligatory) was a nauseating exhibition of unctuous cant.[4] The Tory leader,[5] not to be outdone, proposed that Heathrow Airport be renamed Diana Airport. I suspect that he has forgotten that by now.

---

[1]   Mary R. Lefkowitz (b. 1935), American classical scholar and Andrew W. Mellon Professor in the Humanities at Wellesley College 1979–2005. She was the second wife of Lloyd-Jones, who read Proust or Henry James aloud to her while she cooked dinner. Her book *Not Out of Africa: How Afrocentrism Became an Excuse to Teach Myth as History* (1996) was a critique of Martin Bernal's *Black Athena: The Afroasiatic Roots of Classical Civilization* (1987). She co-edited a volume of essays entitled *Black Athena Revisited* (1996) and wrote an opusculum on the same subject, *History Lesson* (2008).

[2]   The funeral of Diana, Princess of Wales, on 6 September 1997.

[3]   After the death in New York of Rudolf Valentino (1895–1926), his embalmed body lay in state in a bronze coffin festooned in flowers (including a wreath from Mussolini). There was a small riot at the mortuary on the first day of the lying-in-state as hundreds of people fought to see his corpse. Thereafter four black-shirted fascist guards and a bevy of private detectives protected his coffin as mourners filed past at the rate of 80 a minute. The huge crowds in the New York streets on the day of his funeral were solemn and respectful.

[4]   During the princess's funeral in Westminster Abbey, Tony Blair (b. 1953) read 1 Corinthians 1: 3, with pauses for dramatic effect.

[5]   William Hague (b. 1961), Leader of the Conservative Opposition 1997–2001, Foreign Secretary from 2010.

I have been occasionally to the House of Lords, but it is very dull and anodyne. Perhaps it will brighten up when we come to serious matters like fox-hunting and hereditary peers (both now to be branded as politically incorrect).

I apologise for having been so bad a correspondent in the last two years; but you know the cause. I hope to improve now, in order to hear from you again.

yours ever,

Hugh

P.S. Just as I was finishing this letter, I had a telephone call from Isaiah's secretary,[1] to tell me that Isaiah died last night. He had double pneumonia very badly a few months ago and although he recovered from that, he never regained the necessary vital force to keep going: he had lost the will to live. P.P.S. Do you remember Gibbon's footnote on Antinous? This is surely a perfect early instance of the modern use of the adjective 'correct'.[2]

---

*Richard Rhodes (b. 1929) had been a history undergraduate at Christ Church in the early 1950s. In 1952, after Rhodes had been awarded a travel scholarship by Christ Church, Trevor-Roper recommended him to Berenson as a suitable visitor to I Tatti. Rhodes's evocative photographs of the journey were published in his brother Anthony's book* A Sabine Journey: To Rome in Holy Year *(1952). The catholicity of the young man's interests delighted Trevor-Roper.*

*Rhodes has led a versatile life. A classical pianist, he married the daughter of the conductor Leopold Stokowski. He used his experiences as an executive in South America in his satirical novel* Gushing *(1970). As a barrister he practised in Paris and in Geneva, where in his retirement he has been associated with the classics department of the University of Geneva.*

---

[1]   Patricia Utechin, née Rathbone (1927–2008), had been Max Beloff's secretary at All Souls until a quarrel in 1961. Berlin immediately recruited her, and she became his favourite and longest serving secretary (1961–5 and 1972–97). She managed his chaotic academic and social arrangements with aplomb.

[2]   Chapter 3 of *The Decline and Fall*: 'The deification of Antinous, his medals, statues, city, oracles, and constellation, are well known, and still dishonor the memory of Hadrian. Yet we may remark, that of the fifteen emperors, Claudius was the only one whose taste in love was entirely correct.'

# To Richard Rhodes, 11 June 1998

Old Rectory, Didcot

Dear Richard

Your penultimate letter still sits before me awaiting a reply; and now it is succeeded by another, which precipitates that overdue acknowledgment. I greatly appreciate your sympathy on Xandra's death. I miss her dreadfully, especially now that I not only live alone, isolated in Didcot, but am increasingly blind and can hardly read. But I could not wish her life—the half-life that it had become—to be prolonged. One reason for the delay in my correspondence, as in everything else, is that my energies, such as they are, have been almost entirely absorbed, in recent weeks, in organising a memorial tribute to her: not a memorial service—she would not have wanted that—but a memorial concert, which took place in the Sheldonian a fortnight ago and was, I am glad to say (in spite of the forbodings of some defeatist members of the family) a very great success: the Sheldonian was packed and it was a marvellous concert—thanks entirely to the splendid conductor,[1] who did far more than merely conduct: he helped to organise, often from a considerable distance—Mexico, Turkey—being in great demand. He is a Turk, and had become a great friend of ours, and was devoted to Xandra. Yehudi Menuhin sent his best violinist from his school in Surrey,[2] and the organist[3] (whom I have heard described as 'the best organist in *Europe*', recommended by Simon Preston,[4] who couldn't come himself, being in America) is the *assistant* organist at Christ Church.

---

[1]  Cem Mansur (b. 1957), Conductor of Istanbul State Opera 1981–9 and of City of Oxford Orchestra 1989–96, conducted a programme of Mozart, Poulenc, Schubert, and Shostakovich.

[2]  The violinist was Paweł Zatorski, a pupil at the Yehudi Menuhin School of Music at Stoke d'Abernon.

[3]  David Goode (b. 1971), sub-organist at Christ Church 1996–2001, and subsequently organist at Eton College, where he had been a music scholar.

[4]  Simon Preston (b. 1938), Organist and Tutor in Music at Christ Church 1970–81, Conductor of Oxford Bach Choir 1971–4, Organist and Master of the Choristers of Westminster Abbey 1981–7.

The wonderful Ukrainian soprano[1] was supplied by the orchestra. I enclose the programme as a souvenir.

I also enclose—since you asked for it—my old address to the Virgil Society: a pretty trivial piece hardly worth the strain of transport; but I obey your orders.[2]

I am also bold enough to make a request—or rather a suggestion. Owing to blindness, senility, etc., etc., I fear that I may never finish my book on Sir Theodore Mayerne—and thank you for the contributions of Mme Sarasin (a distinguished Genevese name)—but I have the material for it, which, I am bold or rash enough to say, corrects all previous accounts (including—but don't tell her this—her material), and so I would like, if invited, to give a lecture on the subject in Geneva. Do you think that that could be arranged? Mayerne's life has never been written; almost everything published contains grave errors; and it is in fact an interesting story. He was an important figure in Anglo-Genevese relations—indeed in the European world—of politics and diplomacy as well as in medicine, and a very colourful one too. Owing to my blindness, I cannot read a lecture, or even notes; but I have learned the technique of lecturing *apparently* extempore, and have lectured recently in Rome, Oporto and Lisbon. In fact I have just returned from lecturing in Lisbon. I would greatly enjoy a visit to Geneva. Do you think this is a possibility?[3] If it were, it would be a great pleasure to see you. If not, I hope I shall see you on your next visit to England, whether in London or (even) in Didcot.[4]

yours ever

Hugh

—❊—

[1]  Alla Kravchuk trained in the Kiev Conservatoire.
[2]  The presidential address of the Virgil Society for 1990: 'Why Virgil?'
[3]  T-R never made this visit.
[4]  T-R enclosed with this letter a memorandum about his quest for Mayerne's personal archive, and his hope to identify a Geneva advocate named l'Archevesque who acquired an important bound volume of Mayerne's papers in 1711. This memorandum resembles Appendix C, 'Mayerne's Papers', in *Europe's Physician*.

*The sixteenth-century scholar Erasmus was a pre-eminent figure among Trevor-Roper's intel-
lectual heroes: a humanist scholar of European outlook, who championed reason, scepticism,
and tolerance, and withstood prejudice, bigotry, and fanaticism. A portrait of Erasmus hung
on the wall of his study. Trevor-Roper argued that, though Erasmus had died apparently a
failure, his ideas had persisted in both Catholic and Protestant thinking. 'Political programmes
may be defeated entirely,' he wrote in an article on Erasmus in* Encounter *in 1955 (reprinted in*
Historical Essays*), 'but not ideas: at least, not great ideas. Political circumstances may alter
around them, ideological frontiers may be formed against or across them, but such convulsions
merely alter the terrain: they may divert or divide, but they do not permanently dam the
stream.' Trevor-Roper's use of the term 'ideological' to describe ostensibly religious conflicts
was indicative of his secular approach. He readily made analogies between the ideological
struggles of the Cold War and those of the Reformation and Counter-Reformation. The following letter was written in response to an enquiry from Peter N. Miller, a former Harvard
student with a Ph.D. from the University of Cambridge, who was then an assistant professor
at the University of Maryland. Miller was interested in the history of historical research, and
in the ways that historians use evidence. He asked Trevor-Roper to reconstruct the beginnings
of his interest in Erasmianism, Arminianism, 'and those happy early days of confessional peace
between the French wars of religion and the Thirty Years' War'. Miller wondered whether 'the
Laud book had come from the same context'. He mentioned that two of the most persuasive
evocations of this period had come from former Nazis, Gerhard Oestreich and Otto Brunner,
and asked if Trevor-Roper could suggest an explanation.*

## To Peter Miller, 18 March 1999

Old Rectory, Didcot

Dear Mr Miller

You wrote to me on 29 Jan., and I apologise for being so slow to reply. I am
afraid I am a very bad correspondent: I am almost blind, have great difficulty in reading, and now (since my wife died 18 months ago) live alone.
So you will understand my difficulty.

What a difficult question you ask! You ask about my own mental processes, which I have not myself studied or analysed. But I shall try to answer you.

Of one thing I can be certain. However my interest in Erasmianism may have developed, it was *not* a direct result of my work on Laud. I do not think highly of that book, which I wrote, under no supervision, before I had really given any thought to history, historical philosophy, or the history of ideas. (I was trained as a classical scholar, not as a historian—of which I am glad, since I was taught classics well whereas such historical teaching as I had, or would have had, was very elementary). It was only after my book on Laud was published that I really began to think about history and the history of ideas.

But I always had a sympathy for Erasmus: his exact scholarship, his humanist philosophy which rose above that scholarship, his easy Latin style, his wit and scepticism. Then, after the war, I read Marcel Bataillon's great work *Erasme et l'Espagne*, which put Erasmus in a larger context.[1] I was greatly impressed by this, and all Bataillon's work, and visited him in Paris. It was through Bataillon that I saw Erasmus as an intellectual radical and a spiritual thinker—not merely as a humanist writer. But I felt that Bataillon's last chapter, '*Derniers Reflets d'Erasme*', was rather light—perhaps because it was confined to the Spanish world. In the course of my general reading I discovered that the ideas of Erasmus persisted, not merely in the Protestant world, but also in Catholic societies—de Thou, the Dupuy brothers,[2] Gui Patin,[3] etc.—and this led me to see the period of general peace and the relaxation of ideological orthodoxy as a brief age of enlightenment before the renewed ideological wars of the 17$^{th}$ century. So I discovered, through Erasmus and Grotius, something of the character and pedigree of Arminianism which I had not

---

[1]  Marcel Bataillon (1895–1977), of the Collège de France, published the book in 1937.

[2]  Jacques Dupuy (1591–1656) was de Thou's librarian. Together with his historian brother Pierre (1582–1651) he published de Thou's *History*.

[3]  Gui Patin (1601–72), Dean of the Paris Faculty of Medicine and Professor at the Collège Royal; his letters abound in gossip, and in sharp comment on political and medical matters. He was a clandestine book-dealer who aided the publication in France of foreign medical scholarship.

realised when I wrote about Laud, and had accepted the conventional view of it.[1]

This interest in the 'Libertins Erudits'—I had not read Pintard[2]—naturally led me towards Peiresc.[3] But I have to admit that after reading many of Peiresc's letters (and what a lot there are!), I was disappointed in him. He seemed to me too much of an *érudit* and too little of a *libertin*. All roads seemed to lead to him, everyone respected him and his antiquarian erudition, but I could not find in him the intellectual originality that I found in the writings of de Thou and Grotius, Bacon, Camden[4] and Sarpi. In this I may well be wrong—perhaps I did not persist long enough: I am ready to be corrected by you. I saw him as a provincial *savant* whose great reputation depended partly on his eminence in a provincial world. But I hope you will correct me.

You ask when I discovered Pintard's work on *Le Libertinage Erudit*. The answer is, very late: long after I had discovered the *libertins* themselves (who I found through de Thou and his circle).[5] The book is very difficult to find now: I have long been looking for a copy for myself, but have scoured the antiquarian booksellers' catalogues in vain.

A book which quickened my move from political to intellectual history was Marjorie Nicolson's *Conway Letters*, to which I was introduced, during the war, by Logan Pearsall Smith. Do you know it? I urged undergraduates to read it in order to introduce them to the subject. I find the interaction of politics, war and ideas far more interesting than their separate specialisation.

---

[1]  Arminianism, named after the later 16th-century Dutch theologian Jacobus Arminius, attacked the Calvinist doctrine of predestination. Because the ecclesiastical regime of Charles I, which the 'conventional view' presented as a reactionary and oppressive force, was anti-Calvinist too, and so got called Arminian, the intellectual liberalism of the movement was overlooked.

[2]  René Pintard (1903–2002), French linguist and literary scholar, whose *Le Libertinage érudit dans la première moitié du XVIIe siècle* was published in 1943.

[3]  Nicolas-Claude Fabri de Peiresc (1580–1637), classical scholar from Aix-en-Provence, friend of Pope Urban VIII, and of Galileo and the painter Rubens. Miller's *Peiresc's Europe: Learning and Virtue in the Seventeenth Century* was published in 2000.

[4]  William Camden (1551–1623), author of *Britannia* and *Annals of Queen Elizabeth*, on whom T-R wrote 'Queen Elizabeth's First Historian: William Camden' (a lecture reprinted in *Renaissance Essays*).

[5]  'Libertins' was a term of abuse used of various freethinkers in the late 16th and in the 17th century. 'Libertinage erudit' was applied to a group which included the Dupuy brothers and Patin.

I have tried to answer—very imperfectly—two of your three specific questions. Before the third I retreat. I didn't know that Oestreich[1] and Otto Brunner[2] were ex-nazis. But I can see why neo-stoicism could appeal to the defeated Erasmians of the Netherlands—as, of course, did Tacitism:[3] the retreat of the *libertins*, under the pressure of the new despotism, into the citadel of *private* virtue, Lipsius' *de Constantia*,[4] Cremonini's *extra ut moris est, intus ut libet*.[5] But those ex-nazis...! what kind of nazi were they? Disciples of Stefan George[6] perhaps. Where did they stand on 20 July 1944?

It was a pleasure to hear from you and I apologise again for my dilatory reply (which I hope is not too illegible).

yours sincerely

Hugh Dacre

PS. A further general point about Erasmianism. In his last chapter Bataillon referred to Benito Arias Montano.[7] Later, I read B. Rekers' book on Montano[8]— a very unreliable book, but it led me to more reliable works on the Plantin circle[9] and so I was able to observe how Erasmianism, in its native land, was able to survive under Counter-Reformation pressure by outward conformity and inner heresy. I also observed the same phenomenon in Switzerland, where

---

[1]  Gerhard Oestreich (1910–78), German historian of the early modern period, wrote a book on the 17th-century neo-stoic movement, which had some overlap with the Erasmian tradition.

[2]  Otto Brunner (1898–1982), Austrian historian who specialized in later medieval and early modern European social history.

[3]  The Roman historian Tacitus commanded wide and intense interest in the Europe of the wars of religion. In his narratives of the early Roman empire, readers found pressing parallels with the conduct of rulers in their own time.

[4]  *De Constantia* (1586) was a principal text of the neo-stoic movement,

[5]  Cesare Cremonini (1550–1631), an Italian philosopher from Cento.

[6]  Stefan George (1868–1933), lyric poet, whose writings were a protest against materialism and naturalism. His young literary and academic adherents treated him as a prophetic figure. His poetry emphasized self-sacrifice, heroism, and power, and thus attracted some National Socialists, but he was opposed to the political interpretation or application of his ideas.

[7]  Benito Arias Montano (1527–98), a Spanish scholar who under the direction of Philip II of Spain supervised the production of an eight-volume polyglot edition of the Bible.

[8]  Bernard Rekers, *Benito Arias Montano, 1527–1598* (1972).

[9]  The publishing house of Christopher Plantin (1520–89) at Antwerp was a centre of Erasmian scholarship. Montano's edition of the Bible was published there.

the Italian erasmist émigrés sought refuge and sought to survive under an opposite and equally oppressive orthodoxy. From both the Netherlands and Switzerland these heretics tended to converge on England and so strengthened the thin Erasmian current which, within the Church, turned to Arminianism and afterwards to Socinianism, of which both Grotius and Laud were accused: indeed, the stiff Presbyterian persecutor Francis Cheynell[1] accused Laud of organising a Socinian fifth column in the English Church.

I find it interesting that Gibbon, that 'most strong-minded of historians' as Carlyle called him,[2] almost alone in his time saw the long-term revolutionary intellectual tradition begun by Erasmus. Nearly everyone else saw him as a civilised moderate scholar snuffed out by rival orthodoxies.[3]

I apologize for inflicting on you so long and rambling a letter. I hope it is legible, although I am aware that my blindness has played havoc with my handwriting.

---

*The possibility that Adam Sisman might write about Trevor-Roper had arisen in the aftermath of Sisman's life of A. J. P. Taylor, published in 1994. They continued to meet from time to time, and often talked about aspects of Trevor-Roper's past. Sisman began writing Trevor-Roper's biography after his death in 2003; it was published in 2010.*

## To Adam Sisman, undated (April 2001)

[Didcot]

Dear Adam

You are now, I suspect, back from America. I hope your visit was in every respect profitable. Before leaving England you wrote me a charming letter

---

[1] Francis Cheynell (1608–65), uncompromisingly Calvinist theologian.
[2] The impact of Gibbon on Carlyle is described in T-R's article on Carlyle, republished in the posthumous collection *History and the Enlightenment*.
[3] T-R's had already touched on this theme in his 'Desiderius Erasmus', published in *Encounter*, and republished in his *Historical Essays* (1957).

to which I should have replied before now. I crave forgiveness. I am in consequence of my blindness, which is now much worse, hopelessly in arrears with correspondence as with everything else, and writing itself is very difficult. I now find myself identifying—not deliberately, but accidentally, circumstantially—with G. M. Trevelyan. Like him I am a Northumbrian and am reputed a whig (though I think I am less whiggish than he). Like him I have been a regius professor of history and head of a Cambridge college. Like him I am now a widower and blind. And like him— see his autobiographical essay in, I think, *Clio, A Muse*—I would like to disappear without a biography and my letters to be destroyed. All this I have said to Blair, who replies 'but like it or not, someone *will* write about you', to which I can only reply that I cannot control what may happen after my death and that, if so—and Trevelyan did not escape either (and did in fact chance on a good biography)—then I would rather trust myself to you than to anyone else that I can think of. But I do not want to waste part of your life on an unrewarding subject. '*La vie d'un savant sedentaire*', says Voltaire, '*est dans ses oeuvres et non pas dans les événements*' (or words to that effect),[1] and my works are not significant. Surely I would be a steep descent from Boswell,[2] or even Alan Taylor, whose life was at least colourful, not to say outrageous, and therefore readable whereas I am really a very ordinary and conventional person.

So there you have my disclaimer. But if you insist on trying to make something out of me, I shall do what I can to answer your questions. However, before committing yourself, we ought to meet so at least I can show you the scope and limits of the material before you take the plunge.

If you persist in your quixotic desire it will be necessary (and if not it would anyway be a great pleasure for me) to meet; and if so, soon; for I cannot expect to last long, and always at my back I hear Time's winged chariot hurrying near. There is much that I still want to do, but my life at

---

[1] 'La vie d'un écrivain sédentaire est dans ses écrits,' in *Siècle de Louis XIV* (2 vols., 1751). 'The life of a sedentary writer lies in his writings.'

[2] Sisman's *Boswell's Presumptuous Task* had been published the previous year. It was one of the books that T-R chose to have read to him when he could no longer read himself.

present is very difficult. I wish I did not live alone—I miss Xandra dreadfully. I wish I could see to read and write. But my step-children, friends and former pupils sustain me and I have no grounds for complaint. Only I wish I could find an instrument which could write clearly enough for me to read what I have written. I hope you can.

yours ever

Hugh

---

*This letter, written thirteen months before Trevor-Roper's death, was addressed to the retired ambassador 'Nicko' Henderson. In his youth Trevor-Roper had shown little interest in politics until the Munich agreement between Hitler and the British Prime Minister Neville Chamberlain in September 1938 jolted him.*

## To Sir Nicholas Henderson, 21 December 2001

The Old Rectory, Didcot

Dear Nicko

Many thanks for sending me that tape of Chamberlain's Birmingham speech of 17 March 1939.[1] I listened to it fascinated and appalled. I meant to come to the dinner of the Other Club[2] on Wednesday and return it to

[1]  Neville Chamberlain's speech to the annual meeting of the Birmingham Conservative Association was broadcast to the Empire and the United States. It was delivered two days after the German invasion of Czechoslovakia. He explained that he had gone to Munich six months earlier in 'an almost desperate situation that seemed to me to offer the only chance of averting a European war'. By meeting Hitler at Munich, and previously at Berchtesgaden, 'the peace of Europe was saved, and if it had not been for those visits hundreds of thousands of families would to-day have been in mourning for the flower of Europe's best manhood'. He asked: 'what was the alternative? Nothing that we could have done, or France could have done, or Russia could have done, could possibly have saved Czechoslovakia from invasion and destruction.' Chamberlain was speaking, as Alan Taylor noted, 'among his own people—jewellers, locksmiths, makers of pots and pans'. After he sat down, the audience of 2,300 cheered him for several minutes before singing 'For he's a jolly good fellow'.

[2]  A dining club, formed in 1911 by Winston Churchill and F. E. Smith, which meets fortnightly in the Pinafore Room at the Savoy Hotel when Parliament is in session. Henderson had been a member since 1976, T-R since 1978.

you directly, but I have not been well and could not face the journey; so I will send it back when the Christmas mail no longer congests the Post.

I was fascinated to hear again the voice of poor old Chamberlain: strong and resolute in his own conviction; but appalled by the implications.

Still in our ashes live our wonted fires.[1] At the time, in my callow youth, I was deeply shocked by Chamberlain and Appeasement. Afterwards I came to agree that he had little alternative. The pass had been sold; if we had fought then, we would probably have been defeated; we had no Spitfires. But even so, Chamberlain's pretence that Munich was a diplomatic victory, that it had secured 'peace in our time'—when he should have said that it was a defeat, the inescapable result of wasted years whose damage must now be repaired—seemed to me shocking. And now I heard that self-assured, self-satisfied voice still insisting that the surrender at Munich was right and would have preserved peace if only Hitler had not—surprise, surprise—afterwards turned out to be such a cad. So here I am, back again in the mood of 1938. I have been reading—that is, James, my step-son, has been reading to me—Alexander Cadogan's diaries.[2] How I relished Cadogan's explosion on meeting Chamberlain and Halifax on their return from Munich: 'Good God! The PM has been hypnotised by Hitler and Halifax has been hypnotised by the PM!'[3]

Our generation will never escape from the 1930s.

yours ever

Hugh

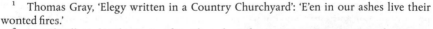

[1]   Thomas Gray, 'Elegy written in a Country Churchyard': 'E'en in our ashes live their wonted fires.'

[2]   David Dilks (ed.), *The Diaries of Sir Alexander Cadogan, OM, 1938–45* (1971). Cadogan was Permanent Under-Secretary for Foreign Affairs 1938–46.

[3]   On 24 September 1938, over a week after Chamberlain's return from Munich, Cadogan noted of Chamberlain's report to the 'Inner Cabinet': 'I was completely horrified—he was quite calmly for total surrender. More horrified still to find that Hitler has evidently hypnotised him to a point. Still more horrified to find P.M. has hypnotised H. who capitulates totally... Ye Gods!'

# INDEX